INSIGHT GUIDES

SOUTH AMERICA

D0652989

Discovery
CHANNEL

APA PUBLICATIONS

Part of the Langenscheidt Publishing Group

INSIGHT GUIDE
SOUTH america

Editorial
Project Editor
Natalie Minnis
Managing Editor
Huw Hennessy
Editorial Director
Brian Bell

Distribution
UK & Ireland
GeoCenter International Ltd
The Viables Centre, Harrow Way
Basingstoke, Hants RG22 4BJ
Fax: (44) 1256 817988

United States
Langenscheidt Publishers, Inc.
36–36 33rd Street 4th Floor
Long Island City, NY 11106
Fax: 1 (718) 784 0640

Canada
Thomas Allen & Son Ltd
390 Steelcase Road East
Markham, Ontario L3R 1G2
Fax: (1) 905 475 6747

Australia
Universal Publishers
1 Waterloo Road
Macquarie Park, NSW 2113
Fax: (61) 2 9888 9074

New Zealand
Hema Maps New Zealand Ltd (HNZ)
Unit D, 24 Ra ORA Drive
East Tamaki, Auckland
Fax: (64) 9 273 6479

Worldwide
Apa Publications GmbH & Co.
Verlag KG (Singapore branch)
38 Joo Koon Road, Singapore 628990
Tel: (65) 6865 1600. Fax: (65) 6861 6438

Printing
Insight Print Services (Pte) Ltd
38 Joo Koon Road, Singapore 628990
Tel: (65) 6865 1600. Fax: (65) 6861 6438

©2005 Apa Publications GmbH & Co.
Verlag KG (Singapore branch)
All Rights Reserved
First Edition 1990
Fourth Edition 1998
Updated 2004. Reprinted 2005

CONTACTING THE EDITORS
We would appreciate it if readers
would alert us to errors or out-
dated information by writing to:
Insight Guides, P.O. Box 7910,
London SE1 1WE, England.
Fax: (44) 20 7403 0290.
insight@apaguide.co.uk
NO part of this book may be reproduced,
stored in a retrieval system or transmitted
in any form or means electronic, mech-
anical, photocopying, recording or otherwise, without prior written permission of
Apa Publications. Brief text quotations
with use of photographs are exempted
for book review purposes only. Information has been obtained from sources
believed to be reliable, but its accuracy
and completeness, and the opinions
based thereon, are not guaranteed.

www.insightguides.com

ABOUT THIS BOOK

This guidebook combines the interests and enthusiasms of two of the world's best-known information providers: Insight Guides, whose titles have set the standard for visual travel guides since 1970, and Discovery Channel, the world's premier source of non-fiction television programming.

The editors of Insight Guides provide both practical advice and understanding about a destination's history, culture, institutions, and people. Discovery Channel and its website, www.discovery.com, help millions of viewers explore their world from the comfort of their own home and also encourage them to explore it first-hand.

How to use this book

This book has been carefully structured both to convey an under-standing of the subcontinent, its people and its culture, and to guide readers through its major sights and activities.

◆ To understand contemporary South America, you need to know something about its past. From the Inca Empire to the Spanish Conquest and from some chilling military dictatorships through to reforming modern democracies, South America has had a dramatic and eventful history.

The **Features** section covers the history and culture of the whole region in a series of lively and informative essays.

◆ The main **Places** section provides a complete country-by-country guide

to all the major sights and areas worth seeing, including opening times of museums, archeological sites, and art galleries.

Places of special interest are coordinated by number with specially drawn full-color maps.

◆ The **Travel Tips** section provides a convenient reference for information on transport, accommodation, restaurants, useful addresses, outdoor activities, language, etc.

Information may be located quickly by using the index printed on the back cover flap.

◆ The **Photographs** have been carefully chosen not only to convey the beauty of the countries, the landscape, the flora and the fauna, but also to give an accurate impression of the people of South America and their everyday lives.

The contributors

This edition was updated by **Jane Egginton** and was edited at Insight Guides' London office by **Paula Soper**. It builds on previous editions by **Tony Perrottet** and **Natalie Minnis**. The editors used writers who combined affection for and detachment from their specialist subjects.

The chapters on South American history were contributed by **Nick Caistor** who also updated the chapter on Peru. Nick is a specialist Latin America analyst. Natalie Minnis wrote about the people of South America, and the music and dance chapter was written by **Shannon Shiell**, a Glasgow-based Latin dance expert who has lived in South America.

The arts and architecture chapters were contributed by **Mike Gonzalez**, a senior lecturer in the Department of Hispanic Studies at Glasgow University. The outdoor sports chapter and new writing on Ecuador were written by **Jane Letham** and **Mark Thurber**, based in Quito, who run their own trekking and mountaineering tours around Peru and Ecuador.

Chapters in the Places section have previously been revised and updated by **Jasper Corbett** (Colombia), **Elizabeth Kline** (Venezuela), **Martin Symington** (The Guianas), **Diana Zileri** (Peru), **Natalie Minnis** (Bolivia), **Patrick Knight** (Brazil), **Dick Barbour-Might** (Paraguay), **Ruth Bradley** (Chile) and **Dr Jill Hedges** (Uruguay, Argentina and the Falkland Islands).

The chief photographers were **Mireille Vautier** and **Eduardo Gil**. Many photographs of Brazil were supplied by **H. John Maier**. Thanks also to **Sylvia Suddes** who proofread the book.

Map Legend

— · · —	International Boundary
— — —	State Boundary
⊖	Border Crossing
— · —	National Park/Reserve
— — — —	Ferry Route
Ⓜ	Metro
✈ ✈	Airport: International/ Regional
🚌	Bus Station
Ⓟ	Parking
❶	Tourist Information
✉	Post Office
✝ ✝	Church / Ruins
✝	Monastery
☪	Mosque
✡	Synagogue
Castle / Ruins	
∴	Archeological Site
∩	Cave
⌶	Statue/Monument
★	Place of Interest

The main places of interest in the Places section are coordinated by number with a full-color map (e.g. ❶), and a symbol at the top of every right-hand page tells you where to find the map.

INSIGHT GUIDE
SOUTH AMERICA

CONTENTS

Maps

Girl from the
Bolivian
altiplano

Travel Tips

Insight on …

Information panels

THE UNDISCOVERED CONTINENT

From the Andes to the Amazon, from dense forests to alluring beaches, South America's diversity is extraordinary

According to the Colombian novelist Gabriel García Márquez, foreigners see South America as "a man with a moustache, a guitar and a revolver." More perhaps than any other continent, South America has been the victim of stereotypes and misconceptions. Most people see it as one huge, mysterious jungle, a mountainous wasteland or a backward rural world languidly lost in an eternal *siesta*.

But from the moment you step out of an aircraft anywhere in South America, it's obvious that the images fail to capture even a fraction of the reality. There are mighty rivers, wilderness areas and final frontiers, but also ancient civilizations and vibrant new cultures. The Amazon Basin and its remote outposts grab the imagination of novelists, screenwriters and adventure seekers, while the elegant salons of Buenos Aires and the stylish resorts along the Caribbean attract a less vocal following. Like the Amazon rainforest, the Andes are home to communities that have barely changed for centuries; unlike the enormous metropolises of Brazil and Argentina, where life is so modern and energetic it will leave you breathless.

The countries in South America share a common history – thousands of years of indigenous cultures broken by European intrusion over 500 years ago; colonial rule followed by bitter wars of independence; then an unsteady progress at the fringe of world events. Despite these shared experiences, each country retains its own character.

On the north coast *(see page 85)*, are Colombia and Venezuela, Guyana, Suriname and French Guiana, racially mixed and geographically divided between rugged mountains, hot equatorial coastline and dense Amazon rainforest. South of Colombia lies the Andean heartland of South America *(see page 139)*: Peru, Bolivia and Ecuador, which have the highest Amerindian populations on the continent, clustered around the barren highlands where the mighty Inca empire once reigned and now the continent's least developed region.

The east *(see page 223)* is dominated by the giant Brazil, in a world of its own, separated from its Spanish-speaking neighbors by a Portuguese heritage – despite bordering on every single country in the continent except Ecuador and Chile. In the cooler southern zones *(see page 259)*, are Paraguay, Chile, Uruguay and Argentina, the most European-influenced and prosperous of South American republics, with vast empty spaces that stretch along the spine of the Andes to the last stop before Antarctica: Tierra del Fuego.   ❑

PRECEDING PAGES: Grey Glacier, Torres del Paine National Park, Chile; the "Devil's Throat", Iguaçu Falls, Brazil; reed boat on Lake Titicaca, Bolivia; beach in Rio, Brazil.
LEFT: "El Tren a las Nubes" ("The Train to the Clouds"), northern Argentina.
FOLLOWING PAGES: Machu Picchu, the Inca sacrificial city on a mountain-top.

20,000-4500 BC

PRE-COLUMBIAN TIMELINE

Human settlement in South America began with nomadic hunter-gatherers traveling southward, and reached its peak with the Inca Empire at the time of the Conquest

EARLIEST ORIGINS
First humans arrive in South America, around 20,000 BC, related to hunter-gatherers who crossed the Bering Straits "ice-bridge" between Asia and the Americas, following herds in search of food.

◁ *Ceramic vessel in a feline form, Chavín culture, Peru, c.900 BC.*

3000 BC–400 AD

POTTERY AND METAL
The first production of ceramics in South America began around 3000 BC, according to carbon-dated remains found in Colombia and Ecuador. These earliest ceramics were fashioned by hand, and were mostly utensils, but highly sophisticated ornamental and ceremonial items were soon being produced, from the Andes to the mouth of the Amazon.

Gold was the first metal known to be worked in the Andes, with remnants found in central Peru dating from around 2000 BC. The practice soon spread to Bolivia and later to Ecuador and Colombia. Gold and silver items of incredible beauty and technical quality were produced in huge quantities, as symbolic decorations of the ruling classes of the emerging state societies.

▷ *Silver breastplate, Chibcha culture, Colombia, c.1200 BC.*

400 BC–1100 AD

MASTER WEAVERS
The earliest textiles, found in central Peru, have been dated from as early as 8600 BC. Around 400 BC, the Nazca and Paracas cultures rose to prominence along the coastal desert of southern Peru. These people were the technical masters at weaving and pottery, much of which has survived in funeral chambers, preserved by the dry air. Some of the textiles found have more than 200 threads to the square

inch – finer than most modern materials. The Nazca culture also produced the famous lines on the desert floor, which still mystify visitors and archeologists alike – with interpretations ranging from a giant astronomical calendar to a landing strip for extraterrestrials.

◁ *Woven cotton cloth decorated with feathers, Paracas culture, Peru c.1000 BC.*

1100–1569 AD

BIRTH OF THE INCAS
c.1100 AD, the legendary appearance of Manco Capac, rising out of Lake Titcaca, hailed as the Sun god and divine leader of the chosen Inca race. The city of Cusco is founded by Manco Capac, legendary first Inca ruler. The Inca state is called *Tahuantinsuyu*, the "Land of the Four

Quarters," with Cusco at its center, as the "Umbilicus of the Universe."
c.1430 AD, Incas defeat Chancas and extend their empire across a huge area of South America, based on military efficiency, road network, terracing, irrigation and stone architecture.

◁ *Quipú knotted cords, used by Inca officials to keep an inventory of goods and produce.*

SETTLING DOWN

Cave remains and shell mounds *(sambaquis)* found in Brazil, and stone tools found in Peru, suggesting earliest humans from c.17,000–5000 BC. But the most reliable evidence of the first human settlement was at Monte Verde in central Chile, where remains have been dated at 12,500 BC.

◁ *Pottery figure of religious leader, Chavín culture, Peru, c.1200 BC*

FISHING AND FARMING

Between 7500 BC and 4500 BC Andean peoples began seasonal cultivation of crops, including the potato, maize, manioc and sweet potato; and domestication of dogs, llamas, alpacas and guinea pigs. Coastal tribes from present-day Ecuador to northern Chile harvested rich marine life of the Pacific, boosted by the Humboldt Current. The fishermen made hooks from shell, bone and cactus spines.

SOCIAL SKILLS

From about 2800 BC, societies began to form in the central and northern Andes. The earliest of these were the Chavín, in northern Peru; the Tiahuanaco to the south of Lake Titicaca and the San Agustín culture in southern Colombia. They built massive ceremonial urban centers in stone, and produced highly sophisticated ceramics, textiles and religious artifacts in gold and other precious metals and stones. They formed large populations of up to hundreds of thousands, organized in complex social hierarchies and covering large administrative regions. Amazonian societies also flourished at about this time, if not earlier. Aruak-speaking people inhabited a region near to present-day Manaus from as early as 3000 BC.

◁ *Gold "Darien pectoral" from Colombia, 900–1200 AD. Figure has alligator-like head, thought to represent a supernatural being, a priest or a shaman.*

IMPERIAL EXPANSION

Based in the deserts of northern Peru, the Moche culture built up an empire from about 100–800 AD, that covered much of the north of the country. Their military and commercial influence was aided by their roadbuilding and irrigation works, skills later picked up by the Incas. Above all, the Moche were superb artisans, producing ceramics and fine metal and precious stone ornaments to a standard never seen before in the Americas. The Moche Empire disappeared dramatically and mysteriously, around 700 AD. From about 600–1000 AD the religious Tiahuanaco culture combined with the militaristic Huari of the central Andean highlands to form an empire that at its peak spread into present-day Bolivia.

◁ *Gold burial mask, Lambayeque culture, Peru, 1100–1400 AD.*

PEAK AND FALL

Around the mid 1400s, the Inca Empire expands rapidly, firstly under Pachacutec and, later, under his son, Topa Inca. The Chimu empire, based in northern Peru, is defeated by the Incas, c.1466 AD. **1532 AD**, the Spanish conquistadors arrive in Peru; Inca Atahuallpa is executed a year later. In 1569, Tupac Amaru, the last Inca, is killed by the Spanish and the Conquest is complete.

◁ *Gold ornament, Sinu culture, Colombia, 1100–1600 AD.*

◁ *European missionaries bring the Gospel to Amazon peoples.*

THE FIRST PEOPLES

Pre-Columbian South America was a place of cultural diversity where enduring traditions and unique lifestyles were forged and great empires were built

The first colonization of South America is shrouded in mystery, as knowledge of those early times has had to be pieced together from archeological finds and linguistic evidence. Experts now believe that the first Americans arrived from the Asian continent, crossing the Bering Straits when they were

solid with ice during the last Ice Age, some 40,000 years ago. These bands of hunter-gatherers gradually spread down America; some sites in Patagonia show the far south was inhabited by around 9,000 BC. Remains of mastodon, sloth and other animals that have since disappeared, found together with arrowheads, demonstrate that these people were hunter-gatherers, but little else is known of their way of life or social organization.

Over several thousand years, these small groups turned from hunting to a more settled farming existence. According to archeological evidence, some lived close to the seashore and subsisted on a diet of fish and shellfish; some

settled in the Andean highlands, and others adapted to the tropical lowlands of the Amazon. These early settlers appear to have grown beans and peppers, and to have used domesticated dogs to help them hunt small game. Maize is thought to have been cultivated from Peru down to Argentina by 3,000 BC, and some of the highland groups also began to herd llama and other camelids. The first pottery remains found date from about 3,000 years ago.

First societies

As these groups became based around seasonal agriculture, population gradually increased, and more complex societies emerged, with officials, including chieftains and priests or shamans. Some of the earliest remains discovered are from **La Tolita** in Ecuador, which date from around 2,000 years ago, but the **San Agustín** culture in southern Colombia appears to have been one of the outstanding early sites. Here, burial mounds and intricate sculptures speak of a high degree of social organization, with religious ceremonies and complex burial rites.

Over the centuries, these small population centers grew into larger regional units, with ceremonial sites that have yielded a great deal of information. In some cases, such as the **Taironas** of the northeastern highlands of Colombia, it is thought that up to 250,000

THE MYTH OF EL DORADO

One of the early Colombian cultures, the Chibcha, gave rise to perhaps the most enduring South American legend, that of El Dorado. The Chibchas were divided into two kingdoms who worshiped the sun as their chief deity, and practiced human sacrifice. The ceremony for appointing a new Chibcha ruler apparently involved throwing gold statues into a lake, covering the new leader in gold dust and immersing him in the water until it had washed off. This made him "El Dorado" – the Golden One, giving rise to the legend.

people lived on one site; by now, the main buildings were made of stone, and gold, emeralds and other precious stones were used both for ornament and for trade.

The great edifices

In Peru and in the Andean highlands of Bolivia, there is evidence that settled occupation began as early as 5,000 BC. By 2,000 BC large monumental structures were being built, by population groups estimated at around 1,000 or 1,500 people. One of the most significant of these early centers grew up around 1,000 BC in the **Moche valley** near the northern Peruvian coast-

superseded in northern Peru by the **Moche** culture, which flourished from AD 200–700. The Moche are known for their prolific production of beautiful stirrup-spouted pottery, which depicted every aspect of their life, from violence and erotica to medical treatments. They also produced fine gold, silver and copperwork. Their imposing capital at **Moche** is dominated by two large structures – the **Huaca del Sol** and the **Huaca de la Luna** – temples of the sun and moon, built around a large plaza or central square. In around AD 500 natural disasters probably forced them to move from Moche; their later center at **Pampa Grande** shows that

line. It is known as the **Chavín** culture, after the archeological site at **Chavín de Huántar**, about 3,000 meters (10,000 ft) up in the Andean mountains, thought to date from 3,000 years ago. The most impressive structure here is a platform of earth and rock with a hollow interior, known as **El Castillo** or The Castle, probably used for religious ceremonies.

The Chavín culture, which also produced fine pottery and intricate stone stelae, is believed to have gone into a decline around 200 BC. It was

LEFT: pre-Columbian artifact from the Gold Museum, Bogotá, Colombia. **ABOVE:** the Gateway of the Sun, Tiahuanaco, Bolivia.

the culture continued to thrive until the 8th century. Later, the **Chimu** culture, based at **Chan Chan** *(see page 165)*, showed a continuity of development in these coastal sites.

At the same period in the south of Peru, the **Nazca** culture came to the fore *(see page 150)*. The Nazca people are best known for the extraordinary lines they drew in the desert, which from the air can be seen to represent figures such as hummingbirds, monkeys or fish, but which do not make sense from ground level. The size and complexity of the lines gave rise to the theory that extra-terrestrials must have visited South America in ancient times: although this idea is now dismissed, as yet there is no convincing explanation as to why a farming community should have spent so much time making such an immense display.

Further inland, near Lake Titicaca in northern Bolivia, the **Wankarani** people who lived by fishing, herding llama and growing potatoes, gave rise to the fascinating society known as the **Tiahuanaco** culture *(see page 181)*. Their main center, **Pukara**, was 3,600 meters (12,000 ft) up on the altiplano of the Andes. Some 40,000 people are thought to have lived in this city, with an impressive ceremonial complex at

> **ENORMOUS EMPIRE**
>
> The Inca empire is believed to have encompassed around a third of South America's population.

the north, so that in two generations the Incas succeeded in taking over the two most important Andean centers. The Incas continued to expand their rule: pushing down into northern Chile, Huayna Capac conquered what is now Ecuador, setting up a second center of empire in Quito. By 1525, the Inca empire extended 4,000 km (2,500 miles) from northern Ecuador to central Chile. Between six and 12 million people are estimated to have lived in the empire known as **Tawantinsuyu** or "Land of the Four Quarters".

its heart. The people of Tiahuanaco are among the first in South America to have used stone to create large permanent buildings; about 1,200 years ago their power and influence reached down as far as the Atacama desert in Chile.

The Incas

The last and most impressive of these Andean highland cultures was the **Inca** empire. This was based in the valley of Cusco, in what is now Peru, and only emerged around AD 1400, during the rule of the semi-mythical leader Viracocha. In 1438 his son Yupanqui defeated the Tiahuanaco people around Lake Titicaca, and Yupanqui's son Topa defeated the Chimu to

At the top of the Inca hierarchy was the emperor, or Sapa Inca, thought to be a descendant of the sun god Inti. The emperor was married to his sister, but had many other wives as well. Beneath him was a complicated priestly and administrative system, designed to keep control over the extensive empire. Communications were based on a 30,000-km (18,640-mile) network of paved roads, many of which still exist, along which relays of runners carried messages.

The imperial language, *Quechua,* was imposed throughout: the sons of royalty among the conquered peoples were taken to Cusco to learn it along with other important elements of

Inca culture. The Incas had no writing as we know it, but used knotted pieces of string to record important dates and numbers, which were memorized by a special group of officials. The Inca ceremonial centers at Machu Picchu, Cusco and elsewhere show their mastery of architecture, based on cutting and fitting large blocks of stone together without mortar.

Lost tribes

There are thought to have been anything between five and 50 million inhabitants throughout South America before the arrival of Europeans. Over the past 500 years, these indigenous

1860s and 1870s. Small groups of people who continued to live similar lives to those of their ancestors thousands of years earlier managed to survive on the distant coasts of Patagonia and Tierra del Fuego.

The prevalent attitude toward them is shown in an extract from Charles Darwin's journal when he visited these coasts in HMS *Beagle* in 1832: "I could not have believed how wide was the difference between savage and civilized man: it is greater than that between a wild and domesticated animal ..." Such attitudes led to the hunting and extermination of the indigenous people of the far south as late as the 20th

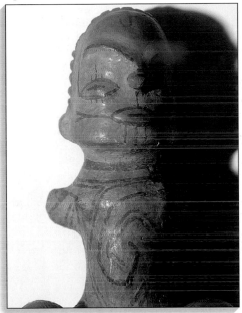

peoples have been incorporated into the dominant system or persecuted, and their own cultures looked down upon. In the 1530s, the great Inca empire was conquered by Francisco Pizarro with just 150 men *(see page 26)*. In the south of the continent, the Mapuche people of Chile resisted the European influence the longest, living independently until the end of the 19th century. In Argentina, the indigenous peoples of the pampas were conquered in what was known as the "War of the Desert" in the

LEFT: Gold treasure from Bogotá Gold Museum.
ABOVE: Inca "Mamacona" or "chosen woman" figure.
ABOVE RIGHT: Marajó figurine, Brazilian Amazon.

century, and a similar ignorance continues into the 21st century, to threaten other survivors of the first peoples of South America from Ecuador to Brazil and Venezuela. It is only in the northeastern Amazonian regions that small tribes who have had no contact with the outside world continue to exist.

Elsewhere, the descendants of the Inca and other Andean highland tribes, the Mapuche of southern Chile, the Tairona and other groups in Colombia and Ecuador live today as part of the mixed European and Latin American civilization around them, and yet they also stand apart, with many of their beliefs and traditions still powerful beneath the surface. ❑

LOST EMPIRES AND DISCOVERED TREASURE

What was life like in South America before the Europeans arrived? It's a mystery that continues to enthrall, and there are some intriguing clues

▷ **GOLDEN YEARS**
Metallurgy flourished in South America long before the Incas, as this Chimu funerary mask shows (Lambayeque Valley, Peru).

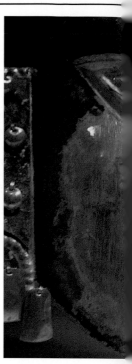

As no writing has been found from pre-Columbian South America, the artifacts left behind are likely to remain mere clues, giving us exciting glimpses into the lives of a host of very different communities that flourished and declined through various times and locations. The central Andes is by far the richest region for finding artifacts of the ancient past – partly because the dry desert conditions prevalent in the area are much more suitable for preserving ancient remains than the humid climate of the Amazon rainforest. But there is no doubt that the central Andes, especially the region that is now Peru, was a center for skilled activity of all kinds for centuries, producing numerous advanced communities long before the great Inca civilization arrived on the scene. Some ancient finds have echoes in the modern cultural practices of local communities, while others, like the mysterious people who built the megaliths of San Agustín, Colombia, seem to have disappeared without a trace.

△ **SAN AGUSTIN**
Little is known about the people who built 500 stone statues at this Colombian site *(see page 99)*.

MAKING SENSE OF THE PAST

Trying to remember all the names of the pre-Columbian groups can be a mind-boggling task. Most were named by archeologists after the locations where their remains were found, and grouped according to type, location and dating. Their complexity can be confusing, but the visitor with enough time to go to the excellent museums and archeological sites from Colombia to Chile will retain a picture of a fascinating era when civilizations waxed and waned, fought and conquered one another, and exchanged goods, skills, and ideas.

▷ **RAINFOREST LIFE**
Remains of early Amazonian cultures have largely perished in the humid climate.

◁ **MADE TO LAST**
This striking belt was woven by the Huari people of ancient Peru – 1,500 years ago.

LIFE AND TIMES OF THE MOCHE

If the Incas were master architects and empire builders, the much earlier Moche culture must be one of the most artistic and intriguing in South America. The Moche settled near the modern city of Trujillo in northern Peru, and flourished for a few centuries before and after the time of Christ. What sets the Moche apart is the high quality and quantity of the artifacts they left behind; from adobe pyramids to finely crafted gold jewelry. The recent discovery of the tomb of the "Lord of Sipán," pictured above, was one of the most important finds ever in the Andes (see also page 167), displaying Moche mastery of metallurgy. The vast collection of Moche ceramics found provide a remarkably accurate and detailed record of life 2,000 years ago, and some superb textiles have also been found.

◁ **MACHU PICCHU**
The most fabulous of all the Inca ceremonial centers, yet just one of many awe-inspiring Andean citadels in near-inaccessible locations.

▽ **GATEWAY OF THE SUN**
The pre-Inca site of Tiahuanaco, near Lake Tilicaca (see page 160) in Bolivia, was built in beautiful and sophisticated masonry.

◁ **INCA HAT FROM CHILE**
In the late Inca period, vicuña wool was worn only by kings, as cloth was a symbol of wealth.

▷ **MAIZE WORSHIP**
This Moche maize effigy may have been a fertility charm, used to help ensure a good crop.

THE EUROPEAN CONQUEST

In the 16th century, most of South America quickly fell to Spain and Portugal,
except for the far south, which would remain unconquered for three centuries

A t the end of the 15th century, Christopher Columbus explored the shores of Central and South America. Soon afterwards another Italian sailor, Amerigo Vespucci, was to give the new continent its name. Both these Italian explorers were in the pay of the Spanish crown, and before long, numerous Spaniards

were arriving. From their bases on the islands of Hispaniola, Puerto Rico and Cuba, they started to explore Central America and the South American mainland.

Gold was the lure that enticed most of them into the unknown territories of the continent. *El Dorado* was the legendary paradise where, Midas-like, everything was made of gold. In 1531 Francisco Pizarro set out to find these fabled riches in the Inca empire, which then stretched from Quito (in present-day Ecuador) in the north down through the areas now known as Peru, Bolivia and northern Chile. With only 150 followers, Pizarro managed to take control of the entire Inca empire in just two years. This

was achieved with ruthless determination aided by the fear that the Spaniards, mounted on horseback and using firearms, struck into the indigenous armies. Also, after years of refined centralization and uniformity, the Inca empire was severely weakened at the very moment that Francisco Pizarro began his conquest.

Downfall of the Incas

Before the Spaniards arrived, the Incas had expanded their empire from Cusco, Peru into Quito. The Inca Tupac-Yupanqui had founded the magnificent city of Tomebamba (now Cuenca) after subduing the southern Cañari people. His son, Huayna-Capac, married the daughter of the Duchicela king to consolidate their kingdoms.

Their son Atahuallpa was to become Huayna-Capac's favorite, but Atahuallpa's half-brother Huascar, descended from Inca lineage on both sides, was the legitimate heir. In 1527, Huascar ascended the Cusco throne, dividing the empire for the first time, between Quito and Cusco. Atahuallpa won the ensuing five-year civil war, killing his brother and establishing the new capital of Cajamarca in northern Peru. But the war had severely weakened both the infrastructure and the will of the Incas.

The Spanish arrived in Cajamarca in 1532. At a pre-arranged meeting, Atahuallpa and several thousand followers – many unarmed – entered the great square, where a Spanish priest called on him to embrace Christianity and accept the sovereignty of the Spanish king, Charles V. When Atahuallpa refused, Pizarro and his men ambushed the Incas. Pizarro was the only Spaniard wounded, when he seized Atahuallpa, while hundreds of Incas were killed.

Pizarro took Atahuallpa prisoner, demanding a room full of gold to pay his ransom. This was done, but the Inca was not freed. During his captivity, Atahuallpa learned to speak and write Spanish and to play chess. After nine months, the Spaniards accused him of treason, and garotted him. The Spaniards then marched on the Inca capital, Cusco, and immediately used the Inca bureaucracy and administrative divisions for their own ends. By 1533 they were in command of the entire Inca empire.

The Spaniards founded the city of Lima in 1535. Lima grew and prospered, as did its religious zeal, prompting some to dub it the "Rome of South America." Churches and monasteries sprang up, each more ostentatious than the next. Nuns, bishops, priests and monks flocked to Lima, and with them, eventually, came the terror of the Holy Inquisition, which meted out its frightful tortures in Peru from 1570 to 1761.

Lima was the seat of the Spanish Empire in South America for several centuries. The jungle

Orinoco and Amazon river systems. This brought the Spanish and Portuguese crowns into conflict over who should be allowed ownership of the new territories. The dispute was settled at the Treaty of Tordesillas in 1494, which established that Portugal should have the right to all lands east of the mouth of the Amazon – which meant the whole of the Brazilian coastline. Pedro Alvares Cabral claimed Brazil for Portugal in 1500. For many years, its most important export was dyewood or Brazil wood, but European settlement was slow, as the Portuguese preferred to trade with their new colony rather than to settle it. Eventually, a system of

city of Machu Picchu was the last redoubt of Inca rule, which ended completely in 1536, when Manco-Capac was defeated and killed.

Further north, Gonzalo Jimenez de Quesada set out to explore New Granada (Colombia). He quickly subdued the Chibcha kingdoms, and in 1538 Santa Fé de Bogotá was founded.

The birth of Brazil

Europeans were soon busy exploring down the Atlantic seaboard of South America and the

"captaincies" was set up, in which ownership of the land was granted by the Portuguese crown to individuals. Many of these people, such as Martim Afonso, brought in cattle and began to cultivate sugar, using enslaved Amerindians initially, and then people shipped from Africa.

The new cities of the south

In the far south, explorers were still seeking a sea route from Europe to Asia. Between 1519 and 1522, Fernando Magellan's fleet rounded Cape Horn and sailed out into the Pacific Ocean, making them the first Europeans to land in Patagonia and Chile. Sailors like Antonio Pigafetta enhanced the mystery of the new

LEFT: Amerindians buckling under the weight of colonial demands. **ABOVE:** the meeting of Pizarro and Atahuallpa at Cajamarca.

lands to wide-eyed Europeans, with lurid descriptions of the strange beings encountered there: giants, men with heads under their arms, or with tails like pigs.

Another wave of Spaniards set out to explore the Rio de la Plata (River Plate) network. Pedro de Mendoza founded Buenos Aires in 1536, and Asunción de Paraguay the following year. But the settlers were soon driven out of Buenos Aires by the indigenous people. It was only in 1580 that colonists sailed down from Asunción and set up the fort on the south bank of the River Plate again, this time successfully.

On the Pacific Ocean side, Pedro de Valdivia

cannon. The Spanish had to make do with maintaining garrison towns on the coast, and making marauding slave runs into indigenous territory.

In Argentina, the "frontier" was no more than 200 km (350 miles) south of Buenos Aires until well into the 19th century.

A Spanish treasure trove

This first wave of conquest of South America lasted for two generations. From then until the beginning of the 19th century, the Spanish and Portuguese crowns sought to administer their vast empires. Economic activity was based on mining – first for gold, then silver, which by

pushed south from Inca territory into Chile, and established the capital city of Santiago in 1541. The Incas had only exacted tribute as far south as the Bío Bío River, and Valdivia fared little better when he marched south of the river, meeting his match in the Araucanian warriors, for whom death in battle constituted a supreme honor. In 1554, they captured Valdivia, bound him to a tree, and beheaded him. Legend has it that the executioner ate Valdivia's heart.

The south (now Patagonia) "belonged" to the Araucanian (or Mapuche as they are known today), and other Amerindians well into the 19th century. They organized a cavalry force of 10,000 men and learned to use firearms and

THE HORRORS OF DISEASE

Diseases carried by Europeans wrought more devastation on the native peoples of South America than the weapons they brought. Indigenous populations, who had evolved over centuries without developing immunity to diseases like smallpox, cholera, syphilis, measles and even malaria, fell by 95 percent in some regions. Further waves of disease were brought with African slaves, and the ensuing reduction in the native population led to the importation of more African slaves, who had built up resistance over the years.

the middle of the 16th century became South America's most valuable export.

Agriculture was developed, with Spaniards being awarded large tracts of land and also "given" large numbers of local indigenous peoples to work it, in what was known as the *encomienda* system, a feudalistic method of securing plantation labor in exchange for a subsistence living. Taxation in the form of animals and vegetables was exacted from the Amerindians, and labor was unrewarded.

But the power in South America was firmly located in the growing towns and cities. It was here that Spanish authority was rooted, and here too that the Catholic church followed in the wake of the conquerors. Most of South America became a viceroyalty based in Lima and its port at Callao. From here, Spain attempted to impose a commercial monopoly on all its South American colonies. The inhabitants of the colonies were only permitted to sell their products to Spain, and could only purchase products from the mother country. A Council of the Indies was set up in Seville in southern Spain to administer the territories. The riches of South America were dispatched back to Europe in yearly fleets, which soon attracted the interest of English, Dutch and French pirates.

A new society

Through the 16th and 17th centuries, the Spaniards consolidated their rule. In each country there were a small number of Spanish-born administrators and clergy. Below them in rank were the *criollos*, people born in South America but claiming both parents as having Spanish blood. But the fastest-growing sector of the colonial population were the *mestizos*, mixed-race people, most of whom were born of a Spanish father and an indigenous mother due to the preponderance of male immigrants. One of the conquerors of Chile, Francisco de Aguirre, admitted to having at least 50 such children, and proudly affirmed that "the service rendered to God in engendering mestizos is greater than the sin incurred in so doing."

Many indigenous groups remained outside Spanish society, or were forced to work in slave-like conditions on the big estates. As

more labor was needed, so the trade in slaves from Africa grew; they were brought mostly to the Caribbean coast of Venezuela and Colombia, and to the coast of Peru. But it was Brazil where African slaves made most impact on the rest of society. As the Brazilian sugar plantations grew in importance, so did the numbers of slaves shipped in from west Africa and Angola, rising to a million by the 18th century.

As the demand for sugar fell, the discovery of gold and diamonds in Minas Gerais led to a further boom in Brazil, and Rio de Janeiro became increasingly important as a port. In 1763 it was made the capital, and its importance increased

still further by the end of the century, with the growth of Brazil's new treasure crop, coffee.

As Brazil's economic strength grew, so relations with Portugal became more difficult. Brazilian merchants wanted to be free to trade with other countries, and local politicians wanted more control over their own affairs.

A similar situation arose in the Spanish colonies. Most of the treasures shipped back to Spain had been used to finance its wars in Europe, but by the end of the 18th century, Spain had fallen behind both France and Great Britain as an industrial and colonial power. By the 19th century, European wars were to lead to the loss of its South American empire. ❑

LEFT: Pukara (fortress), the last Inca stronghold in Chile. **RIGHT:** Pedro de Valdivia, who was put to death by the Mapuche after invading their territory.

INDEPENDENCE

Spain's defeats on the battlefields of Europe led to the loss of all its South American territories, but independence for the criollos *brought neither peace nor democracy*

When the Emporer Napoleon invaded Spain in 1808, the consequences were felt all over "Spanish America", as *criollos* took advantage of Spain's weakness to free themselves from the demands of the Spanish Empire. In previous decades, republican ideas from the revolutions in North America

commanding a British naval squadron on the way home from South Africa, decided to capture Buenos Aires and open it up to British trade. He occupied the city for several months until the *porteños* (inhabitants of Buenos Aires) rose in rebellion and captured the whole enemy force. Reinforcements from Britain were

and in France had been taken up enthusiastically by many South Americans, who wanted to be able to trade freely with countries other than Spain, and to elect their own leaders.

Rebellions in the south

In the 18th century, Buenos Aires (the modern-day capital of **Argentina**) was a thriving smuggling center, allowing trade to enter South America without having to pass through Lima or Panama, as the Spanish Crown had decreed. The city grew in importance with the creation in 1776 of the Viceroyalty of La Plata along with the relaxation of trade restrictions.

In 1806 an Englishman, Sir Home Popham,

defeated by a popular militia. The victory gave *porteños* extra confidence in their ability to govern themselves.

The fortunes of Asunción, which is now the capital of **Paraguay**, were tied by the Rio de la Plata (River Plate) to those of Buenos Aires. When the Spanish colonial seat in Lima closed the port of Buenos Aires to ensure that trade (and taxation) would pass through Lima, Paraguay suffered as well. As the power of Buenos Aires grew, the leaders of Asunción began to resent their own growing insignificance, refusing to go along with the Argentine declaration of independence in 1810. A military junta led by Fulgencio Yegros declared the state of Paraguay independent on May 14, 1811.

Montevideo, the modern capital of **Uruguay**, had also been in British hands for a brief period, in 1807. Later, dictates from Spain and Buenos Aires aimed at limiting contraband and expelling small landholders from the great *estancias* caused growing resentment in the region. In 1811 revolutionary forces representing the interior and led by José Gervasio Artigas, a *criollo* army commander, rebelled against the Spanish authorities in Montevideo. One of the aims of the revolution was to redistribute wealth to the poor, including Amerindians and freed slaves.

With the assistance of Buenos Aires, the revolutionary forces managed to eject the Spanish authorities, but Artigas and a growing number of *orientales* (easterners) did not want to substitute the old colonial power with the newer power of Buenos Aires. In 1815 he succeeded in ejecting the *porteños* and establishing his authority throughout the new country.

In 1816 the Portuguese invaded, fearing the spread of revolutionary ideas to Brazil. They defeated Artigas in 1820, with support from sections of the upper class who resented his confiscation of their lands. The country remained in Brazilian hands after Brazil's independence, in 1822. However, many *orientales* were becoming disillusioned with the Brazilian influence, and in 1825 a revolt, led by the legendary "Thirty-three Orientales" began against Brazil. Independence was finally declared on August 25, 1825.

Britain played a part in Uruguay's independence and in mediating a peace settlement. The River Plate was one of the most important trading channels to South America, and British trade interests did not want it to be controlled by Argentina alone, or disrupted by Brazil.

The wars of independence

The collapse of the Spanish monarchy when Napoleon's troops entered Madrid had dramatically shown *criollos* all over the American continent that Spanish rule could be defeated.

By 1810, these political leaders had declared autonomous governments or juntas in many parts of Spanish South America. When Spain attempted to repress these movements, the real wars of independence broke out. In the south

LEFT: early painting of Punta Arenas, Chile.
RIGHT: General Simón Bolívar, *El Libertador*.

these were led by the Spanish-born general José de San Martín. He managed to defeat Spanish forces in Argentina, and then in 1817 led his army across the Andes – a tremendous feat of organization – to help the Chileans in their struggle. In 1811, **Chile** had opened its ports to neutral countries, in defiance of Spain's monopoly on trade. But forces loyal to Spain had regained control, and the Chilean insurgents had been forced into exile in neighboring Argentina. Many of them returned to Chile with General San Martín, and this time were successful in overthrowing Spanish rule.

In the northern part of South America, the

independence struggle was led by *El Libertador* – "The Liberator" – Simón Bolívar. The struggle began in his native Venezuela, where he successfully fought off the Spanish loyalists to become Dictator. He was very successful at first, winning six battles against royalists in 1813, but with the defeat of Napoleon in 1815 and the restoration of the Spanish monarchy in Europe, the fight to recover the colonies began in earnest. Bolívar was forced to retreat to Haiti and Jamaica: letters he wrote from exile were to become the fundamental ideology behind the independence struggle. Three years later, he was back on the mainland, leading a force of Venezuelans and British veterans from the

Napoleonic Wars. The Battle of Boyaca in northern Colombia on August 17, 1819, marked the end of royalist resistance there, and not long afterwards, Bolívar entered Santa Fé de Bogotá in triumph.

Peru had been the center of the Spanish empire in South America, and it proved the hardest country of all to liberate. Gradually San Martín's forces advanced from the south and Bolívar's from the north, and independence was declared in Lima in 1821, but parts of the country remained in Spanish control until 1826.

> **VENEZUELAN HERO**
>
> Simón Bolívar was an inspiration to even foreign romantics. The English poet Byron named a boat after him and planned to sail it to Venezuela.

Disillusioned and dying, Bolívar spent his last days at Santa Marta in Colombia. His verdict on his life's dream was harsh: "America is ungovernable. He who serves the revolution plows the sea". San Martín had a similar experience in Argentina, discovering that the new generation of politicians had no place for a troublesome general. Eventually he left his home in South America and lived out his last years in France.

It was only years later that these heroes of independence were honored: every country in

When General Antonio José de Sucre's victories in Peru helped Bolívar put an end to Spanish rule there, the provinces of "Upper Peru" were declared a new republic named in honor of the Liberator: **Bolivia**. Although they had nothing in common, these disorganized territories, stretching from the Amazon to the icy sierra, were now forced to fuse and develop as a nation.

The immediate years following independence were in many ways more difficult than the battles themselves. Bolívar dreamt that the different countries could stay united as **la Gran Colombia**, but within a decade **Ecuador** and **Venezuela** had seceded.

South America now has statues, street names, and even currencies named after them.

Rise of the dictators

For several decades after Independence, there was virtual civil war in most of the emerging republics. The fight for control was usually between two groups: those from the interior who wanted some kind of loose federal political arrangement, and those from the cities who traded more with the outside world and wanted strong central control of the new nation. Those groups were usually identified with conservatives and liberals, allegiances which survive to this day. Often the struggle for power between these two factions was only settled by the emergence of a strong autocratic leader, which hindered the growth of democratic rule. By the mid-19th century, many South Americans found they had thrown off the tyranny of rule from Spain for a more brutal local variety.

Brazil: independence without war

Portugal, Brazil's imperial power, was also invaded by Napoleon's troops. The Portuguese Emperor Dom João fled and moved his entire court to Brazil in 1808. Brazil then became a dominion in its own right, until the Emperor returned to Portugal in 1821, leaving his son

Pedro's son took over the Brazilian throne, and outlawed the importation of slaves in 1850, but the practice continued in the country. Brazil was dominated by the large estate owners of the north, who employed huge numbers of slaves to grow sugar and other crops without much concern for efficiency or social progress. Dom Pedro II deliberately set out to encourage European immigrants to settle in the south of Brazil. This new population settled in Rio Grande do Sul and made São Paulo a new pole for development. There were increasing tensions between these two power groups, with the question of slavery being at the center of

Dom Pedro I in charge. When Pedro was recalled to Portugal in 1822, he rebelled, replacing the Portuguese insignia with the new national colors of yellow and green, and shouting, "Independence or death!" This, in effect, was Brazil's declaration of independence, celebrated each year on September 7.

In the early 19th century, Brazilian society was made up of about a million people of European ancestry, the local indigenous groups, and some 2 million black slaves. In 1847, Dom

---

LEFT: the Llanero Lancers in Venezuela's wars of independence. **ABOVE:** many blacks freed from slavery were press-ganged into the Brazilian army.

the debate over what kind of country Brazil should be. Eventually in 1888 the Brazilian Parliament voted to abolish slavery, making Brazil the last country in the western hemisphere to do so. This move brought the conflict in Brazilian society out into the open, and the following year Pedro II was deposed and a constitutional republic created. As in many other countries of South America, the new parliamentary regime was weak compared to the real power that the military had, which was often used to impose their own solution to political problems.

The battles of independence were over, but the struggle for power in South America's new republics had only just begun. ❑

INTO THE 21ST CENTURY

*The republics of South America have trodden a rocky road to a tenuous stability,
and many have failed to prosper, despite being rich in natural assets*

By the late 19th century, South America was completely free of Spanish rule, but power and influence were still in the hands of a privileged minority. The land was largely under control of the owners of huge estates, who were usually resistant to any change. The economies were dominated by and Chile eventually occupied the whole of the territory of Patagonia, finally subduing and largely destroying the indigenous cultures in the process. In Argentina, General Julio Roca's "Conquest of the Wilderness" in the 1880s opened up the pampas and Patagonia. Any native standing in his path was killed, the rest

exports, whether of products like coffee in the case of Brazil and Colombia, wheat and beef from Argentina, or minerals such as copper from Chile and later, oil from Venezuela. Governments found it easier to tax these exports and buy imported goods than to encourage local industry. Britain took the lead in selling products to South America.

Despite this new kind of dependency, the independent South American countries quickly forged a strong sense of their own identity. Wars consolidated national boundaries, but could be extremely destructive to populations as well as burgeoning economies.

In the south, the governments of Argentina

BUYING BRITISH

Britain did brisk trade with South America in the 19th century. In the 1850s the British Consul in Argentina wrote the following about the *gauchos*, wild horsemen of the Argentinian pampa:

"Take his whole equipment, examine everything about him – and what is there not of hide that is not British? If his wife has a gown, ten to one it is from Manchester. The camp kettle in which he cooks his food, the common earthenware he eats from, his knife, spoon, bits and the poncho which covers him – are all imported from England".

herded into reservations. The land was used to raise cattle for European markets, taking advantage of new methods of freezing meat.

By the end of the century, the ten republics of South America were firmly established. But the struggle for power in the relatively new nations had only just begun, and would overshadow the events of the following century, with the result that for much of the past 100 years, South America has found itself on the sidelines of world history. Its involvement in the great wars of the 20th century was minimal – few South Americans fought in them, and the continent suffered no occupation or damage. But the in 1900 there were around 40 million South Americans. In the 21st century it is nearly ten times that figure. In a relatively short time, South America has evolved into a continent where more than two-thirds of the population live in towns or cities. But with ownership of many national assets in foreign hands, profits were rarely invested in the country, and rural poverty was not alleviated, which further fueled the trek to the cities.

The haves and have-nots

In the towns and cities, the 20th century saw a powerful growth of both the middle and work-

ideological battles that divided Europe and the rest of the world for many years were reflected in the region. Its military rulers often brought in fascist ideas formulated in Spain or Italy, whilst guerrilla groups with Marxist ideologies sought to bring revolutionary change.

An urban society

These political developments were responses to the challenges and tensions within South American society. The population has grown rapidly:

LEFT: mine workers in Chile's northern desert.
ABOVE: the Peróns on the balcony of the Casa Rosada, Buenos Aires.

ing classes. Argentina's booming beef industry and conquest of more territory in Patagonia meant that more labor was required, and in the 1880s thousands of European immigrants flocked to the country, mainly poor peasants from Italy and Spain. It was the greatest influx of immigrants in relation to population patterns in world history. But the immigrants usually arrived penniless, and did not get to share in the country's boom wealth, as the great landowning families refused to break up their massive holdings and snapped up even more land by using false names. The immigrants were given small plots, but only to work for three to five years before moving on. Unlike North America, which was settled by millions of small landowners, Argentina remained the property of around 200 close-knit families referred to simply as "the oligarchy". The new immigrants remained in the urban areas, and the population of Buenos Aires grew from 750,000 in the early 1900s to more than two million in 1930.

As the economy expanded, the moneyed classes looked to Europe for their inspiration, and largely ignored the social inequalities and growing protest movements around them. The Great Depression of the 1930s ushered in a period of political instability and military rule characterized by the typical alliance of the

trade unions and organized labor. During his 15 years in power, Vargas built up a strong state and promoted Brazilian industry, in ways reminiscent of Mussolini in Italy.

After Vargas' fall, a long period of constitutional rule followed. Brazil's economy and population grew rapidly, a growth symbolized by the construction of Brasilia as the country's new capital in the late 1950s *(see page 239)*. But as in the rest of South America, the growing numbers of landless people in the rural areas, added to increasingly militant political groups in the major towns and cities, began to pose a threat to stability – or so it appeared

armed forces with conservative elements in society to try to halt political reforms or any of the new ideas finding political expression.

In **Brazil** the pattern was also one of economic instability leading to periods of military dictatorship. In the early part of the 20th century, most of the country's wealth came from the export of rubber and coffee. But Malaysia began to grow rubber too, and in 1930 the world price of coffee fell dramatically. With military backing, Getulio Vargas seized power from a weak civilian government. The so-called "father of the people" used a populist rhetoric to win the support of poor workers and peasants, and brought in legislation that encouraged

to the armed forces, who took over Brazil's government once more in 1964.

Foreign ownership

Many South American countries saw the wealth generated within their own borders trickle away overseas. **Bolivia** is arguably the worst example, with most of its silver going to Spain where it was used to finance European wars *(see page 173)*, and the profits from its massive tin wealth staying in the hands of a few entrepreneurs and mostly being squandered abroad, leaving it today one of the world's poorest countries.

Another country which is still extremely poor, **Ecuador**, did brisk international trade in bananas, coffee, cocoa pods and Panama hats. The sole beneficiaries, however, were a few hundred *criollo* families and the foreign companies who controlled the industries. For decades Ecuador has been the world's largest exporter of bananas, but until the 1960s the entire industry was owned by the Boston-based United Fruit Company. Until the recent growth of the oil industry, bananas accounted for most of Ecuador's export earnings – and the fact that all the profits left the country is one reason why Ecuador has remained so poor for so long.

Colombia's wealth was also traditionally based on the export of bananas and coffee. But was found in Lake Maracaibo. At that time, Venezuela was ruled by the dictator Juan Vincente Gomez, who had no scruples about siphoning off a large part of this new wealth, nor about rewarding his family and cronies with lavish gifts (including the archbishop who gave him special dispensation to eat meat on Good Friday). Little of the profits from the "black gold" found their way to the vast majority of Venezuelans, who moved in increasing numbers from the poor, backward countryside to the attractions of the capital city, Caracas.

The death of Gomez in 1935 led to riots and strikes until the typical combination of military

these industries were either owned by foreign companies like the United Fruit Company, or by a small number of national landowners who had control of vast plantations. As the population grew, poverty increased, as did social tensions, exploding in 1948. Years of violence and civil war followed *(see page 91)*.

Neighboring **Venezuela** suffered political turmoil in spite of the discovery of huge oil deposits, which did bring great wealth to the country – but not without a struggle. In 1917, oil

LEFT: Brazil's President Juscelino Kubitschek at the 1960 inauguration of Brasília. **ABOVE:** the bombing of La Moneda, Santiago, Chile, during the 1973 coup.

officers and conservative landowners took power. Eventually one strong man emerged – Colonel Pérez Jimenez, who brought in a series of populist measures, allowing labor organization and investing some of the oil profits into public works and low-cost housing. Once again though, this autocratic rule led to instability.

In 1958, after riots which caused the death of 600, Jimenez was overthrown. Elections heralded an unbroken period of parliamentary rule.

Territorial conflict

North America had one major civil war, but many of the republics of South America have been severely weakened by repeated territorial disputes. Some benefited – in the 19th century, Chilean dictator Diego Portales won a war with a Peru/Bolivian Confederation (1836–39), taking Antofagasta, later claiming Patagonia, Tierra del Fuego and Magallanes, and founding Punta Arenas in 1847.

In the 1879 War of the Pacific, Peru and Bolivia declared war on Chile, resulting in a Chilean takeover of southern Peru, along with its valuable nitrate and mineral mines, and Bolivia losing its only access to the sea. And in 1903, Brazil annexed a vast stretch of Bolivia's Amazon basin, known to be rich in rubber trees.

Wars could be costly for the winners too.

Paraguay won much of the southern Chaco from Bolivia in the 1932 Chaco War. While Bolivia held on to its Chaco oil fields, no oil has ever been found in the Paraguayan Chaco lands. The desperately fought war bled both countries dry economically and in manpower.

Tension still exists between Peru and Ecuador over a conflict which began in 1942, when Peru annexed most of Ecuador's southern jungle region, El Oro. This area is rich in precious metals and oil, and was where Ecuador's best coffee was grown. A three-month conflict in 1995 cost both sides hundreds of casualties and had a very damaging effect on the Ecuadorian economy.

A turbulent decade

Ironically, it was the countries with the most stable political traditions and the biggest economic growth which suffered the most brutal military dictatorships in the 1970s. Uruguay had the longest democratic tradition and one of the world's first welfare states, but the 1950s and 1960s saw economic downturn, social disruption and the rise of guerrillas. A military takeover in 1973 led to 12 years of dictatorship with widespread repression and torture (*see page 313*).

In the 19th century, Chile was the most stable nation in the region. In 1970 the Socialist party was elected under Salvador Allende, but in 1973 the military wrested control under General Pinochet, once again with the backing of conservative forces (*see page 280*).

Pinochet remained in power for 17 years, bringing in the free-market economic model that has since been adopted by practically all the other countries of South America. In many ways, this has meant their economies have come full circle: earnings once again mainly come from exports. Local markets have been opened up to all kinds of foreign goods, with the result that national firms have either gone out of business or have been bought up by larger and more efficient foreign concerns. This has led to a new economic stability, but with high levels of unemployment.

The new challenges

The early years of the 21st century promise a bright future, if South America learns to integrate as a region, realizing Bolívar's dream of unity. In 2003, Brazil's President Lula pledged to revitalize the South American alliance, Mercosur. The trading bloc currently has Argentina, Brazil, Paraguay, and Uruguay as members. If Lula has his way, Mercosur will take as its model the European Union, expanding to include Chile, Bolivia and Venezuela as members.

Sadly, chronic poverty and unemployment are causing massive unrest in some countries, and governments need to do much more to narrow the huge gap between the rich and poor, to harmonize life in the cities and the countryside, and to offer the continent's young population – almost 40 percent of the total – the chance to realize their full potential. ❑

LEFT: Alberto Fujimori, president of Peru 1990–2000; allegations of bribery forced him to flee to Japan.

The Drugs Trade

A common sight in Bolivian street markets is huge sacks of coca leaves for sale. The local people buy them to make tea or to chew in order to stave off the effects of altitude, cold, or lack of nourishment *(see page 188)*. In many highland and jungle areas of South America, indigenous groups use their knowledge of plants and essences to concoct drugs for use in ceremonies.

But in the past 40 years, with the spectacular growth of the export of refined drugs to the United States and Europe, drugs and drug-trafficking have become a huge problem for the region. Coca leaves are converted into the basic paste for cocaine in distant hideouts (chewing coca leaves does not have the same effect as taking the powdered drug, as massive amounts are needed to make cocaine).

In the 1970s, the fight for control of the production and distribution of cocaine for foreign markets led to increased violence. Hoodlums from Colombian cities such as Medellín and Cali made vast profits out of the shipments, and showed little mercy for rivals or anyone trying to maintain the rule of law. They formed "cartels" to keep prices up and competitors out, and soon drugs became Colombia's most valuable export. Colombia produces 80 percent of the world's supply of cocaine and over a third of the heroin.

Successive United States governments, aware that the problem was manifesting itself on the streets of their own cities, tried to harness attempts to control the trade. They insisted that South American governments carry out programs to "eradicate" the plantation of crops like coca; that police and armed forces co-operate with the Drug Enforcement Administration in tracking down the traffickers; and that governments be willing to extradite those convicted of trading in illegal drugs.

This led to a virtual civil war in Colombia at the end of the 1980s, as traffickers like Pablo Escobar took on the state in their efforts to avoid arrest. Escobar and his followers are believed to have blown up a passenger aeroplane with 200 people on board, and several hundred policemen among others were killed in their war against the state. Escobar was finally killed after escaping from jail, and the power of the Medellín and Cali drugs cartels was tamed. This did not mean the problem

went away – new people took over, and the trafficking moved to other countries – Brazil, Ecuador, and Mexico, which shares a long border with the principal client, the United States.

Throughout South America today, the drugs trade is still a huge if largely invisible presence. Drugs money has financed new banks, hotels, and buildings from expansive beach resorts in Chile or Uruguay to high-rise blocks in downtown Bogotá and Caracas.

It is one of the chief reasons for the high levels of corruption in government and other offices – in Colombia for example, President Ernesto Samper, who was in power from 1994 to 1998, was never

able to shake off allegations that his successful election campaign benefitted from several million dollars' worth of contributions from the drugs bosses *(see page 92)*. From poorly paid border guards and customs officials, to equally badly paid police and army recruits, to politicans and high-ranking officers, money from the illegal trade perverts the system.

The US war against drugs in South America continues, with the result that 2 million Colombians have been displaced. Meanwhile, the fragile economies of many South American countries continue to depend on the drug trade, and the trafficking persists in creating social disruption around the world. ❑

RIGHT: coca leaves from the Andes, which can be used to produce cocaine.

A LAND OF MANY FACES

The people of South America are as diverse as the countries many of them came from, yet they also share a distinctive Latin American heritage

Ever since Colombus landed in what is now the Bahamas and thought he had arrived in the East Indies, the indigenous peoples of the Americas have been lumped together and collectively termed Indians. Today, indigenous farmers in the Andes are described as *campesinos* – this term has been made official in Bolivia. The number of terms used to describe ethnicity in South America may daunt the visitor – it's an indication of not just the continent's racial diversity, but also of the importance of ancestry here.

Mestizo, or *mameluco* in Brazil, describes someone who is part indigenous, part European. *Mulatto* describes someone whose origins are African and European. In Brazil, *cafuso* describes someone of Amerindian and African heritage.

All this complex ethnic terminology probably grew out of people's attempts to define their identity in a continent that has seen so much immigration in the past 500 years, and where national boundaries have only been defined in the past few centuries and are often in dispute. This is a continent where people from the world's most diverse nations and cultures meet, mix and intermarry, and where the Japanese ancestry of Alberto Fujimori in Peru or the Syrian descent of Carlos Menem in Argentina raised few eyebrows. Yet the surface multiculturalism of South America hides a complex mesh of social and racial hierarchies.

The new arrivals

South America's ethnic make-up changed dramatically after the arrival of Europeans in the 16th century, who were predominately Spanish and, in Brazil, Portuguese. They initially arrived as single men, intermarried with the indigenous women, and brought in slaves from Africa. By 1888, when slavery was finally abolished in Brazil, immigration from Europe was

PRECEDING PAGES: Quechua people at a wedding near Cusco, Peru; Carajás boy, Amazon. **LEFT:** Quechua woman. **RIGHT:** teenage girls, Santiago, Chile.

being actively encouraged, particularly to Brazil and Argentina. Most of the immigrants initially came from Spain and Italy, but there were also Germans, eastern Europeans, Syrians, Lebanese, Japanese and Chinese.

The people of the Andean countries – Peru, Colombia, Ecuador, Bolivia and Chile – are

predominately *mestizo*. These countries also have the highest "full-blood" Amerindian populations, partly because there were a lot of indigenous people living in this region at the time of the Conquest, and partly because of the large-scale destruction of the indigenous societies in the southern regions and lowlands.

People of African descent are concentrated in northern Brazil and parts of Colombia, Venezuela and the Guianas, places where their ancestors were taken as slaves. Argentina and Southern Brazil are predominately caucasian, and Chile is roughly 20 percent white.

Guyana, Suriname and French Guiana, on the north Caribbean coast, have a particularly interesting ethnic make-up, due to their histories as crop-producing outposts of three world empires – Dutch (Suriname), British (Guyana) and French (French Guiana). African slaves were brought in to work the plantations, and many then fled into the rainforest to form "Bush Negro" communities, retaining many of their African traditions.

After the abolition of slavery, indentured labor was imported from other parts of the empires, leaving all of these countries with highly mixed populations composed of

> **SPEAKING OF ...**
>
> There are at least 82 different indigenous language groups in South America.

Asians, Amerindians, Africans, Portuguese *mulattos* and Europeans.

New communities

The Bush Negroes are not the only group to have taken advantage of South America's formidable territory in order to pursue their chosen lifestyle. This continent has a number of discrete independent communities which often transcend national boundaries, such as the *gauchos* of Argentina *(see page 338)*, and the fundamentally religious Mennonite groups *(see page 274)*. Don't be surprised if you come across lederhosen on the Caribbean Coast, or Welsh hats in Patagonia – these are the legacy

of groups of immigrants who might have felt restricted in their country of origin, or who just wanted to build a new life in a new country.

The continent's racial diversity is reflected in its languages. Although Spanish is by far the dominant language in South America today, and Portuguese is the official language of Brazil, many other languages are spoken.

Native American languages are frequently spoken in the Andean regions, and in Bolivia, Spanish, Quechua and Aymara are all official languages. In Peru, Spanish and, since 1975, Quechua, are both official languages. In Paraguay, Spanish is the official language, but most people speak Guaraní. The Guianas follow a colonial pattern, with English the main language of Guyana, Dutch the main language of Suriname, and French the language of French Guiana.

The racial hierarchy

In many areas the melting pot has been blended so completely that local people are unexpectedly homogeneous. In the cities of northern Chile, Bolivia and Peru, for example, pale European tourists are distinctive enough to turn heads, as do people with darker skin coloring, who will frequently hear themselves described as *moreno* or *negrita*.

In many South American countries, skin color and racial origins have a distinct bearing on status. The palest people are frequently concentrated in the professional establishments, behind the counters of smart department stores or in front of television cameras. In bars, restaurants and on long-distance buses you can often detect a striking color difference between the faces that appear on the television screen and the faces watching it, with the few dark or black faces on screen usually relegated to servile roles.

Off the screen, indigenous people – particularly in the Andes region – are usually seen laboring in the fields or behind market stalls. Many indigenous people have steadfastly continued to practice their ancient customs and traditions, often in the face of strenuous opposition. The distinctive dress of Bolivian *campesina* women is believed to have developed as a response to the conquistadors' prohibition of tradtional dress. The death penalty was imposed in many cases for Amerindians who resisted conversion to Christianity, so it's not surprising that the countries of South America are overwhelmingly Catholic (except for Guyana, previously a British colony.) Yet many communities have incorporated their religious traditions into Catholicism, producing hybrid religions in some areas, like *Macumba* in Brazil *(see page 246)*.

In the years following the Conquest many indigenous societies were forced to either adapt or be obliterated. The tribal societies in the low-lying Amazon regions were devastated by European disease and violence. Some of the

Lifestyles under threat

People who live in South America's urban regions may feel economically and socially under pressure to deny their Amerindian ancestry, but for many tribal peoples of the Amazon, their heritage and distinctive traditions are among the few resources they have left in their struggle for the survival of their communities. Many of these lifestyles are constantly evolving and adapting in response to their changing environment, which is particularly vulnerable to the encroachments of the technological age.

In some areas, tribal groups are benefitting

numerical reduction may be explained by the fact that Amerindian heritage persists in being seen as a stigma in most South American countries, to the extent that most people prefer to describe themselves as white rather than *mestizo*, particularly in urban areas. Take the typical response to a question frequently asked of tour guides by admiring tourists, enthralled by the history of the Inca or the Aymara:

"And are you descended from the Incas?"

"Oh, no! My grandparents were Spanish – in fact, my sister's baby is as white as you!"

LEFT: Peruvian boy in the Sierra.
ABOVE: young street vendors in Brazil.

BRAZILIAN HOLOCAUST

In 1639 the Spanish Jesuit Cristóbal de Acuña wrote that "Amazon Indian settlements are so close together that one is scarcely lost sight of before another comes into view." But this state of affairs was not to last – 17th-century officials in Brazil boasted that they killed 2 million Amerindians in the lower Amazon. Brazil's indigenous population was estimated at 2½–6 million at the time of the Conquest. Although numbers fell by around a third in the 20th century, tribal groups have grown in recent years and now account for 350,000 of the population.

from an increased tourist interest, which brings in some income while encouraging the continuity and development of their way of life. Some such schemes are criticized as creating tribal theme parks, but there is reason to believe the alternatives for the tribes concerned could indeed be oblivion.

Some indigenous groups, like the Mapuche of southern Chile, have found it necessary to take political action to ensure their survival. But in a few cases, ethnic and social unrest have been left to foment, spawning guerilla movements, notably in Peru, where the Sendero Luminoso ("Shining Path") terrorized locals

and visitors for years, and where another guerrilla group, Tupac Amaru, seized worldwide headlines with their seige of the Japanese Embassy in Lima in December 1996.

Social hierarchies

The middle classes are becoming more influential, but in many South American countries, old social hierarchies refuse to shift. Numerous revolutions and government coups have failed to dislodge the influence of the handful of old family names that still wield formidable influence.

These social hierarchies often originally derived their power from the old feudalistic *encomienda* system, whereby families of Span-

ish conquistador origin would control huge estates, worked by indigenous serfs who would provide labor in return for being allowed to work small plots of land for their own use. This system was still officially condoned in Ecuador until 1971.

Women's changing roles

South America has an increasing number of independent businesswomen, but their status is often questionable in this predominantly Catholic continent, where children, children and more children are the focus of every family. In some countries, jobs advertizsed on television are divided into separate sections for *chicos* (boys) and *chicas* (girls). Women traveling alone may sometimes feel ignored by staff in public places – not out of deliberate rudeness, more likely because a man is expected to return and speak for them! A woman staying in a hotel alone may encounter raised eyebrows, propositions, or even late-evening demands from hotel staff to change rooms.

These attitudes seem more pronounced the further up the price scale you go, especially in institutions used to catering for business*men*. Just as was the case in Europe and America, it takes quite a few pioneers to break stereotypes that have accumulated over generations.

There may be more independent businesswomen, but the respectably employed woman is nothing new. South America has a long-established class of women who regularly and visibly combine motherhood with a full day's work, out in the fields surrounded by their children, or managing a busy restaurant or café while feeding and entertaining a noisy brood.

THE YANOMAMI

The Yanomami people of northern Brazil and Venezuela were undiscovered by the rest of the world until the 1970s, when "civilization" began to encroach on their Roraima rainforest home. Latter-day gold miners moved in and, in 1993, 20 Yanomami were massacred by them. The Yanomami have managed to publicize their plight, but attempts by the rest of the world to do something about it have not been so successful, notably since the disastrous Amazon rainforest fires that broke out during the drought of early 1998 destroying an area the size of Belgium.

Young people

At all levels of society, it seems, children are the focus of South American life. Families are large, contraception is often frowned upon, and women tend to start producing children at a lower age than in Europe and North America.

Some visitors might be alarmed at the incessant noise of children's exuberant shouts, which will often continue late into the evening – these playful noises are not tolerated or endured but indulged and encouraged, with the adults often joining in! The best thing to do for everyone's peace of mind is to shrug your shoulders, join in, and put off any quiet-time activities you

publicize and alleviate the situation, but for many children of poor families in South America, life can be a very hard slog indeed.

Music and dance is an outlet for all levels of society in exuberant South America. Youth is celebrated and indulged, not by prolonging it with plastic surgery, but more through the feelings of youth, recaptured throughout life at fiestas and in the dance clubs, where anyone can dress up in tight Lycra and get away with it. Youth brings romance, often rapidly followed by procreation and more children. But there is nothing perfunctory about this eternal cycle. Try to count the number of times you hear the

planned until the next day's *siesta*. Or invest in a good pair of earplugs.

The importance of children in South America makes the plight of the street children, orphaned and abandoned to scavenger lifestyles on the streets of big cities like Rio de Janeiro, seem all the more shocking. This is another case of social status coming into play, with the children forced to carry the burden of their parents' social disgrace. People from inside and outside South America have worked hard to

LEFT: chieftain and his wife, western lowlands, Ecuador. **ABOVE:** Venezuelan farmer.
ABOVE RIGHT: Guajira woman, Venezuela.

words *"mi corazon"* ("my heart") in popular songs. Latin American men may have a reputation for *machismo*, but it's probably just a front to disguise the very obvious passion for romance that pervades this emotionally charged part of the world.

Fun, pleasure and romance are of the highest priority in South America, and can transcend the boundaries of religion, race, politics, and social standing. Everyone, whatever their background, is expected to indulge in the lighter side of life at least occasionally. Music, dance, a determination to enjoy life whatever the burden – the diverse people of South America are clearly linked with a common bond. ❏

THE IRRESISTIBLE LURE OF THE UNKNOWN

From gold-crazy conquistadors to modern eco-adventurers, South America has attracted a long line of explorers in pursuit of elusive dreams

The earliest Spanish and Portuguese explorers were primarily concerned with charting the length and breadth of the newly discovered continent. In 1520, the great ocean navigator Fernando Magellan rounded the globe, giving his name to the stormy straits he passed at the southern tip of present-day Chile. In the same era, conquistadors Gonzalo Pizarro and Francisco de Orellana led arduous expeditions into the Amazon jungle in search of the mythical city of gold, El Dorado. They never found much gold but, in 1541, Orellana's expedition sailed down the world's mightiest river to the sea, becoming the first Europeans to cross South America.

SCIENTIFIC EXPLORATION

In the 18th century, the Age of Enlightenment in Europe sparked off a new, scientific interest in the little-known South American wildlife.

One of the foremost European explorers was Alexander von Humboldt, a Berlin-born student of botany, chemistry, astronomy and mineralogy. With his companion, French botanist Aime Bonpland, Humboldt set off on an expedition from Venezuela to Ecuador in 1799, charting the link between the Orinoco and Amazon rivers. He assembled meticulous lists of plants and animals, which led to the publication of *Essays on the Geography of Plants*, pioneering studies into the relationship between a region's geography and its flora and fauna.

△ **SURVIVAL RATIONS**
Humboldt and Bonpland were reduced to a diet of ground cacao beans and Amazon River water when damp and insects destroyed their supplies.

△ **CHARLES DARWIN**
The originator of the theory of evolution was inspired by studies made during an expedition to the Galápagos Islands in 1835.

▷ **MARINE IGUANAS**
Whilst on the Galápagos Islands, Charles Darwin observed these unique reptiles, which have a breathing system that has adapted to life in the ocean.

▷ FALKLANDS FOUNDER

As well as having the Bougainvillaea plant named after him, the 18th-century French navigator, mathematician and soldier Comte Louis Antoine de Bougainville also first colonized the Falkland Islands for France. He then made his name by becoming the first Frenchman to successfully circumnavigate the globe.

△ AMAZON CRUISE

Despite the harsh realities met on arrival, expeditions were often well-funded and publicized, to considerable popular enthusiasm.

▽ GREEN HELL

Early explorers endured long, mosquito-ridden journeys, with little food, and fear of attack by fierce beasts, and even cannibals.

THE ORIGINAL INDIANA JONES

In 1906, a British army officer, Colonel Percy H Fawcett, went to South America, contracted by the Bolivian and Brazilian governments to help demarcate their jungle borders.

Fawcett's own plan, however, was to locate the fabled continent of Atlantis. He arrived armed with an 18th-century Portuguese document, and a stone idol thought to be of Brazilian origin and identified by psychics as having come from Atlantis.

On Fawcett's second expedition in 1925, he was accompanied by his son Jack and a man called Raleigh Rimell. The three men all vanished, the predators swallowed up by their prey. But the story did not end there. Subsequent tales of Fawcett's quest attracted more explorers over the years, many of whom sent back mysterious reports of white men living with jungle Amerindians; none, however, succeeded in finding him.

Fawcett's mystery and fame live on today, and he is credited as being the inspiration behind the Hollywood hero, Indiana Jones.

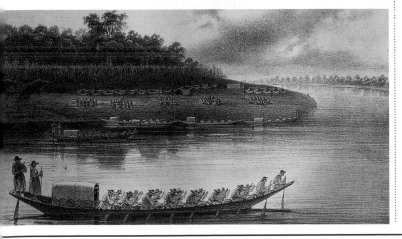

MUSIC AND DANCE

*South America pulsates to the beat of many rhythms as, through music and dance,
people express their joys, their struggles and often their longing for home*

A bus journey in South America can be a whole new experience; a bumpy ride from somewhere you can't remember to somewhere you can't pronounce. Your driver will probably make numerous unscheduled stops to pick up passengers, call over a friend or jump out on an errand, and may also want to demonstrate his DJ skills to his captive audience. As your bus pitches and thunders down perilous mountain trails or bleak, dusty stretches, local musical delights blare at deafening volume from crackling speakers. For the driver, savoring the delights of his playlist, staying on the road is not always top priority.

Music is considered a staple in the Latin American diet, being as important as food itself, feeding and replenishing the soul. Popular Latin music is laden not just with passion, sentiment, happiness and anguish, but with history and nostalgia. Just as early musical expression symbolized resistance for slaves and fueled struggles for independence in the 17th and 18th centuries, music and dance is revered by the underdogs of modern Latin American society. It is a tonic to counteract the harsh socio-economic realities of everyday life.

Dancing for everyone

Dancing serves as a pressure valve, a reprieve from life's chaos or a celebration that tomorrow it's Friday and you feel lucky. Throughout Latin America dance is viewed as a fundamental right that may be expressed freely and openly at any hour or occasion of the day. It offers a refreshing change from attitudes in many northern hemisphere countries, where dance seems so often to belong exclusively to youth and beauty, and has subsequently been exiled to nightclubs.

To understand the evolution of musical and dance forms on the continent is to attempt to fathom the tremendous demographic upheaval that took place over 500 years. The richness

and diversity of Latin music is indicative of the many colonizing and colonized forces present over the centuries. Along with native South America, Africa , Europe, and the United States all had a hand in the shaping of this magical land and its music.

Music grew from a brutal and loveless relationship, out of enslaved Amerindians and Africans, early European settlers and colonial powerbrokers. Often oceans away from their homelands, these early inhabitants all had their music and dances. They were a way of remembering home and who you were in an uncertain landscape. Thrown together in an ethnic melting pot, many traditions were either discarded or bonded together. It makes for an enthralling tale of survival of the fittest, triumphant underdogs, resistance and compromise.

Out of this struggle was born regional and national musical traditions which, in a sense, represent different colonial experiences and development. So there are historical reasons

LEFT: the exuberant display that is *Carnaval*, Brazil.
RIGHT: traditional dancing in Trujillo, Peru.

for the tango belonging to Argentina, the samba to Brazil and the cumbia to Colombia.

A spicy mix

Arguably the most international of all Latin American rhythms is what we now call **salsa**. The term itself is really nothing more than a marketing ploy adopted by the United States music industry in the late 1960s, which assumed that people could not cope with the many different types of music Latin America had to offer. Son, mambo, guaracha and many other styles were lumped together so that they could be easily packaged for consumption.

rhythms of regular pulses provided by the *clave* (two sticks that beat at a 2–3 or 3–2 tempo) and the *campana* (cowbell), and accents that are off-beat (piano, bass and brass). This is all useful to know if you want to blame your dance partner for messing up when they are clearly the better dancer.

If salsa means sauce then the musical ingredients in these complex arrangements need a master chef to work. As music is food for the soul to Latin Americans, culinary references in the lyrics are compulsory. *¡Azucar!* (sugar) is salsa legend, Celia Cruz's trademark exclamation, while other musicians will call out for salt,

Salsa means "sauce" and the name was inspired by many musicians who would scream "Salsa!" at a pulsating audience to excite them even further. This artificial grouping of many different styles means that most discussions about the origin of salsa become as hot and spicy as the dancing that the music inspires. Most unbiased opinion, however, follows the view that today's salsa is really a jazzed-up version of **son**, whose origins date back to Eastern Cuba in the 1880s.

Son intermingled African rhythms with Spanish verse forms, and its early means of expression were drums, maracas, Cuban tres guitar and claves or sticks tapping out the beat. The beat is syncopated and loaded with poly-

pepper, and other seasonings as an invitation for a particular instrument or singer to join in. This seems perfectly natural, so long as the chops cut the mustard.

Modern son and salsa, predominant in Colombia, Venezuela and throughout Central America, have been enhanced by the addition of the piano, bass and heavy brass sections. Cuban **charanga** replaces the brass instruments with violins and flutes, but the structure is similar. In Cuba the accent remains heavily on improvization, and the force of this and fluctuations in the salsa rhythm has caught out even the most expert musicians. Whilst jamming with some Cubans even the great Dizzy

Gillespie couldn't keep up, famously crying out in bafflement "Where's the beat?"

The accompanying dance may look easy but it is as intricate and erratic as the music, fluctuating between regular and counter movements. Salsa is electrifying, sensual, and dynamic, yet it can be cheeky and passionate at the same time. Don't be discouraged by the stylish, fast footwork, for much of the rhythm is contained within set steps. You will get as much of a kick out of observing the rhythmic exchange between the couples spinning and strutting their stuff or caught in a swaying embrace as from actually taking part.

foreign intervention in the 20th century as well as being a vehicle to address social problems.

Its infectious rhythm adheres to a frenetic, repetitious "thump, thump, thump" beat present in disco and rock music. An ensemble of guitar, *guira* (scraper), tambour and *marimba* (African piano) or accordion traditionally plays the merengue. The beat is crisp, accelerated and at times chaotic, with one beat suddenly dropped and another picked up. Merengue is less intense than salsa and it starts with a bang and adrenaline rush, making you feel instantly giddy and producing a strong urge to jump about in a silly fashion or run around the room.

A crisp, frothy beat

Merengue came to South America via the Dominican Republic in the Caribbean. It comes, as you might expect, from the French "meringue", meaning "whipped egg whites and sugar". Both the dessert and the dance have a frothy, exciting mix. From its origins in the formalized 18th-century dances of the French court, merengue acquired African influences as it settled in the Dominican Republic. It provided the beat for many protest marches against

LEFT: belting out rhythms in a Caracas nightspot, Venezuela. **ABOVE:** strumming up a storm in Porlamar, Isla Margarita, Venezuela.

The lyrics adopt a tongue-in-cheek tone, heavy with double meaning and conveying either a social critique or commentary on everyday life. Native Dominican superstars Juan Luis Guerra and Wilfredo Vargas command great respect among their audience for their musical creativity and brazen addressing of the country's social and political problems in their lyrics.

The dance that compliments merengue is easily picked up compared to salsa. The basic version consists of bending one knee then the other forward and then back in clockwork alternate movements whilst not lifting your heels off the ground. Couples mirror each other, as in salsa, and when dancing close together, the woman places her right foot in between the man's feet. The couples resemble palm trees swaying in the breeze as they move to the beat.

Recent adaptations have seen merengue embracing North American crazes such as rap, hiphop and techno music. This has proven highly popular among the youth in Dominican and Caribbean *barrios* in the United States, who see hiphop merengue as a Latin expression of the "brotherhood" practiced by their African-American counterparts. The new sound was first introduced by a group of young people of Dominican descent calling themselves *Proyecto Uno*. The adaptability of the rhythm

initial disdain on the immodest hips and swift foot movements of a dance whose sexual connotations could only arouse dismay and moral approbation. Indeed, it was to be a long time before tango was considered sufficiently refined to be acceptable in higher social circles. In fact it wasn't until tango caused a sensation in the dancehalls of pre-First World War France that it gained international acceptance.

Today, tango is enjoying an extraordinary resurgence. Following on from the dance form's global appeal, a whole new generation of young Argentines are ensuring the survival of tango in the steaming cafés and clubs of Argentina.

and the facility of the dance has given it the upper hand over salsa in many Latin communities in the US and in Andean South America.

A dance for lovelorn men

The **tango** is closely associated with Argentina (*see page 330*). To many the most sensual and erotic of all South American dances, its origins lie in the Buenos Aires slums of over a century ago. There, lovelorn male migrants, bereft of female company, would re-enact the intimacy of man and woman. Hence, the tango was a dance of men. One male would play the part of the female coquette whilst the other represented the rough wooer. The upper classes looked with

Samba-mania

If the tango is Argentinian, the samba belongs to Brazil. **Samba** comes from an African word, *semba*, meaning "a type of belly dance". It originated in Africa as a reel dance and is first recorded in the 1875 festivals in Bahia in northeast Brazil. Samba today takes many forms. Ballroom, carnaval, and pagode (a slower São Paulo version) are just a few. It is universally popular and has influenced the **bossa nova** musical form, the first recording of which was made by Elizabeth Cardosa in the 1950s.

The samba danced at *Carnaval* differs from one city to the next. Its proper name is *samba enredo*. First introduced in the 1930s, this is the form of samba most of us would associate with phenomenal footwork and bottom-shaking. Samba dancers are reminiscent of leaves quivering violently in the wind as they are driven along by the feverish beat of the *bateria* (rhythm section) of drums and percussion.

Brazil's biggest show

It was the Portuguese who brought the practice of *Carnaval* to Brazil at the end of the 17th century as a festivity celebrated by pelting each other with flour and water bombs *(see page 236)*. The music and dance is essentially African in origin. *Carnaval* is undoubtedly one of the biggest displays of modern Brazilian popular culture, blending festivity with show, and art with folklore, as everyone takes to the streets in extravagant and colorful costume.

The excitement escalates from the Christmas period and Lemanjá New Year celebrations. In the run-up to Lent, an eerie hysteria hangs heavily in the air like the tension before a monsoon. The observer is washed along by a wave of infectious anticipation and then buffeted by relentless musical elements for four days and nights as this tropical storm sweeps over the country. It is a test of stamina that leaves you feeling numb, exhausted and giddy whether you participate or are kept awake by it.

Carnival in Rio is distinct from the rest of the country with its purpose-built Sambadrome stadium and world-famous samba schools of up to 4,000 participants each, who jealously compete for the title of champion. The din filling the Sambadrome comes from the samba percussion *baterias* and sounds like torrential rain beating down on a tin roof. Scantily clad women shake violently as if possessed, and a chorus of several hundred voices chant responses to the samba caller.

The rest of the country prefers a giant street party. In recent years the Bahia carnival, which is held in the colorful northeastern city of Salvador, has grown in popularity. Held as a massive street party, *trio electricos* – floats which transport deafening speakers pumping out 100,000 watts of **samba**, **axé** and **frevo** music – lead the processions through the winding cobbled streets. The air dances and heads undulate. The smell of *vatapá* – a maize and shrimp

dumpling dish – forms a haze, served by mountainous Baiana women swathed in traditional white dresses.

Home to Brazil's acclaimed writer Jorge Amado, who died in 2001, and international musical exports Olodum, with their army of drummers who have played with Michael Jackson and Latin music superstars Daniela Mercury and Caetano Veloso, Bahia is the bastion of Africanism in Brazil. It is also home to the Santeria religion known as **Candomblé** and the African martial arts dance **capoeira**. Bahia is considered the center of musical innovation in Brazil, and draws heavily on its African roots.

Many dance crazes originate in the northeast before being eagerly snapped up by the rest of the country.

The plaintive panpipes

A world away from the samba drums and salsa tambours is the haunting, plaintive sound of Andean panpipe music – **peña**, played in such countries as Ecuador, Bolivia and Peru. Drums, rattles, flutes, panpipes and the famous *charango* (a miniature guitar made from an armadillo shell) characterize it. Peña is a mixture of pre-Columbian and Spanish instrumentation, which traditionally involves no lyrical accompaniment – but this has changed

LEFT: tango, the passionate dance.
RIGHT: a fruity night out in Rio.

recently. The music is now accompanied by ballads sung most often in Quechua, Aymara and Spanish. These plaintive yet raucous songs record the daily lives, romances and ribald interludes of rural Amerindian communities.

It is music to dance to. Andean music is a foot-stomping version of a barn dance. It is very moving. It shakes the soul and makes the air jump. The sound can be frenetic, accelerating from a ballad to a musical duo reminiscent of that classic country piece *Duelling Banjos*. The pitch becomes feverish and your feet seem to move of their own accord. This kind of indigenous folk music attests to the survival of the ordinary, compromised history of local populations. Music is, in a sense, the last place to hide what is left of yourself.

Songs of struggle

Used by dictatorial powers as a propaganda tool, traditional music has, nevertheless, also been a useful source of social revolution and protest. The **Nueva Canción** (New Song) movement that emerged in Chile in the 1960s and 1970s put music at the forefront of the struggle in Latin America. One of the leading lights of *Nueva Canción* was the musician and poet Violeta Parra, who received little recogni-

PANPIPES OF THE ANDES

The panpipe dates back at least 2,000 years. Ecuadorian panpipes were named *rondador* after the nightwatchmen in colonial Ecuador who played the instrument on their rounds. A typical *rondador* is made of varying lengths and widths of cane or bamboo that are tied together in one long row; the different lengths and diameters produce unique and distinct tones. The *zampoña* is the panpipe typical of Peru and Bolivia; it is tuned quite differently from the *rondador* and usually has two rows of pipes that are lashed together, to produce a deeper and more breathy sound.

tion in her own country, Chile, until after her death by suicide in 1967. *Nueva Canción* was to voice the struggle and suffering of those Chileans who were persecuted during the dictatorship of the 1970s and 1980s. Cuba's equivalent, *Nueva Trova*, produced Sylvio Rodríguez and Pablo Milanes, two of Latin America's most respected musicians. Milanes has only recently returned to Chile after vowing never to appear there when the brutal dictator Augusto Pinochet was in power.

General Pinochet was aware of the danger that *Nueva Canción* posed to his regime when he imprisoned Chile's geatest prize, singer Victor Jara, in the notorious football stadium in

Santiago. The inspirational Jara sang to his fellow activists, and for his crime Pinochet had his hands smashed, his tongue cut off and then had him murdered.

Another important Chilean dance style is **la cueca**. It began as a pantomime; a game of coy evasion and rebuttal by women and playful conquest by men. The woman holds a white handkerchief. It was at one time a dance of remarkable restraint. There was no physical contact between the pair until the point of the *vacunao* when the man claims the woman with a pelvic movement, gentle kick or swat.

What is more moving about the **cueca**, however, is that it was employed by women to protest the mass disappearances of their sons and husbands under Pinochet's regime during the 1970s and 1980s. La cueca became a dance of anger and grief. The women danced alone, their partners lost, disappeared. Their plight was brought to world attention when the British artist Sting paid tribute to them in his song *They Dance Alone*.

Dances of the countryside

On a more cheerful note, the giddy **cumbia** is a popular coastal dance from Colombia. It consists of a rousing, regular beat with a steady "molasses" bass line and brassy horns.

Urban myth has it that the movements to the cumbia reflect gender-based rural activities. The man makes a sweeping movement with his hand that mimics the machete cutting a path through the bush. The woman, with one hand, raises her petticoats, and with the other hand, holds a candle. This purportedly alludes to her guiding the man through the wilderness.

There is a close relation between the cumbia and **vallenato** *(see page 103)*; both come from the coastal regions of Colombia. Traveling *vallenato* musicians would move from one small town to another. They were gossips. They shamelessly drafted local scandal and intrigue into their songs. The lyrics were built piece by piece from the feckless lives of isolated communities. Crowds would gather and eagerly devour the news brought by these musicians. This was before the era of telephone, and the gossip was juicier.

In recent years *vallenato* has enjoyed a surge in popularity. Maybe the phone isn't what it used to be. Carlos Vives spirited this revival with his modern sound. He appeared in a Colombian television soap opera as a wide-eyed *campesino* called upon to defeat Lucifer in a singing contest. The fate of a village lies in his hands. At first things don't look good for Vives. You worry about the village and his dubious wardrobe. Still, Vives and his accordion manage to deal a fatal blow to Lucifer by striking an original chord, securing the future of the village and the vallenato. As is so often the case in South America, music conquers all.   ❏

LEFT: dancing the *cumbia*, Colombia. **RIGHT:** singer Violeta Parra, often described as the "mother" of Chile's *Nueva Canción* movement.

ARTS AND CRAFTS

Visitors to South America will find art all around them – indigenous crafts, pre-Columbian treasures, colonial baroque art, and powerful modern paintings

For over five centuries, Latin Americans saw themselves through the eyes of others. In 1492 Spain conquered a continent it had not known to exist; within a few short years it had overwhelmed the population who already lived there – the 30 million or so indigenous peoples of Latin America – and made them "disappear". Those 20 percent or so who were not killed or assimilated were pushed into the background, seen as "barbarians" and savages.

The native population of South America and the black African communities imported as slaves were rarely painted after the Flemish artist Theodore de Bry produced his famous engravings of the Conquest. When they did appear it was usually as curiosities, exotic figures in the landscapes of European travelers documenting this New World after Spain finally lost its South American empire in the early 19th century – artists like Jean-Baptiste Debret in Brazil, or Camilo Fernández in Colombia (his watercolors can be seen in Bogotá at the Biblioteca Nacional).

Occasionally you can catch glimpses of the work of anonymous indigenous artists – in the paintings of the Cusco school in Peru, for example, with its black Madonnas and curious Amerindian faces painted in the background or carved into the frames. Yet the arts of the native and the black population did survive, in what we now call craftwork or folk arts – papier-mâché figures, painted gourds, fine weaving and so on. In a way, contemporary crafts represent a continuous line from that past, although at the same time they have changed beyond recognition from their original models.

A new conciousness

It was not until the mid-19th century that Latin American painters began to see their own world as worthy of attention. José Correia de Lima painted Brazil's black people for the first time (Museu de Belas Artas, São Paulo), while in Peru, Pancho Fierro recorded the Amerindian and *mestizo* people on Lima's streets (Museo de Arte de Lima). In the Museo Nacional de Artes Plasticas in Montevideo, Uruguay, the paintings of Juan Manuel Blanes record the inhabitants of the pampas, the open grasslands

ECHOES OF THE PAST

Many of the contemporary crafts and traditions of the Andes have clearly evolved from pre-Columbian times. By studying local culture, art, architecture, and artisans, modern archeologists have been able to advance their understanding of ancient artifacts. The people of northern Peru still regularly use ceramic pots surprisingly similar to their ancient Moche precursors. Similarly, the backstrap loom, which is attached to the weaver's back so that she can adjust the tension by moving her body, is still used in modern Peru, yet much earlier models are depicted in 2,000-year-old ceramics.

LEFT: modern art captures an age-old scene, Peru.
RIGHT: making *shigras* (sacks), Ecuador.

where the *gauchos* lived. Pedro Figari, painting much later, created delicate and evocative images of a life of poverty in a similar world.

Change was coming – and it exploded upon South America at the beginning of the 20th century. After a century of political independence, the ties of external domination were still strong. Any bid to find real freedom meant turning the artistic gaze inward and rediscovering both the reality and the traditions that were authentically Latin America's own.

Ironically, the new cultural nationalists were often artists who, as their contemporaries so often did, first traveled to Europe in search of

berated around the whole continent, influencing university students, who began to demand an art and an education that reflected their own reality.

The *Semana de Arte Moderna*, a famous exhibition that took place in São Paulo in 1922, announced the new movement in music, literature, and all the arts. Most representative of its extraordinary innovations was the work of painter Tarsila do Amaral. Her famous painting *Central Railway of Brazil*, like much of her work, marries bright colors and geometric forms set in a primitive landscape; it is on display in the Museo de Arte Contemporáneo of

culture. Many became involved in the new modernist movements there and brought the avant garde back to Latin America, where it came face to face with a different and dramatic reality. Latin America's modern art movements were born out of that encounter.

The past rediscovered

The 1910–1920 period was a time of political and social upheaval – and of nationalism above all. Every country of Latin America began to rediscover – unearth almost – its past; Hiram Bingham's "rediscovery" of Machu Picchu in Peru in 1911 was a signpost to what was to come. In 1910 the Mexican Revolution rever-

the University of São Paulo. Amaral, with contemporaries such as Anita Malfatti, represented one face of the new movement; beside them Emiliode Cavalcanti and Cándido Portinari used the mediums of etching, woodcutting, and engraving to portray the experience of the ordinary people of Brazil.

European influences

Joaquín Torres-García, like his contemporary Barradas, returned from Europe and the United States to his native Uruguay in 1932, and began to generate his own version of the geometric three-dimensional designs learned from the Constructivists. The exciting and inventive

MADI group, founded in Buenos Aires in 1945, developed that work in entirely new directions.

The extraordinary purity of Armando Reverón clearly owes its origins to Manet and the post-Impressionists, searching as it does for the perfect expression of light and color that led him finally to the blinding whites of his last canvases. Reverón's claim was to have captured the essential atmosphere of his own coastal town in Venezuela – an achievement far removed from the innovative and daring new directions for which his country earned an international reputation. For in the capital, Caracas, the architect Carlos Raul Villanueva

dimensions in the museums and streets of Rio, where much of their work may still be found. In Chile, Roberto Matta drew on European surrealism to create a universe of mysterious gardens and landscapes full of color and menace.

The *Indigenista* movement

Yet even the most non-representational kind of painting in Latin America has wrestled with the past, the "invisible" South America. The powerful *Indigenista* movement that began in the late 1920s in Peru, Ecuador, and Bolivia sought out the indigenous communities in all its artistic expressions – in music, literature, and in

was building a new university and inviting a younger generation of exciting new artists to participate in the design of new and very modern spaces *(see page 69)*. This invitation was eagerly accepted by artists like Alejandro Otero, Jesús Rafael Soto, and Carlos Cruz Diez, whose disturbing optical games with light, movement, and geometric form can be seen in their settings in Caracas Central University.

The "neo-concrete" artists of Brazil – Lygia Pape, Lygia Clark, and Helio Oiticica among others – explored space and color in several

LEFT: masks from Terra Nova, along the Amazon near Manaus, Brazil. **ABOVE:** woodcarving in action, Peru.

painting. José Sabogal was the doyen of *indigenismo* in the visual arts, influencing a whole generation in Bolivia and Ecuador. But for some he was too close to an exaggerated socialist realism that owed much to the Mexican muralists.

A newer generation of artists took that brute realism in new directions – particularly the controversial artist Oswaldo Guayasamín, who moved toward a kind of primitive abstraction, his paint piled on the canvas as if the physical gesture of painting itself conveyed the emotions it contained. His enormous popularity and commercial success have invited the accusation that he paints to pander to the metropolitan world's vision of the south.

Satires on complacency

Colombian artist Fernando Botero's bitterly satirical portraits of a plump and complacent Latin American bourgeoisie have brought him both success and the enmity of some of his subjects. This variety of individual expression has its counterpoint in movements whose object is to create art that is collective in its nature.

The radicalization of Chilean political life between 1968 and 1973 produced a mural art reflecting a movement in the streets. This movement was founded by the group Brigada Ramona Parra, named after a young art student who was killed in a demonstration. Else-

where, that impulse took art into the realms of sculpture and performance – art as a kind of public statement, ranging from Chilean Eugenio Dittborn's poignant "airmail paintings", mailed to exhibitions around the world, to Argentine Antonio Berni's provocative and highly political collages.

A meeting of art and crafts

In another direction, art left the studio to reconnect with a completely different, popular tradition – colorful, naïve, passionate. It had its representatives in Brazil, and in Chile in the work of Luis Herrera Guevara.

It was here that art met "craft". In the aftermath of the Chilean military coup of 1973, for example, groups of women began to make *arpillerías* – patchworks – that employed traditional skills to make powerful symbolic statements about freedom, pain, and the search for the "disappeared". Of course, these crafts had evolved and changed from their origins in pre-Columbian America or in Africa, yet they remained the property of the poorest sections of South American society.

They often produced useful items – beautifully woven *ruanas* (capes) in Ecuador, sweaters of llama or alpaca wool in Peru, woolen ponchos, hats, and gloves in the Andes – all are functional as well as beautiful. The growth of tourism has often contributed to the resurgence of some of these traditional domestic crafts – in the Ecuadorean community of Otavalo, for example *(see page 202)*. But it has almost certainly changed them too.

Hand-made clay sculptures with enormous hands and feet can be bought everywhere in Peru – their faces are those of the highland peoples. The beautifully painted scenes inside bamboo stalks or hollowed-out nuts are survivals of authentic skills as well as attractive mementos for sale to tourists.

In the greatest markets of Latin America, like Huancayo in Peru, plastic items and tacky electronic goods cohabit on blankets on the street with delicate paperlace cutouts or fine ceramics. This coexistence of dramatically different levels of life and methods of production is the the contradictory reality of South America. ❑

CHECK YOUR SOUVENIRS

It's not difficult to find good reproductions of the featherwork of Paracas or the fine beaten gold of the Inca highlands. But it's illegal to take authentic historical artifacts out of most South American countries. So many have already been hoarded in Europe and North America that visitors are strongly discouraged from continuing the depletion of the historical past – and there are stiff penalties for those who are caught. It's also illegal – as well as irresponsible – to export certain materials such as the feathers of protected bird species, which are sometimes found in handicrafts at local markets.

LEFT: *Maternity*, woodcarving by R.P. Athyde, Ceará Museum, Fortaleza, Brazil. **RIGHT:** tapestries in an Otavalo market, Ecuador.

ARCHITECTURE

South American cities have been at the forefront of modern architectural movements, and there are also much older architectural wonders to be seen

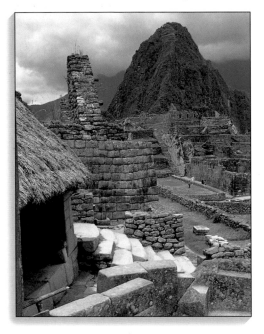

We do not know the names of those who built the extraordinary Inca cities – Cusco and Machu Picchu – or the magnificent ceremonial structure of Sacsahuayman in Peru. Pablo Neruda, the great Chilean poet, called them only "John Stonesplitter and John Woodheaver". But whoever they were, their constructions were built to last forever. In Cusco, the Spanish colonialists built their houses on the walls of the Inca city, for example.

There are still remains of older ancient cities like Chan Chan on the coastal plain. Elsewhere, the ancient indigenous peoples of what are now Argentina, Chile, and Brazil, did not leave monumental signs of their passing. Mostly they were hunters, gatherers, or fishermen without imperial ambitions. But Cusco was built at what the Incas saw as the center of the world, and to symbolize this, it is divided into four districts representing each corner of the empire, surrounding a central square.

The Spanish influence

When the Spanish conquered South America, they brought their own values, their own religion and their own forms of artistic expression. Where they could, as in Mexico, they destroyed the buildings they found and used the stones to make their own, Christian, cathedrals. Where they could not move the stones, as in Cusco, they built their own cities on Inca foundations. But they were able to preserve the structure of the cities, since Spain built its cities on a grid system around a central square. For in a real sense, Spain's was an urban culture and, apart from the great plantation houses, rural building was left to the communities who lived there, relying on their skill in using local materials.

For more than 300 years, Latin America's building styles originated in Spain – at first, the highly decorative *plateresque* style; later there were echoes of European baroque, where elaborate decorated surfaces and cascades of gold reflected the confidence of a colonial order. Compared with the first imperial buildings in Mexico, Quito's churches were austere in their facades; yet inside, they could be exuberant – sometimes blue and red washes were added to the endless swirling gold; sometimes they were influenced by *mudejar* (Moorish) styles, and incorporated wooden beams, carved closed balconies, and geometrical patterns.

Despite the codes of austerity that were

MASTERS OF MASONRY

Stone was considered sacred, or *huaca*, to the Incas. Hundreds of sites display the outstanding masonry skills of the Incas, *such as the famous 12-angled stone at Cusco, or *Inti-huatana* at Machu Picchu, the "hitching post of the sun". The Incas were also expert at earthquake-proofing their buildings. The colonial church of Santo Domingo was built on top of Qorincancha, the Inca Temple of the Sun, at Cusco. Over the centuries the Inca foundations have proved much more resistant to earthquakes than Spanish constructions.

imposed by the Spanish imperial center in Madrid, Latin America did adapt these received styles, particularly in the late 17th- and 18th-century baroque edifices.

The Amerindian influence

Indigenous craftsmen in Bolivia left their mark on Sucre Cathedral and the churches of San Lorenzo in Potosí or San Francisco in La Paz, and in Peru in the carved soft lava stone used in Arequipa. Bright colors, animals and plants, and occasional dark-skinned faces carved into the stone are testimony to their presence, for example in the facade of the old Jesuit University in

the statues of the Prophets at Congonhas do Campo *(see page 243)*.

Looking to Europe

Landscape and geography affected construction too. New Granada (as the Andean republics were called under Spanish rule) lay across an earthquake zone, to which many of Lima's buildings have fallen victim. The Torre Tagle Palace (now Peru's Ministry of Foreign Affairs) is one of the few colonial buildings to have survived in the city.

Once freed from Spain, the leaders of a newly independent sub-continent turned their

Cusco's central square. And in Brazil, where the imported Portuguese style encountered no local architecture to stand in its way, the reality of the tropics found its way into the baroque facades of Pernambuco or the extraordinary San Francisco da Penitencia churches of Recife and Bahia.

The most outstanding expression of this "tropicalized" baroque is the work of the crippled sculptor-architect Aleijadinho on churches and other buildings throughout Ouro Preto. His most enduring and idiosyncratic expression are

LEFT: Machu Picchu, Peru: a miracle of architectural achievement on an Andean mountain top.
ABOVE: twelve-angled Inca stone in Cusco.

attention to other parts of Europe. The 19th century produced an imitative grandeur, mimicking the wide boulevards and grand palaces of France and London and their new enthusiasm for neo-classical styles. La Moneda, the famous presidential palace in Santiago, Chile, that was destroyed by bombing during the 1973 military coup against Salvador Allende, was a typical example of this trend.

In Buenos Aires, growing to dominance in the latter half of the 19th century, the newly wealthy bourgeoisie used architecture to emphasize their European roots, producing their own versions of the Champs Elysées – usually called La Alameda. In Lima this change was exemplified by the demolition of the old city walls to make way for the new avenues.

Outside the planned, structured heart of Latin American cities, buildings tend to be somewhat improvized and transient. By the late 19th century the spaces between the grand houses and tenements had themselves become living places for a poor immigrant population. In the 20th century these areas swelled, spreading like mushrooms (*callampa*, the name for a shanty town in some South American countries, means mushroom) around and through the burgeoning metropolises. The hillside *favelas* of Rio *(see page 238)* are extreme examples.

planners, and Brazil's 1930 revolution, which was led by young military officers promising to modernize and industrialize at every level, provided the opportunity. The architect Gregorio Warchavchik set out the new ideas: architecture would be functional and geometric, celebrating the materials and structures of a new urban and industrial world.

The Ministry of Education and Health in Rio was the landmark of the new movement. Completed in 1937 by a team that included Lucio Costa and Oscar Niemeyer, it was the center of a completely urban utopia. Not just buildings, but whole cities would be built like efficient

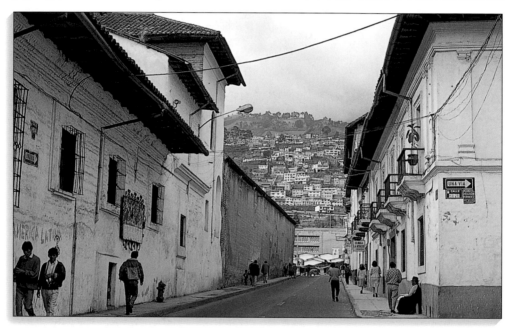

Beacons of the technological age

The past 70 years have brought Latin America – and in particular Brazil and Venezuela – to the very center of innovation in architecture. The architects responsible for the modernist revolution in Brazil traveled to Europe and brought back new and experimental ideas. They seized on the ideas of the great Swiss architect Le Corbusier and the Dutch architect Mies van der Rohe as they imagined great modern cities. They hoped the sub-continent would be catapulted into the 21st century by gilding its new urban spaces with the most daring "machines for living". Le Corbusier's lecture tour of Argentina and Brazil galvanized local urban

machines with clean lines, open and flexible spaces set in planned landscapes like those designed by the Brazilian architect and landscape gardener Roberto Burle Marx. The high blocks along Rio's Copacabana beach are one such example; the recreational complex at the suburb of Pampulha another. The church of São Francisco de Assis at Pampulha, decorated by Portinari, symbolized the marriage of plastic and the constructive arts.

The triumph of the idea was Brasília *(see page 239)*, the most ambitious of several new cities purpose-built in the late 1950s that illustrate the meeting of architecture and sculpture. Oscar Niemeyer, the principal architect, imagined a city that would in turn create a way of living. In just ten years the Brazilian movement transformed architecture everywhere, as the 1943 "Brazil Builds" exhibition at New York's Museum of Modern Art testified.

Modern icons

Less well known abroad, but equally dramatic in its significance, was the movement led by Carlos Raul Villanueva in Venezuela, and in particular, Caracas. Villanueva's first major projects – the El Silencio (Silence) and El Paraiso (Paradise) workers' housing complexes built in the 1940s – symbolized a utopian and optimistic

buildings – this was a landscape where natural lines and plants and trees were symbolically represented in concrete and metal.

In Argentina, where the neo-classical forms persisted longer than elsewhere, the Teatro Colón (see page 328) expressed both the high point and the ending of the movement. The next generation of architects were as responsive as their colleagues elsewhere to the modern movement as the country began its process of industrialization. Clean sharp lines and open space characterized the work of new architects like Amancio Williams, whose house in Mar del Plata for his brother, the composer Alberto, was

modernism. As in Brazil, the mass housing projects represented the promise of an organized and smooth transition to urban growth; the concrete and glass that were its chief materials were not indigenous but they were cheap and readily available. Like the Brazilians, Villanueva saw architecture as a meeting point between spatial and visual arts. The new Central University, the construction of which began in the early 1950s, expressed the confidence of a newly oil-rich country. In a sense, Villanueva created more than

entirely functional and without artistic pretensions. In Chile the long, low buildings of Emilio Duhart and Alberto Piwonka reflected an adaptation of the same ideas to the earthquake-prone Santiago valley.

In the 1980s and 1990s, architectural innovation took place largely in the commercial sphere. However, Niemeyer – who planned Brasilia – continues to design in his unique style. In the late 20th century, he completed the Museum of Contemporary Art in Rio – an enormous, sculptural flying saucer. At the age of 96 he was invited to design the 2003 Serpentine Gallery Pavilion in London; an indication of his ongoing international appeal. ❑

LEFT: colonial buildings, Quito, Ecuador. **ABOVE LEFT:** statue honoring the workers who built Brasília. **ABOVE RIGHT:** Casa Natál, Bolívar's birthplace, Venezuela.

THE GREAT OUTDOORS

Not all outdoor activities in South America center on the rainforest – increasingly sophisticated leisure facilities are available, from sand-skiing to paragliding

South America is a paradise for outdoor enthusiasts. Down the spine of the continent is the Andes, the longest continuous range of mountains in the world. This lofty landscape has snow-capped peaks for mountaineers, trekking, horseback riding, mountain biking on remote trails through isolated villages, and world-class kayaking and river rafting.

Within the Amazon basin to the east lie thousands of miles of virgin rainforest best explored by dug-out canoe. Beaches offer excellent surf and the northern Pacific and Caribbean reefs are great for scuba diving. Adrenaline sports such as snowboarding, paragliding, and bungee jumping are on the increase. But there is little regulation of the adventure travel business, so care needs to be taken in finding a reputable company.

National parks

Nahuel Haupi, the first national park in South America, was created in Argentina in 1903. Since then hundreds of parks have been established throughout the continent, protecting beautiful wilderness. Access to parks is becoming easier with improved transportation and infrastructure. In the more developed countries, notably Chile and Argentina, the parks have established trail systems with visitor centers.

Cusco in Peru is the Mecca for outdoor adventure, the most popular excursion being the Inca trail trek to Machu Picchu *(see page 158)*. Cusco's surrounding mountains are also perfect for mountain biking. There is a popular ride to the Inca terracing and salt ponds at Moray. Instead of a bus tour, the Sacred Valley can now be experienced by rafting the Urubamba River, on horseback, or paragliding from the cliffs.

Further south, the spectacular alpine and coastal wilderness of southern Chile brings in visitors from October through April. The town of Pucón is a good base for hikes, climbs, river rafting, mountain biking, and horseback riding into the nearby national parks of Huerquehue

and Villarrica. Even further south is spectacular Torres del Paine National Park *(see page 298)*.

Mountaineering

The high peaks of the Andes attract high-caliber international climbers every year. Acclimatization, proper equipment, and preparation are para-

mount. The highest of these peaks is Aconcagua (6,962 meters/22,841 ft) in Argentina. In northern Peru, from June through September, the small town of Huaraz is filled with climbers organizing expeditions to the many glaciated peaks in the Cordillera Blanca, the highest being Huascarán at 6,768 meters (22,200 ft). Snowboarders sometimes precariously descend its slopes. Ecuador's volcanoes can offer the novice a taste of high-altitude mountaineering.

Skiing

The world's highest ski run is at 5,420 meters (17,782 ft) in La Paz, Bolivia, on the slopes of Chacaltaya *(see page 180)*. It was developed in

LEFT: Argentina: a climber contemplates Mt Fitzroy.
RIGHT: tackling the Urubamba River, Peru.

the 1930s and is still accessed by the oldest ski lift in South America – horror stories abound regarding its safety. More sophisticated ski areas have been developed in Chile and Argentina, with the huge ski area of Las Leñas in Argentina considered the most prestigious. The resorts near Santiago such as Valle Nevado and Portillo also have many challenging slopes. The best time to go is June through October.

Cycling

Every year a few serious cyclists pedal the length of the Andes to the southern tip of the continent, Argentinian Tierra del Fuego. Most

canyons" in southern Peru, said to be twice as deep as the Grand Canyon. Condors soar above, a volcano smokes in the distance and sheer cliffs tower hundreds of meters on either side. The Bío Bío River in central Chile has a temperate climate, excellent white water, spectacular gorges and waterfalls, and Mapuche settlements, making it one of the most exciting rivers in the Andes to run.

Paragliding

In Rio de Janeiro, Brazil, you can paraglide tandem over Atlantic rainforest, soaring above the skyscrapers and landing at Pepino beach, São

recommend taking detours off the Pan-American Highway, for example up into Cajamarca or the Cordillera Blanca in northern Peru, for the best views and to avoid traffic. For the less serious cyclist there are one-day cycle tours coasting down the flanks of the active Cotpaxi volcano or pedaling from the mountains of Baños to the jungle town of Puyo in Ecuador.

Rafting and kayaking

Beginners can descend the fun and safe class III rapids of the Upper Napo River, near Tena, Ecuador. More experienced rafters can run the Colca River floes down the "Everest of river

Conrado. Paragliders are often seen flying off the coastal cliffs of Miraflores in Lima, Peru. The craze has also hit Mérida in Venezuela and Tucumán in Argentina. You can also have a go at ballooning in Rio from the Autodromo de Jacarepaguá, a half-hour ride ascending to 1,500 meters (4,921 ft).

Beach and watersports

Crazy *buggeiros* (buggy drivers) will take you out on their buggies along the beaches and sand dunes of Brazil. The noise may disturb people trying to relax on the beach, but others love the wild spins in the dunes and dodging incoming tides. Some of the most popular areas are the

Natal Beaches of Río Grande do Norte. The massive sand dunes in the desert of Huacachina near Ica in southern Peru offer a different kind of dune-fun. All you need is a board (cheap to rent) for sliding down the sand and to be prepared to walk to the top of the dunes.

Surfing

The Humboldt Current brings constant surf to the west coast of South America. Various towns along the Pacific coast such as Montañita, Ecuador and Huanchaco, northern Peru, have become hip places for foreign surfers to hang out. Puerto Chicama, set in the arid coastal desert of northern Peru, has become famous for its long left point break.

Snorkeling and diving

You can snorkel with hammerhead sharks, rays, starfish, seals, and penguins off the Galápagos Islands, Ecuador; scuba diving is also possible. Along the Caribbean coast, palm-fringed beaches offer the perfect start for snorkeling and scuba diving. The small coral islands of Los Roques, off the coast of Venezuela, are teeming with marine life. Morrocoy National Park is also a popular center for snorkeling and scuba diving off Venezuela's coastline.

Jungle trips

Dug-out canoe trips along small tributary rivers in the Amazon basin are far more exciting than floats along the wide Amazon River where the banks are too far off to see any wildlife. Adventure trips into the Cuyabeno Nature Reserve in Ecuador, Manu National Park in southern Peru, and from Rurrenabaque, Bolivia offer real jungle experiences, with piranha fishing and hiking through swampy forests. ❏

LEFT: birdwatching along the Ariau River, Amazonas state, Brazil. **ABOVE:** a party of trekkers pitch camp in an Andean valley.

SOUTH AMERICAN EXPLORERS CLUB

The South American Explorers Club is an invaluable resource for anyone planning adventure excursions and expeditions. This is a non-profit organization with clubhouses in Lima and Cusco in Peru, and Quito in Ecuador offering travelers advice. The clubhouses share detailed information on members' experiences, and it's also a good place to meet people and compare notes with other travelers.

There is a yearly membership fee of US$50 ($80 for couples.) The SAEC can be contacted at in the US at 126 Indian Creek Road, Ithaca, NY 14850; tel 607-277-0488; fax 607-277-6122; www.samexplo.org

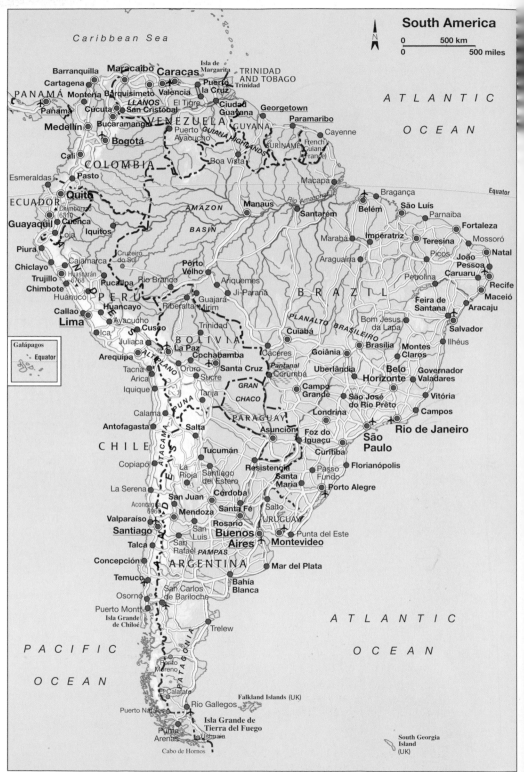

PLACES

A detailed guide to the whole of South America, with major sites cross-referenced by numbers to the maps

First-time visitors may be daunted at the range of sights and new experiences on offer in this diverse region. On a short visit it's best to confine yourself to a limited geographical area, or to certain types of experience, and there are many to choose from: rainforest expeditions, archeological tours, adventure sports, tropical beach life, subantarctic forays, music and nightlife, and much more.

To help you plan your South American itinerary, we have divided the subcontinent into four sections, devoting a chapter to each country. We start at the north coast: Colombia, Venezuela, Guyana, Surinam and French Guiana, countries which run from west to east. Colombia and Venezuela have an abundance of tropical white-sand beaches as well as large modern cities. All of these countries have densely forested interiors which harbor a plethora of exotic species and are home to some of the world's most traditional communities.

Next, we come to the countries of the Andean Highlands, Peru and Bolivia, linked by enormous Lake Titicaca, and Ecuador. In this region – also in Colombia – are found the treasures of fascinating ancient civilizations, as well as the distinctive living cultures of the Andean people. These countries are also known for their natural diversity, with mountains, tropical lowlands and desert. Ecuador in particular is a Mecca for wildlife enthusiasts, who flock to the famous Galápagos Islands, 970 km (600 miles) off its coast.

From the Andes we move west to Brazil, which sprawls over an area nearly half the size of all South America. Everything in Brazil seems to be on a large scale: its massive Amazon rainforest in the north, the huge and vibrant cities of the east coast, its passion for football, sensual music and dance culture, and of course its world-famous carnival.

Finally we head south, to the Southern Cone, where long, thin Chile lines the west coast from tropical to subantarctic latitudes. The Atlantic coast is covered by the relatively small Uruguay and huge Argentina, which shares the Lake District, Patagonia and the island of Tierra del Fuego with Chile. Landlocked Paraguay, directly north of Argentina, is also bordered by Bolivia and Brazil. The Southern Cone countries are characterized by large urban centers, wide open spaces, sheep and cattle ranching and a pioneering tradition.

The tiny Chilean islands of Juan Fernandez lie 670 km (415 miles) west of Valparaiso, and 3,790 km (2,355 miles) west of the Chilean coast lies Easter Island, one of the most isolated inhabited islands in the world, and a colony of Chile since 1888. Some 500 km (300 miles) east of Argentinian Patagonia lie the chilly Falkland Islands, Great Britain's most far-flung colony. ❑

PRECEDING PAGES: Moreno Glacier, Glacier National Park, Argentina; the Amazon rainforest; the colonial city of Potosí, Bolivia.

THE NORTH COAST

*Great adventures start here – on the balmy Caribbean Coast,
or in the remotest reaches of the rainforest*

Hot palm-fringed beaches, languid lifestyles, and fast nightlife characterize South America's northern Caribbean Coast, but just inside the coastal belt are miles of tropical rainforest, and mountain ranges high enough to provide some cool respite in these equatorial zones. Both Colombia and Venezuela attracted gold-seekers in colonial times, and later fortunes were made from Venezuela's oil, or "black gold", while in Colombia it was drugs that made fortunes – and unfortunate headlines. Today, gold and diamond hunters are causing controversy in Venezuela's rainforest.

The people who live in the highland regions are mostly *mestizos* – mixed European and Amerindians – while on the coast, African heritage bears testimony to the slavery of colonial times. In Guyana, Suriname and French Guiana, fascinating communities of African descent have settled in the interior, living in the traditional manner of their ancestors. There are also Amerindian communities in these regions and in Venezuela also, some of whom were unknown to the rest of the world until the 1960s.

Colombia, in the northwest, is notorious for its guerrilla networks and urban violence, but most of the country is safe for visitors, and it is becoming an increasingly popular destination among tourists for its friendly people, exciting dance culture, and breathtaking scenery. Colombia has some remarkable historical sites, including the ancient ruins of San Agustín *(see page 99)*, the Spanish fortress city of Cartagena *(see page 103)*, and the finest gold museum on the continent *(see page 94)*, which is in the capital city, Bogotá.

Venezuela is an oil-rich country with beautiful beach resorts, many of which surround the paradise island of Margarita *(see page 120)*. Venezuela is also a naturalist's dream, with some magnificent wildlife and dramatic scenery. The landscape of the central regions around Mérida and Trujillo *(see page 116)* is alpine and picturesque, with many outdoor sports on offer in the hills. The remote, Guayana Region *(see page 121)*, where the world's highest waterfall, Angel Falls *(see page 122)* cascades, are characterized by enormous sheer rock formations, golden savannah and dense jungle.

East of Venezuela lie three smaller and less well-known countries – Guyana *(see page 127)*, Suriname *(see page 130)* and French Guiana *(see page 132)*. These sparsely populated lands mainly attract visitors who want to explore their extensive rainforest hinterlands, inhabited by people who lead very distinctive and traditional lives. All five continents are represented in the populations of these countries, due to their histories as plantation outposts for three different world empires. ❏

PRECEDING PAGES: young boy in a colorful Caribbean restaurant.
LEFT: a perfect morning on a perfect Venezuelan beach.

COLOMBIA

Map
on page
90

Despite its initial notoriety as the land of El Dorado and latterly the drugs capital of the world, this is still a beautiful, friendly country of enormous natural diversity and historical treasures

olombia has gained a fearsome reputation as the world's foremost producer of cocaine and for relentless violence and civil unrest. This, however, tells only part of the story of a country where myth and modernity mingle to produce a diversity of culture which can be matched by few other countries. This is where the myth of El Dorado and the lure of untold riches caught the imagination of the Spanish conquistadors. Miners still pursue this dream, in search of emeralds as well as gold. Modern and outward-looking on the surface, the architectural and social legacy of Spanish colonial rule is here for all to see, as well as the remains of some of the great pre-Columbian civilizations.

Geographically, Colombia is the fourth-largest country in South America and is unique in having both a Pacific and Atlantic coast. In the south lies the forbidding Amazon jungle. Three *cordilleras* (mountain ranges) stretch north from the southern border with Ecuador to meet the lowland plains of the Caribbean. Most of the country's 44 million inhabitants live in the central region, which incorporates the capital, Santa Fé de Bogotá, set high amid the mist and rain of the eastern cordillera, and the two modern cities of Medellín and Cali. In between the cordilleras lie the valleys of the Cauca and Magdalena rivers, the most fertile agricultural areas. Eastern Colombia is made up of vast, largely uninhabited grasslands known as *Los Llanos*, stretching down to the Orinoco basin. The northern Sierra Nevada of Santa Marta is the highest coastal mountain range in the world. On a clear day you can stand on a Caribbean beach and see snow-capped mountains.

While Bogotá is undoubtedly the cultural center of the country, each region has developed a distinct identity that is reflected in almost every strand of life. Musical styles range from the traditional string-based forms of the Andes to the accordion-led *vallenato* and *cumbia* of the Caribbean coast. One of the country's most popular figures is the Nobel Prize-winning writer Gabriel García Márquez with his particular brand of "magical realism". Other writers such as Alvaro Mutis are less well known but have helped place Colombian literature firmly on the map.

Soccer is by far the most popular sport; the country has also produced several world-class cyclists.

Colombia's exports include coffee, oil, emeralds, cut flowers, bananas, coal, and small quantities of gold. The population is predominantly *mestizo*, although there are sizable Afro Caribbean populations on the Caribbean and Pacific coasts and around Cali, and more than 50 indigenous groups.

PRECEDING PAGES: Bogotá by night. **LEFT:** Bogotá Cathedral, Plaza Bolívar. **BELOW:** Puerto del Reloj, Cartagena.

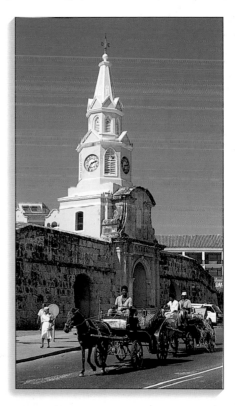

The turbulent past

Colombia has a turbulent political history. The 19th century was marked by 50 insurrections, eight civil

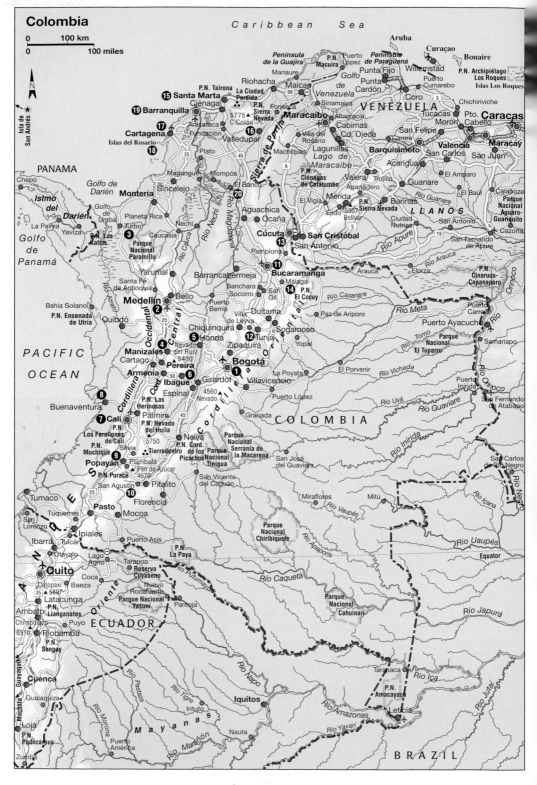

Colombia

0 ——— 100 km
0 ——— 100 miles

Map on page 90

wars and several constitutions. The most violent civil war, the War of the Thousand Days, began in 1899, but the ensuing bloodshed and loss of 130,000 lives wrought few changes. The government remained in the hands of a *criollo* (European) minority who paid scant attention to the *mestizos*, mulattos, blacks, and Amerindians who formed the bulk of the population.

Meanwhile, the United States took advantage of Colombia's chaos to foment a secessionist movement in Panamá, then a Colombian state. Soon afterwards, work began on the Panamá canal. Before receiving the Nobel Peace Prize, President Theodore Roosevelt boasted: "I took the Canal Zone and let Congress debate." The Colombian government grudgingly accepted the loss in 1921.

The United Fruit Company of the United States created huge banana plantations along the coast, paying starvation wages and, in 1928, ending a long-running strike by using the Colombian Army to machine-gun unionists. As the banana boom died, coffee became the new hope for the economy, but the pattern of large plantations repeated itself. Small fluctuations in the world price would devastate whole areas of the countryside.

By the end of the 1980s, Medellín drugs cartel boss Pablo Escobar had an estimated wealth of US$3 billion, making him the 14th richest man in the world, according to Forbes magazine.

Unprecedented brutality

In 1948, Jorge Eliecer Gaitan, a popular Liberal politician pushing for real political change, was gunned down in the streets of Bogotá. A spontaneous explosion of frustrations known as *La Violencia* (the violence) ensued, bringing angry crowds to the streets of the capital. Civil war in the countryside followed (the *Bogotazo*), with fighting between peasants, police, and soldiers reaching unprecedented levels of brutality. At least 300,000 people lost their lives. By 1953, armed peasant groups were beginning to develop a clear revolutionary philosophy. The Liberals and Conservatives quickly united in fear of a communist advance. In 1957, they agreed to share power for the next 16 years. Once again, the same politicians were back in power, ensuring that nothing would really change. Meanwhile, the various peasant armies in the countryside dragged on their battle with the armed forces, a fight that continues to this day, giving Colombia the dubious honor of having the oldest guerrilla forces in the continent.

Sporadic efforts to bring peace and greater democracy failed in the early 1980s, when the M-19 guerrilla group took over the Palace of Justice, central Bogotá. In the ensuing battle, more than 100 people lost their lives, including 11 judges of the Supreme Court.

BELOW: the *Bogotazo*, 1948.

Drug economy

The presidency of Virgilio Barco opened the way for full competition in democratic elections but the government now had a battle against a new force – the Medellín drug cartel headed by Pablo Escobar that controlled 80 percent of the world traffic in cocaine; this illegal trade undoubtedly helped the economy.

Escobar died in a hail of bullets in 1993, putting more business in the hands of the Cali barons. Over the next two years the authorities had a number of successes, not least when the treasurer of the Cali cartel gave himself up to the US Drug Enforcement Adminstration. Among the damaging claims he made was that President Samper's 1994 election campaign was funded by US$6 million of drugs money. Samper's term of office was dogged by these accusations, but he managed to survive an investigation relatively unscathed. The country suffered a recession and unemployment rose, while left-wing guerrillas, right-wing paramilitaries and the security forces fought on, and ordinary Colombians suffered.

Andres Pastrana won the presidency in 1998, promising economic regeneration and peace. To fight drug problems, Pastrana's government introduced the "Plan Colombia", costing US$7.5 billion – partly financed by the US and the European Union, but with little success. In May 2002 right-wing lawyer Alvaro Uribe, who has close ties with the paramilitary United Self Defense Forces and whose campaign was supported by the Bush administration, won a landslide victory, and vowed to get tough on FARC (the Marxist rebels). By 2004, the number of Colombians displaced as a result had jumped from 1 to 2 million in 4 years. Violence and kidnapping are still serious issues and foreign visitors are urged to avoid traveling on public transport at night and, because the situation is not static, to seek official advice before visiting what is otherwise a most beautiful and fascinating country.

Bogotá, capital and intellectual hub

Shrouded by clouds in the midst of the northern Andes (and beset by air pollution), the city of **Bogotá ❶** grew 20-fold in the second half of the 20th century. Layers of history peel away like the rings of an onion: outlying slums give way to towering skyscrapers of polished steel and glass; grand government palaces tower over quaint English mansions. The center is colonial Spanish with flower-covered courtyards and vice-royal monuments of stone and weathered brass.

This highland city, 2,642 meters (8,670 ft) above sea level, is often viewed with incomprehension by people of the Colombian coast, who see its inhabitants as cold and aloof. Reflecting a popular view, Gabriel García Márquez once described Bogotá as "a gloomy city where on ghostly nights the coaches of the viceroys still rattled through the cobbled streets."

The image has never worried *bogoteños*, who see themselves as intellectual, cultured, and cosmopolitan. Anything and everything can be found in Bogotá's chaotic avenues: opulent restaurants, teams of homeless children, vendors selling emeralds, peasants in ponchos, endless traffic jams, and walls covered with graffiti. Above all, it is the intellectual hub of Colombia, a place where – despite a complete lack of government aid to the arts – you can find dozens of theaters, vibrant university life, classic museums, streets full of bookshops and avant-garde art galleries, all joined in a creative tumult.

Orientation

Bogotá's El Dorado airport is impressively efficient, with the world's second-largest landing field. Miles of glasshouses surround the airport, growing some of Colombia's lesser-known exports – flowers.

The best view of the city is from the top of **Cerro de Montserrate**, which can be reached by a funicular railway and cable car. Every Sunday, *bogoteños* stroll to the summit, where an amusement park is set up

BELOW: traditional dance in a Bogotá nightclub.

alongside a statue of *El Señor Caido* (the Fallen Christ). Below, the city is arranged in a grid, with numbered *calles* running east–west and *carreras* running north–south. On the way down, call in at the **Quinta de Bolívar** (open Tues–Sun), a magnificent colonial mansion with expansive gardens, once the home of Simón Bolívar. It is full of paintings depicting Bolívar's life as well as many of his personal effects.

Map on page 90

To the west of the city, the **Jardín Botánico Jose Celestino Mutis** are the nation's botanic gardens (open Tues–Sun 8am–noon, 1.30–4pm). The extensive grounds have an impressive collection of Colombian flora.

The city center

In 1538, three conquistadors met at what is now the heart of the old city, the **Plaza de Bolívar**, to found a town in the fertile lands of the native Muisca people. Despite killing off the locals and later each other with surprising rapidity, the outpost grew, and became capital of Gran Colombia. The plaza has a statue of Bolívar, the Liberator, at its center. To the south, the **Capitolio Nacional**, where Congress sits, looks like a classic Greek temple. Beyond is the **Palacio Presidencial**, sacked in 1948 during the *Bogotazo* uprising. Every day at 5pm there is a changing of the guards, whose uniforms were modeled on pre-World War I Prussian outfits, complete with shiny silver spikes on their helmets.

On the western side of the plaza is the **Catedral**, which was begun in 1565, destroyed by an earthquake two centuries later and only completed after Colombia's independence. Alongside are the **Capillo del Sagrario** and the sumptuous **Teatro Colón**, the city's principal theater, which can only be visited during performances.

Painted interior, Puracé National Park, near Popayán (see page 98).

BELOW: hotel interior, Villa de Avila, near Bogotá.

A Golden Heritage

Protected like Fort Knox, the Museo del Oro (Gold Museum; open Tues–Sun) in the heart of Bogotá, is unsurpassed. Its collection of bracelets, earrings, masks, statues, and rings runs to more than 36,000 pieces from a dozen pre-Columbian cultures, all revealing a mastery of technique that leaves modern jewelers astounded.

Even before many of its pieces were revealed to be false, the Gold Museum in Lima was a pale collection in comparison to this one. This is largely due to the impatience of the gold-crazed Spanish conquistadors, who were too busy plundering the Inca empire to the south to search deep below the surface of the earth for the occasional piece of jewelry from long-forgotten cultures. Thus the great art of the Incas and other Peruvian cultures, easily robbed by the Spaniards, was melted down into gold bars to be shipped back to the royal coffers, while the jewelry of the Colombian cultures was left to be discovered by the archeologists of later

years and also, sadly, by the ever-present *guaqueros* or grave robbers who have scoured the countryside for generations.

The metal-working tradition of the Americas developed from the middle of the 2nd millennium BC up to the 16th century. The gold technology of ancient Colombia is considered remarkable, embracing all the known gold-working techniques then available in the New World. Its diversity is extraordinary: each of the cultures, isolated by the country's wild and inhospitable geography, developed its own peculiar style.

Hammering was the most primitive technique for making gold objects, although great skill is required to manage the metal. Some cultures in Colombia developed smelting, using combinations of alloys to strengthen the gold. Joining techniques were perfected to connect sheets of gold into more complex figures, and it is probable that the technique of lost-wax casting – using molds of wax models which dissolve on contact with the alloy – was first developed in Colombia.

Pre-Columbian people used gold for decoration and religious rites, recognizing the value of a metal that did not tarnish. Clear guidelines were laid down as to who could and could not wear the metal, while in some areas it was also used as an item for trading.

Run by the government-owned Banco de la República, the Museo del Oro is in the Parque de Santander. On the first level there is an excellent model of La Ciudad Perdida, the lost city of the Taironas *(see page 102)*.

One of the museum's prize possessions is a tiny boat created by the Muisca people, showing the ritual of throwing gold into Lake Guatavita as an offering to the gods, while the chief gilded himself with gold, giving rise to the first myth of "El Dorado."

The climax of any visit is the huge strongroom on the top floor. Only 20 people at a time are allowed to enter the room, which is in complete darkness, until lights are turned up to reveal more than 12,000 pieces, almost blinding in their brilliance. Atmospheric piped music transports visitors to the mysterious golden world, the reality of which can now only be imagined. ❑

LEFT: native Muisca turn their king into "El Dorado," the Gilded One.

Map on page 90

The colonial quarter

A short stroll from the Plaza de Bolívar takes you to Bogotá's colonial quarter, **La Candelaria**. Single-story whitewashed buildings seem to creep up a hillside, their red tile roofs and decaying cupolas stretching out to the city center.

Like all of South America's colonial cities, Bogotá has a wealth of religious art. **Iglesia de Santa Clara** (Calle 9/Carrera 8), built during the 17th century, has a sumptuous interior with works by the most famous of Bogotá's painters at the time, Gregorio Vasquez de Arce y Ceballos. On a less sublime note, history records that the church became notorious for the kidnapping of several novices – on one occasion Vasquez himself was implicated and imprisoned.

Heading back into the modern city, wander along Avenida 19 to see the amazing range of books on display. Colombia is South America's largest exporter of the printed word. Nearby, on Calle 18A/Carrera 1, is the campus of the **University of the Andes**, one of the sub-continent's most respected centers of learning.

To get a taste of the flourishing emerald business, head for the corner of Avenida Jimenez and Carrera 7. Colombia controls 60 percent of the world's production of these precious gems, and fortified shops sell them to travelers with a few thousand dollars to spare. Emeralds are graded by their brilliance, color and purity, but beware of fakes.

Bogotá's most famous and unmissable museum is the **Museo del Oro** *(see opposite)*. The **Museo Nacional** (open Tues 10am–8pm, Wed–Sat 10am–6pm), housed in the Panopticon building, was designed as a prison by Englishman Thomas Reed in the early 19th century, and was built so that each of the 200 cells could be observed from a single vantage point. It was used as a prison until 1946, and has been lovingly restored. Each corridor displays a different episode from Colombian history. The lower level is devoted to art.

Cathedral of salt

Traveling along a highway 48 km (30 miles) north of Bogotá, through lush countryside once ruled by the native Muisca, a morning excursion can be made to the **Cathedral of Zipaquira**, carved out of salt (check locally to see if open). The salt mines had been worked for centuries by the local people when the Spanish took them over. By the 1920s, such a large cavern had been dug that the Banco de la República decided to build a cathedral inside. Carefully cut from a mountainside above the small town of Zipaquira, a tunnel leads into a sulfur-laden darkness. Finally an altar appears silhouetted in the distance: the cathedral is 25 meters (78 ft) high and has held more than 10,000 people at one time, but the walls are black, giving the unsettling sensation of walking through space. Despite the lack of color, they are 75 percent pure salt – as can be affirmed by a quick taste – and mining is still going on elsewhere in the mountain. Colombians will proudly tell you that the mountain could keep the world supplied with salt for more than 100 years.

The other side of Medellín

Four hundred kilometers (250 miles) northwest of Bogotá is **Medellín ❷**, Colombia's second-largest

BELOW: altar of the Salt Cathedral, Zipaquira

city and the capital of Antioquia province. The city has done its best to shed its infamous image as murder and kidnap capital of the world and the home of the country's main drug cartel. Violence is less common than it was, but it is still a place where foreign visitors should be careful. Medellín is sometimes known as the "city of eternal spring" due to its pleasant climate. Residents have a reputation for being passionate about most things, including business, food, and enjoyment. One of the best ways to see the city is on the metro, much of which runs above street level. Don't expect too much in the way of colonial architecture – Medellín is above all a modern city – but the red-brick cathedral on **Parque Bolívar** is interesting. There is a permanent exhibition of the work of Colombia's best-known sculptor and artist, Fernando Botero, in the **Parque San Antonio** (Calle 46/Carrera 46).

Bananas and coffee

For a more relaxed pace, head northwest on the road toward Turbo to **Santa Fé de Antioquia**. Set among rolling hills, Santa Fé is a beautifully preserved colonial town. Two-story houses with brightly painted balconies line the streets. At weekends people travel in from the countryside, often on *chivas* – open-sided buses covered in gaudy paintings. From Santa Fé the road continues northward to the port of **Turbo** ❸ in the banana-growing region of **Urabá**. Unless you are going to the World Heritage Site of **Parque National Los Katíos** this area is best avoided. In recent years the region has seen some of the country's worst violence and human rights abuses. A few travelers pass through the region heading overland to Panama but this is not recommended as armed groups operate in this region.

South of Medellín lies the main coffee-growing region, the *zona cafetera*.

TIP

Medellín's annual flower festival in mid-August is one of the most colorful events in Colombia.

BELOW: coming home from market, San Agustín.

Coffee remains Colombia's biggest export and almost all the hillsides around here are dotted with small coffee farms. **Manizales ❹**, some 270 km (168 miles) south of Medellín, is regarded as the capital of the coffee-growing zone. It is a modern city, founded in the mid-19th century when Antioquian farmers migrated south in search of new agricultural land. The city suffered several fires and earthquakes in the early 20th century, but its huge cathedral survived. Its streets are built on steep hills – strolling can be tiring. From Manizales you can gain access to **Parque National Los Nevados** via the village of **La Enea**. This is a trekker's paradise, but take local advice about routes. The park's highest peak is the **Volcán Nevado del Ruiz**, which erupted in 1985, wiping out the town of Armero on the other side of the cordillera.

From Manizales the road to Bogotá passes through **Honda ❺**, a picturesque colonial town and weekend resort on the Río Magdalena. Directly south of Honda is **Ibagué ❻**, a rapidly expanding, but still pleasant, industrial city.

Salsa city

Going west from Ibagué the main road ascends steeply to cross the central cordillera. The pass can be freezing cold and for much of the year it is shrouded in mist. The Pan-American Highway then heads south and descends into the fertile valley of the Río Cauca where sugar, rice, and cotton are grown, providing important sources of income for **Cali ❼**, Colombia's third-largest city.

Cali was founded in 1536 but remained relatively small until the early 20th century when, with the arrival of the railway and the growth of the sugar industry, the city expanded at an unprecedented rate. Today it is the most important commercial center in southeast Colombia, and this is reflected in the modern

Map on page 90

Cali is famous for its nightlife, in particular its salsa scene. The city's annual festival is held between Christmas and New Year, with bullfighting, beauty contests, and impromptu salsa parties.

LEFT: mysterious statue in the Magdalena Valley. **RIGHT:** the muddy streets of San Agustín.

Fruit and vegetable market, Popayán.

architecture and high-rise office buildings around the city center. When the drug cartels of Cali were partly broken up during the mid 1990s, the city declined somewhat, as unemployment and crime soared. There are several interesting colonial churches such as **San Francisco** (Carrera 6/Calle 10) and **La Merced** (Carrera 4/Calle 7), as well as **La Ermita**, in Gothic-style but §built in the 1930s, the star of numerous postcards of the city. A short walk north from the center is the church of **San Antonio**, built in the mid-18th century on a hill, the **Colina de San Antonio**, with good city views. In the main square, **Parque Caicedo**, tall, arching palm trees can provide shade from the heat and humidity that smothers the city during the day. At night, fanned by cooling winds, the city comes alive and its numerous dance clubs can be heard from miles away.

For a more relaxing pace, visit one of several *haciendas* (farm estates) north of the city. One of the most interesting is **El Paraíso**, a beautifully preserved colonial mansion where the writer Jorge Isaccs wrote *María*, a highly regarded work of romantic realism. The house and its garden have been turned into a museum (closed Mon). Nearby is the *hacienda* of **Piedechinche** with a sugar refinery and sugar museum (closed Mon). The *haciendas* can be visited on a tour with a Cali travel agent, or take a bus to Amaime on the road between Buga and Palmira and walk from there (but don't travel alone).

BELOW: Cali: drug money is often laundered through construction projects.

Traveling northwest from Cali for 120 km (75 miles) takes you to the Pacific coast port of **Buenaventura** ❽. The town looks fairly ramshackle, but some of the country's best salsa musicians were born here, so there is usually something going on at night. From here, launches run up the coast to the fishing villages of **Juanchaco** and **Ladrilleros**, which have dark sandy beaches.

A few hours south of Cali by road is the city of **Popayán** ❾, founded in

Map on page 90

1536 following a brutal campaign to exterminate the indigenous Pubenza. The town prospered in colonial times due to its location on the road between Lima, Quito and Cartagena. In 1983 its Holy Week processions ground to a halt when a massive earthquake struck the region, reducing most of the city's oldest buildings to rubble. Almost all have been painstakingly restored. One of the most successful restorations is the white cathedral on the main square, the **Parque Caldas**. Behind the altar there is an impressive statue of the Madonna. Other churches worth visiting include **La Encarnación** (Calle 5/Carrera 5), **San Agustín** (Calle 7/Carrera 6), and **Santo Domingo** (Carrera 5/Calle 4). Popayán's Holy Week processions are famous throughout the Catholic world.

Silvia, a small village in the hills north of Popayán, is home to the culturally distinctive Guambiano, who come to sell their goods at the market on Tuesdays. Just northeast of Popayán, near **San Andrés de Pisimbalá**, is the National Archeological Park of **Tierradentro**. This World Heritage site is made up of a number of pre-Hispanic burial chambers, some of which have motifs and figures carved onto the walls, and stone statues. Little is known about the culture that built the tombs, but the statues are believed to have been carved at a later date, probably around the same time as those further east at San Agustín.

Some of Colombia's richest and most aristocratic families lived in Popayán, and the city proudly proclaims to have produced 11 Colombian presidents.

Natural beauty and ancient wonders

From Popayán a poor road goes east to **Parque Nacional Puracé**, an outstandingly beautiful spot with volcanoes, lakes, waterfalls, thermal springs, and many species of wildlife, including bears, condors, and tapirs. The park's altitude, from 2,500 to 4,800 meters (8,202 to 15,748 ft), accounts for the natural diversity. There are tourist facilities at **Pilimbalá**, at the northern end of the park.

Southeast of Popoyán is the small village of **San Agustín** ⑩, famous for its ancient stone statues, mysterious remnants of a lost culture from one of the most important archeological sites in South America. Layers of red-tiled roofs lead past a white church tower to the surrounding hills, covered with banana trees. The mountains beyond are a rich green because it rains every day for nine months of the year in a light, erratic drizzle. The village, with its laid-back atmosphere and beautiful surroundings, has long attracted tourists. Transport is mostly by horse: on every corner, cowboys in ponchos, wide-brimmed hats, and leather boots stand by their trusty steeds.

BELOW: selling lottery tickets, Cali.

Baffling figures

The statues of San Agustín have continued to baffle archeologists. Around 500 figures have been found in the surrounding Magdalena Valley: some resemble masked monsters, others eagles, jaguars, or frogs. Nobody knows who carved the statues or for what reason. Even today, investigators can only date the civilization from between the 6th and 12th centuries. Some experts argue that it was earlier, others that it grew later and was suppressed by the Incas, since this was the northernmost point of their empire.

Some of the statues are arranged neatly in archeological parks near the village. Within walking distance are the **Bosque de los Estatuas**, with more than 35

figures, and the **Alto de los Idolos**, where the largest statue is 7 meters (23 ft) high. Nearby are four *mesitas*, ancient burial sites with mounds, statues, and funeral temples. Most exciting to visit are the statues deeper in the country-side. Many can be reached only on horseback as the paths are difficult and often knee-deep in mud, though the landscape is spectacular.

Cradle of liberty

North from Bogotá the rugged eastern cordillera runs for just under 1,000 km (620 miles) to the modern industrial city of **Bucaramanga** , known for a local delicacy – the *hormiga culona*, an edible species of ant. Before the Spanish arrived much of this area was populated by the native Muisca. There is little evidence left of their culture but the wild, mountainous landscape is arguably the most dramatic in Colombia.

North of Bogotá, the first major city you encounter is **Tunja**. The Spanish founded the city in 1539, but there was a settlement here long before that. A monument and bridge commemorates the Battle of Boyacá, the decisive battle in the independence struggle, which was fought just south of the city. For a short time after independence, Tunja was the capital of Nuevo Granada. Simón Bolívar referred to it as his "cradle and workshop of liberty". The capital shifted south when a number of important families moved to Bogotá. A measure of Tunja's importance during colonial times lies in the number of churches that were built – anyone interested in religious art should visit Tunja. The cathedral contains several paintings by Gregorio Vasquez. Also worth visiting are, between Calles 19 and 20, the churches of **Santo Domingo** (Carrera 9), with its ornate wooden interior, and **Santa Clara** (Carrera 7), with a 16th-century convent.

TIP

Every August a festival of kites takes place in Tunja's main square, and in December there is a festival of lights.

BELOW: villages in the Nariño region, southwestern Colombia.

Tunja is a good base to explore the small villages and towns scattered around the Boyacá highlands. One of the most popular is **Villa de Leyva** which, with cobbled streets lined by low, whitewashed, tile-roofed houses, has become a national monument. The main focus of the town is the wide central square with a museum dedicated to the work of well-known painter and sculptor Luis Alberto Acuña (open Wed–Sun). The town is deeply rooted in national history. Antonio Nariño, an intellectual and statesman who led the call for independence at the end of the 18th century, lived and translated Thomas Jefferson's *Declaration of the Rights of Man* at a house on Carrera 9/Calle 10.

There are several other buildings worthy of note, including the **Carmelite monastery** and its church opposite in the Plazuela del Carmen. But what makes this town special is its unhurried atmosphere, particularly during the week. From Villa de Leyva buses and *collectivos* leave for nearby towns like **Ráquira**, known for its pottery; and **Chiquinquirá**, where pilgrims from all over Colombia converge to visit a painting of the Virgin, supposedly Colombia's oldest painting, by Alonso de Narváez. From Chiquinquirá, the lawless emerald mining towns of **Muzo** and **Coscues** can be reached, although the journey, on an unpaved road, can be arduous in the rainy season.

From Tunja a twisting road goes northeast for 460 km (286 miles) to the Venezuelan border at **Cúcuta** . The scenery along the route is spectacular and passes through several whitewashed towns such as **Málaga** ⑭ before arriving at **Pamplona**, which has one of the oldest universities in Latin America. The main road from Tunja goes north to **Santander**, a province filled with old colonial towns, most notable of which are **San Gil**, **Barichara**, and **Socorro**, from where the *comuneros* led the first revolt against the Spanish in 1781. This

Floral cowboy, Medellín flower festival.

BELOW: pueblo Paisa, near Medellín.

event is remembered in the town's **Casa de Cultura** (open daily), housed in a colonial mansion on the Calle Real beside the brick cathedral.

The Caribbean coast

Arriving from Bogotá to Colombia's Caribbean coast is like stepping into a completely different world. It is as if there were two separate countries: one cool and remote, the other tropical and sensual.

A gateway to the coast and many attractions of the north is **Santa Marta** ⓯, capital of Magdalena province. One of the most pleasant cities in Colombia, it was founded by the Spaniards in 1525, but there are few colonial relics in the popular modern resort town. Visitors come here to loll in the sun along **El Rodadero Beach**, considered one of the best in Colombia; to stroll up and down the tourist promenade while being bombarded with salsa; or simply sit in a pavement bar and enjoy the view across the bay to the rocky island of **El Morro**.

Santa Marta is a convenient jumping-off point to **Parque Nacional Tairona**, with its string of stunning, pristine and often deserted white-sand beaches. This stretch of untouched jungle, once the territory of the native Tairona population, is at the foot of the **Sierra Nevada de Santa Marta**, a pyramid-shaped mountain that drops sheer into the Caribbean Sea. Further east is the **Santuario de Flora y Fauna Los Flamencos**, a nature reserve which, as the name suggests, is full of pink flamingos.

Santa Marta is also the place to reach **La Ciudad Perdida**, the Lost City of the Tairona that was only found in 1975. Larger than Machu Picchu in Peru, the discovery is considered one of the most important of the 20th century in South America, confirming that the Tairona were not just accomplished craftsmen

BELOW: classic Caribbean sunset.

but built one of the largest cities on the sub-continent, with wide boulevards and road links. The city was discovered by *guaqueros* (grave robbers) in the tropical jungle of the Sierra Nevada. Calling it *El Infierno Verde* (Green Hell), they fought over the finds until the government intervened. In the absence of any written records, archeologists can only guess when the city was built – probably the 13th century – and what disaster led the inhabitants to disappear without trace. Today this legendary city can only be reached by a six-day trek.

García Márquez country

The first image many foreigners have of South America comes from the Caribbean coast of Colombia, thanks to the works of author Gabriel García Márquez. His writings have preserved the life and history of the region, and today the small town of **Aracataca** where he was born and raised – and which he fictionalized as the town Macondo in his 1967 novel *One Hundred Years of Solitude* – can be visited for a glimpse of coastal life. Buses leave several times an hour from the Santa Marta terminal. Aracataca has a plaza with a statue of Bolívar, an old church tower, several shabby billiard halls and a couple of empty restaurants. Tucked away in a back street is a modest building with the sign "GGM Museum." In a garden full of chickens is the house where Márquez was born in 1928 – wooden, whitewashed, and without a stick of furniture.

A few hours south of Aracataca is the city of **Valledupar** ⓰. Founded in the mid-16th century, there is little evidence of its colonial past apart from the main square, where people sit around a giant mango tree to shelter from the searing midday heat. Every year this space becomes the focus of the country's attention during the festival of the Legend of the Vallenato. For five days at the end of April Colombia's top accordion players battle it out in Valledupar to be crowned King of the Vallenato, a popular style of music which originated here. The festivities are fueled by rum and large quantities of *aguardiente* ("fire water").

Cartagena, Spain's New World fortress

Of the many colonial jewels in South America, **Cartagena de Indias** ⓱ is perhaps both the most romantic and the least known. Placed on the tropical Caribbean coast, saturated by heat, music, and feverish dreams, this fortress city of the Spaniards is a living museum. It is recognized internationally as a World Heritage Site. Just walking its streets recalls the days of bloodthirsty pirates, galleons full of bullion, and swordfights beneath the palm trees. Founded in 1533 by the first of Spain's scurvy-ridden conquistadors, the town quickly blossomed to become the main colonial port on the Caribbean and the gateway to the whole South American empire. But as the wealth plundered from the local populations piled up in galleons to be taken to Cádiz, the city became a target of every pirate and desperado cruising the Caribbean seas.

During the 16th century, Cartagena was besieged five times by buccaneers and cut-throats. The Spanish decided to create fortifications so powerful that the port would be impregnable. Stone ramparts and battlements were constructed over many decades, the

Map on page 90

Sir Francis Drake sacked Cartagena in 1586 and extorted a 10-million peso ransom from the inhabitants. This was shipped back to England for Queen Elizabeth, along with the bodies of several crocodiles, blasted from nearby swamps with cannons and stuffed with straw.

BELOW: taking a break on the Caribbean coast.

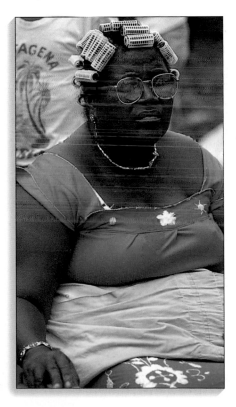

like of which had never been seen in the Americas. The pirate attacks continued, but never with the same success – Cartagena was even able to survive several sieges by the English and the French.

Exploring the old city of Cartagena

Arriving from the airport, a highway passes along Marbella beach toward **Las Murallas**, the stone ramparts that still surround the old city. Many small forts, where cannons and other defensive weapons were placed to ward off sea attacks, remain intact. The colonial section of Cartagena is only a small part of the metropolis, but it contains enough relics to warrant several days' exploration.

Farmer stitching a saddle blanket, Antioquia province.

BELOW: fortress at San Fernando, Cartagena.

Facing the **Plaza de Bolívar** is the **Palacio de la Inquisición**, one of Cartagena's finest buildings. Its museum recalls the fearful proceedings of the Holy Inquisition, during which 12 people suffered a public *auto-da-fé* in the plaza. When Cartagena declared its independence, this palace was one of the first places that the angry crowd came to sack.

Adjoining the Plaza Bolívar is the fort-like cathedral. Three blocks south is the **Plaza de la Aduana**, once used as a parade ground for troops, and now based around a statue of Christopher Columbus (Cristobal Colón, in Spanish). Call in at the **Museo de Arte Moderno** in the former Royal Customs House, then take a stroll under the **Puerto del Reloj**, which once linked the inner walled town to the poorer Getsemaní district by a drawbridge over a moat. Following the city wall closely around to the south, you will run into the **Iglesia y Convento de San Pedro Claver**, named after a Spanish monk who spent his whole life looking after African slaves. Nicknamed the "Slave of the Slaves", St Peter Claver (1580–1654) was the first person to be canonized in the New

World. Today the monastery is a haven of solitude and peace, with arched stone patios built around a garden of flowers and foundations.

There are dozens of other colonial houses, churches, and monuments worth visiting in Cartagena. Drop in at the colonial **Casa de la Candelaria** – once a noble's mansion, now a restaurant but also open to non-diners – then stroll around the city walls to **Las Bovedas**, built two centuries ago as dungeons, with walls 15 meters (50 ft) thick. Today they are home to tourist shops and bars.

Map on page 90

Barriers of stone

To keep their stolen gold extra secure, the Spanish built even more extraordinary fortifications in key points. Looming over the city from the San Lorenzo Hill is the impregnable **Castillo de San Felipe de Barajas**, a complicated system of batteries, tunnels, and hiding places engineered from massive chunks of stone. The tunnels, which can be visited, were constructed so that any sound would echo and warn guards of approaching soldiers. The view over the old city from the castle is one of the best in Cartagena.

At the entrance to Cartagena Bay is the **Fuerte de San Fernando**, a fort which can only be visited by water. A huge chain was hung between it and another outpost across the bay to prevent surprise attacks. Many films have been shot in its well-preserved interior. On top of a large hill behind the city is the **Convento de la Popa**. The Augustinians built a wooden chapel at the summit in 1607, soon replaced by a monastery with an image of the patron of Cartagena, La Virgen de la Candelaria.

Near the Puerto del Reloj is the city's dock area, **La Muelle de los Pegasos**, where you can sit at a juice stall and watch the port life go by. La Muelle is the departure point for tourist boats to the idyllic **Islas del Rosario** ⓲, just a couple of hours away. For a cheap seafood dinner, stroll up **Avenida Venezuela** and call in at the *ostrerias*, small booths selling delicious shrimp and oyster cocktails. For more sophisticated nightlife, head for **Bocagrande**, a resort suburb several minutes out of town by taxi. The food and dancing are the best Cartagena can offer.

BELOW: Spanish tunnel inside the San Fernando fortress, Cartagena.

Around Cartagena

Heading northeast along the coast is the large port city of **Barranquilla** ⓳, famous for its magnificent carnival held in February. **Mompós**, 240 km (150 miles) south of Cartagena on an island in the Río Magadalena, was declared a World Heritage Site by UNESCO in 1995. In the 18th century the Río Magdalena changed course, isolating Mompós, which had flourished in the Spanish era as the river provided the most important line of communication between the interior and the north coast. The city now has some of the finest examples of colonial architecture in Colombia.

Of particular note is the yellow church of **Santa Barbara**, with a Moorish octagonal tower. The **Casa de Cultura** (open daily) stands beside the church of **San Agustín**, where crowds gather during the town's impressive Easter processions. Buses and launches depart from here for the hot, dusty, and decaying town of **El Banco** ⓴. ❑

VENEZUELA

*This Caribbean country, struck by disaster in December 1999,
still has a wealth of fabulous natural treasures
to offer both beachcombers and adventurers*

Map on pages 110–11

The Caribbean shoreline and adjacent islands that once provided Venezuela with tantalizing warm-water beaches, excellent sailing, and underwater delights, plus some of the world's best bill and bonefishing, is on the road to recovery after nature's fury left a path of devastation along the central coast. The popular beaches bore the brunt of the weather system and were severely damaged by the storms; inland attractions avoided much of the destruction. They range from the snow-capped Andes to vast plains with sprawling cattle ranches, from quaint villages to modern metropolitan areas with non-stop nightlife. Venezuela still has immense natural beauty, with virgin tropical rain-forests inhabited by indigenous tribes, the Guayana Region rich in gold and diamonds, and famed Gran Sabana, a paradise for bird-watchers and anglers.

As one of the world's largest oil-producing countries, petroleum has been an influential element in Venezuela's recent history. During six decades of boom, beginning in the 1920s, money flowed freely. With the seemingly bottomless pot of "black gold", agriculture was virtually abandoned as people left farms to get a piece of the pie in the principal cities. Development of national industry waned as imports soared, and no one took note of growing government corruption and lack of investment in the country's basic structure. But petroleum prices began to tumble in the early 1980s and, with the infamous "Black Friday", February 18, 1983, hard reality hit. The value of the national currency was slashed and exchange controls were imposed. The party was over.

The real crisis was not felt until Carlos Andrés Pérez returned for a second presidential term in 1989, riding on the popularity from his first time in office in 1974–79. His tough economic measures led to two bloody military coup attempts that year. Pérez survived, but on May 20, 1993, he was indicted by the Supreme Court on charges of corruption for alleged misuse of secret funds. The Senate voted to remove him from office and he was convicted in 1996.

Rafael Caldera, president 1969–74, was re-elected in 1994. Faced with mounting foreign debt, the failure of 17 financial institutions representing nearly half the total of the nation's deposits, massive capital flight, and the public's lack of confidence, the value of the bolívar was slashed and exchange controls imposed from June 1994 to April 1996. The devaluation of the currency hit Venezuelans hard.

Talk rather than action followed promised spending cuts, and the country's public debt increased. Plummeting real earnings and high unemployment have since placed 85 percent of Venezuelans below the poverty line. Robberies directed against the "haves" have turned them into prisoners of their privilege, living behind guarded doors. Meanwhile, violence among the poor in

PRECEDING PAGES:
La Llovizna,
Guayana Highlands.
LEFT: Parque
Central, Caracas.
BELOW: taking it
easy in Ciudad
Bolívar.

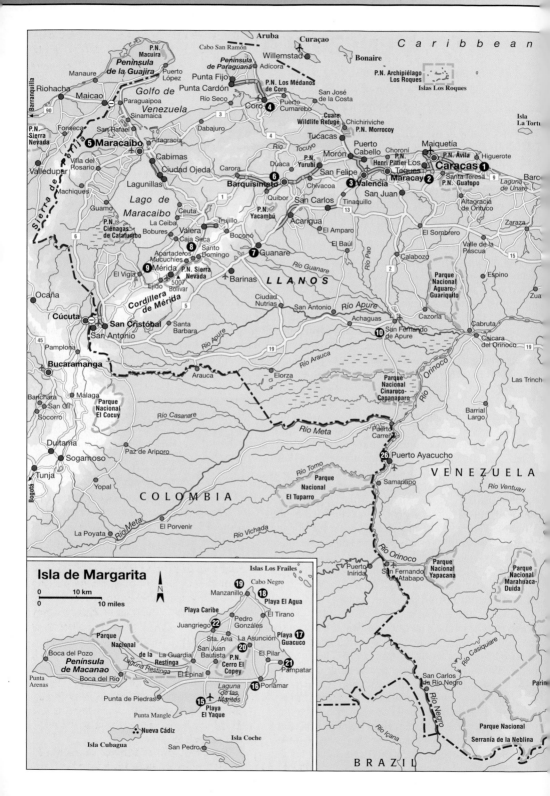

the *barrios* of Caracas is on the increase.

Since 1997, Venezuela has been on the difficult road to recovery: rebuilding national industry, working to stimulate agriculture, dealing with inflation that surpassed 100 percent in 1996, learning how to be competitive with the elimination of price controls and a shift to a free market economy. In 1998, Colonel Hugo Chávez Frías won the presidential election and overhauled Venezuela's political system. He was re-elected in July 2000 with 60 percent of the seats in a new unicameral parliament, amid demontrations by protesters who claimed votes had been rigged. Despite enormous windfalls from the quadrupling in price of Venezuela's oil, falling inflation and the increased public spending of Chávez's Plan Bolívar 2000, the president was unable to bridge the gap between rich and poor. Civil protests culminated in a nationwide strike and mass demonstrations. In 2002 the bolívar was devalued; a huge decrease in foreign investment, mounting military discontent and a general strike led to the president's forced resignation on April 12, although he was reinstated two days later. In June 2004 it was announced that Chávez would face a mid-term recall referendum on August 15.

Caracas: city of fortune

The first view of the country for most visitors is El Litoral – the central coast location of Simón Bolívar International Airport and adjacent National Airport. This area was struck by disaster in 1999, when torrential rain turned gentle mountain streams into swollen rivers surging down ravines, picking up ancient trees, giant boulders, and tons of earth as they rushed to the sea. Homes and businesses were destroyed and this idyllic landscape was all but ruined. Venezuela's capital, **Caracas ❶**, is 27 km (43 miles) away across the coastal mountain range. Sadly, **Macuto** and **Caraballeda**, some 40 minutes to the east, were obliterated in the floods, although the latter has started to come back to life.

The mountains of **Parque Nacional El Avila** form a dramatic backdrop for Cara-

Inhabitants of Caracas are known as Caraqueños.

cas, called home by some five million inhabitants. The hillsides surrounding the airport road and slopes ringing the metropolis are blanketed with haphazardly constructed *ranchos* (shanty towns), inhabited largely by illegal immigrants and poor rural folk who came to seek their fortune, but quickly found that without marketable skills, formal jobs were not available. The central valley and upscale residential areas of the east and south show a modern, dynamic, and affluent side.

Centro is the traditional heart of the city and **Plaza Bolívar** is the core of its historic zone, with treasures including the 19th-century **Capitolio**, the 17th-century **Catedral** and adjacent **Museo Sacro** (open Tues–Sun). **Casa Natal** was the birthplace of South America's liberator, Simón Bolívar. Next door, there is military memorabilia in the **Museo Bolivariano** (both open Tues–Sun; free). **Concejo Municipal** was the birthplace of Venezuela's call for independence. Visit the **Museo de Caracas** (open daily; free) inside, which has a display of miniatures created by Raúl Santana depicting every aspect of *criollo* life at the end of the 19th century, along with paintings by the impressionist Emilio Boggio.

Casa Amarilla, formerly a jail and presidential residence, now houses the Foreign Ministry. Facing the northwest corner of the plaza is the **Gobernación**, seat of government of the Distrito Federal. The **Iglesia de San Francisco**, dating from 1575, has walls lined with gorgeous gilded altars and is connected to the **Palacio de las Letras**, the academies of history, language, and science. Several blocks north of the cathedral is the striking pink and gray **Panteón Nacional** (open Tues–Sun; free), resting place for over 130 of the nation's greatest heroes.

The excellent colonial art museum, **Quinta de Anauco** (open Tues–Sun), in San Bernardino, is well worth a visit. Surrounded by gardens full of plants of the period, this elegant building has been restored with outstanding art and furnishings.

BELOW: hats and hammocks, Ciudad Bolívar.

Financial hub

Interspersed with colonial gems in Centro are sleek glass-faced skyscrapers, harboring the nation's financial, business, and political movers and shakers. Shoppers here can delight in the nine-story gold center **La Francia**, facing Plaza Bolívar, and small shops selling shoes, clothing, and jewelry stretching east from the plaza to the **La Hoyada** metro station.

Chuao has one of the city's largest shopping centers, housed in an attractive mall, **Centro Ciudad Comercial Tamanaco** (**CCCT**), filled with top-of-the-line shops, restaurants, nightclubs, travel agencies, Viasa's office with advanced luggage check-in service, a supermarket, and a four-star hotel. Facing it is the distinctive **Cubo Negro** (black cube) office building, one of the many examples of attention-grabbing contemporary architecture in the city, with a dramatic hanging kinetic sculpture by Venezuelan artist Jesús Soto.

Traffic and parking are perennial headaches in Caracas but the fast, clean, economical subway system, the Metro de Caracas, takes you across the city in minutes. Though a slower option, there is also a non-stop flow of dirt-cheap buses that go everywhere. Taxis are numerous and inexpensive, but few drivers speak English, so have your destination written in Spanish if you can.

A few minutes east from Centro is **Parque Central**. This massive urban renewal project has 53-story twin towers, seven 44-story apartments, and the outstanding **Museo de Arte Contemporáneo de Caracas Sofía Imber**, with sculpture garden and restaurant. Visitors can go up to the 52nd floor of the East Tower for 360-degree views of the city. There is also a fabulous hands-on museum for children, **Museo de los Niños**, and the **Museo Teclado**, a keyboard museum with weekly concerts. Nearby is the spectacular **Teatro Teresa Car-**

TIP

The best way to get around Caracas is by the metro (subway). To save money, buy *ida y vuelta* (round trip tickets for one destination), *multi abono* (10 rides of any distance for a discounted rate), or *integrado* (metro plus metrobus).

LEFT: old and new in Caracas.
RIGHT: Los Caobos Park, Caracas.

Colonial facade, Coro.

reño and the **Teatro Rajatabla**, home of a popular alternative theater group. Other attractions are three great museums (all open Tues–Sun; free): the **Museo de Ciencias Naturales**; the **Museo de Bellas Artes**, with international contemporary art; and the **Galería de Arte Nacional**, showing Venezuelan artists. Behind them is the sprawling **Los Caobos Park** and in the background the **Ibrahim bin Abdulazis al Ibrahim Mosque**, the largest in South America.

Continue on the metro to **Plaza Venezuela**, then walk east to **Chacaíto** along the kilometer-plus "gran avenida" of **Sábana Grande**. This wide pedestrian boulevard is lined with shops, cafés, and chess tables, where office workers often spend their lunch hour. It is delightful by day, but at night hookers and transvestites take over and the adjacent hotels are primarily rented by the hour.

A little further east, exit the metro at **Parque del Este** to explore the 81-hectare (200-acre) park by Brazilian landscape architect Roberto Burle Marx, with planetarium, mini-zoo, and artificial lake. The **Museo de Transporte** (open Wed–Sun) facing its east side is connected by walkway over the busy freeway.

Among the city's other parks, two blocks south of **Plaza Venezuela**, with a giant central fountain, is the **Jardín Botánico** (open daily), which has extensive gardens, an arboretum of some 100,000 trees, and sculptures by national artists. Or take the No. 2 spur of the metro from Capitolio to the **Zoológico** stop to visit the 486-hectare (1,200-acre) "no cages" **Parque Zoológico Caricuao**.

The greatest concentrations of upscale restaurants are found in the commercial zone of **Las Mercedes** in the shopping center of the same name. **La Candelaria**, just east of Centro, is an eminently Spanish sector famous for its traditional restaurants and *tascas*, bars which feature many *tapas* appetizers.

Map on pages 110–11

West of Caracas

Colonia Tovar, about an hour away by car, is a village high in the mountains that was founded in 1843 by Germans from the Black Forest, who transplanted their architecture, language, cultural practices, farming tradition, and cuisine. On weekends, *Caraqueños* jam the narrow streets lined with produce and crafts stands. It has numerous cozy hotels and a yearly international chamber music festival in March or April. **Maracay ❷**, 90 minutes west of Caracas via freeway, is the entry point for **Parque Nacional Henri Pittier**, Venezuela's oldest protected environmental zone (since 1937), renowned among bird-watchers for over 550 species seen here, and by non-birders for its winding scenic routes surrounded by bamboo groves, cloud forests, and mammoth vine-draped trees.

Entry via **El Limón** leads to the beautiful palm-lined arc of **Bahía de Cata**. A short distance before the park is **Ocumare de la Costa**, with various lodging options. Continuing past **Cata**, the beach of **Cuyagua** is a favorite for surfers. Follow the route via Las Delicias to reach the picturesque colonial village of **Choroní** and the coast at the fishing village of **Puerto Colombia**, with many *posadas* (guest houses), a few kilometers on. The broad, palm-shaded swimming beach is about 1 km (⅔ mile) to the east. Local fishermen offer boat transfers to the popular beaches of **Chuao** and **Cepe** from Puerto Colombia.

From **Valencia ❸**, Venezuela's manufacturing capital, take the road north for a 20-minute mountain drive to the coast, passing the hot springs of **Centro Termas Las Trincheras**. From there, turning east takes you to **Puerto Cabello**, Venezuela's most important port. Here, a beautiful waterfront colonial zone faces **Castillo Libertador**, an impressive fort built in 1732. **Fortín Solano**, the last colonial fortification erected in Venezuela, completed in 1770, stands on a hill in the background.

Turning west at the coast brings you in 40 minutes to **Tucacas**, the first entrance to **Parque Nacional Morrocoy**. Alternatively, continue to another entrance via **Chichiriviche**, with the bonus of a drive through **Cuare Wildlife Refuge** where the flashiest inhabitants are scarlet ibis and a flock of some 20,000 flamingos. The park is also popular for its white sand, palm-fringed islands and keys. Boat shuttles are available from Tucacas and Chichiriviche.

The westbound coastal highway traverses desert plains to reach **Coro ❹**, which was declared a World Heritage City by UNESCO for its concentration of outstanding colonial structures, including an exceptional **Diocesan Museum**. A side trip north to the windswept **Paraguaná Peninsula** takes you past the towering sand dunes of **Parque Nacional Los Médanos de Coro** to **Adícora**, a windsurfer's paradise. Fans of colonial architecture can admire houses that demonstrate the Dutch influence of the nearby islands of **Curaçao** and **Aruba**.

Source of the black gold

Arriving at the country's westernmost state, Zulia, one encounters **Lago Maracaibo**, the largest lake in South America (and one of the world's most valuable, with the greatest portion of Venezuela's enormous oil reserves and some 40 percent of the country's gas

BELOW: Guajiro woman at a market north of Maracaibo.

TIP

For a fast route to Táchira, take Highway 6 along the west side of Lake Maracaibo, following signs out of town indicating Machiques.

reserves). Cross the **Rafael Urdaneta Bridge**, the longest pre-stressed concrete span in the world, to reach the state capital, **Maracaibo** ❺, Venezuela's second-largest city. Maracaibo is the center for the nation's oil industry, with a core of upscale residential areas and multi-national company offices. It is also populated by thousands of native Guajiro and Paraujano, the women proudly wearing traditional long flowing dresses.

Near the seven-block long **Paseo Ciencias** park is the colonial **Catedral** and the **Casa de Capitulación**. The **Basílica de Nuestra Señora de la Chiquinquirá** honors Zulia's beloved patron saint, nicknamed "La Chinita." **Calle Carabobo** (or Calle 94) is a street of colorful "Maracaibo-style" houses, now mainly shops and restaurants, and a huge, handsome, former municipal market restored and converted into the **Centro de Arte de Maracaibo Lia Bermúdez** (open daily; free). In the Santa Lucia district, along with good shops and popular restaurants, is the **Museo de Arte Contemporáneo del Zulia** (MACZUL), the second-largest contemporary art museum in Latin America.

A cheap shuttle boat service runs from El Mojón to the colonial fort and extensive beach of **Isla San Carlos**. At nearby **Laguna de Sinamaica** boat excursions with Amerindian guides visit communities of native Paraujano who live in houses built on stilts in the lagoon.

Where the Andes begin

The Andean states of **Tachíra** and in particular **Mérida** and **Trujillo**, are the most picturesque in the country. Though accessible by air, this area should be visited by car to appreciate the stunning landscapes of glacier-fed lakes bordered by colorful flowers. There are quaint villages with traditional architecture, and

BELOW: drilling on Lake Maracaibo.

Map
on pages
110–11

wayside restaurants where you can savor trout or smoked cheese on a wheat flour *arepa* washed down with warm, spiked *ponche andino* or *calentado*.

Taking the Transandean Highway from the coast through **Barquisimeto** ❻, with side trips to the weavers' colony in **Tintorero** and to **Quibor**, known for its ceramics and ancient indigenous heritage, you will enter the area from **Guanare** ❼, in the heart of the central farmlands. Here, you can visit the impressive **Templo Votivo Nacional de la Virgin de Coromoto**, inaugurated in 1996 by the Pope and dedicated to Venezuela's patron saint.

Alternatively, go via **Boconó**, driving through coffee plantations, or approach from **Barinas** via **Santo Domingo**. Because of their isolation (roads here were not surfaced until the mid-1950s), the Church became the center of social as well as religious life for the *andinos*, and this is still evident. Visitors are likely to encounter some sort of religious or folkloric celebration during their stay.

Paso El Aguila crowns the highest paved road in the country at 4,007 meters (13,146 ft). The surrounding *páramo* (high moorland) is dominated by the tall *frailejón*, with fuzzy silver-green leaves and bright yellow flowers (best in October). Near **Apartaderos** ❽ is the **Observatorio Astronómico Nacional del Llano del Hato**, with four giant telescopes and public viewing.

East of the highway from **Santo Domingo** lies **Parque Nacional Sierra Nevada**. Principal entrances to its many hiking trails are at **Laguna Mucubají**, the largest of Mérida's 200 glacial lakes, most full of trout, and **Mucuy Alto**.

A rather touristy but nonetheless interesting stop, about 20 minutes north of Mérida city, is **Los Aleros**, the reproduction of an entire Andean village as it would have looked before the highway came through. Along with traditional construction and period artifacts, participants carry out daily chores, and live

BELOW: national observatory near Apartados, Mérida state.

music of the era and even a wedding are performed daily. Park creator Alexi Montilla followed up with the all-encompassing **Alexi's Venezuela de Antier**, between Mérida and the restored colonial village of **Jají**.

Views of Venezuela's snow-capped peaks, the highest of which is Bolívar, at 5,007 meters (16,427 ft), can be enjoyed in the year-round spring-like weather of the city of **Mérida ❾**. *Posadas* around **Plaza Las Heroinas** (by the cable car station) are the gathering places for those in search of mountain activities such as trekking, climbing, and paragliding, with equipment rental, guides, and *Toyoteros* – drivers of four-wheel-drive vehicles who take visitors to the remote mountain villages of Los Pueblos del Sur, or to entry points for excursions.

Mérida has the world's highest (4,765-meter/15,633-ft) and longest (12.5-km/8-mile) cable car, completed in 1999. The city has 43 parks and plazas, including **Parque Zoológico Chorros de Milla**, with a mini zoo, pretty gardens, and its namesake cascade; and **El Acuario**, which has an aquarium and vignettes with life-size figures showing life in the Andes of the past.

Roadside basket shop in the Andes

The **Museo de Ciencia y Tecnología** is also well worth a visit, as is the **Museo de Arte Moderno** (daily; free) and the massive, eclectically styled **Catedral Metropolitana** on **Plaza Bolívar**.

No state more fully epitomizes the unique character of Venezuela's vast *llanos* (central plains) than **Apure**. Huge *hatos* (cattle ranches) covering thousands of hectares, the *llaneros* who work them, moriche palms, the traditional *joropo* music and dance, and an incredible abundance of wildlife are its trademarks. Some *hatos* can be reached by road, via the state capital of **San Fernando de Apure ❿** from the east, or **Ciudad Nutrias** from the west; others are accessible only by private plane, boat, or four-wheel drive.

BELOW: Plaza Bolívar, Mérida.

The Eastern Gold Coast

The marine paradise of **Parque National Los Roques Archipelago** is only 35 minutes away by air, though both day-trips and overnight stays are very expensive. Along with excellent diving and beautiful (but shadeless) beaches, Los Roques offers unparalleled game-fishing. From Caracas to the "Route of the Sun", between Puerto La Cruz and Cumaná, follow the eastern coastal highway (but not during public holidays, as traffic comes to a standstill for hours). While most people head directly to Barcelona and Puerto La Cruz, other great beaches en route include the outer banks of the **Laguna de Unare** (enter via Boca de Uchire) and **Puerto Píritu**.

Barcelona, Anzoátegui state's capital, has a well-preserved historic zone with such attractions as the **Museo de Tradiciones**, along narrow streets bordered by vintage architecture. At the other extreme, beaches along a narrow neck of land lead to the mammoth **El Morro Tourist Complex**. Some 12 km (7½ miles) east along the coast lies **Puerto La Cruz** ⑪ – action never stops along its beachfront boulevard, **Paseo Colón** (but leave swimming to island beaches, since the water here is contaminated). **Pozuelos Bay**, dotted with luxury yachts and traditional fishing boats, and the dramatic rocky islands of **Parque National Mochima**, forms the seaward backdrop for the boulevard. A shuttle service is offered by a boatmen's union from the eastern end of the beach to the island beaches, with the best snorkeling and diving spots.

Continuing eastward along the coastal highway, you can stop off at beaches like **Playa Colorada** and **Arapito** on the way to **Cumaná** ⑫, Venezuela's oldest continental city (founded in 1521). A ferry crosses from Cumaná to the **Araya Peninsula** ⑬, landing near ruins of a colonial fort and pretty beach.

Map on pages 110–11

TIP

The dry season (mid-November to the end of April) is the time to visit Los Llanos, when wildlife is concentrated around shrinking watering holes – the rest of the year, rain is incessant and many places are inundated (or closed), with fauna widely dispersed.

BELOW: Caribbean islands of Los Roques Archipelago National Park.

Further east still, try the fabulous beach of **Playa Medina** near the Río Caribe.

To the south, near **Caripe** , is the **Cueva del Guácharo** (officially Monumento Natural Alejandro Humboldt), the country's largest cave, named for the *guácharos* (night-flying oil birds) that call it home.

Margarita and the Pearl Islands

*La Asunción church,
Isla Margarita.*

Isla Margarita, less than an hour by air from Maiquetía or two to four hours by ferry from Puerto La Cruz, is the main attraction of the three-island Pearl group which constitutes Nueva Esparta state. Water temperature varies from 23–30°C (73°F–86°F) around the island's numerous white sand beaches. Activities include watersports, fishing and horseback riding. The island is beginning to rival Hawaii as a windsurfing hotspot – **El Yaque Beach** ⓯ is considered one of the world's top beaches for the sport. With numerous historical sites, a rich tradition of crafts, shopping (the island has more than 2,000 duty-free shops), lodging ranging from intimate *posadas* to luxury resorts, a multitude of restaurants, and a lively nightlife, it is little wonder that Isla Margarita has become a prime tourist destination.

Spanish settlement of the **Pearl Islands** in 1500 was the first in all South America. The colonizers were attracted by the discovery of the first pearls found in the New World in the rich oyster beds surrounding the island of **Cubagua**. However, greed leading to over-harvesting, a devastating storm leveling the stone buildings, and pirates who took whatever the storm had not destroyed, brought an end to the settlement barely four decades later. Pearl fishing continued, but was banned in 1962 and is now permitted only in season (Jan–Apr) every other year.

BELOW: Playa El
Agua, Margarita.

Map on pages 110–11

Ruins of the site (along with pristine beaches) on this nearly uninhabited island can be visited on day tours from **Porlamar** ⓰, Margarita's largest city. Most of the island's hotels and shops, plus numerous restaurants, nightclubs and casinos are concentrated in downtown Porlamar. The city also has a ferry service to **Coche Island**, which is just beginning to develop its great tourism potential, with excellent windsurfing and several small resort hotels.

The majority of accommodation on Margarita is near the most popular beaches. North of Porlamar, **Playa Guacuco** ⓱ has some tourist facilities. Further up the coast, **Playa El Agua** ⓲ is the most popular (a beautiful beach, but with a treacherous undertow). The beaches continue to **Manzanillo** ⓳, the islands's most northerly point, and down to the west.

The capital city **La Asunción** ⓴ is smaller and more peaceful than Porlamar. Sights in this historical town include the 16th-century colonial cathedral (one of the oldest churches in Venezuela); the **Museo de Nueva Cádiz** (open Tues–Sun; free), which depicts the history of the town of the same name, destroyed by an earthquake in 1541; and the colonial **Castillo de Santa Rosa** fort (open Mon–Sat; donation) some 10 km (6 miles) northeast, **Pampatar** ㉑ also has some interesting colonial buildings including a pretty church and fortress.

The town of **Juangriego** ㉒, famed for its sunsets, offers a tranquil beach and nearby communities known for handicrafts. Pottery is made at **La Vecinidad** and **El Cercado**; basketry is the craft at **Pedrogonzález**; hammocks can be purchased at **Tacarigua**; and straw hats at **San Juan**. Within the town of **Tacuantar** is the **Taller de Arte Así con las Manos – Tierra, Agua y Fuego** artisan village. Contrasting with the bustling eastern half is the island's rugged, scarcely populated **Macanao Peninsula** to the west. **Parque Nacional Laguna La Restinga** lies along the narrow link between the two sections. Boatmen can take you through channels among mangrove swamps en route to the spectacular beach along the outer banks of the lagoon.

The Guayana Region: the last frontier

Venezuela's vast southern sector (covering Delta Amacuro, Bolívar, and Amazonas states) is known as the Guayana Region, named for the Guayana Shield, composed of pre-Cambrian rock, among the oldest on the continent at 1.2 to 2.5 billion years. The unique features in Bolívar and Amazonas are *tepuyes*, towering mesas of ancient rock. The most famous are **Roraima**, subject of Sir Arthur Conan Doyle's *Lost World* and **Auyantepui**, from which Angel Falls drops.

Except for a few roads near the state capitals of **Delta Amacuro** (Tucupita) and **Puerto Ayacucho** (Amazonas), travel is almost exclusively by boat. Difficult access has been the greatest factor in maintaining the mystery, natural state, and allure of the region. The tourism potential in the huge delta of the **Orinoco River**, making up most of Delta Amacuro state, has only recently been exploited. Now some half a dozen rustic tourist camps operate here, with emphasis on observation of fauna and visits to the indigenous Warao, principal inhabitants of this unique ecosystem. Warao means "the boat people", and their crafts, particularly basketry, are highly prized.

BELOW: young salespeople on the "Route of the Sun", east of Caracas.

Obelisk marking the meeting place of three countries: Venezuela, Guyana, and Brazil, on top of Roraima Tepuy.

BELOW: water-logged plant life on Roraima Tepuy.

Bolívar, Venezuela's largest, and one of the most richly endowed states, has huge reserves of gold, diamonds, iron, bauxite, hardwoods, and water power from its great rivers. **Ciudad Guayana ㉓**, on the northern border, was created in 1961, as headquarters for development of Venezuela's heavy industry. Mammoth steel, iron, and aluminum plants use electricity generated at **Guri Dam**, one of the most powerful hydroelectric plants in the world, an hour to the southwest, with a visitor center and interesting tours. Tourist attractions include the waterfalls in **Parque Cachamay** and **Parque Llovizna** and ruins of the colonial **Caroní Mission Church**. About an hour away are the 17th- and 18th-century forts, **Los Castillos de Guayana La Vieja**, overlooking the Orinoco.

An hour west of Ciudad Guayana by freeway is **Ciudad Bolívar ㉔**, the state's capital. Founded in 1764 on the banks of the Orinoco, it became a patriot stronghold, Simón Bolívar's base of operations, and capital of the Third Republic, 1817–21. It was also a gold center, and a thriving river transport hub.

The opening of the highway joining San Fernando de Apure with the central coast spelled the demise of the river trade and its commercial importance. But evidence of the city's prosperous past can be seen in the impressive architecture, including the colonial **Catedral**, the **Museo Etnográfico de Guayana**, the **Casa del Congreso de Angostura**, and the **Museo Manuel Piar**. Other worthwhile stops are the **Museo de Arte Moderno Jesús Soto** (honoring the city's most famous modern artist) and the **Quinta de San Isidro** (where Bolívar often stayed and now the **Museo Casa San Isidro**). The **Angostura Bridge** can be seen from the river banks, the only span across the 2,140-km (1,330-mile) length of the Orinoco (other crossings are by ferry). The rest of the state is mostly accessible only by small plane, with vast unexplored areas and a population of scattered indigenous groups and miners.

The paved road, completed in 1991, linking Ciudad Guayana with **Santa Elena de Uairén**, by the frontier with Brazil, permits even city cars to traverse the length of **Parque Nacional Canaima** and **La Gran Sabana**. Along the highway, observe gently rolling hills of this vast savannah dotted with moriche palms; settlements of native Pemón with thatch-roofed, mud-walled dwellings; and stately *tepuyes* in the distance (among them **Roraima**, the highest in the Guayana Region). There are numerous impressive falls along the roadside, including **Kama Merú** and **Quebrada de Jaspe**. The mission of **Kavanayén** and the spectacular falls of **Chinak-Merú** can be visited by four-wheel-drive vehicles.

Canaima ㉕, one of the first areas in Venezuela to be developed for adventure travel, and a principal tourist destination, is in the northwest corner of the 30,000 sq. km (11,500-sq. mile) Canaima National Park. The park is only accessible by air, and visitors can take day tours from Maiquetía, Porlamar, or Ciudad Bolívar, or stay overnight. Canaima's principal draw is its proximity to **Angel Falls**, named after the American bush pilot Jimmy Angel, who "discovered" them in 1935. The falls are the world's longest, at 979 meters (3,212 ft), of which 807 meters (2,648 ft) are free fall, and cascade over the edge of **Auyantepui**, the park's largest *tepuy*, which covers 700 sq. km (270

Map
on pages
110–11

sq. miles). Weather permitting, visitors may get a look at the falls from the air. Excursions are offered from Canaima in the rainy season, May to November.

Despite fierce opposition, Venezuela has built electricity pylons and transmission lines through Canaima National Park and La Gran Sabana to transport hydro-electric power to Brazil. As well as the irreparable impact on the delicate ecosystems and beautiful scenery of the region the power lines have also allowed the possibility of full-scale mining within a supposedly protected reserve.

A tenuous wilderness

Flying over Amazonas, with a vista of virgin tropical forest, interrupted only by the snaking black lines of rivers, engraves a lasting impression of the vastness of the state and the magnificence of nature it embraces. Though it covers an area larger than Portugal, Holland, and Denmark put together, Amazonas only has about 45,000, mostly indigenous, inhabitants. Paved roads extend only 100 km (60 miles) from the capital, **Puerto Ayacucho** ㉖, in its northwestern extreme. The rapids of the Orinoco long prevented extensive penetration. The construction of tourist camps has allowed visitors to savor this extraordinary territory. Independent travelers can reach Puerto Ayacucho by car (or bus) from Caracas via Caicara del Orinoco in about 10 hours, passing through landscapes dominated by enormous sandstone formations called *laja*, and Panare and Guahibo communities. Do not miss Puerto Ayacucho's outstanding **Ethnological Museum**. Near the capital are the giant petroglyphs of **Tobogán de la Selva**, and the indigenous Piaroa and Guahibo settlements. More distant (and costly) excursions by boat or charter plane include trips to **Autana**, the sacred mountain of the Piaroa, and to the native Yanomami (*see page 48*). ❑

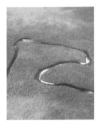

Outline formed by Caroní River, near Angel Falls.

BELOW: awesome Angel Fallo.

GUYANA

This lush, exotic, and richly forested former British colony is geographically larger than Britain, but has a mere fraction of its population

Map on page 128

G uyana means "Land of Many Waters" in a local Amerindian language. Life in this country on the northeast shoulder of South America is indeed dominated by its mighty rivers – the Essequibo, Demerara, and Berbice. They act as highways into the rainforests, mountains, and savannahs of the interior, regions which are, in turn, dissected by a network of lesser tributaries and creeks. Initially colonized by the Dutch in the 17th century, the territories which make up present-day Guyana came under British rule in 1814, and remained so until independence in 1966. It is populated mainly by the descendants of African slaves and indentured indigenous workers, together with smaller numbers of Chinese and Portuguese, brought to work the sugar, coffee, and cotton plantations of the coast. Amerindians, the original inhabitants, number just 5 percent.

Because of her colonial history, modern Guyana is South America's only English-speaking country, and is Caribbean in culture and outlook. However, unlike her Caribbean neighbors, Guyana has no palm-fringed powdery sand or limpid waters. Instead, the narrow coastal belt consists mainly of reclaimed swamps, marshland, and deltas of the great rivers, rich in alluvial soil and intensively cultivated. These areas, and small towns such as **New Amsterdam ❶** and **Charity ❷**, are protected from the sea by a system of dams and dikes (a practice initiated by the Dutch). Ninety percent of the population, a mere 627,570 in a country larger than Britain, live on this coastal belt.

Georgetown ❸, the capital, lies below sea level on the east bank of the Demerara River. The city is laid out in a grid with wide streets lined with colonial buildings constructed of tropical hardwoods. The skyline is dominated by **St George's Anglican Cathedral**, said to be the world's largest wooden building; and the tower crowning the immense, covered Stabroek Market where the full pageant of Guyana's ethnic mix barters goods of every conceivable desciption, from manioc flour to gold. The **Georgetown Cricket Club** where test matches are played, and the pan-yards where steel bands prepare for the annual carnival, speak loudest of Guyana's Caribbean identity. Georgetown also has comfortable modern hotels and a lively nightlife. However, it is to explore the interior that the great majority of visitors travel to Guyana.

Towering forest and fabulous falls

Kaieteur Falls, the world's highest single-drop waterfall, is at the top of most visitors' lists. It is feasible to journey overland to the falls by driving to **Linden ❹**, the bauxite mining town, then continuing along a track through the rainforest to join the Potaro River for four days' struggle by boat against the current. It is

PRECEDING PAGES: Rupununi River, Guyana. **LEFT:** close to the edge, Kaieteur Falls, Guyana. **BELOW:** Bartica, Guyana.

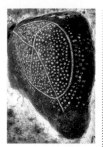

Turtle petroglyph.

also just possible, at certain times of the year, to journey to **Kangaruma** ❺, near Kaieteur. The easier option is to fly by light aircraft from Georgetown. For about an hour and a half passengers gaze down at a disk filled to the horizon in every direction with forest, interrupted by glinting hairs of water. Occasionally they might identify tiny riverside settlements where solitary gold panners and diamond prospectors sieve for their fortunes.

Abruptly, the forest rises about 300 meters (1,000 ft) at the point where two folds of the earth's crust overlap. The Potaro River flows calmly through the forest, spills over and plunges down, uninterrupted for 226 meters (740 ft) of its 250-meter (820-ft) fall. Airborne tourists are usually treated to a full-frontal vista of the entire falls, before sweeping low over the foaming white cauldron and dropping down on a strip of jungle cleared for a runway. A forest trail leads to the falls, as the gathering roar seems to come from every direction, including below ground. The viewing promontory is just meters from the falls. A huge volume of black water flows over the lip every second, seemingly in slow motion, turning copper, yellow, and finally a foaming white frenzy.

If this doesn't give you your fill of falls, you can fly for 30 minutes on to **Orinduik Falls**. Here the Ireng River thunders over a series of steps and terraces on a fold of rock which marks Guyana's border with Brazil. Although Orinduik does not offer the full, elemental drama of Kaieteur, the location is stunningly beautiful with views over the rolling, grass-covered Pakaraimae Hills.

Rainforest idyll

A stay at a rainforest lodge is another feature of Guyana's fledgling tourist industry. The most comfortable and genuine of these is **Timberhead**, reached

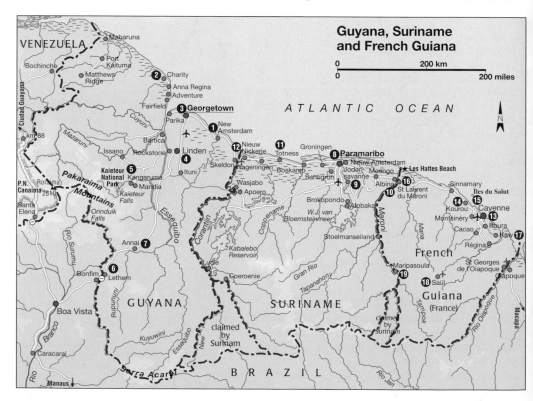

Map
on page
128

from Georgetown by whooshing up the wide, aptly brown sugar-colored Demerara River, then chugging up the oozing Kamuni Creek, its waters blackened by decomposing vegetation. The banks are overhung with undergrowth supported by aerial roots. Enormous Blue Morpho butterflies flitter about in abundance. Parrots and toucans flash in the foliage, and troupes of monkeys can be heard crashing through the branches overhead. There are jaguars, pumas, tiger cats, and bush pigs in the forest, though sightings are rare.

Further south, along the upper reaches of the Rupununi River, the landscape changes dramatically into savannah grassland bordered by a ridge of mountains pricking the horizon. Here *vaqueros* (cowboys) ride across the plains, barefoot in the stirrup, rounding up their cattle.

A flight over the rainforest to the airstrip at **Lethem ❻** near the Brazilian border takes you to the heart of this region. A trip across the savannahs by open-backed jeep reaches Dadanawa Ranch. From here, visitors ride horses into the mountain foothills, where streams refresh the scenery. Nights can be spent under the stars, after a supper of beef roasted on an open fire. The area is a bird-watchers' and naturalists' dream. The most dedicated book into the Rock View Eco-Tourism Resort at **Annai ❼**, where the savannah meets the Pakaraima Mountains. Harpy eagles and giant otters are among the trophy sightings.

As you fly over Guyana's endless rainforest, it's easy to believe that there are forest-dwellers who have never had contact with the outside world. In fact, in the 1960s, contact was made for the first time with the Wai-Wai, a tribe living as hunter-gatherers between the Essequibo and Amazon watersheds. To minimize the impact on their culture, very few expeditions into their territory are permitted, and every potential participant is interviewed.   ❏

Jungle lodges are rustic but with basic comforts.

BELOW: Orinduik Falls on the Guyana-Brazil border.

Map on page 128

SURINAME

This little-known former Dutch colony has a fascinating cultural mix in its sleepy coastal towns and vast swathes of rainforest

The 1667 Peace of Breda treaty granted New York to Britain and Suriname to The Netherlands. In the intervening centuries the two places have become, respectively, perhaps the most renowned city on Earth, and one of the world's most obscure countries. The irony is not lost among Surinamese, for many of whom it is self-evident that the Dutch got the better deal.

Suriname is the former Dutch Guiana, sandwiched between Guyana (formerly British Guiana) and Guayane, or French Guiana, which remains officially a *département* of France. The Suriname coast was first settled by English and Dutch merchants in 1613, followed by Jews from Holland, Italy, and Brazil. Slaves were shipped from West Africa to work the plantations, mainly of sugar and cotton. Imports of slaves were banned in 1818, and slavery itself abolished in 1863. During this period, Indians, Pakistanis, Chinese, and Javanese from Dutch Indonesia arrived as indentured laborers. Add to these the indigenous Amerindians, and the result is one of the most extraordinary ethnic cocktails in the world.

Suriname gained independence from Holland in 1975. Since then, relations between the two countries have rollercoastered, reaching a low point in 1982 when military dictator Colonel Desi Bouterse, who had seized power two years earlier, had 15 opposition leaders executed. Economic aid was terminated and diplomatic relations severed, not to be restored for five years, when democratic elections were held. Huge numbers of Surinamese emigrated to The Netherlands, leaving a depleted population which today numbers just under 435,000. The official language is Dutch, while Sranan Tongo, an English-based creole, is widely used as a lingua franca. Runaldo Ronald Venetiaan of the New Front has been head of state and government since 12 August 2000.

Suriname's sleepy capital

As in the other Guyanas, roughly 90 percent of the people live in towns strung along the loamy mud flats of the coast. The capital, **Paramaribo ❽**, is a small, quiet city of faded and peeling colonial wooden buildings arranged in a grid pattern, on the west bank of the Suriname River. It is hard to comprehend the violence and upheavals of the 1980s as you wander the sleepy squares graced by statues of Simón Bolívar and Mahatma Gandhi. (Home-grown Surinamese heroes and potentates are thin on the ground.)

Suriname is remarkably free of racial tension. The synagogue stands fraternally next to the mosque. Down the road, restoration of the wooden **Saint Peter and Paul Cathedral** is due for completion. The **museum**, in the old Dutch **Fort Zeelandia** is a modest affair. The **central market** is more lively; the

BELOW: Islamic mosque, central Paramaribo.

aroma of spices brought from India and sold by sari-clad women mingles with the smell of fresh shrimps sold by African fishermen.

A popular day trip from Paramaribo is to cross the Suriname River by ferry to the Dutch fort of **Nieuw Amsterdam** and drive eastward along the coast, through the old Jewish settlement of **Jodensavanne** ❾ and the bauxite-mining town of **Moengo**. The road ends at **Albina** ❿, a thriving little frontier town on the Marowijne, the river border with French Guiana. Another road, westwards, passes through the village of **Totness** ⓫, curious only for its name, which dates back to a Scottish settlement that has long since dispersed. The only other town on the road is **Wageningen**, the rice-growing center, before **Nieuw Nickerie** ⓬, the border town with Guyana at the mouth of the Corantijn.

Into the forest

Like its neighbors, the majority of Suriname's territory is covered by dense, virgin rainforest, cut through by great, black rivers. In "Operation Grasshopper", a government-sponsored scheme in the 1950s, a few short airstrips deep in the darkest interior have been hacked out of the forest. Near three of these, the Movement for Eco-Tourism in Suriname (METS – owned by Suriname Airways), have built simple lodges where visitors can experience life in the rainforest.

Central market, Paramaribo.

BELOW: Suriname River

Two of them are on islands in the **Gran Rio**, in the heart of Saramaccan country. The Saramaccan are a tribe of so-called "Bush Negroes", the descendants of African slaves who escaped as rebellions swept through the plantations on Suriname's coast. They speak a hybrid language of West African dialects, smattered with English, Dutch, and Portuguese words. Many of their practices – drum-playing, dancing and animist religious beliefs – can be traced directly to West Africa. Other means of forest survival were learnt from indigenous Amerindians. For example, they cultivate manioc on small slash-and-burn clearings, and build houses roofed with plaited palm.

A typical visit to this area begins with a light aircraft flight to **Kayana Airstrip**, and transfer in a motorized dug-out canoe up to **Awarradam Lodge** at some impassable rapids. Here, the air is heavy and moist. The double wolf-whistles of Screaming Piha and a cacophony of croaks, caws, and the occasional growl of a howler monkey, float over the canopy. Sightings of larger creatures are rare – unless you count the peccary (bush pig), shot or trapped in the forest, which the lodge's Bush Negro staff roast on open fires. However, the Black Caiman, an Amazonian crocodile up to 2 meters (6 ft) long, is common. They are often seen lazing by the bank during the all-day canoe trip to **Kavalu Island**, facing the Bush Negro village of **Asidonopo**. Outsiders are usually welcomed by the village chief or "Kapiteni" and introduced to villagers who sing as they spin cotton or grate manioc, while mischievous naked children follow.

Palumeu, the third lodge, is next to an Amerindian village deeper into the interior on the Tapanahony River, a tributary of the Marowijne. Palameu is the most stunningly located of all the lodges, on a broad hillside clearing with sweeping river views, but the people are shyer and interaction can be awkward. ❑

Map on page 128

FRENCH GUIANA

Formerly home to a notorious penal colony, this heavily forested and naturally diverse département *of France is today the launch site for Europe's Ariane rockets*

To the east of Suriname lies the small French colony of French Guiana (Guayane), almost a fifth of the size of France with more than 300 km (190 miles) of coastline. Eighty percent of the inhabitants live in the coastal regions, as beyond the coast lies a dense carpet of Amazon rainforest.

Ancient petroglyphs near the village of Kaw bear testimony to thousands of years of human habitation in the area, but as in neighboring countries, European colonization, from the early 17th century, dramatically changed the ethnographic make-up of the region. The territory was tenuously held by the French in the face of short-lived appropriations by the British, Dutch, and Brazilian-Portuguese. African slaves were brought in to work the plantations, to be replaced when slavery was abolished by indentured laborers from other parts of the French Empire, notably Indo-China. After a minor gold rush in the 1850s the territory became best known as a brutal penal colony, immortalized in the novel *Papillon* by Henri Charrière, and in the famous film of the same name. The Jewish army officer Alfred Dreyfus, whose imprisonment for treason in the 1890s caused a political storm, was held at the notorious Devil's Island.

French Guiana became an overseas *département* of France in 1946. In the 1960s a satellite and space exploration center was established at Kourou, which

BELOW: Devil's Island.

brought jobs and urban development, but the rest of the country has suffered unemployment and economic stagnation. The population is highly racially mixed, with input from Africa, Europe, native South America, China, and Vietnam. There are many Amerindian groups living in the rainforest areas, and also communities of "Noir Marrons", or Bush Negroes, descendants of African slaves, who live along the banks of the River Maroni in a traditional African manner with Amerindian influences .

Cayenne ⑬, the capital, has some interesting colonial buildings, but is a relatively expensive town. The **Musée Départemental** has a mix of historical and archeological artifacts including exhibits on the penal colonies. There is a vegetable and flower market, and a fish market on Wednesday, Friday, and Saturday.

The town of **Kourou ⑭**, 55 km (34 miles) northeast of Cayenne, revolves around the **French Guiana Space Center**. There is a **Space Museum** (Mon–Fri and Sat afternoons; entrance fee), from where rocket launches can be witnessed. Europe's largest and most expensive satellite was launched from the center in March 2002. The modern part of town, known locally as the "white city" due to the preponderance of families from mainland France, is very different from the more traditional old village at the mouth of the Kourou River. Boats are available from here to the three **Îles du Salut ⑮**, which lie 15 km (9 miles) to the north. The famous **Île du Diable** (Devil's Island) is inaccessible due to hazardous landing conditions, but accommodation is available on the Île Royale.

The Transportation Camp at **St Laurent du Maroni ⑯**, 250 km (150 miles) northeast of Cayenne, was the largest prison in the territory, and can be visited. Dugout canoes can be hired from the town for trips on the Maroni River. About 40 km (25 miles) north of St Laurent, at the mouth of the Maroni and Mana rivers, is **Les Hattes Beach**, which is a breeding site for leatherback turtles. The laying season is from April to July and hatching takes place from July to September. The turtles have no shell but a dark blue leathery skin, and measure up to 170 cm (67 inches) long when fully grown. Nearby is the Amerindian village of **Awala Yalimapo**.

The interior of French Guiana has much to interest naturalists and adventure seekers. Roughly 60 km (40 miles) south of Cayenne are the **Kaw Marshes**, an area of forest and mangrove swamps rich in birdlife and inhabited by the rare black caiman. Houseboat accommodation is available in the village of **Kaw ⑰**. At **Montsinéry**, 43 km (27 miles) southwest of Cayenne, a botanical hiking trail leads to the **Annamite Penal Colony**, where deported Indo-Chinese were detained. Other hiking trails lead to waterfalls and wildlife-infested creeks. The interior can also be explored by *pirogue*, or dugout canoe.

South of Cayenne, the village of **Cacao** is inhabited by a Hmong community of Laotian descent. Visitors can sample traditional Hmong cuisine, and Hmong handicrafts can be bought. There are inland jungle expeditions centered around the gold-mining village of **Saül ⑱**; in the west, the town of **Maripasoula ⑲**, home to Bush Negro communities, is a popular expedition destination. ❑

Painted "maluana" disk of the Wayana people.

BELOW: children in the Place Leopoldo, Cayenne.

ANDEAN HIGHLANDS

The ancient heart of the subcontinent, these high-altitude countries continue to fascinate, both for their imperial past and for the rich cultural heritage they proudly maintain

Clustered around some of the most inhospitable territory in South America are the countries of the Andean highlands: Peru, Bolivia, and Ecuador. The area was home to some of the world's most extraordinary civilizations for thousands of years before being finally united by the Inca empire in the 14th century. Although the Incas were the most famous rulers of South America, they had a relatively brief moment of glory before the Spanish conquistadors crushed them into submission *(see page 26)*. The colonists subsequently kept themselves distant from their subjects and to this day the old Inca lands are dual societies: one Amerindian, impoverished and traditional; the other *mestizo* or white, looking to Europe or the United States for cultural inspiration.

Nowhere is this more so than in the Inca heartland of Peru. The capital, Lima *(see page 146)*, lies on the barren coast facing the sea, while the ancient capital of Cusco *(see page 151)*, regarded by the Incas as the navel of the world, remains in the mountains, nursing its shattered past. From these two cultural poles Peru's many wonders can be reached: the ancient Inca Trail leads from Cusco to Machu Picchu *(see page 158)*, arguably South America's most spectacular ancient city. In the south are the baffling Nazca lines *(see page 150)*; in the north the ancient adobe city of Chan Chan *(see page 165)*. The world's deepest canyons are near the colonial city of Arequipa *(see page 157)*. Peru's Amazon region *(see page 161)* is unforgettable, despite being opened up to settlement at breakneck speed.

Across from Lake Titicaca *(see pages 168–9)* is the land-locked mountain country of Bolivia. The most ethnically native American and the poorest of South America's republics, this is a land of ancient traditions and colonial relics. Carved from the bleak *altiplano* or "high plain", La Paz is the highest capital city in the world *(see page 177)*. In the shadow of spectacular peaks, the nearby Yungas *(see page 182)* is a sub-tropical region of banana, coffee, and coca leaf. Back in the windswept heights is the town of Potosí *(see page 189)*, once the Spanish empire's main source of silver and still a mining town.

To the north of Peru is the Republic of Ecuador. This compact country can be explored in short trips from the mountain capital Quito *(see page 201)*, a colonial gem now placed on the World Heritage list. Nearby is the town of Otavalo *(see page 202)*, famous for a remarkable weaving tradition which is attracting new wealth, while around the capital are mountains and nature reserves *(see page 205)*. A short jump east lands you in the steamy Oriente jungle *(see page 209)*. In the west lie the Pacific beaches of Ecuador's coast *(see page 211)*, 965 km (600 miles) beyond which are the country's pride and joy: the wildlife-rich Galápagos islands *(page 214)*. ❏

PRECEDING PAGES: pre-Columbian gold mask; Peruvian llamas.
LEFT: traditional weaver, near Cusco.

PERU

*The birthplace of ancient empires, Peru has towering mountains,
steaming rainforests and parched deserts. It's the ultimate
destination for culture seekers, adventurers, and eco-tourists*

Map on page 144

No other country in South America, possibly in the whole world, has such an astonishing archeological heritage as Peru. Most tourists come to see the monumental citadel of Machu Picchu – the other big archeological attraction is the mysterious desert lines of Nazca, which can only be viewed from the air. This is a country packed with archeological wonders – the fabulous remains of Inca and pre-Inca civilizations housed in numerous museums, as well as countless pyramids and ruined cities, many still unexcavated. Then there are the treasures of the colonial period which gild the magnificent cities of Cusco and Arequipa. Lima, the capital, once the center of the Spanish empire in South America, is an exciting city that moves at a frenetic pace. Many of its colonial buildings fell victim to earthquakes and urban planning, but it still has some beautiful architecture and an enormous range of museums.

Peru is an exceptional country even for those who don't have an interest in history or archeology. Arid desert in the south and the splendid Pacific coastline with beaches that attract surfers from around the world give way abruptly to the snowy heights of the Andes mountain range that edges along the country's coastal belt. Beyond the Andes lies the Amazon basin, a rainforest area teeming with exotic plants, insects, birds, and animals.

PRECEDING PAGES: the Colca Canyon. **LEFT:** portal of Lima Cathedral. **BELOW:** Quechua girl.

Tourism is rapidly developing as this is a country that recognizes the importance of protecting its rich natural and historical heritage. But poverty is still widespread, from the poor indigenous communities eking out a living in the barren Andean plains to the people who inhabit Peru's volatile coastline, which is frequently hit by drought, earthquakes, and by the floods brought by the El Niño current.

Peru is a developing country, but lingering poverty together with the residue of unresolved social and political conflict and guerrilla activity have left a legacy of lawlessness in some areas, and visitors should check the situation with their country's embassy before they go. Most areas of tourist interest are safe, although there have been reports of mugging in and around Cusco and Lima – personal effects should not be flaunted. Take care, but don't let such reports spoil your trip – most tourists enjoy the wonders of Peru without encountering any trouble at all.

Peru after independence

José de San Martín proclaimed Peru's independence in Lima on July 28, 1821, although most of the country was still held by the Spanish crown. Simón Bolívar finished the job of freeing the country and, in 1826, the last Spanish troops surrendered. The first years of independence saw few real changes in the way that Peruvians lived. But midway through the

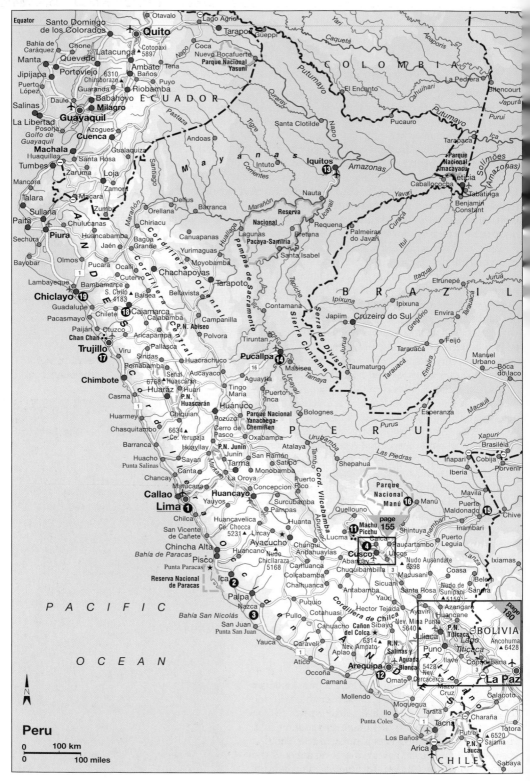

Peru

0 ___ 100 km

0 ___ 100 miles

century, military leader Mariscal Ramón Castilla took over the presidency, and under his rule modernization shook the country. Basic services such as water and street lights were installed in Lima and a rail track – the first on the sub-continent – linked the capital with the nearby port of Callao. Castilla abolished slavery and directed approval of the 1860 national Constitution. But setbacks were incurred in the bloody War of the Pacific, which lasted from 1879 to 1883. Despite these tumultuous changes, life in the 19th century continued much as in the 17th for the bulk of the population – the native peoples living in the highlands. The two worlds of Peru, the "Indian" and the "European", were drifting further apart.

A divided nation

Of all the nations of South America, Peru saw the most important clash between native and European cultures – a clash that continues today, proving fertile ground for terrorism in the highlands, an energetic chaos in Lima, and an amazing creativity. Peru has been run by a number of military strongmen. Most intriguing among them was the left-wing military dictator General Juan Velasco Alvarado, who, in the 1970s, undertook a flawed agrarian reform program, temporarily turned over the biggest newspaper – *El Comercio* – to a peasant group and renamed all of Lima's streets after national heroes. For example, Avenida Wilson, named after the US president, was relabeled Garcilaso de la Vega after the *mestizo* poet who chronicled the Spanish conquest of Peru.

Colonial door knocker.

Sprinkled amongst these dictators have been 30 elected presidents, all of them conservatives until the 1985 election of left-of-center Alan García Pérez. The charismatic García drew popular support from the poor and rural dwellers who cheered his decision not to pay the foreign debt incurred by past governments.

But the US cut-off in development aid, the unwillingness of businesses to invest in the country, and political maneuvering by the far left and far right sent the nation into an economic crisis in late 1988 after two years of growth. Food and gasoline prices doubled overnight more than once, the currency devalued rapidly, and people headed abroad in search of jobs.

The political division and social upheaval accompanying García's presidency opened the way for an independent candidate, Alberto Fujimori, to take over as president. His government waged a savage campaign against the guerrilla group *Sendero Luminoso* (Shining Path), whose activities had severely affected tourism in the 1980s, and captured their leader, Abimael Guzmán, which led to the collapse of the group. In December 1996, the Movimiento Revolucionario Tupac Amaru took hostage nearly 500 guests during a siege of the Japanese ambassador's residence. One hostage died during the siege, which ended on April 22, 1997. Fujimori won a controversial third term in 2000 amid allegations of electoral fraud, but leaked videos implicating him in bribery brought down the government and Fujimori fled to Japan. In June 2001 Alejandro Toledo, leader of the Peru Posible party and the first Peruvian president of Andean indigenous extraction, won 52 percent of the vote, and formed a government, although he was forced to rely on the support of other parties to rule the country.

Lima: capital of the New World

Spanish conquistador Francisco Pizarro considered the site where he founded **Lima** 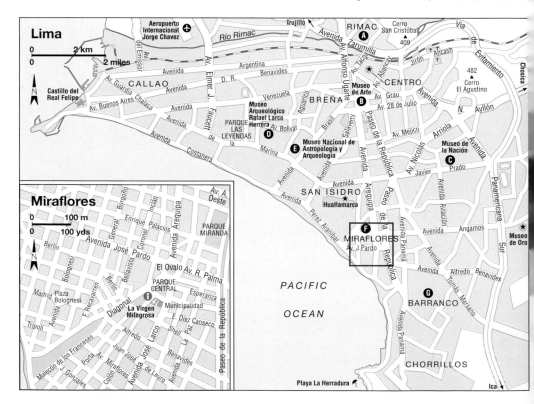 on January 18, 1535, inhospitable: rain seldom fell, earthquakes were common and winter was a time of gray skies and dreary fog. But his soldiers saw it as the best place for a quick sea escape in the event of a native uprising. Little did they suspect this open plain would become the political and military capital of the New World, seeing the reign of 40 viceroys before the "City of Kings" was declared capital of an independent Peru in 1821.

The **Plaza Mayor** is where for centuries the power of the new colony was concentrated, and it remains one of the city's most active and attractive squares. At its center are rose gardens, a stone fountain and park benches that draw young couples, shoeshine boys, and families in their Sunday best posing for photos. The foundations of the **Palacio de Gobierno** are from Pizarro's time, but its facade was changed in the early 1900s. Every day at noon there is a ceremonial changing of the guard, with a band playing, but visits to the palace have to be pre-arranged in the Oficina de Turismo of the Municipalidad. The best spot for viewing the ceremony is the wide front balcony of the **Palacio Municipal**. The original structure used as a city hall burned down in 1923, but its neoclassical replacement is impressive, with marble stairways, gilt mirrors, and crystal chandeliers. The library, with massive leather chairs, huge wooden tables, and a smell of old books offers a calming respite from the traffic outside. Its circular stairway was hand-carved from a single piece of Nicaraguan cedar.

Across the square, the **Palacio del Arzobispo** has one of the most beautiful wooden mudejar-style balconies in the city. Take a peek in the archbishop's patio before heading next door to the **Cathedral** (open Mon–Sat), which contains

Pizarro's remains. A block away is the **Museo Banco Central de Reserva**, with a small but impressive pre-Columbian collection (open Tues–Sun). Nearby is the splendid **Palacio de Torre Tagle**, constructed in 1735, now used as the Foreign Ministry. A few blocks to the northeast is the jewel of Lima's old churches, the **Monasterio de San Francisco**. Lovingly repaired after every earthquake that damaged it in the past four centuries, this cloister features fine mosaic tiles from Seville, frescoes discovered when an earthquake demolished portions of an outer wall, and an impressive collection of religious art. Most fascinating are its catacombs, stacked with skulls and bones from the colonial period.

Maps
Area 144
City 146

Saints and sinners

Behind the Palacio de Gobierno is **Estación Desamparados** (railway station), the city's first iron building. Brought in pieces by boat from England and rebuilt here in 1908, it was formerly the depot for all trains out of the capital, but is no longer in operation. Also behind the president's office is the bridge that leads to **Rimac Ⓐ**, one of Lima's oldest neighborhoods, named after the river that flows along its edge. A working-class *barrio*, where women in doorways chat with their neighbors while children play soccer in the streets, it once was the city's top spot for promenading. Then, the stars were the *tapadas (see box, page 148)* – seductive women whose skirts shamelessly showed their tiny feet, whose necklines were scandalously low and whose faces were covered by a veil that bared only one eye. In the afternoons, they were likely to be found on the **Alameda de los Descalzos**, courting and flirting but never lifting their veils to reveal their identities. This promenade, built in 1611, is lined with Italian marble statues representing the months of the year and bordered by lawns and flowers.

BELOW: changing of the guard, Plaza Mayor, Lima.

It leads to the **Monasterio de los Descalzos** (Monastery of the Barefoot Friars; daily 9.30am–1pm), recently restored and well worth the walk to get there.

Lima was home to two of South America's most famous saints: Rosa de Lima and Martín de Porres. Rosa, who died of tuberculosis at age 31, had a fervent following during her lifetime and was credited with curing thousands, performing innumerable miracles and even saving the city from pirate attacks. For Martín de Porres, fame came after his death. He lived in the **Santo Domingo** monastery in Jirón Camaná, but was barred from becoming a priest because he was black. His duties included working as the janitor, and statues and paintings of the saint usually show him with broom in hand. Both saints are buried in Santo Domingo, which is open to visitors.

Lima's religious devotion may have been proportional to the terror inflicted by the Holy Inquisition. Chills will run up your spine when you descend into the depths of the **Museo de la Inquisición** in Plaza Bolívar (open Mon–Sat). Gruesome tortures were inflicted to obtain "confessions" of heresy, Judaism and witchcraft. The "guilty" had their property confiscated and were marched off to the Plaza de Armas (now Plaza Mayor) to await their fate, which ranged from public flogging to burning at the stake.

Lima's most active square is **Plaza San Martín**, linked to Plaza Mayor by the pedestrian walkway **Jirón de la Unión**. Plaza San Martín is where most of the money-changing houses are located (alongside the Gran Bolívar Hotel). A few hundred meters south of the plaza, the **Museo de Arte ❸** (open daily except Wed; free on Mon) contains an extensive collection of Peruvian art from the Conquest to the present day. The Filmoteca here is a low-price cinema club. It has two auditoriums where concerts are given, and is surrounded by a public park.

BELOW: the scandalous *tapadas*, or "covered ones."

THE SCANDALOUS TAPADAS

If the 17th century was Lima's religious period, the 18th century was its romantic era when poetry, promenading and pomp were the mainstay. It was during this time that the *tapadas* appeared, the shockingly sensual upper-class *mestizo* women. It wasn't long before a rivalry arose between these flirtatious *tapadas* and the more reserved Europeans. While the Spanish females cinched their skirts to show their tiny waistlines and fluttered fans before the eyes of admirers, the *mestizos* narrowed their skirts to emphasize their ample hips and bared their arms. But they always kept their faces veiled – with the exception of one eye. French feminist Flora Tristan, visiting her father's homeland, described the *tapadas'* Moorish costume as a "skirt... so tight that it allows just enough room to put one foot in front of the other and to take very little steps. This costume so alters a woman – even her voice since her mouth is covered – that unless she is very tall or very short, lame, hunchbacked or otherwise conspicuous, she is impossible to recognize. I am sure it needs little imagination to appreciate the consequences of this time-honored practice which is sanctioned or at least tolerated by law." Those "consequences" ranged from men unknowingly flirting with their own wives, to infidelity.

Outside the city center

Some of the most interesting museums, shops, and beaches are in Lima's suburbs, accessible by bus or taxi from downtown. Just south of the city center, on Avenida Javier Prado Este, is the excellent **Museo de la Nación** ☉ (open daily; small fee), with artifacts from prehistoric times to the present day (Spanish only). The once-popular **Museo de Oro** (Gold Museum) on Avenida Alonso de Molina in the Monterrico district fell from grace in 1998 with the startling revelation that a large proportion of its artifacts were fakes. After a brief enforced closure it re-opened, and claims to have removed all non-authentic items from display. However, the museum also has a collection of textiles, stone carvings and ceramics on display.

Southwest of the center, in Pueblo Libre, the **Museo Arqueológico Rafael Larco Herrera** ☉ (open Mon–Sun) has a fascinating display of pottery spanning 3,000 years, including a huge collection of pieces from the Moche, Sican, and Chimú cultures of northern Peru. In 2002 the museum opened a new pavilion dedicated to the gold and silver of ancient Peru. A blue line painted on the sidewalk leads to the **Museo Nacional de Arqueología, Antropología y Historia** ☉ (open Tues–Sat), with pre-Columbian displays and colonial paintings.

In the suburb of San Isidro, bougainvillea grows beside the pre-Inca burial site of **Huallamarca** (open daily), with a small museum of mummies and artifacts.

In **Miraflores** ☉ suburb, stomping ground of the children of Peru's wealthy families, you can people-watch at outdoor cafés, shop or enjoy good meals and music. The pretensions of the Miraflores youths – the *miorafloriños* – are described with precision in the novels of Mario Vargas Llosa. Miraflores is the best place for theaters, trendy boutiques and nightclubs. Nearby is **Barranco** ☉, the bohemian neighborhood made immortal in Peruvian waltz and still home to the city's best artists, poets, and jazz bars. Here you'll find the lover's lane, **Puente de los Suspiros** (Bridge of Sighs), lined by fragrant jasmine and hyacinth bushes. It heads down to a lookout point over the Pacific Ocean, and to a steep stairway to the beach. Strolling here at sunset you may hear Peruvian flute music or Argentine tangos wafting from open windows.

The most important archeological site near Lima is **Pachacámac**, 31 km (19 miles) south of the city and accessible by bus or tour from the city center. Rising to prominence around AD 700, this pre-Inca shrine was later used as an Inca temple for adoration of the sun god, and there is also a reconstruction of the Templo de las Virgenes (House of the Chosen Women), also known as *Mamaconas*.

Some 220 km (135 miles) south of Lima, and worth visiting if you are traveling by road to Nazca, is **Ica** ☉, famous for its vineyards and March wine festival, but especially for the **Museo Regional**, one of Peru's most interesting small regional museums. Exhibits include mummies, ceramics, and skulls from the Paracas, Nazca, and Inca cultures; an excellent collection of Paracas textiles and feather weavings; and a number of *quipus*, the knotted strings believed to have been used to keep calculations and records for the Incas.

Outside Ica, **Las Dunas** is a luxurious resort and hotel complex that pioneered the sand-surfing frenzy in this dune-covered area. Cerro Blanco, some 14 km

Craftsman with gold jewelry.

BELOW: elaborate colonial facade.

(8 miles) north of Nazca, is purportedly the world's biggest sand dune. Nearby is **Laguna de Huacachina**, a green lagoon of sulfur waters that Peruvians claim has medicinal value. The colonial-style Hotel Mossone is an idyllic place to stay. Next door, the Salvatierra offers a cheaper alternative.

The mysterious Nazca lines

Until the 1930s, **Nazca** ❸ was like any other small Peruvian town, with no claim to fame except that you had to cross one of the world's driest deserts to reach it from Lima. Since then, the pampa, or plain, north of the city, has become one of the greatest scientific mysteries in the Americas. The Nazca lines are a series of drawings of animals, geometric figures, and birds up to 300 meters (1,000 ft) in size, scratched on to the arid crust of the desert and preserved for 2,000 years owing to a complete lack of rain and unique winds that clean, but do not erase, the pampa. The huge figures can only be seen from the air.

In 1939, North American scientist Paul Kosok, flying over the dry coast, noticed the lines that were previously believed to be part of a pre-Inca irrigation system. A specialist in irrigation, he quickly concluded that this had nothing to do with water systems. By chance, the day of the flight coincided with the summer solstice and, on a second flight, Kosok discovered that the line of the sunset ran tandem to the direction of one of the bird drawings. He called the Nazca pampa "the biggest astronomy book in the world." However, it was a young German mathematician who became the expert on the lines and put Nazca on the map. Maria Reiche was 35 when she met Kosok, and he encouraged her to study the pampa. Reiche, who died in 1998, devoted her life to studying the lines, which she measured, cleaned, analyzed, and charted daily from the air and

BELOW: aerial view of hummingbird design, Nazca lines.

Map on page 144

from a 15-meter (49-ft) high platform. She developed the most widely accepted theories on the hundreds of drawings that cover a 50-km (30-mile) belt between Nazca and Palpa, describing them as an "astronomical calendar". For example, she speculated that the drawing of the monkey was the Nazca symbol for the Big Dipper, the constellation representing rain. When rain was overdue – a common occurrence here – the monkey was sketched so that the gods would be reminded that the earth was parched. Because the drawings are only visible from the air there are those who do not accept Reiche's theories, denying that the Nazca people would have drawn something they could not see.

The most damaging theory about the Nazca lines came seven years earlier, when Erik Von Daniken published *Chariots of the Gods*, in which he proposed that the pampa was part of an extra-terrestrial landing strip – an idea that Reiche discarded impatiently. Von Daniken's book drew thousands of visitors, who set out across the pampa on motorcycles and four-wheel drive vehicles, leaving unerasable marks. Now it is illegal to drive or even walk on the pampa: Reiche used the profits from her book, *Mystery on the Desert*, to pay four guards to keep a constant watch on the plain.

There is a metal ladder and viewing platform at the side of the highway, but there is not much to see. The only way to capture the impact of the lines is to fly over them. AeroCondor do a day-long package from Lima that includes a flight over the lines, plus lunch and a visit to the Museo Arqueológico in Nazca; or flights can be booked at the Hotel Alegría or Hotel Nazca Lines, in Nazca. They last from 30 to 45 minutes and can be bumpy. If you want to make the trip more economical, some of the pilots at the Nazca airstrip may be open to offers.

Pre-Columbian mummy, Chauchilla cemetery, Nazca.

BELOW: detail from an ancient Paracas textile.

Cusco: capital of the Inca Empire

The stallholders in Cusco's market speak Spanish with tourists and Quechua with one another. The buildings behind them are colonial, built on Inca foundations. The elaborately carved facades on the city's churches have detailed scenes of angels and saints – with Amerindian facial features. **Cusco ❹** stands as a living testimony to the fact that the Inca civilization, one of the world's most sophisticated, could not be erased.

Of course, the Cusco of today is dramatically different from the awesome city that Francisco Pizarro and his conquistadors found when they reached the capital of the Inca Empire, home to that kingdom's noblemen, priests, and their servants. Five hundred years ago, an estimated 15,000 people lived in the city, which was linked to the rest of the empire by way of *chasquis* – long-distance runners who carried news and messages from the four corners of Tawantinsuyo to its capital. It is now a fairly modern Andean community with a population of about 200,000 and daily plane, and bus services to Lima.

When the Spanish headed here after executing Atahuallpa in Cajamarca, they entered the fertile valley where Cusco is located to find a lush, green countryside filled with fields of corn and golden and purple patches where *kiwicha* and *quinua* – varieties of amaranth, a high protein grain – were planted. Corn was perhaps the most valuable crop in the kingdom. It was

Ceramic bull on a rooftop for good luck, Cusco.

used for bartering and as a food staple that appeared in everything from main dishes to the alcoholic *chicha*, prepared by young women who chewed the corn, then spat it into jars where it fermented with their saliva. The amaranth, which grows well despite extremes in temperature and moisture, nearly fell victim to the Spaniards' attempt to "civilize" the local population. The conquistadors called it the "subversive grain", as it made the Amerindians healthy, and thus harder to enslave. Pressured by the Spanish, the Vatican outlawed its cultivation and consumption. But now, four centuries later, *kiwicha* and *quinua* once again flourish in the Sacred Valley, and are used in everything from soup to cookies.

In pre-Columbian times, anyone entering Cusco was greeted with the phrase, "*Ama sua, ama quella, ama lulla*" – "Don't lie, don't steal, don't be lazy", summing up what was important in this cooperative society. Laziness was a capital offense punishable by death. Everyone in an Incan community – except for royalty and priests – was required to work on projects such as roads, irrigation ditches, and aqueducts owing to a philosophy that if all participated, all would take care of the finished product. When the Spanish took control of this country those cooperative projects – known as *mingas* – were replaced by forced labor. But they were not completely erased; today there are still *mingas* in the Peruvian highlands. Women begin preparing a community meal on *minga* day while the townspeople, regardless of age, set to work.

At its peak, Cusco was a city with sophisticated water systems, paved streets, and no poverty. But its leaders were not all wise and competent. One Inca chief, Urco, perpetrated such atrocities that his name was erased from Incan history and his mention forbidden. Another hung his enemies along the roadsides in the empire's cities. Yet another had the entire population of a nearby city executed

BELOW: hilltop view of Cusco.

for the rape of a virgin selected to dedicate her life to the sun cult. But these excesses fail to overshadow the magnificence of a civilization whose architecture could not be destroyed and whose feats could not be matched.

Map on page 144

Walking into the past

The most startling and curious characteristic of Cusco at first glance is its architecture. Huge walls of intricately fit stone pay testimony to the civilization that over 500 years' ago controlled much of the South American subcontinent. The Spaniards' attempts to destroy every trace of the "pagan" Inca civilization proved too ambitious a task, and the Europeans ended up erecting their own buildings on the indestructible Incan foundations, often using the same huge rocks that had been cut by the Incas. The cathedral in Cusco is made in part from stones hauled from Sacsayhuamán, the Inca fortress outside the city.

To explore this intriguing city, the **Cathedral** (which closed in 2001 for extensive restoration but was scheduled to reopen in 2002) is a perfect place to start. It is located on the north-east side of the **Plaza de Armas** which, in Incan times, was known as Huancaypata and in addition to being the exact center of the empire was the spot where the most important religious and military ceremonies were held. Although the most spectacular view of the cathedral comes after dark when its lights turn the plaza into a breathtaking sight, its interior can only be seen during the day – and you won't want to miss it. Built on what was once the palace of Inca Viracocha, the cathedral mixes Spanish Renaissance architecture with the stone-working skills of the Incas, and took a century to build. Its María Angola bell in the north tower can be heard up to 40 km (25 miles) away. Made of a ton of gold, silver, and bronze, hthe bell, which is more than 300 years old, is reportedly the largest on the continent.

El Triunfo (open Mon–Sat, at rather irregular hours), to the right of the cathedral, was built to commemorate a Spanish victory over the Amerindians, who unsuccessfully tried to burn the thatched roof chapel that originally stood on the site. On the other side of the cathedral is the church of **Jesús María** (irregular opening hours). At only 250 years old, it is one of Cusco's newer structures.

TIP

An excellent value US$10 ticket allows entry to many highlights of Cusco and the Sacred Valley, including the cathedral, the Regional History Museum, Coricancha, Sacsayhuamán, Qenko, and Pisac.

BELOW: colorful Andean market.

A mingling of cultures

Turn left from El Triunfo and walk one block up to the corner of Calle Hatunrumiyoc, literally "the Street of the Big Stones", and Calle Palacio, to the **Museo de Arte Religioso del Arzobispado** (open Mon–Sat). This Moorish building with complicated carvings on its doors and balconies was constructed on the site of the 15th-century palace of Inca Roca, under whose rule Cusco's schools were initiated. The museum displays a fine collection of paintings in the style known as the School of Cusco, which flourished from the 16th–18th centuries – a mingling of indigenous and Spanish cultures in which archangels are dressed as Spaniards carrying European guns, surrounded by cherubs with Amerindian features, and the Last Supper shows Christ and his Amerindian-looking apostles dining on roast guinea pig and Peruvian cheese. Outside is the **Twelve-Angled Stone**, a tribute to the skill

of Inca masons, proving that no piece of granite was too irregular to be fitted without mortar and every piece slotting together like a jigsaw puzzle.

In a city with so many churches, it is an honor to be dubbed the "most beautiful" but that is the title given to **La Compañía de Jesús** (open Mon–Fri), sitting on what was once the palace of Inca Huayna Capac on the southeast corner of the Plaza de Armas. Construction of the church, with its intricate interior, finely carved balconies and altars covered in gold leaf, took nearly 100 years, and is a fine example of Andean baroque.

The street to the side of the church leads to what was the most important place of worship in the Inca Empire. The **Iglesia Santo Domingo** (open daily), was once **El Templo del Coricancha** (or Qoricancha) – the Temple of the Sun – the most magnificent complex in Cusco. Its walls were covered in gold, and its windows were constructed so the sun would cast a near-blinding reflection of golden light from the precious metals inside. Spanish chronicles describe the astonishment of the Europeans when they saw Coricancha's patio filled with life-sized gold and silver statues of llamas, trees, flowers, and delicate butterflies. Current excavations promise to reveal more of the temple's mysteries.

Coaxing a llama.

LEFT: Cusco's narrow, cobbled streets.
RIGHT: street vendors, Cusco.

Retrace your steps toward the Plaza de Armas, and on Calle Arequipa you will find another Christian enclave that was formerly an Inca holy place. This is the **Convento y Museo de Santa Catalina** (open Mon–Thur and Sat). Now a colonial-style building occupied by Roman Catholic nuns, this was home to the Chosen Women, virgins who were trained to serve their heavenly husband, the sun, or attend to the pleasure of his earthly son, the Inca. The museum contains a fine collection of School of Cusco art. Most of the sites can be seen on a combined Cusco Visitor Ticket, which is far more economical.

The valley of ruins

The megalithic fortress of **Sacsayhuamán** ❺ is a bold example of Inca archi-tectural skills. Constructed from massive stones, this military complex over-looking Cusco has a double wall in zigzag shape. It also marks the birthplace of the river that runs under Cusco, channeled through stone conduits honed by the ancient Incas, invisibly supplying the city with water. Archeologists estimate that tens of thousands of workers labored on this massive structure for more than seven decades, hauling the immense stone blocks that make up its double out-side walls and erecting the near-indestructible buildings that made the com-plex one of the most wondrous in all the empire. Inti Raymi, the Inca feast of the winter solstice, is celebrated every year on June 24 at Sacsayhuamán, with a procession, ceremony and much merrymaking.

Some 7 km (4 miles) from Sacsayhuamán, **Qenko** ❻ is an Inca shrine that has a 5-meter (18-ft) high stone block that *cusqueños* claim looks like a puma. Its name means labyrinth, and this ceremonial center, dedicated to the worship of Mother Earth, has water canals cut into solid rock and a subterranean room. Farther along the road to Pisac is a smaller fortress, **Puca Pucara** ❼, believed to have guarded the road and the Sacred Valley of the Incas. It has hillside ter-races, stairways, tunnels, and towers. To the north, **Tambo Machay** ❽ is sacred bathing place of the Inca rulers and their royal women. A hydraulic engineering marvel, its aqueduct system still feeds water into a series of showers.

From there head down 400 meters (1,500 ft) into the valley on the curvy road leading to **Pisac** ❾, a friendly village known for its fishing, Sunday market, and the ruins above the town. To reach the ruins, climb past the mountainside ter-races (local children will serve as guides for a small fee). It's a high-altitude hike

TIP

If you decide to take the short hike to Sacsayhuamán, keep in mind that it is uphill from the city. Alternatively, take a minibus tour, or hire a cab to take you up and wait for you. This is one of the area's most spectacular spots to take photos at dawn.

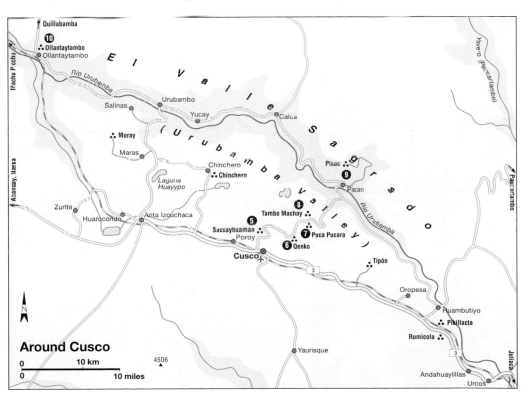

Around Cusco

0   10 km
0   10 miles

that may leave your heart pounding. The stones in Pisac's buildings are smaller than those at Sacsayhuamán, but the precision with which they are cut and fit will amaze you. If you plan to do a full circuit of the valley, continue to the great fortress of **Ollantaytambo** , 72 km (45 miles) from Cusco. This elegant and intricate granite complex has temples, baths, and impressive military installations. Both Ollantaytambo and Pisco can be seen on the Cusco Visitor Ticket.

The massive stone ramparts at Sacsayhuamán.

The Andes

At 7,200 km (4,500 miles), the Andes, the longest mountain chain in the world, forms the backbone of South America. The range stretches from Colombia down to southern Chile and Argentina, and is made up of dozens of parallel mountain ranges known as *cordilleras*. In Peru, these ranges cluster together, providing trekkers with easy access to some of the world's highest peaks outside the Himalayas. Except for the most rugged and remote areas, the Peruvian Andes are not an untouched wilderness. Every single piece of arable land is farmed by local *campesinos* (peasants).

The formidable Peruvian *sierra*, or mountainous region, was conquered by the Incas, whose terraced system of agriculture enabled large areas of steep yet fertile land to be cultivated. This ancient system is still employed in some areas, and countless remains of ancient terracing give an insight into the productivity achieved by this civilization. Passing through these remote, yet populated areas is a bit like stepping back into the past. One- or two-room huts constructed of crude adobe bricks and topped with *ichu* grass have changed little in design since Inca times. There is no electricity, and water is drawn from a nearby stream. Small courtyards house chickens and *cuy*, or guinea pig, considered a delicacy in the sierra. Corn and other grains can often be seen drying in the midday sun.

BELOW: the fortress of Sacsayhuamán, near Cusco.

The Inca Trail

Of all the popular treks in South America, the three- to five-day hike along the Inca Trail (following the course of an old Inca roadway) to Machu Picchu is the best known. The adventure from Cusco begins with a four-hour overcrowded train ride along the Urubamba River, known by the Incas as the **Sacred Valley**. It is no longer possible to walk the Inca Trail independently; you must pre-arrange the trip either at home or in Cusco. (If you want to avoid several days of arduous trekking, the train also stops at Aguas Calientes, 8 km (5 miles) from the Lost City, and you can get off there, but you will miss out on some stunning scenery.)

The first 12 km (7 miles) of the trail meander through easy terrain of dusty scrub, low-lying hills, and hut dwellings. Then comes the **Warmiwañusqa Pass**, beyond which lies a wealth of Inca ruins. Struggling to the top of this 4,000-meter (13,000-ft) pass is no small challenge. The hiker soon identifies with its name, which translates as "Dead Woman's Pass". The small guard post of **Runkuraqay**, often shrouded in mist, is the first reward of the Inca Trail. Further along, the more elaborately constructed ruins of **Saya-jmarka** ("Dominant Town") perch on top of a narrow cliff. The fine stonework for which the Incas are

famous is apparent. An incredible paved highway snakes along the valley below, masterfully constructed by a people the Spaniards did not consider civilized. **Puyapatamarka** (Cloud-level Town) is fascinating for its circular walls and finely engineered aqueduct system, which still provides spring water to the ancient baths. Along the road to **Wiñay Wayna**, a long stone staircase leads down into dense jungle. Clinging to a steep hillside, the last set of ruins is the most stunning. That something so complex was constructed in a ravine so vertical is almost beyond comprehension.

Map on page 144

An hour away lies the jewel in the crown – **Machu Picchu** ⑪. To see it at sunrise, most trekkers stay at the camp beyond Wiñay Wayna, where rainy nights are filled with the howls of campers trying to sleep in leaky tents. The high pass of **Intipunku**, the Sun Gate, provides the first glimpse of the fabled city. Arriving as the Incas did centuries ago, the trekker begins the final descent into Machu Picchu. However, the sheer number of visitors hiking up the trail (up to 1,000 per day) has caused the tourist board to contemplate controversial changes, such as increasing the hiking trail fee and constructing a cable car from Aguas Calientes to Machu Picchu.

Cusco means "navel" in Quechua, because the Incas considered the city the center or source of their universe.

Arequipa: the "white city"

Although **Arequipa** ⑫ was far from Lima and isolated between desert and mountains when the country was young, it was on the route linking the silver mines of Bolivia to the coast. For that reason, the oasis at the foot of the Misti volcano grew to be the Peruvian town with the largest Spanish population and the strongest European traditions. Today, with buildings of white volcanic stone lending it the name "white city", it remains Peru's second most important city.

BELOW: craft stall and assistant, Chinchero.

TREKKING IN THE ANDES

One of the best places for trekking information is the South American Explorer's Club in Lima. Membership fee is US$40. Their office at Avenida República de Portugal 146, Breña, tel: 425-0142, keeps reports on trails, maps, and books. Another good place for advice is the Casa de Guías in Huaraz (Parque Ginebra 28G, tel: 72-1811, fax: 72-2306). Bring a down jacket and plenty of warm clothes for very cold nights at 4,000 meters (13,100 ft) and above. A tent and a good sleeping bag are essential. To be certain of good-quality equipment, it's best to bring your own, but it can be hired in the major trekking centers. Check the quality, since items are often the worse for wear.

Before setting off, spend a couple of days getting used to the thin, high-altitude air around Cusco and Huaraz, or you will quickly become exhausted. If you are trekking independently (no longer possible on the Inca Trail), stock up on food – you won't be able to buy anything on the way. A stove for cooking is essential: there is no wood for fires at higher altitudes, and using up scarce reserves at lower levels only adds to the serious problem of soil erosion in the area. And of course no litter whatsoever should be left behind. A guide who knows the area well can be invaluable – ask around, as competence varies.

Machu Picchu

The mystery of Machu Picchu did not start in 1911 when Hiram Bingham stumbled on the snake-infested mountaintop citadel hidden by a vast tangle of vines and trees. This site on the steep summit overlooking the raging Urubamba River was always a mystery – because only a chosen few in the Inca Empire were allowed to glimpse it. To call it a "lost city" is misleading; it was more like a sanctuary.

Machu Picchu means "Old Peak", and the higher Huayna Picchu (Young Peak), stands vigil over it. The site is accessible on the four-hour bus and train service from Cusco or by hiking the Inca Trail *(see page 156)*. The area is semi-tropical, at 900 meters (3,000 ft) lower than Cusco.

Machu Picchu was home to priests, high functionaries, craftsmen, and servants and, most importantly, the *mamacunas*, or virgins chosen to dedicate their lives to the sun god. It was a city of streets, aqueducts where

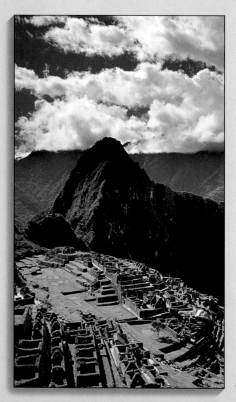

crystal clear waters still run, of liturgical fountains and walkways. Even after Bingham's discovery, the city remained inaccessible until the 1940s, when an archeological expedition working at the site discovered the Inca Trail cutting through the valley.

The fate of this city's inhabitants remains unknown. Spanish chronicles of the Cusco area make no mention of it. Theories of its demise range from epidemics to suggestions that the occupants were ostracized and forgotten in the bloody political disunity sweeping the empire before its fall.

Excavations have only added to the mystery. The skeletons of 173 people were found, 150 of whom were women. No gold objects were discovered. At the tomb of the high priestess, as Bingham called it, the remains of a woman and a small dog were found with some ceramic objects, two brooches, and woolen clothing. The woman had suffered from syphilis.

Today's visitors enter the ruins near the hotel, but the only entrance to the city in ancient times was the narrow doorway at the southwest section of the citadel. The city's cultivated land was farmed on narrow terraces on the steep slopes of the mountaintop, and the thousands of steps connecting them have survived for centuries.

The city is divided into sections: the cemetery, jails, small dwellings, and temples. The Temple of the Three Windows allows sunlight to pass through its windows to the Sacred Plaza. Climbing higher is the astronomical observatory and *Intiwatana*, the curiously shaped stone block believed to have been a solar clock or, as some claim, "the hitching post to the sun", where the sun's rays cast shadows used in planning seasonal activities and religious ceremonies.

Some of the buildings in Machu Picchu were two stories high, originally topped with sharply peaked straw roofs. What amazes architects today is the precision with which building stones were cut and assembled.

A steep and perilous path rises from the site to the top of Huayna Picchu. At the skirt of Huayna Picchu is the construction known as the Temple of the Moon, and from the summit there is an extraordinary view of the ruins and the Urubamba valley. ❏

LEFT: Machu Picchu.

Map on page 144

Arequipa's **Plaza de Armas** is one of Peru's most beautiful. One full side is occupied by the massive **Cathedral** (open daily), rebuilt twice in the early 19th century after it was destroyed by fire and earthquake. Its clock is the city's unofficial timepiece. Make sure you see the cathedral's organ, brought from Belgium, and the elaborately carved wooden pulpit, the work of French artist Rigot in 1879. Two-story arcades grace the other three sides of the plaza, with palm trees, old gas lamps, and a fountain set in an English garden.

The city is full of patrician homes built in the 18th century which have withstood its frequent earth tremors. The one-story colonial structures are replete with massive carved wooden doors, grilled French windows and high-ceilinged rooms around spacious patios. The best for visiting are **Casa Ricketts** (open daily), built as a seminary in 1738 and now used as a bank; the 200-year-old **Casa de la Moneda** or former mint; and the **Casa Moral** (open daily), named after the venerable mulberry tree on its patio, which has also become a bank.

No visit to Arequipa would be complete without a stop at **La Compañía** church. The sacristy's ceiling is covered with miniature paintings and carvings in crimson and gold. The view from the steeple is fabulous, especially at sunset when the fading light gives a rosy glow to the city's white rock buildings.

The most astonishing stop in Arequipa is the **Monasterio de Santa Catalina** (open daily), opened in 1970 after 400 years as a cloister for nuns. Although they lived behind closed doors, the nuns paid little heed to the traditional vows of poverty and silence. During its heyday, this convent's sleeping cells were furnished with English carpets, silk curtains, cambric and lace sheets, and tapestry-covered stools. Each nun had her own servant and dined off porcelain plates using silver cutlery. At its peak nearly 500 nuns were housed in the convent.

When the convent opened its doors again, its anecdotes and scandals were resurrected. But don't believe it when they tell you the story of Sister Dominga, the 16-year-old who entered the convent when her betrothed left her for a rich widow, then staged her own death to escape. This beautiful young woman really did place the body of a deceased Amerindian woman in her bed one night then set the room on fire, but it happened at the **Convento de Santa Rosa** (which is still cloistered).

Two other places worth visiting nearby are the **Museo Histórico Municipal** (open daily), which is interesting for an overview of the city's history. From here it is only a few yards to the **Iglesia de San Francisco** (open daily 7–11am and 5–8pm), the focus of attention every December 8 during the Feast of the Immaculate Conception, when a coach topped with the image of the Virgin Mary is paraded through the streets in a colorful procession. The most interesting museum in the city, the **Monasterio de la Recoleta** (open daily), lies across the Río Chili (use the Puente Grau or Puente Bolognesi). The monastery has a vast library of 20,000 books, many of them very old.

Independent spirits

Outside Arequipa, set in beautiful countryside, is **Sabandía** and a flour mill that was restored, stone by stone, in 1973. Three hours' away and drawing nearly

BELOW: walking the Inca Trail.

Convent of Santa Catalina, Arequipa.

as much tourist attention as the city itself is the **Colca Canyon**. From the Colca River at its base to the mountains above, the chasm reaches depths of 3,400 meters (11,000 ft). Even more remote than Colca, the **Cotahuasi Canyon** has only recently been exposed to tourism. Now believed by many to exceed Colca in depth, making it the world's deepest canyon, it is a pristine area of great natural beauty ideal for adventurers and nature lovers.

At the Cruz del Condor viewpoint you may see a condor, soaring on the warm thermal currents produced in the early morning or the early evening. The Cruz del Cóndor is included in a variety of one- and two-day trips, which can be organized in Arequipa. En route, many of the tours take in the **Reserva Nacional Salinas y Aguada Blanca** (at 3,900 meters/12,800 ft you'll notice how thin the air is), where groups of shy vicuñas can often be seen. The area is also accessible by bus from Arequipa then switching to *burros* (donkeys).

To unwind in Arequipa after a hard day's sightseeing, do what the locals do and head to a *picantería* for a cold Arequipeña beer and some spicy stuffed peppers, rabbit, or marinated pork.

Puno and Lake Titicaca

Lake Titicaca's great size and breathless altitude, its mysterious antiquity, and even its steamships constitute an exotic legend. At 174 km (108 miles) long and up to 64 km (40 miles) wide, Titicaca is South America's largest lake. The lake moderates the climate and facilitates cultivation around its shores, despite the frosty nights and short growing season. Peru and Bolivia share this lake peacefully, but in bygone times it was at the heart of warring tribalism and imperial ambition. About 1,500 years ago the powerful Tiwanaku civilization

BELOW: Plaza de Armas, Arequipa.

built a vast city on the Bolivian shore; its collapse led to centuries of sectarian strife. At Sillustani, the towering tombs of the Colla kings, whose armies fought the Incas, can still be seen. Today, Quechua- and Aymara-speaking Amerindians occupy discrete stretches of Titicaca's shoreline.

Map on page 144

You can visit two very different island communities that subsist on the lake. The Uros islanders, dwelling on spongy reed masses, live on the waters of **Puno** bay. This tourist hub is an old, cold town on the lake shore that has, thanks to the tourism industry, undergone something of a revival. Puno now offers a good selection of comfortable hotels, as well as lively bars and decent restaurants.

On solid **Taquile**, a traditional way of life manages to survive in spite of the steady flow of fascinated visitors. Taquile is a traditional Quechua-speaking community. The island is best known for its weaving, and two co-ops in the central square sell superb handicrafts. Overnighters should have sufficient time to climb to the highest point on the island. Follow a footpath that turns uphill off the street between the village and the main archway, allowing about 30 minutes to reach the top. Toward the summit there are some tombs dating from pre-Inca times. The summit views of Lake Titicaca, with Amantaní island to the north, are superb. In fine weather you can see a dazzling horizon of snowy peaks, the Cordillera Real, on the Bolivian shore.

Condor over Colca Canyon.

The lake's hinterland is a great plateau studded with isolated mountains known as the *altiplano*, the high plain. **Juliaca** is its hustling commercial capital, known for its textile and leather goods, while the charming town of Lampa is becoming a center for tourism.

The Peruvian Amazon

Three-fifths of Peru is jungle – the Amazon. Despite the encroachment of modern life, this is where adventures can still occur and the exotic reigns. Here the roads are rivers and the vehicles are motorboats and canoes. It is the home of many natural healers, who say that its unique fauna might contain anything from new contraceptives to a cancer cure. The Amazon is the one place the Incas never managed to penetrate. When the Spanish conquistadors arrived, they heard wild tales of a golden city hidden in the heart of the jungle. In their search for El Dorado, they found nothing but disease and hostile tribes, although the legend lives on.

The Spanish explorer Francisco de Orellana is credited with discovering the Amazon River. He named it after the fierce female warriors of Greek legend when he mistook the long-haired Yagua men, who confronted him wearing fiber skirts, for women. A later Spanish expedition was fictionalized in the 1973 Werner Herzog film *Aguirre, the Wrath of God*, about the demonic conquistador Aguirre, who killed for pleasure during his 1560 trek along the Amazon. The search for gold was replaced by missionaries' quest to convert the indigenous population; from the late 1600s to the mid-1700s, thanks to an uprising led by Jesuit-educated Quechua Juan Santos, the jungle was kept free of Europeans, but the missionaries eventually returned, and the Catholic presence in the rainforest has received strong competition from Protestant evangelists.

BELOW: Colca Canyon.

The rubber barons

The colonization of the Amazon was consolidated at the end of the 1800s with the rubber boom. The period was one of overnight wealth for European and US rubber barons and overnight enslavement for the people of the rainforest. The best-known of the rubber barons was Carlos Fitzgerald, the son of an English immigrant and a Peruvian. Accused of spying for Chile during the 1879 war, Fitzcarraldo fled to the Amazon where he made a great fortune in rubber and became obsessed with a plan to travel from the Ucayali River (which flows into the Amazon) through the Madre de Dios River by steamship. Although Fitzcarraldo's quest failed, steamships later made the trip, effectively linking the Atlantic and Pacific oceans – with thousands of Amerindians hauling the ships across the isthmus. Fitzcarraldo and other rubber barons had no cause to miss Europe; they imported every luxury that struck their fancy, from Paris fashions to imported wines, and European theater and opera stars regularly performed in the midst of one of the world's densest jungles. But the opulence ended in 1920 when rubber grown in Asia and Africa began to compete on the world market.

Boom towns and exotic wildlife

Peru's most important rubber boom city – and the largest city in the Peruvian Amazon – is **Iquitos** ⓭. The old days of wealth are still evident in the houses covered with Portuguese tiles and, on the **Plaza de Armas**, in the ramshackle two-story metal house designed by Gustave Eiffel for the Paris Exhibition of 1889 and transported to Iquitos piece by piece by rubber magnate Jules Toth. On the waterfront is the colorful **Belén** port, where the houses float on rafts. From here, irregular riverboat services run to Leticia in Colombia and onward to

BELOW: local riverboats carry both passengers and cargo.

Map
on page
144

Manaus in Brazil, preserving a taste of the days when air travel was unknown and the only way to reach Iquitos was through weeks of journeying overland and upriver. Although it is a bustling city of 400,000 one only has to go a short distance from Iquitos on the Amazon, Yanamono or Manatí rivers to be in virgin jungle. On the way are the wood and palm houses on stilts inhabited by the *ribereños – mestizos* who speak a lilting Spanish reminiscent of Brazilian Portuguese. Exotic birds fly in and out of vine-covered trees, while brilliantly colored butterflies, tapirs, monkeys, peccaries, and pink river dolphins fascinate visitors. Only 100 km (62 miles) from Iquitos is the biggest national park in Peru, the 2-million hectare (5-million acre) **Reserva Nacional Pacaya-Samiria**, a wildlife-packed lowland jungle area that can only be reached by hiring a boat and a guide, in either Iquitos or the village of Lagunas.

Tourists generally stay in lodges in the jungle, the oldest and most recommended being the three Explorama complexes, ranging from the ultra-modern Explorama Inn with 24-hour electricity and private bathrooms in every cabin to the primitive Explornapo camp, where kerosene lamps, night walks, and mosquito netting tents add to the mystique.

The people in this part of the Amazon live isolated lives, except when they head off in their dugout canoes or hitch a ride on the "river buses" – boats that cruise up and down the river collecting passengers and their cargoes of bananas, yucca, corn, dried fish, and chickens headed for Iquitos.

Another important Amazon city is **Pucallpa** ⑭, a frontier lumber town and the last navigable port for ocean-going vessels on the Amazon. It is 9 km (6 miles) from **Lago Yarinacocha**, a 22-km (14-mile) body of water luring tourists fascinated by its spectacular sunrises and sunsets, its fishing and the undis-

LEFT: Amazon Amerindians still use blow darts to shoot their prey. **RIGHT:** young puma, a rare sight

San Pedro cactus, Chiclayo.

turbed native Shipibo villages along its banks. Its forests are full of cedar, pine, mahogany, and bamboo and serve as home to nearly 1,000 bird species, endless varieties of butterflies and exotic mammals – including sloths. Local boats called *pekepekes* are available for hire for day trips to some of the isolated villages or to visit the Shipibos and buy their hand-painted pottery and textiles. In nearby **Puerto Callao** you can visit the fascinating artisanal cooperative Maroti Shobo, where high-quality ceramics and weavings made by the Shipibo from the surrounding villages are displayed and sold, and sent to museums all over the world. Further south is **Puerto Maldonado** ⓯, just a few hours by river from one of the world's most important wildlife reserves and capital of the least-populated, least-developed and least-explored province in Peru.

At 1.8 million hectares (4½ million acres), the **Parque Nacional Manu** ⓰ is one of the largest conservation areas in the world. Founded in 1973, it was declared a Biosphere Reserve in 1977, and a World Natural Heritage Site 10 years later. Parts are accessible only to biologists and anthropologists with permits, one zone is set aside for two local native groups, and the reserve zone is aimed at eco-tourists. The excellent **Manu Wildlife Center** allows visitors to meet researchers and scientists on-site. Closer to Puerto Maldonado is the second-largest reserve, the **Reserva Nacional Tambopata Candamo**. Created by the Peruvian government in 1989, this 1.5-million hectare (3.8-million acre) zone has been set up both as an extractive reserve (for rubber, Brazil nuts, and other products) and for eco-tourism. The reserve encompasses the entire watershed of the **Río Tambopata**, one of the most beautiful and least-disturbed areas in Peru, and protects the largest macaw lick in South America, the **Colpa de Guacamayos**, where hundreds of parrots and macaws gather daily.

BELOW: girl at a fiesta, Trujillo.

Peru's historical north

Trujillo ⓱, the "travelers' resting place" along the Spaniards' route between Lima and Quito, is a graceful coastal city. Founded in 1535 and named after Francisco Pizarro's birthplace in Spain, it soon became worthy of the title the "Lordliest City", and even today its well-preserved Andalusian-style wooden balconies pay testimony to the colonial days.

The city is famous for being the first in Peru to declare independence from Spain in 1820, and in the 1920s it was the birthplace of APRA (Alianza Popular Revolucionaria Americana) – Peru's longest-standing political party.

The best place to start exploring Trujillo is the **Plaza de Armas**, bounded by the city hall, the bishop's palace and the recently renovated cathedral with its marble pillars and gilt hand-carved wooden altars. The colonial building next to the cathedral is now the **Hotel Libertador Trujillo**. Off the main square, colonial mansions abound, although earthquakes have taken their toll. Most have been elegantly restored by national banks or other private enterprises (most open Mon–Fri and Sat am). **Casa de la Emancipación** is typical of the houses built in the 16th and 17th centuries and contains much of its original furniture. **Casa de Mayorazgo, Casa Urquiaga, Casa Bracamonte,** and **Casa de los Leones** (also known as the

Casa Ganoza Chopitea), now an art gallery, are all worth a look. The **Palacio Iturregui** houses the Club Central, with a permanent exhibition of ceramics. Trujillo's pre-Hispanic past is on display at the University of Trujillo's **Museo de Arqueología** (irregular hours, ask at tourist office). The **Museo Cassinelli** (open Mon–Sat) in the basement of the Cassinelli gas station, holds a fascinating private collection of Moche and Chimu ceramics.

Map on page 144

An ancient adobe city

On the northwest of Trujillo are the ruins of **Chan Chan**, which was one of the world's largest adobe cities at its discovery by the Spanish. Made up of seven citadels spread over 20 sq. km (8 sq. miles) and enclosed by a massive wall, Chan Chan was home to the Chimu people, who fished and farmed, worshiped the moon, and left no written records. On the city walls are carvings of fish, sea birds, fishing nets, and moons. The Chimus had such a sophisticated irrigation and aqueduct system that they were able to turn the arid wasteland around them into fertile fields of grains, fruits, and vegetables.

About 10 km (6 miles) southeast of Trujillo lie **Las Huacas del Sol y de la Luna** (the Tombs of the Sun and the Moon). You can get there by minibus or go on an organized tour. These pyramidal temples were built by the Moche people (100BC–850AD). The Huaca del Sol (arguably the largest pre-Columbian building in the Americas) is unexcavated, but at the smaller Huaca de la Luna, 10 years of archeological work have begun to unveil a series of temples superimposed on one another to form a pyramid covered in beautiful, bright murals. Archeology enthusiasts should visit the Huaca el Brujo, a recently discovered site a few hours from Trujillo in the Chicama Valley. Ask at the tourist information office for details.

BELOW: the "House of the Grandson" near Huaraz.

Where the last Inca leader met his fate

Historically, the most important northern city is **Cajamarca** . This is the city where the Incas and Spaniards had their final confrontation. According to Spanish chronicles, the Inca Atahuallpa *(see page 26)* was taken prisoner after offending the Europeans by accepting a preferred Bible then tossing it to the ground. To pay the ransom demanded by the conquistadors, people from all over the Inca empire brought gold and silver, filling **El Cuarto del Rescate** (the Ransom Room; open daily), a block from the Plaza de Armas. But the effort was futile and the Spaniards garrotted the last Inca on the main square.

The **Plaza de Armas** is the hub of this slow-paced city of 120,000 and is ringed by colonial buildings and churches. Opened in 1776, the **Cathedral**'s carved wood altars are covered in gold leaf and its facade is of intricately sculpted volcanic rock. The **Iglesia San Francisco**, older and more ornate than the cathedral, is home to the **Museo de Arte Religioso** (open Mon–Fri) and some eerie catacombs. Also on the plaza is Restaurante Salas, the place to eat the city's best home cooking. Cajamarca is ideal for exploring the province of **Amazonas**, home of the Chachapoyan, who built several pre-Incan cities, including **Kuélap**, a great walled city perched high above the Río Utcubamba. Minibuses leave in the morning for the village of **Tingo**, from where a road goes to within 15 minutes' walk of the fascinating site.

Gold figure, Vicus culture, Brüning Museum.

BELOW: the ancient adobe citadel of Chan Chan.

Digging for the past

The Moche burial area at **Sipán** (open daily; guided tours available), about 30 km (18 miles) south of **Chiclayo** , is the largest tomb excavated in the Americas. Known as the tomb of El Señor de Sipán, it was uncovered in the late

Map on page 144

1980s, originally by *huaqueros* (grave robbers), before the excavation was taken over by the director of the Brüning Museum *(see below)*, Dr Walter Alva. He became aware of unusual objects on the black market and realised that a burial site was being ransacked. It is 15 meters (50 ft) deep and contained the remains of a high priest or prince wearing a spectacular gold mask with emerald eyes. In his tomb were numerous artifacts including gold and copper, and gilded cotton cloth. There were also the skeletons of 24 women. The whole burial complex comprises 14 tombs, one of which contained 50 kilos (110 lb) of gold. The continuing excavation at Sipán promises to provide crucial new evidence about the life of the Moche, a sophisticated pre-Columbian civilization that flourished from 100–700 AD.

The nearby **Sicán** site, the first to be excavated using radar, disclosed similar riches from the period betweeen the Moche and Chimu civilizations (9th–10th centuries). The artefacts and remains found are on the same scale as those found in the tomb of Tutankhamun. The site is well worth visiting, but to see the stunning contents of the tomb of the Lord of Sipán, when they are not touring the world's museums, you should go to the tiny town of **Lambayeque** nearby to visit the remarkable **Museo Brüning** (open daily), which has Peru's finest publicly owned gold, silver and ceramic collection as well as the fabulous finds from the Sipán dig.

One of the most intriguing projects in the area was set up under the direction of the Norwegian explorer, Thor Heyerdahl. His archeological dig at **Túcume**, near Sipán, brought together a team of European and Peruvian archeologists. Túcume is a plain with 27 hills that are actually pyramids covered by centuries of dirt, and can be explored with the help of guided tours from Chiclayo. ❑

Although Peru has strengthened its laws on the sale of archeological artifacts, large quantities are still smuggled out of the country. Ancient ruins are also plundered by squatters in search of materials to construct their own dwellings.

BELOW: totora reed boats, Huanchaco.

A REMARKABLE CRAFT

In 1948, a Norwegian expedition led by Thor Heyerdahl embarked on a voyage that would take it from Callao in Peru to French Polynesia in a balsa raft, the *Kon-Tiki*. Heyerdahl's intention was to prove that Amerindians could have colonized the Pacific Islands on balsa rafts, and his expedition launched a whole area of scientific investigation. His theory has since been discredited, but interest in the sea-going craft of the pre-Columbian South Americans and Pacific Islanders has increased. Many modern adventurers have their rafts built by Bolivians from the Lake Titicaca region, who are considered the best balsa raft craftsmen in the world.

When the Spanish first reached the Americas they recorded these craft in detail, which ranged from the totora reed bundle rafts used today by the fishermen of Huanchaco, Peru, to huge cargo-carrying rafts. Chronicler Augustín de Zárate described rafts that could carry 50 men and three horses. In the 17th century, European navigators began to understand the "guara", or centerboard, a navigation instrument used by the Amerindians. Visitors to Peru today can witness the ancient craft in action around Lake Titicaca, or at Huanchaco, near Trujillo.

LAKE TITICACA: PERU'S LEGENDARY WATERWAY

Surrounded by snow-capped Andean peaks, this lofty expanse of clear, fresh water has fired the imagination for generations

Linking Peru and Bolivia, the world's highest navigable lake is a large, remarkably clear blue body of water covering more than 8,000 sq. km (3,000 sq. miles) with more than 30 islands. The lake may look inviting, but bathers beware – at 4,000 meters (13,000 ft) above sea level, its waters are freezing all year round. Lake Titicaca is full of history, ancient legends, sacred sites, and living history, as age-old traditions are continued and developed on and around its waters.

BIRTHPLACE OF THE INCAS

The Isla del Sol, in the middle of the lake, is at the center of the Inca creation myths as recorded by 16th-century Spanish chroniclers. One myth tells of the emergence of four sisters and four brothers from a stone door on the island, two of whom were the Incas Manco Capac and Mama Ocllo (or Huaca). Another legend relates that the sun was born on a sacred rock on the island. Ruined Inca temples and sacred sites can be visited on the Isla del Sol and the nearby Isla de Luna *(pictured above)*. Inca history holds that when the Spanish reached Cusco in Peru, the Incas took the 1,800-kg (2-ton) gold chain of Inca Huascar from Qoricancha, and hurled it into the lake. The late French oceanographer Jacques Cousteau spent two months exploring the lake with a mini submarine. He found no gold but he did discover a 60-cm (24-inch) tri-colored frog that apparently never surfaces. In 1996 the oldest known temple in South America was found near the lake, occupied between 1500 and 1000 BC, nearly 2,500 years before the Incas. Its discovery adds to the fascination of this remarkable region.

▷ **REED BOATS**
People of the Lake Titicaca region have been building tortora reed boats since time immemorial to sail the vast expanses of the lake.

△ **GATHERING REEDS**
Although the last full-blood Uros died in 1959, modern Uros islanders still use reeds to build homes, boats, islands, and even for food.

◁ **TAQUILE TRADITIONS**
The colorful text[il] designs of Isla Taquile are not just for decoration but can denote social or marital status. Some are reserved for special times of the year.

THE WEAVERS OF ISLA TAQUILE

On the Peruvian side of the lake is Isla Taquile – the island of weavers. Under the Spanish it was a *hacienda*, and later it became a prison, but the Taquile people have managed to regain ownership. Since 1970 they have been running their own tourism operations to ensure their old traditions are not lost.

There are no hotels, but islanders open their homes to overnight guests, and there are small eating establishments specializing in lake trout.

Poverty has bred a cooperative lifestyle, which has won the islanders their reputation for hospitality. Textiles can be purchased from the weaving cooperatives, most knitted from finely spun sheep's wool dyed bright red and blue – the colors and weaves can reveal age, social position, and marital status. More textiles can be purchased at Amantaní, a peaceful island with temples and a carved stone throne on one shore.

◁ **FRESH FISH**
Lake Titicaca has waves, and can get very choppy! Trout from the lake can be tasted at restaurants in Copacabana and elsewhere.

∇ **UROS ISLANDERS**
The Uros Islands have become a popular tourist attraction. Islanders make small model boats out of reeds to sell to tourists.

◁ **FIESTA OF THE VIRGIN**
The quiet Bolivian town of Copacabana, beside the lake, bursts into life at fiesta time.

▷ **TIAHUANACO**
This mysterious pre-Inca site has advanced stonework that is over 2,000 years old.

BOLIVIA

Map
on page
174

Landlocked and isolated, Bolivia is one of South America's most unlikely treasures, attracting the most intrepid visitors for its rich cultural heritage and literally breathtaking mountain scenery

Geographically, Bolivia takes you from the heights of the *Altiplano*, the Andean plateau which elevates northeastern Bolivia, down to the balmy valleys of the Yungas and east to the fertile lowlands of the *Oriente*. Linking these physically dissimilar territories are, in the north, hair-raising zigzag roads which cling to near-vertical cliffs. Further south, the plateau shelves off a little more gently, in the area known as the *Valles*.

Bolivia is also noted for its material highs and lows, particularly the vast gulf between rich and poor. The poverty is obvious – just look around on the streets of La Paz, behind the cheerful smiles of the traders and colorfully dressed *campesinos* (farmers), or drive past families toiling in the fields early in the morning. Bolivia's wealth is not so obvious, but is hinted at in certain genteel cafés in La Paz. Much of it, like the riches of the silver and tin mines, was concentrated in the hands of a few, and spirited away to Europe. Much of the country's physical wealth was taken by neighboring countries in a succession of disastrous wars. Today, Bolivia is the sub-continent's poorest nation, with about two-thirds of its population, many of whom are subsistence farmers, living in poverty, and the highest infant mortality rate in South America.

A sizeable part of Bolivia's wealth is generated in the coca fields of the Oriente and turned into cash on the streets of North American cities In 2001, farmers rejected an offer from the government of US$900 each, annually, in exchange for destroying coca crops.

The country has been plagued by protests in recent years – which can affect tourists, but generally the atmosphere is peaceful.

The lust for silver

In 1544 an Amerindian named Diego Huallpa discovered silver in the Cerro Rico of Potosí, and from that moment, the country's fate was sealed. For the next two centuries, everything in Bolivia was geared toward extracting this vein of precious metal, the greatest ever discovered. Towns were founded for the sole purpose of supplying Potosí with goods traded from other parts of the empire or to transfer silver back to Europe. Nothing mattered to the Spanish except the ore and its transportation from the freezing wilderness, least of all the fate of the local people: the magnificent Inca systems of terracing and irrigation fell into disrepair and Christianity was imposed, although the conversion was at best superficial. More obvious was the imposition of a new form of dress for native women. Layered dresses, derbys (bowler hats), and plaited hair typify the most common tourist view of the Bolivian people today – this appearance actually came about by Spanish decree in the 18th

PRECEDING PAGES: musicians, La Paz. **LEFT:** La Paz seen from the rim of the altiplano. **BELOW:** Aymara man playing the *zampoña*.

century. The local populations were theoretically free subjects of the Spanish crown, but in reality they were forced to pay massive tributes, lived at the beck and call of brutal overlords, and were regularly dragged from their agricultural communities to work in the mines of Potosí. Amerindians died by the thousands in the harsh and brutal conditions while colonial Potosí grew to match any city in the Old World.

Two-thirds of the Bolivian population are of native origin, the highest proportion of any country in South America.

The amount of silver that was taken from Potosí is staggering: 16 million kg (16,000 tons) arrived in Seville between 1545 and 1660, three and a half times the entire European reserves of the day. The wealth was squandered on Spain's futile religious wars, or wasted by the extravagance of its nobles and clergymen, almost all of it ending up in the coffers of Flemish, German, or English bankers.

The creation of Bolivia in 1825 *(see page 32)* launched the country into an apparently endless series of military governments, mostly bloodless reshufflings in the palaces of La Paz, with wealth and control being kept in the hands of a small number of families of Spanish descent. Meanwhile, the country proceeded

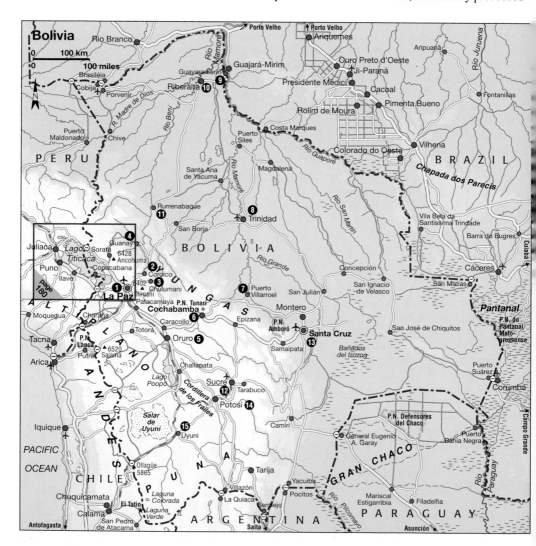

to loose large chunks of its territory in wars with its neighbors. The only good news seemed to be the discovery of rich veins of tin in Oruro and Potosí, by a prospector named Simón Patiño. But Patiño amassed a personal fortune from this new boom, becoming one of the ten richest people on earth by the early 1900s. While Patiño lived in luxury, he kept miners on starvation wages and he quashed industrial disputes by organizing massacres as he vacationed in Europe.

Map on page 174

Moves for change

A period of intense self-reflection followed the 1930s Chaco War, creating a movement for change, culminating in the Revolutionary Nationalist Movement (MNR) behind Victor Paz Estenssoro. Winning the elections of 1951, the party was blocked from office by a military coup and Paz Estenssoro was forced into exile in Buenos Aires. But the miners began an armed revolt and after heavy fighting defeated the military. Paz Estenssoro returned to La Paz and the MNR began to put its reforms into action. In the following years Bolivia saw the nationalization of tin mines, the granting of votes to Amerindians and extensive land reform. Unfortunately, the mines were still dependent on foreign capital and land given to indigenous peoples was in plots too small to be productive. The economy began sliding and the MNR was ousted in another military coup.

Dictator followed dictator with monotonous regularity. The country's most infamous dictator came to power in 1980 in a coup that cost hundreds of lives: General Luis García Meza sent his tanks into La Paz, shot left-wing leaders, and bombed mining camps in Oruro. He ran an extraordinarily corrupt regime, inviting ex-Nazi Klaus Barbie to help organize his security forces and selling off national assets to line his own pockets. Finally García Meza was driven from

Stone cross on Chacaltaya, with Huayna Potosí in the background.

BELOW: colorful cemetery near La Paz.

power and in 1982 democracy was restored under Dr Hernán Siles Zuazo, who is unfortunately best remembered for leading Bolivia into one of the world's highest inflation rates, hitting a mind-boggling 35,000 percent a year.

Tin price collapse

In 1985, with the economy on the verge of collapse and cocaine the major export, Paz Estenssoro returned as president. He embraced conservative policies recommended by the IMF and, with the collapse of tin prices, sacked 20,000 miners from the state-run COMIBOL, using the military to head off union protests. Inflation ground to a halt, at the price of massive unemployment.

Inconclusive results in the 1989 elections led to a congressional vote to elect the president, and center-left Jaime Paz Zamora came to power under an alliance with right-wing ex-dictator Hugo Banzer Suárez. Unemployment boosted cocaine manufacture as people looked for new sources of income, and in the early 1990s the US embarked on Operation Support Justice, an anti-narcotics program in Bolivia, tied to US$78 million in aid. But high-profile raids on illegal laboratories led to few arrests and the Americans were shortly asked to leave. Such programs have often provoked violent demonstrations by angry *campesinos*. Many defend their traditional right to grow coca for uses other than drug production. Others, desperately poor, defend the chance to grow a crop that is more durable than rice or potatoes and which can be many times more lucrative.

The 1993 elections brought to power the MNR, led by millionaire Gonzalo Sánchez de Lozada, but opposition to his program of aggressive economic and social reform led to social unrest. In March 1997, Bolivia negotiated an agreement with Mercosur, the Southern Cone trade organization. Ex-dictator Hugo

BELOW: woodcut of Potosí from 1555, the earliest known drawing of a New World mining enterprise.

Banzer Suárez formed a coalition to take power. Banzer's government pledged to end drug production and trafficking and succeeded in eliminating about 25 percent of the coca crop. In June 2002 Gonzalo Sánchez de Lozada was returned to power. In February the following year, Bolivia's most violent protests in decades were sparked when Sánchez de Lozada's government tried to introduce income tax. Among others, the police went on strike. The army was called in to restore order but used bullets to control the crowd, resulting in 33 deaths. Income tax proposals were withdrawn, five ministries were abolished and ministers were replaced.

Sánchez de Lozada was forced to resign due to public protest and was succeeded by Carlos Mesa in 2003. He too has been dogged by dissent and demands have been made for his resignation. The International Monetary Fund (IMF) lent Bolivia US$118m in April 2003. The loan came shortly after a US$10m loan from the USA, but Bolivia is still South America's poorest country, with a per capita GDP of US$2,600. Although there is some scope for optimism, the country still has a long way to go before it can begin to solve its economic inequalities and to improve the dismal statistics of unemployment and child deaths from malnutrition.

Map on page 174

Elegant colonial streetlight in La Paz.

La Paz: the highest capital

If you're going to fly to Bolivia's unofficial capital, **La Paz ❶**, try to get a window seat. The views are extraordinary as the aeroplane sweeps across Bolivia's highest mountain ranges to dive into the city, which sits in a natural canyon. The one disadvantage is that some travelers arriving in the airport, at an altitude of almost 3,600 meters (12,000 ft), are struck by the nausea and headaches of *soroche*, or altitude sickness. A day or two of taking it easy is a certain cure.

BELOW: Bolivian girl.

In such a magnificent setting, La Paz at first seems an ugly blur of orange brick and gray corrugated iron roof. But on much closer inspection, it is one of South America's most unusual and lively cities. The streets of La Paz, made of slippery bricks, are steep and tiring in the thin mountain air. They meet at the **Plaza San Francisco** with its huge stone church containing a statue of Jesus with a blue fluorescent halo.

The snowcapped **Mount Illimani**, at over 6,000 meters (19,000 ft), dominates the skyline from most parts of La Paz. The modern city center has a collection of shabby skyscrapers and broad streets often clogged with traffic. The city's traditional center is the **Plaza Murillo**, where the Italianate **Presidential Palace** is located – often referred to as the *Palacio Quemado* (Burnt Palace), twice gutted by inflamatory crowds since it was first built in the 1850s. Nearby is the modern **Cathedral**. The surrounding streets are the most atmospheric in the city: **Calle Jaén** is still cobbled and without traffic, lined by preserved colonial buildings. Another atmospheric area is behind the church and monastery of San Francisco near the upper end of Avenida Mariscal Santa Cruz. Dating from 1549, the carvings are rich and ingenious.

The café of the **Club de La Paz**, on the corners of avenidas Camacho and Colón, is a cultural landmark.

A Night at the *Peña*

After a long day of sightseeing, the best place to head for is the local *peña*, or folk nightclub. Here, you can sit and enjoy the haunting music of the altiplano while sipping a cold beer, glass of wine, or potent *pisco sour*, made from grape brandy.

Starting off at around 10pm, *peñas* are usually relaxed, informal bars which offer set musical programs. Up to a dozen groups can play on a single night, giving an idea of the range and variety of Andean music; while the rhythms of the altiplano are related, every region has its own unique sound. A group from Potosí is quite different to one from the shores of Lake Titicaca, and different again to one from Cuzco in Peru. The musicians are often accomplished mimics and the show generally includes a few comic turns, which can be quite hilarious, even if you don't understand the language.

In La Paz, one of the best *peñas* is the Naira at Sagárnaga 161, a dark and intimate venue with a fine repertory of musicians. Other well-known *peñas* are in the restaurants Los Escudos on M. Santa Cruz and La Casa del Corregidor on Murrillo 1040.

The basic instruments used are the single-reed flutes known as *quenas*, *zampoñas* (deep wooden pipes), drums, and rattles. The famous *charango* is a miniature guitar made from an armadillo's shell, with 15 strings with which the player creates a penetrating, tinny sound. Along with the Andean harp, the *charango* is an unusual example of the local culture mixing successfully with the Spanish. Stringed instruments were one of the few cultural innovations that the Andean peoples were glad to accept from Europe. The effect of these instruments is mesmerizing and evokes the loneliness and austerity of the bleak and harsh altiplano. The music is traditionally played without vocal accompaniment, but in recent decades ballads – called *waynos* – have been added, sung mostly in the Quechua or Aymará tongues, or in a mixture of native languages and Spanish. They often deal with the daily lives of *campesinos*:

> Do you want me to tell you
> Where I'm from?
> I'm from behind that hill,
> Amid the carnations,
> Among the lilies
> My sling is of Castilian fabric,
> And my lasso of merino wool:
> Very long-lasting,
> Very strong.

Others are much more progressive:

> The priest of Andahuaylas
> Keeps telling me to get married.
> Maybe he knows, maybe not,
> Where I went last night.

As an expression of Indian culture, the music has often had a mixed reception from the country's rulers. On radio, it must compete with modern pop, as well as salsa and samba. At its worst, it has "crossed over", producing Western songs on Andean instruments – even *Rock Around the Clock* on panpipes. But as native cultures are increasingly gaining acceptance, the presence of altiplano tunes is definitely growing. ❏

LEFT: *zampoña* player, La Paz.

Map
on page
174

This antique wooden retreat has seen innumerable business and political deals, and was probably where many of Bolivia's coups were hatched. It was a favorite hangout of Klaus Barbie before he was arrested in the early 1980s and returned to France for trial as a Nazi war criminal.

Witches and markets

The real attaction of La Paz is the street life. Narrow alleyways stretching up the hillside behind the Plaza San Francisco are generally packed with brightly dressed Bolivian *campesinas* selling blankets, nuts, herbs and – for the *gringos* – woolen jumpers with llama motifs. Near here is the famous **Mercado de Hechicería**, or Witchcraft Market, where elderly ladies sell magic charms for every possible occasion. You can pick up a small bottle full of colored pieces of wood and oil which, depending on its contents, will give good luck with love, money, or health. A somewhat macabre market specialty is the dried llama fetus, traditionally buried in the foundations of a new building to bring good fortune to the occupants. Also available at many markets are plaster figures of the native household god Ekeko, a red-nosed grinning character who is believed to bring prosperity. During the Alacitas Fair, at the end of January, you can buy toy houses, sheep, or tiny airline tickets for this Bolivian version of Santa Claus – and he will grant you a real one before the year ends.

When visiting these markets, food turns out to be one of La Paz's most unexpected attractions. Street vendors sell papaya milkshakes, spiced chicken and rice, fried trout caught in Lake Titicaca or pieces of heart with hot nut sauces skewered on a wire. The markets near Plaza San Francisco have a particularly good range of delicacies, served by ladies grown large on their own cooking.

Bolivian folk musicians have penned many unforgettable tunes, including El Condor Pasa, *which became a huge hit for Simon and Garfunkel in the 1970s, and more recently, the* lambada.

BELOW: *cholas* (indigenous women of the city) selling vegetables.

Take a seat at one of the booths for tea and goat cheese in the early afternoon – the perfect vantage point to watch Bolivian life go by. Later on, a potent *chicha* (fermented maize drink) might be more appropriate, or the excellent local beer.

La Paz has an unusual collection of museums, such as the **Museo Murillo** on Calle Jaén, in an old mansion owned by one of the country's greatest heroes, Pedro Domingo Murillo, who led an unsuccessful revolt against the Spanish in 1809 and was hanged for his efforts. There is a good collection of colonial furniture and a room devoted to medicine and magic. In the same street, the **Museo de Litoral** has artifacts from the War of the Pacific, which deprived Bolivia of its only access to the sea. A defiant emblem over the cashier reads: "Bolivia Has Not Lost and Will Never Lose Its Right to the Pacific." The **Museo Nacional de Arte**, in the 18th-century baroque palace of the Count of Arana, near the cathedral at Calle Socabaya 432, has colonial and local paintings, and the **Museo Nacional de Etnografía y Folklore**, in the palace of the Marquis of Villaverde, Calle Ingavi 915, has good Ayoreo and Chipaya exhibits.

Beyond the city

La Paz is the perfect base for exploring the Bolivian highlands. The easiest excursion is to the **Valle de la Luna** (Valley of the Moon) **A**. Only 11 km (7 miles) from downtown La Paz in distance, but light years away in appearance, this is a bizarrely eroded hillside full of pinnacles and miniature canyons. Known technically as "badlands", its desert formations are constantly shifting and can be explored for hours.

Chacaltaya B, an hour and a half by bus from the city center, is the world's highest developed ski area. The ski slopes, at between 5,200 and 5,420 meters

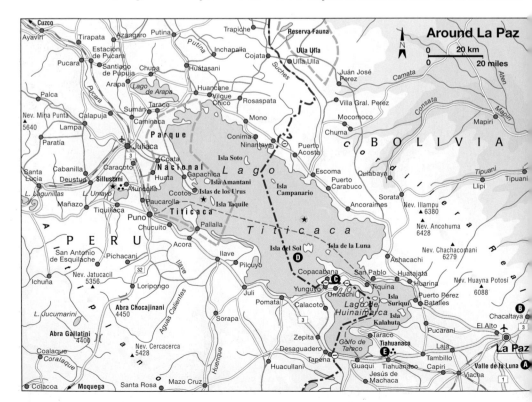

Map on page 180

(17,000 and 17,782 ft) above sea level, are definitely only for those acclimatized to the altitude. For those less interested in snow sports or who tire quickly at such dizzy heights, the peak still provides some spectacular views of the Andes.

Most visitors to La Paz use the opportunity to visit the Bolivian side of nearby **Lake Titicaca** *(see page 168)* the great high-altitude expanse of water shared with Peru. One easy excursion is to the small village of **Copacabana** , famous for its miracle-working Dark Virgin of the Lake, the patron saint of Bolivia. An image of the Virgin was taken to Río de Janeiro in the 19th century and the village later found itself giving its name to a Brazilian beach. The Bolivian Copacabana is a quiet and relaxing place, where visitors can stroll along the lakeside or loll in one of the many fish restaurants. But it comes alive during its fiestas, when the Virgin is paraded through the streets, a copious amount of alcohol is consumed and new buses and trucks are solemnly blessed with beer poured over their bonnets.

A boat trip to the lush and idyllic **Isla del Sol** (Island of the Sun) ❶ is well worth it. The sacred rock is where the Incas believed that their founding parents, Manco Capac and Mama Ocllo, emerged from the waters of Lake Titicaca at the call of the sun god. The Inca Utama Hotel and Spa and **Andean Roots Cultural Complex** is an oasis on the lakeshore at Huatajata, which provides a fascinating insight into the culture, lifestyle and values of the native Andean people.

Glimpses of an ancient civilization

The splendid ruins of **Tiahuanaco** ❷ *(see page 22)*, located on the southern tip of Lake Titicaca, are easily accessible from La Paz. This site is fast becoming one of the most important in South America. Tiahuanaco has a magnificently carved Gate of the Sun, the Acapana Pyramid, and chambers cut from stone with faces

BELOW: baptismal goods for sale, Copacabana

staring from the walls. For those who enjoyed their visit to the ruins, many of the finds are now housed in La Paz, in the **Museo Nacional de Arqueología** (located on the corner of Federico Zuazo and Tiwanaku streets).

Down to the valley

Sweeping down from the Andean heights near La Paz to Bolivia's steaming Amazon basin is the lush, sub-tropical region known as the **Yungas**. The combination of a warm climate with magnificent mountain views has made the zone a favorite for short visits from the capital and for the growing number of trekkers now flocking to Bolivia.

The Yungas – the name means "hot valleys" – is in a completely different climatic zone to the Bolivian capital, less than 100 km (60 miles) away on the bleak, barren *altiplano*. The drive from La Paz is one of the most spectacular in South America, going over a high-altitude mountain pass to dive into fertile valleys with drifting tropical mists, ancient Inca terraces, and abundant fruit.

At 1,500 meters (5,000 ft) above sea level, the small town of **Coroico** ❷ is the zone's main commercial center. Coroico itself is little more than a tidy main square surrounded by a few cheap restaurants and hotels. But there are plenty of tranquil walks in the dripping green countryside near the town, beyond the plantations growing coffee, coca, and bananas. The gentle strolls provide spectacular views of snow-capped mountain ranges on the horizon leading to jungle-covered valleys, as well as to several rivers for swimming. The best views of the Cordillera Real are from the little church located above the town, at the top of Cerro Uchumachi. Also worth a visit is the **Mothers of Clarissa Convent**, where the nuns make peanut butter, biscuits, and quite drinkable wine.

BELOW: llama traffic, Yungas.

The nearby towns of **Sorata** and **Chulumani** ❸ are equally relaxing places to visit – both are villages with small guesthouses and walks. The roads to both places are magnificent and Sorata in particular is said to have the most beautiful setting in Bolivia. A day hike from Sorata leads to the bat-filled **San Pedro cave**, or the more energetic can embark on the Mapiri trail, a strenuous eight day hike. Less adventurous spirits will be content with strolls through the flower-filled valleys that locals insist was the original site of the Garden of Eden.

Bolivia's "Inca Trail"

Coroico is enjoying a new popularity as a starting point and a goal for two popular treks, neither of which need any special experience to tackle. The most popular walk begins at **La Cumbre**, the highest point of the road from La Paz to the Yungas. It takes about four days, following an ancient Inca road that is in better repair than the path to Machu Picchu in Peru, though it lacks any sites as magnificent as the Inca ruins along the way.

Starting in the freezing and treeless heights, this path quickly descends into the more lush and habitable Yungas. Most walkers advance slowly at first, gasping in the thin mountain air and rhythmically plodding over the chilly pass. At this altitude, there are no signs of human habitation. But further into the valleys, small villages begin to appear, which are often inhabited by numerous yelping dogs but few people. More villagers can be seen walking along the path at lower altitudes, usually Bolivian women weighed down with sacks of potatoes or sticks. Finally the Inca path gives way to rough, landslide-prone Bolivian roads, where passing trucks head to the town of Coroico.

A popular trip for adrenaline-junkies is the 64-km (40-mile) downhill cycle ride from La Cumbre to Coroico. Following the road that plunges 5,000 metres (16,000 ft) 5 km provides thrilling gravity-assisted mountain biking.

The Gold-Diggers' Trail

Another trek begins where the last left off, in Coroico. Taking a road back into the mountains, the trail runs further down into the **Beni jungle** along the so-called "Gold-Diggers' Trail". It follows the **Tipuani Valley**, a region first fossicked by the Incas. They exhausted all the surface gold, which was used for ornamental purposes in their temples and art. Today thousands of Bolivians have tossed in their old lives in cities to try their luck in the jungle, and are now digging tunnels in the hope of instant wealth.

The trail once again follows an ancient Inca road, this time mossy and crumbling, through a beautiful landscape of jungle-clad mountains and dramatic gorges. Locals still use the trail today as a kind of highway. Residents come panting down the mountainside after trips to the capital carrying portable cassette decks and non-stick frying pans. It passes many small mining communities that can only be reached on foot, like the village of **Fátima**, put together from bamboo and corrugated iron only a few years ago.

The path ends at the hot and dusty town of **Guanay** ❹, a rather unsalubrious Amazon outpost. From Guanay there are buses back to Coroico and La Paz.

Map on page 174

BELOW: devil dancer in the *Diablada* parade, Oruro Fiesta,

Heading south: Bolivia's most famous fiesta

The town of **Oruro** ❺, 230 km (143 miles) south of La Paz, originally came to prominence as a mining town, but its mines are now redundant. Its past is remembered in the **Museo Etnográfico Minero**. Other places to visit include the **Casa de la Cultura**, a former residence of tin baron Simón Patiño, **Museo Antropológico** (ethnic history), and the **Museo Mineralógico** (minerals).

Oruro is best known today for its annual fiesta, **La Diablada**, the most famous in Bolivia, held eight days before Ash Wednesday. The celebrations begin the night before. At dawn on the big day, eager spectators take their places early, huddling against the cold mountain winds. Soon the street vendors are out in force, selling cans of beer. Older people turn up their noses at tinned drinks, preferring a more potent breakfast of *chicha*, the local maize beer. By 10am the crowd is ready for the Devil Dance.

Satan and Lucifer lead a procession of hundreds of dancing devils in fantastic outfits, leaping and pirouetting along the steep roads. Other dancers are dressed as pumas, monkeys, or insects. The lead is soon taken by China Supay, the Devil's wife, who tries to seduce the Archangel Michael with her wiles.

Some dancers dress as the Incas, in headdresses shaped like the condor, while others appear as black slaves brought over by the Spaniards, clanking through the streets in chains. Bolivian girls in pink and black mini-skirts bounce along the steep streets, dancing with men dressed as giant white bears. The procession ends up at a football stadium, where dancers perform two masques. The first is a re-enactment of the Spanish Conquest, performed, naturally enough, as a tragedy. In the second, the Archangel Michael defeats the forces of evil with his flaming sword, taking on the devils and the Seven Deadly Sins. The result is

BELOW: preparing for the procession at the Festival of Jesús, La Paz.

announced by the Virgen del Socavón, the patroness of miners, and the dancers enter a chapel to chant a hymn in Quechua.

Despite the Christian gloss over the proceedings, the Diablada is a pagan ceremony of thanks to Pachamama, "Earth Mother", to commemorate the struggle between the forces of good and evil. The conquering Spaniards were only able to convert the Amerindians superficially, changing a few names of deities to fit the formulae of the church. The *diablada* survived and grew during colonial times as an expression of the locals' frustration. The Europeans sat on their elegant balconies and looked on, while the subjected peoples were allowed their annual dose of freedom – an act of rebellion that became a safety valve.

Central city

Bolivia's third-largest city, **Cochabamba ❻**, 160 km (100 miles) east of Oruro, lies in a fertile area known as Bolivia's granary, at an altitude of 2,400 meters (9,200 ft). This city is an intriguing mix of old, entrenched tradition and burgeoning new energy. The heart of traditional Cochabamba revolves around the **Plaza 14 de Septiembre**, with its typical mélange of elegant and imposing edifices, street vendors, busy office workers and the more elevated personages, defiantly braving the cloying weather in wool and tweed. Notable buildings include the **Cathedral** and the colonial churches of **Santo Domingo** and **San Francisco**. In the evening, trendy bars and pizza restaurants around **Avenida España** fill with young people with disposable incomes. Out in the wealthy northern suburbs there are some unexpectedly snazzy office buildings, restaurants, and shopping malls, a world away from the gently decaying city center.

Tin baron Simón Patiño left his mark on Cochabamba in the form of the

Llama fetuses and other fetishes are sold in street markets all over Bolivia.

BELOW: yet another bus breakdown.

Palacio de Portales, built between 1915 and 1925 – all the furniture was imported from Europe. The **Museo Arqueológico** has an excellent selection of pre-Columbian artifacts dating back to 15,000BC.

Just south of the city center, perched on a hill, the **Heroínas de la Coronilla** monument commemorates the female independence fighters who defended Cochabamba from Spanish forces in 1812. East of the city center, at the end of Avenida de las Heroínas, a statue of Christ stands atop the **Cerro San Pedro**.

There are a number of Inca ruins in the vicinity of Cochabamba, and though none rival Machu Picchu or Tiahuanaco, they are worth visiting. **Inkallajta**, described as the "frontier post of the Inca Empire", is an extensive site located on a turn-off from the old Cochabamba–Santa Cruz road. If you don't have your own transport, you may well have difficulty finding someone to take you there; however, there are some guided tours available. **Inka Rakay**, 27 km (17 miles) west of Cochabamba, is better known for the wonderful views of the Cochabamba Valley than for the ruins themselves.

Along the Río Mamoré

Puerto Villaroel ❼ is the departure point for boats heading north to Guayaramerín on the Río Mamoré. It's a cozy little village where everyone seems to know everyone else, and from **Ivirgazama** (last opportunity for river trippers to purchase mosquito nets and hammocks) the road becomes a dirt track. **Trinidad ❽**, in the heart of the Bolivian Amazon, is the capital of Beni Province, with airport connections to Cochabamba and La Paz. The **Laguna Suárez**, 5 km (3 miles) away, is a popular wildlife-spotting and rest spot. Wildlife can also be seen at **Chuchini**, 17 km (11 miles) from Trinidad.

LEFT: open-air transport.
RIGHT: *campesinas* in their distinctive dress.

Chuchini has an archeological museum displaying remnants of the ancient Beni culture. The 300-km (200-mile) trip along the Río Mamoré to **Guayaramerín** takes three or four days. This bustling frontier town at the northern tip of the country is split by the river. The Brazilian side is known as Guajará-Mirim. The Bolivian side is an incongruous mix of dusty backstreets and brash duty-free shops selling perfume, jeans, and flashy electronic goods.

Riberalta ⑩, three hours away by bus, is a pleasant, slow-paced and friendly little town, with a cluster of low-key restaurants grouped around the main plaza, ideally placed for perusing the town's social circuit. Towards dusk, motorbikes begin to trundle around the square. Once an important river port, since the road to La Paz was constructed, Riberolta's significance has declined.

It is possible to travel between Riberalta and **Rurrenabaque** ⑪ by boat along the Río Beni, but you'll probably have a long wait for a boat. Boat traffic suffered due to the construction of a road link. However, the road is unsurfaced and can be a very sticky experience, especially during the rainy season – be warned. Rurrenabaque is a very pretty small town that has been enjoying a tourist boom due to its lush rainforest location, which makes it an ideal center for jungle and pampas expeditions and boat trips on the Beni and Tuichi rivers. The town has some good restaurants and abundant low-budget accommodation.

The Oriente and Bolivia's official capital

The city of **Sucre** ⑫, 600 km (370 miles) southeast of La Paz, is Bolivia's official capital, although much government business is based in the big city on the

BELOW: barges on the Río Mamoré, Trinidad.

GENTLY DOWN THE STREAM

Taking a river boat trip is one of the best ways to sample real Bolivian life. But be warned – if bucket toilets and tummy troubles give you nightmares, this is definitely not the trip for you! Barges chug up and down Bolivia's Río Mamoré from Puerto Villaroel to Guayaramerin on the Bolivia-Brazil border, delivering fuel and fruit. Bookings are informal – ask around in the village of Puerto Villaroel and people will tell you if a boat is due to leave. If you're in luck, it will have room for passengers. The most important things to bring with you are a mosquito net, hammock, and binoculars – beds may be in short supply. It's also a good idea to bring food and water, as supplies of these may be limited too. There may be occasional trading trips to jungle villages along the river bank, but passengers are not always taken along.

Don't expect any cruise-style entertainment either – you have to find your own way to fill the days. This is not as difficult as it might initially seem – you can catch up on your reading, chat to the crew and polish up your Spanish or Quechua as well as doing a bit of bird-watching or dolphin-spotting. At dusk, if the weather is clear, find a comfortable spot on deck, lie back, and prepare yourself for a truly star-studded evening's entertainment!

Coca Leaves

To the outside world, the small green coca leaf is best known as the raw material for cocaine. But in the highlands of Peru, Bolivia, and Ecuador, it has been part of Amerindian culture for more than 4,000 years. Coca leaves are on sale in any mountain town market. Ask at a café for *maté de coca*, and you will get a hot, refreshing drink of coca tea, said to be the best cure for *soroche* (altitude sickness).

Some three million South Americans chew coca regularly, adding a little bicarbonate of soda to get the saliva going. It gives energy and dulls the senses against cold. Miners chew up to 1 kg (2.2 lb) a day.

Coca is used at every stage of life. Before giving birth, a woman chews the leaves to hasten labor and ease the pain. Relatives celebrate the birth by chewing the leaf together. When a young man wants to marry a girl, he offers her father coca. When somebody dies, *maté de coca* is drunk at the wake and a

small pile of leaves is placed in the coffin. Local *yatiris* (soothsayers) use coca to tell the future, after scattering the leaves over a woolen blanket and reciting a prayer.

Coca was first cultivated in the Andes around 2,000 BC. Three millennia later, the Incas turned its production into a monopoly – just one more way to control the population. Its use was restricted to royalty, priests, doctors, and the empire's messenger runners, known to travel up to 250 km (150 miles) a day aided by chewing the leaves.

By the arrival of the first Europeans, the Incas had relaxed their monopoly on coca and its use had spread beyond their empire. Italian explorer Amerigo Vespucci, arriving in the Caribbean in 1499, noted with distaste that the islanders "each had their cheeks bulging with a certain green herb which they chewed like cattle." But within months of Pizarro's arrival at Cuzco in 1533, he found some of his own men secretly chewing coca.

The Catholic church first tried to ban coca chewing, denouncing it as "the delusion of the devil." They quickly changed their tune when it was found that Amerindians needed it to survive the brutal conditions in colonial mines and plantations. To keep the captive labor force under control, the church then went into the coca business itself.

Coca was almost unheard of in Europe and the United States until the mid-1800s, when Parisian chemist Angelo Mariani marketed a wine made from the leaf. Immensely popular, this *Vin Mariani* quickly inspired several American soft drink companies to produce drinks based on coca.

At the same time, cocaine was first being developed. It was quickly taken up by such luminaries as Sigmund Freud, who called it a "magical substance." Sir Arthur Conan Doyle wrote of his fictional character Sherlock Holmes regularly partaking of cocaine. But moves were already afoot to ban the drug.

Scientists agree that there are no dangers in chewing the leaf, nor is it addictive, but because of its association with cocaine, coca leaves are banned in most countries. Taking home just a strip of coca leaf chewing gum or a coca teabag could get you into trouble. ❑

LEFT: bags of coca leaves, commonly seen at Bolivian markets.

Map on page 174

altiplano. Sucre is a small, elegant city of great historical significance. Notable buildings around the **Plaza 25 de Mayo** include the **Casa de la Libertad** where Bolivia's declaration of independence was signed, and the **Cathedral**, with nearby Museo de la Catedral. The city has many interesting religious buildings, including the churches of San Miguel, San Francisco and Merced, and the Convento de San Felipe Neri. The Franciscan monastery of La Recoleta and its museum are on top of the Cerro Dalence hill to the southeast of Sucre, and afford excellent views of the city. There is also a Natural History Museum and the very interesting **Museo Textil Etnográfico** (San Alberto 413), which displays Andean textiles traditionally woven from llama and alpaca wool. Some 5 km (3 miles) south of the city, the **Castillo de la Glorieta** was built in a mixture of European styles by the Argandoña family.

Traditional textiles can be purchased at the typically Andean village of **Tarabuco**, 65 km (40 miles) east of Sucre, which is renowned for its weaving. South of Sucre is the Cordillera de los Frailes mountain range, with trekking, rock paintings, and hot springs. Dinosaur bones have been found at **Cal Orko**, 7 km (4½ miles) from Sucre (guided tours to see them are available from Sucre). Che Guevara memorial tours are also available in Sucre, visiting some of the locations the revolutionary passed through on his final journey, including the small village of **La Higuera**, where he was killed.

Some 500 km (300 miles) east of Cochabamba is **Santa Cruz** ⓭, Bolivia's boomtown. Its first, shortlived boom came from rubber in the late 19th century. The current growth spurt was encouraged by a government-led "March to the East" from the 1950s and has been powered by petroleum and tropical lowland crops like soybeans, sugar, rice, cotton, and last but not least, cocaine. Santa Cruz is not a popular tourist destination, though it does have some interesting museums and a rich ethnic mix due to the numbers of people who swarmed to the city to take advantage of its economic success. There is a sizeable Japanese community and a strong Andean cultural presence, with *peñas* and an abundance of nightclubs and karaoke bars. Santa Cruz is linked by rail to Brazil and Argentina – a journey that is best described as an endurance test.

City of silver

Perched at 4,000 meters (13,000 ft) above sea level in the shadow of a cursed mountain, **Potosí** ⓮ is located in the south west of Bolivia, 550 km (340 miles) southeast of La Paz. It is the highest city of its size in the world, and was built in this inhospitable location by Spanish conquistadors for just one purpose: silver mining. Today, Potosí is only a shadow of its former self – during the 1600s it was as large as London and many times more opulent. Nevertheless, anyone visiting Bolivia should make the journey to this remote Andean city. Not only is it one of the least-touched colonial cities on the continent and a World Heritage Site, but it has become, for many, a symbol of Latin America's fate, and shows that the richest regions in colonial times tend to be the poorest today.

In 1967 the hero of the Cuban revolution, Che Guevara, was hunted down and killed in eastern Bolivia, where he was trying to incite the campesinos to rise in revolution.

BELOW: entrance to the Casa de Moneda, Spain's New World mint, Potosí

"As rich as a Potosí"

Appropriately, **El Cerro Rico** (Rich Hill) is always visible from the city's streets. The Incas had known that there was silver in the bare red mountain but did nothing to exploit it. The Spaniards, however, were quick to begin mining, soon discovering that the hill held the largest silver deposit the world had ever seen. A frontier city was quickly created on the bleak mountainside, with conquistadors and missionaries flocking from Spain to win a slice of the fantastic wealth. Local Amerindians were press-ganged to work in the mines, dying by the thousands in horrific conditions.

Even today, people in Spain use the phrase "as rich as a Potosí" when they try to describe an unimaginable fortune. The city's churches were built with silver altars and the lavish feasts of Spanish nobles glittered with the precious metal. Even the horses were said to be shod with silver in Potosí. When the silver gave out, and the Spaniards left, the city survived on tin mining. Now tin is almost worthless, and Potosí has become a fascinating relic.

Testimony to the former riches are the scattered crumbling villas, stone carved doorways and forgotten abbeys of the city. Ancient houses teeter from both sides to nearly meet in the middle of narrow, winding streets. Potosí is still crowded with masterpieces of colonial architecture and artworks blending the styles of medieval Europe and pre-Conquest South America.

Potosí's most impressive building, considered one of the finest examples of Spanish civil construction in Latin America, is the **Casa Real de Moneda**. First built in 1542 and reconstructed in 1759, it was used as a mint by the colonizers. Now a museum, it has rooms full of religious art, collections of colonial coins, and the original wooden minting machines once worked by African slaves.

BELOW: Tarabuco festival.

Guided tours take up to three hours to work through the many exhibits, which contain anything from altars removed from collapsed churches to relics of Bolivia's foreign wars. One of the prize displays is a pair of iron strong boxes used to transport silver from the New World to Spain, using no less than 15 locks to secure them, while a huge gallery makes a valiant, but still incomplete attempt to provide portraits of the country's many presidents. Wear plenty of warm clothes, as the museum is like a refrigerator inside.

Many of Potosí's churches are crumbling into disrepair – in fact, some are dangerously close to collapse. A stroll through the city will take you past **San Francisco**, **La Compania**, and **San Lorenzo**, as well as the **Cathedral** and **Cabildo** (the town council) in the main plaza. Wandering through the town, look out for old mansions such as the **Casa de las Tres Portadas** on Calle Bolivar 19–21 and the **Crystal Palace** at Calle Sucre 148–56.

A city drained of its wealth

Potosí is much more than a collection of ruined colonial buildings. Many of the Andean Amerindians in the area live in a way that has changed little over the centuries. The **Town Market** is a fascinating place to explore, full of women selling produce and butchers carrying whole animal carcasses over their shoulders – usually covered in flies and with the beast's hairy tail still dangling from the meat. But there are few signs of the city's past wealth. The poorest parts of the city, closer to the Rich Hill, were traditionally occupied by miners and their families. A monument to the Bolivian miner has been set up in one of the squares. The mining unions of Potosí and Oruro, once the most powerful force in Bolivian politics, were all but destroyed

Map on page 174

TIP

At more than 4,200 meters (13,780 ft) above sea level, it's a good idea to acclimatize to Potosí's altitude with a day or two of relaxation around the city before you expose your lungs to the exertion of a trip down the mines.

BELOW: Cerro Rico, Potosí.

Miners' shrine to El Tío, Potosí.

with the collapse of tin prices in the 1980s. There are few mines in operation these days, and unemployment stalks the streets. The wealth of Potosí proved a curse that is still with the indigenous population today. The city which helped finance the economic development of Europe in centuries gone by has slid deeper into Third World oblivion.

Realm of the Devil

Deep in the heart of Potosí's "Rich Hill", dust-covered miners were laughing with the Devil. Chewing coca leaves in a candlelit recess full of putrid air, they paid their respects to a small horned statue, the perceived owner of the silver beneath the ground. The miners visit El Tío – "the Old Fellow" – every day to leave a drink or burn a cigarette for luck. "El Tío has always liked tobacco," joked one of the miners, "but these days he only accepts filter tips."

The image of the Devil in the Incarnación mine was made 300 years ago by Amerindian slaves press-ganged by the Spanish to dig silver in Potosí. Shockingly, working conditions in the mines have changed little since those days. With the collapse of the tin market in 1985, the state mines of Cerro Rico were closed, but since then Bolivian miners have been re-opening old shafts to find the silver that the conquistadors left behind. The digging is being carried out in such a primitive and dangerous fashion that many miners accept their work as a kind of death sentence.

Every day at dawn, the miners gather outside the mines on El Cerro Rico. The mountain that once held the world's greatest silver deposit is now a giant slag heap, an unnaturally symmetrical peak riddled with more than 5,000 shafts.

BELOW: mining in 18th-century conditions, Potosí.

Inside a mine in Cerro Rico

There are several private mines still operating, to which guides from the city will bring visitors for a small fee. Most people bring a few packets of cigarettes to share with the miners as they spend the first hour of their day sitting in the cold sun, chatting and chewing coca leaves, which have been in use long before the Incas to ward off hunger and fatigue.

Visiting a mine is absolutely not for asthma sufferers or those not acclimatized to the altitude. Claustrophobics won't like it either – you need to crouch just to enter the mouth of the tunnels, while the miners' antique carbide lamps barely dent the darkness.

Ancient wooden shaft supports often sag in the middle. Stalactites hang from the rough walls of the tunnel near its mouth, but as the mine descends into the mountain, polar cold shifts to sub-tropical heat. Many of the shafts can only be passed on hands and knees. The air becomes thick and stale. Workers from the last shift become visible down cracks, stripped to the waist and hacking away with picks.

There are no power tools and no engineers in these mines. Blasting is done with dynamite bought in the supply store in Potosí, and the miners simply withdraw around a corner as the charge goes off. Each worker keeps the ore he finds himself. Miners on the lowest levels must climb long ladders to the surface with sacks of rocks on their backs.

Map on page 174

The real enemy here is silicosis, caused by fine dust gathering in the miners' lungs. Within a few years of entering the pit, many feel a heavy weight on their chests. A few years later, they die coughing blood. Little wonder that tradition holds the metals of Potosí to be the property of the Devil, or that the miners give El Tío his daily cigarette for luck.

Group tours lasting four to five hours are organized by recognized guides. Put on your old clothes and take a handkerchief to keep out the dust. A helmet and lamp will be provided. Apart from the cost of the tour, a donation to the miners' cooperative would be appreciated.

Lake district with a difference

In the west, near the frontier with Chile, is one of Bolivia's most popular tourist destinations. The **Salar de Uyuni** is said to be the largest salt lake in the world, at 10,500 sq. km (4,054 sq. miles). More desert than lake, it's an eerie sight, lying 3,653 meters (11,985 ft) above sea level – bring plenty of warm clothes, as temperatures can plummet at this altitude. Also don't forget sunglasses as the sun reflection on the salt can burn your eyes. There is accommodation available in the town of **Uyuni** ⓯, including the Hotel Playa Blanca, which is built out of salt. Tours of the area can also be arranged from Potosí or Sucre. Most tours include the option of visiting **Laguna Colorada**, a bright red lake patronized by pink flamingoes that lies 346 km (215 miles) southwest of Uyuni, and **Laguna Verde**, a chilly aquamarine lake at 5,000 meters (16,400 ft) above sea level. Other attractions in the area close to the Chilean border include geysers at Sol de Mañana and hot springs at Aguas Termales Chalviri. ❑

BELOW: salt mining, Uyuni salt bushi.

ECUADOR

Despite being one of the smallest South American countries, Ecuador has plenty of attractions: smoldering volcanoes, rainforest reserves, Amerindian markets and, of course, the Galápagos islands

Map on page 198

Ecuador is one of the easiest and most rewarding countries to explore in South America. Small (just 283,500 sq. km/110 sq. miles) but geographically varied, Ecuador's incredible natural diversity has made it the focus of worldwide biological research. The country has more species of plants (25,000) and birds (over 1,500) than the United States, which is 34 times larger. Sadly, these precious ecosystems are being degraded by a rate of deforestation higher than any nation in South America (280,000 hectares/692,000 acres per annum), but INEFAN, the Ecuadorian National Park Service, with the help of national and international conservation organizations, currently protects 17 percent of the total landmass in national parks and ecological reserves. For a developing nation with a per capita GDP (Gross Domestic Product) of US$2,160 these conservation efforts are admirable.

Outdoor activities are Ecuador's biggest tourist draw. Within a day's drive or flight from the capital city of Quito you can experience virgin Amazon jungle, snow-capped peaks, tropical sandy beaches, and Darwin's Galápagos Islands. Outfitters are set up for mountaineering, trekking, jungle canoe trips, mountain biking, rafting, paraskiing, scuba diving, and horseback riding.

Eight active volcanoes periodically erupt, spewing columns of ash and melting glaciers that cause mud flows to destroy Sierran villages. When the Andes are uplifted along geological faults from the coastal plain, powerful earthquakes can shake the hillsides. A costly earthquake in 1987 broke the trans-Andean oil pipeline in several places, crippling the national economy for six months. Landslides are common during the rainy season, closing roads. Floods due to El Niño in 1982–83 and 1997–98 virtually paralyzed coastal communities.

But Ecuadorians have a tremendous capacity to bounce back and rebuild their country. The tradition of the *minga* (an obligatory community work project), inherited from the Incas, continues to draw citizens together to overcome the challenges of nature and political and economic turmoil.

A nation in movement

Although the country is traditionally divided into four regions – Sierra, Coast, Oriente, and Galápagos – these regions blend at the margins to form a rich mosaic. Perhaps most telling of Ecuador's identity is the flow of goods and people between regions. Trucks filled with *plátanos* (green bananas) daily climb the cloud forests of the western slope of the Sierra to stock Quito's cool open-air markets, while sacks filled with endemic varieties of potatoes are transported down to the hot and humid *barrios* of Guayaquil. The Oriente pumps vital oil exports through a pipeline

PRECEDING PAGES:
Zumbagua market.
LEFT: Mount Sangay eruption.
BELOW: reveler in the Mamá Negra parade, Latacunga.

*The important Inca
sun god Inti is often
subtly portrayed in
religious colonial
art, and in return the
Catholic celebration
for Saint Peter is
associated with the
Inti Raymi festival
(Winter Solstice).*

which crosses the Andes to tankers docked at the port city of Esmeraldas. It is
not uncommon to see a colorfully dressed highland *Otavaleño* on the coast selling woven goods, as well as a coastal *moreno* (Afro-Ecuadorian) on a bus on the
Pan-American highway offering traditional homemade *cocada* (coconut candy).

The majority of Ecuadorians are Catholics but there is a growing number of
Protestants (now estimated at more than 10 percent), due to missionary efforts
which began after freedom of religion was guaranteed in 1945. Pre-colonial
indigenous religions are rarely practiced in their pure forms except in isolated
pockets in the Oriente, but elements are incorporated into modern Christianity.

Pre-Inca civilizations

In the 10th century AD, the Caras – forefathers of the modern *Otavaleños (see
page 202)* – settled in the Quito area. They built an observatory to mark the
solstices, and identified the equator as "the path of the sun." They were animists
who worshiped the sun, and believed the moon to be inhabited by humans.

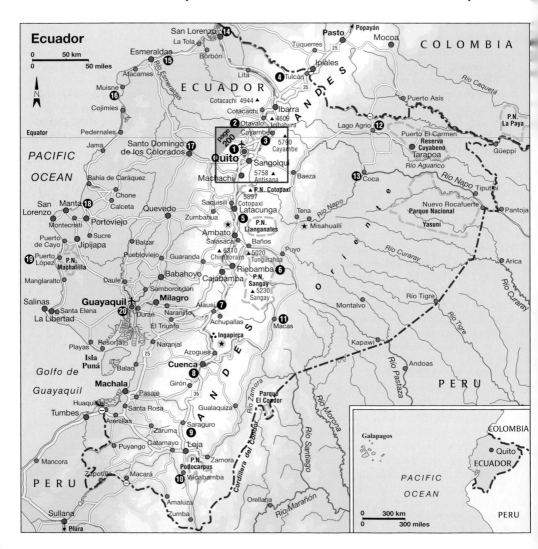

Their economy was based on weaving, and the law required women to spin wool whenever possible, even when walking mountain trails.

Their successors were the Duchicela dynasty, who established the powerful Kingdom of Quitu, which was eventually conquered by the Inca Tupac-Yupanqui. Ecuador soon played an important part in the collapse of the Inca Empire *(see page 26)*, with the execution of the Inca Atahuallpa by the Spaniard Francisco Pizarro. While Pizarro plundered, his lieutenant Sebastián de Benalcázar battled northward to the city of Quito. Arriving in late 1534, he found the city in ruins: Rumiñahui, Atahuallpa's general, had destroyed and evacuated it rather than lose it intact to the Spaniards. Benalcázar refounded Quito on December 6, 1534. Rumiñahui was captured, tortured, and executed the following month.

Ecuador was initially administered by the Spanish as a province of the Vice-Royalty of Peru, and was the site of the first cultivation of wheat and bananas in South America. Colonial administration was based on the *encomienda* system, which was preserved after independence in the form of huge estates or *latifundis* owned by a tiny percentage of Ecuador's wealthiest *criollo* families. The injustices of Spanish rule prompted several violent uprisings. The first of these was the so-called Alcabalas Revolution of 1592–93, when the populace, with the active support of the lower clergy, rebelled against increased taxes on food and fabrics. The reprisals were brutal.

Land reforms were not enacted until 1964, freeing the indigenous population from compulsory agricultural labor. Often, however, it was the most unproductive land which was redistributed, and many *haciendas* (ranches) remained intact, governments being reluctant to attack the wealthiest and most powerful class, the landowners.

Map on page 198

BELOW: Spanish engraving of conquistadors on the march.

The first president of Ecuador, Juan Jos Flores, arranged with his successor, Rocafuerte, to alternate occupancy of the presidency, but then broke the deal, retained control of the army, and bribed Rocafuerte into exile. Finally ousted in 1845, he organized a Spanish invasion of Ecuador which was only averted by Great Britain's intervention. National development since then has been sporadic. Two of the best-remembered presidents, Moreno and Alfaro, were both assassinated.

Stumbling through the 20th century

Twentieth-century Ecuador experienced mainly military rule, the last period of which was from 1972–79. In 1978, the army drew up a new constitution and an election was held the following year. Ecuador became the first Latin American country to return to democracy after the military era that engulfed most of South America during the 1970s, and national politics have since been stable.

Girl from Esperanza.

León Febres Cordero, a Conservative elected in 1984, was kidnapped by troops loyal to a high-ranking general who was in jail for attempting two coups. Febres secured his release after just 11 hours, by granting the general an amnesty. Elections in 1988 brought to power President Rodrigo Borja Cevallos, a Social Democrat who boosted the tourist trade and lowered inflation. Such trends continued under his successor, Sixto Duran Ballen, of the Christian Social Party, who introduced an unpopular privatization program. Many people were surprised that Abdala Bucaram, "El Loco" (the Crazy One), was elected in 1996. The corrupt Bucaram was ousted in February, 1997, after thousands marched through the streets demanding his impeachment. After the interim president, Fabián Alarcón, was democratically installed by the congress, in 1988, Jamil Mahuad of the Popular Democracy Party was elected as president and the new constitution came into effect. Mahuad

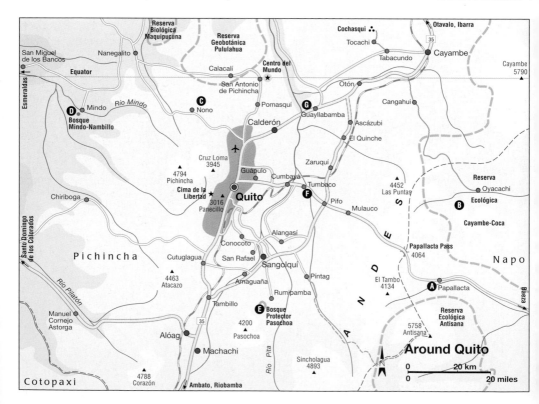

concluded peace with Peru in October 1998, but his popularity fell due to economic difficulties and in 2000 he fled as thousands of indigenous protesters stormed the Congress Building. Power was ceded to the Vice President, Gustavo Noboa, who faced a radicalized indigenous movement and the country's worst economic crisis in 70 years. Soon afterwards, the sucre was replaced by the US dollar as the official currency. Ecuador's economy has been transformed by low inflation and millions of dollars of foreign investment in oil exploration and production. However, many Ecuadoreans have felt no benefit from the recovery. In late 2002 Leftist and former coup leader Lucio Gutierrez won the presidential election. In 2003, the second transandean oil pipeline was completed and Gutierrez pledged to pay off foreign debt with the increased revenue. He signed a US$205 million loan with the IMF and in 2004 was met with widespread protests and demands for his resignation.

Map on page 198

Quito: Ecuador's expanding capital

Modern **Quito ❶** spreads north and south into the intra-Andean valley each year, gobbling up rural farms. Most visitors stay in the **Mariscal** neighborhood, north of **Parque El Ejido**, where old Quito meets new, as the city's old colonial center is more pleasant to explore than the polluted modern sprawl. Hotels, restaurants, and stores bulging with handicrafts line **Avenida Amazonas** and nearby streets.

La Casa de la Cultura housing the **Museo del Banco Central**, just off Parque El Ejido, is Ecuador's most comprehensive museum, with pre-Columbian treasures and ornate gold, along with republican, colonial, and modern art. Rivaling this is the smaller **Museo Guayasamín** in the Bellavista neighborhood. Oswaldo Guayasamín, Ecuador's most renowned painter *(see page 63)*, displays his bold portraits of indigenous people and his collection of pre-Columbian artifacts.

BELOW: Quito's modern district.

The Otavaleños

O tavalo is a modern miracle of economic achievement that grew out of colonial oppression. Forced to become weavers by the Spanish, about half of Ecuador's *Otavaleño* people are today involved in weaving, which has made them the most prosperous indigenous group in Ecuador, possibly in all of South America.

Otavalo lies betwen Quito and the Colombian border. There are expatriate communities in Colombia, Brazil, and Spain. They export their fine-quality textiles to the United States, Canada, and Europe, while the bulk of their business remains in South America.

The modern *Otavaleños* are descended from the Cara tribe, which expanded from Colombia to the Ecuadorian sierra about 1,000 years ago. The Cara established trade links with neighboring tribes, and bartered cotton and blankets, along with dogs and salt, in exchange for *achiote* (a plant from which dyes are extracted), parrots, and mon-

keys. The arrival of the Incas in the late 1400s marked the beginning of 500 years of colonization and imposed labor and beliefs. After 17 years of fighting, the Inca Huayna Capac took Caranqui and massacred thousands of Cara. Large numbers of Cara were transported to Peru, while loyal Inca subjects were settled on Cara territory. The Incas introduced coca and llamas, an excellent source of wool, but they were too short-lived to seriously influence *Otavaleño* culture.

Under the Spanish, the *encomienda* system was established in Otavalo, putting Spanish settlers in control of an area and its indigenous inhabitants. The first weaving *obraje* (workshop) was set up in the 1550s with 500 workers, some as young as nine years old. Modern tools were introduced and within 50 years the Otavalo *obraje* was the most productive in Ecuador. *Otavaleños* labored 14 hours a day manufacturing cloth, woolen blankets, and rope for export. In 1648 an *obraje* in Peguche was closed, because the number of suicides among workers had grown to alarming proportions.

The *Otavaleños* were forced to learn Spanish to facilitate their conversion to Christianity, although their Catholicism today incorporates ancestral beliefs.

Land reforms enacted in Ecuador in 1964 abolished the *wasipungo* system, based on enforced indigenous labor. The first store selling woven products opened in Otavalo in 1966, and within a dozen years there were 75. Weaving has decentralized from the savage *obrajes* and is now a cottage industry. Over the years, the ingenuity of the Otavalo weavers has brought them worldwide fame.

Every Saturday morning, the usually quiet streets of Otavalo teem with the life. By 9am Market Square, known as Poncho Plaza, is a feast of colors and textures: rolls of cloth, thick blankets, tapestry wall hangings, chunky sweaters, long patterned belts or *fajas,* and *cintas* – tapes the women use to bind their long hair. Most *Otavaleño* textiles are made of sheep wool, though some *alpaca* sweaters can be found. The mechanization of the modern textile industry, potentially disastrous for the *Otavaleños*, has been compensated by tourism and an emphasis on quality goods produced naturally.   ❑

LEFT: an *Otavaleña* displaying her wares.

Map on page 198

Back down the hill, fast food joints, shopping malls and trilling cellphones are evidence of the Ecuadorian middle-class fascination with American culture. Quito has a selection of international restaurants, folkloric ballet shows, and salsa bars.

Further north, 24 km (15 miles) out of Quito, the **Centro del Mundo** (middle of the world) monument marks the equator. Here you can straddle the equator with feet planted in both hemispheres. The obelisk houses a museum with displays of the different ethnic cultures of Ecuador.

Old Quito: a walking tour

Old Quito displays Spanish colonial architecture at its finest. Walls of brilliant whitewash, deep blue railings and green tile rooftops dazzle the eye, reminiscent of a period when the city was a peaceful provincial capital. Earthquakes in 1587, 1768, and 1859 caused severe damage to many churches, but nevertheless there are still 87. In 1978, UNESCO declared Old Quito a World Heritage Site.

The Spanish past blends with modern cultural migration as members of Ecuador's many ethnic groups make Quito their home. Life on colorful **Calle Cuenca** contrasts with the city's relative affluence. Fleshy black women sell tropical fruits, while an indigenous newspaper vendor with a baby at her breast cries "Comercio, hoy!" in a nasal refrain. Above it all stands the church of **San Francisco**, the first major religious construction in the continent and the spiritual heart of the city. Begun a few days after Spanish settlement in 1534, it took 70 years to complete. The creaking wooden floor contrasts with the spectacular baroque carvings and the statue of **Our Lady of Quito**, a fine example of the "Quito school of art", blending Spanish and Moorish techniques with the indigenous imagination.

Statue of the Virgin, Panecillo, Quito.

BELOW: the Plaza de la Independencia, Quito.

Corn on the cob sculpture, Quito.

BELOW: interior of the lavish church of La Compañía.

From San Francisco, it is a short walk through the clothes market on Calle Cuenca to **La Merced**, which contains paintings depicting scenes from Quito's past: Sucre riding gloriously into battle, volcanoes erupting, and suspiciously docile Amerindians being converted. Two blocks away is the **Plaza de la Independencia**, where the heroes of 1809 are immortalized. Today, *Quiteños* sun themselves, read the morning newspapers, and put the swarming shoeshine boys to work.

The **Palacio de Gobierno** (Presidential Palace) has traditional guards and a mural by Guayasamín depicting Orellana's descent of the Amazon. The adjacent **Cathedral**, finished in 1706, is where Ecuador's illustrious lie, including Sucre. Among its collection of paintings is the *Descent From The Cross* by Caspicara, perhaps colonial Ecuador's best indigenous artist.

One block south of the church of **San Augustín**, where the first declaration of independence was signed, is the pedestrian thoroughfare **Calle Eugenio Espejo**. Nearby is the magnificent **La Compañía**, built by the Jesuits between 1605 and 1768. Containing an estimated seven tons of gold, it is Ecuador's most ornate church. The remains of the *Quiteño* saint Mariana de Jesus lie beneath the solid gold main altar, and there is a bizarre collection of colonial art: one painting graphically depicts the grades of punishment reserved for sinners in Hell, with the most unpleasant fate reserved for adulterers and fornicators.

From 1828 until his death in Colombia two years later, Sucre lived a block from here: his house, the **Casa de Sucre Museo Histórico**, affords a rare glimpse of period aristocratic home life. A statue of Sucre occupies the Plaza of Santo Domingo, opposite the church of the same name, which is best seen at night when its domes are floodlit. Inside is an altar to St Judas, patron saint of "desperate causes," where satisfied worshipers have posted "thank you" notices.

TAKING THE TRAIN

Rail travel began in Ecuador in 1910, when the line between Quito and Guayaquil opened, reducing to two days a former nine-day trek along a mule path which was impassable for half the year due to rain. The train rattles along the "Avenue of the Volcanoes" from Quito as far as Riobamba, before descending a series of marvelously engineered switchbacks, which allow breathtaking views of the western Andean slopes. Fields of potatoes and corn give way to tropical lowlands.

The northern line starts in Ibarra, a sleepy, provincial mountain town, ending 193 km (120 miles) and anything between 7 and 10 days later in the lively port city of San Lorenzo in the north west. The train descends from rugged, dry scrubland to fields of sugar cane and coffee, papaya, and bananas, and through dense rainforest.

The Riobamba–Guayaquil and "Devil's Nose" section is the most popular route, where travelers sit on the roof or rub shoulders with farmers and their livestock inside open-sided trains trundling slowly through narrow valleys. Trains leave Riobamba on Wednesdays, Fridays and Sundays at 7am

Note that all railway lines are subject to disruption and closure because of frequent flooding and landslides.

The best-preserved colonial street is **Calle Ronda**, south of Plaza Santa Domingo, which is entered down a ramp at the motley open-air market on Avenida 24 de Mayo. A quiet, narrow, cobbled lane, it is lined with 16th-century houses with overhanging balconies and heavy grilled doors. This brings you to the **Bridge of the Black Vultures**, where you can climb to the Virgin of Quito at the summit of **El Panecillo** (Little Bread Roll), with sweeping views of the valley and, on a clear day, the peaks of **Pichincha** and **Cayambe**.

The **Sierra** is actually two mountain ranges (Western and Eastern Cordilleras) divided by a series of central valleys running north–south. The major highland cities are spaced along the Pan-American Highway in these valleys, 2,000–3,000 meters (6,500–9,800 ft) above sea-level, and are blessed with temperate climates. This beautiful patchwork of fields is very productive due to rich volcanic soils and little variation in air temperatures. The flat lowland plains are intensely farmed by modern methods, especially for the booming flower export industry. In the past few years, hundreds of automated greenhouses have been constructed to feed the world's demand for roses and carnations.

The steep hillsides above the valley floor are owned by Quichua indigenous cooperatives, working small parcels of land, which tractors could never till, with hand tools. Their crops of potatoes, carrots, beans, wheat, and corn supply 75 percent of Ecuador's needs. Above are the cold, windswept *páramos* (alpine grasslands), home to grazing horses, cattle, and sheep. Still higher, the craggy and glaciated volcanic peaks that dominate the skyline are home to some of the few remaining Andean condors, which share it with intrepid mountaineers.

Excursions near Quito

The main road to the Oriente climbs to the continental divide at the headwaters of the Amazon basin. The village of **Papallacta** is located below the pass. Here you will find tastefully constructed thermal spring pools surrounded by lush cloudforest. The area is also known for some of the country's best fresh trout, introduced from North American stock. *Quiteños* escape here on the weekends for walks or horseback rides in the nearby **Cayambe–Coca Ecological Reserve B**.

Toward the coast, two hours by bus from Quito, are **Nono C**, **Tandayapa** and **Mindo D**, villages that are becoming favorite birding spots. Private reserves and lodges have been set up to cater for visitors keen on exploring the forests. The **Bosque Protector Pasochoa E** (contact Fundación Natura, at República 481 and Almagro, Quito, tel: 503385, for excursions) is a pleasant nature reserve southeast of Quito. Some of the last intra-Andean cloudforest is protected on the slopes of the ancient volcano. Native trees and plants thrive on the rich volcanic soil and are home to 120 species of birds. A half-day hike on Ilaló, near the valley suburb of **Tumbaco F**, is worth it for the views of northern Ecuador's main peaks.

North of Quito

The Pan-American highway heading north first passes through the agricultural town of **Guayllabamba G**,

Map on page 200

TIP

Take a taxi to the summit of El Panecillo – but don't go alone as numerous thieves are at work on the way up.

BELOW: bargaining for a cow.

several hundred meters lower and much warmer than Quito, which hosts crops of avocado and chirimoya (custard apple). Restaurants are full at the weekends with *Quiteños* who stop off for the town's specialty of *locro*, a hearty cheese and potato soup with optional avocado and pork skin. The **Zoologico Metropolitano** (open Tues–Sun 9am–5pm; entrance fee) here houses the Galápagos tortoise, jaguar, several species of monkeys, and the Andean spectacle bear.

Further north, before reaching **Otavalo ❷** *(see page 202)*, you pass near the town of **Cayambe ❸**. This area is historically known for cheese-making, but the flower industry has surpassed cheese factories in economic importance. These large plantations can be toured, and a dozen roses costs about US$1. Cayambe is also the jumping-off place for excursions to the climber's refuge on the flanks of **Nevado Cayambe** (5,790 meters/19,000 ft), the wood-working indigenous community of **Oyacachi**, and the Inca ruins of **Quitoloma**.

The oldest *hacienda* (farm estate) in Ecuador, **Guachala**, built in 1580, is just outside Cayambe on the equator. In earlier times it was a textile factory producing Scottish-style tweed. Several other important *haciendas* open to visitors are scattered around the Otavalo area, including **Cusin** and **Pisanqui**, offering a glimpse into the wealth and privilege enjoyed by estate owners in the recent past.

About 5 km (3 miles) from Otavalo is an ecologically constructed mountain lodge, **Casa Mojanda**, with spectacular views from its adobe cottages of the nearby volcano, **Cotacachi** (4,940 meters/16,220 ft). Beneath the volcano lies **Laguna Cuicocha**, a collapsed caldera that is now an azure lake.

In the villages surrounding Otavalo the cottage crafts industry is flourishing. **Cotacachi** is most famous for its leather work, **Peguche** and **Agato** for their weaving, and **Iluman** for its double-sided ponchos and felt hats. To the north,

In 1917, a local weaver started to copy the famous Scottish tweed. His commercial success led to the worldwide recognition of the weaving skills of the Otavaleños.

BELOW: one of the Lagunas de Mojanda, near Tabacunda.

Ibarra is a pleasant colonial town with many inexpensive restaurants and hotels, known locally as "La Ciudad Blanca" (The White City) for its whitewashed walls and red-roofed colonial buildings. For a challenging but rewarding excursion, climb **Cerro Imbabura** (4,610 meters/15,120 ft), just south of town, with views of surrounding villages. This peak was once glaciated, and Amerindians harvested ice from the slopes. Twentieth-century climatic change has melted away the glaciers. A few hours west by bus, the subtropical **Chota Valley** is the only place in the Sierra that is populated by Afro-Ecuadorians.

On the road to San Lorenzo is the **Reserva Cerro Golondrinas** cloudforest. A four-day trek descends from the *páramo* through pristine submontane cloudforest and farmland. Visitors will see the positive effects of the conservation efforts in the area, such as the orchid farms, tree nurseries, and reforestation projects. At the Colombian border is **Tulcán ❹**, the provincial capital of Carchi, best known for cypress trees in the graveyard, which are elaborately carved to resemble animals, houses, and geometric figures. At **Reserva Ecológica El Angel**, nearby, you can see the giant *frailejon* plants, members of the daisy family, standing out of the *páramo* vegetation up to 2 meters (6 ft) tall.

Tafi *nougat shop, Baños.*

South from Quito

Heading south from Quito takes you along the "Avenue of the Volcanoes", with excellent views of all the major peaks. Several *haciendas* have been converted into first-class hotels, notably **La Cienega**, steeped in 400 years of history. From **Lasso** a dirt road heads up into **Parque Nacional Cotopaxi**, which encompasses the peaks of Cotopaxi, Rumiñahui, and Sincholagua. Cotopaxi is one of the world's highest active volcanoes and attracts thousands of climbers to its 5,900-meter (19,350-ft) summit every year. At its base, **Laguna Limpio Pungo** harbors Andean gulls, Andean lapwings, and the Andean fox. It is one of the best locations to observe *páramo* vegetation and recent volcanic features.

Just off the Pan-American highway on Thursdays at dawn, the quiet village of **Saquisilí** comes alive with Ecuador's largest indigenous market. People from outlying communities fill the streets and plazas with their local produce. A little further south is **Latacunga ❺**, destroyed three times by mud flows from Cotopaxi in the 18th and 19th centuries. In September the streets are filled with processions, dances, and fireworks in honor of the black-faced Virgin Mary, an event known as **La Fiesta de la Mamá Negra**.

To the west is the Amerindian-populated village of **Zumbahua**, which hosts a colorful vegetable market on Saturdays. An hour's drive away is the starting point for walks to the deep blue volcanic lake of **Quilotoa**. This area is one of the few places where llamas are still employed as pack animals.

The capital of Tungurahua Province, **Ambato**, was leveled by an earthquake in 1949 and rebuilt with concrete buildings that lend a drab feeling to the city. This is an important industrial and fruit-growing area. Between Baños and Ambato lies the resilient Quichua community of **Salasaca**, whose tapestries are sold throughout the country. Tourism remains a small

Map on page 198

BELOW: Baños thermal baths, possibly the best hot soak in the country.

industry in the immediate area, primarily because the Salasacas ship most of their handiwork out to the Saturday Otavalo market. The small outdoor market is open at weekends, and it is possible to see artists at work in their homes.

Hot springs and erupting volcanoes

Baños is a very popular tourist destination for Ecuadorians and foreigners alike. Named after the thermal springs in town, it is graced with a semitropical climate but in October 1999, 20,000 locals were evacuated when the active **Volcán Tungurahua** (5,020 meters/16,470 ft), threatened to erupt. The area was spared but remains on "yellow alert". There are numerous walks in the hills, a zoo, restaurants offering Ecuadorian and foreign cuisine and horseback-riding trips. The **Basilica** houses a statue of **Nuestra Señora de Agua Santa** (Our Lady of the Holy Water). Paintings hang on the wall depicting the miracles accredited to her. Baños is also a great place to shop for local handicrafts and experience locally organized rafting, jungle trips, horseback riding, and mountain biking.

Further south, **Riobamba** ❻ sits on the flanks of **Chimborazo**, the highest mountain in Ecuador (6,310 meters/20,700 ft) and starting point for rail trips to the coast which pass through the town of **Alausí** ❼. Before the Inca period Puruhua people lived in the region, but during Inca rule they were moved away and people from northern Peru were ordered to move here. Today the region is dominated by different indigenous groups and the variety of hats and traditional dress reflects these strong cultures.

To the west of Riobamba is the expansive and remote **Sangay National Park**, home to the mountain tapir and Andean spectacle bear, and the daily erupting volcano **Sangay** (5,230 meters/17,160 ft). On the edge of the park is part of an

Girl from Imbabura.

BELOW: Riobamba, beneath Mount Chimborazo.

old Inca highway that once ran from Quito to Cusco in Peru. Visitors can hike along the trail from **Achupallas** as far as the Inca ruins of **Ingapirca**, built in the 15th century to control the native Cañari living in the area.

The Pan-American highway continues south to **Cuenca ❽**, the third-largest city in Ecuador and formally the Inca town of Tomebamba. Most of the Inca stonework was destroyed by the Spanish and replaced by colonial architecture and cobbled streets. Today, patios, plazas, whitewashed buildings, and red-tiled roofs make Cuenca probably the most attractive Ecuadorian city to visit.

Nearby **Parque Nacional Cajas** with Inca ruins and more than 200 lakes is a popular retreat for fishermen and hikers. Since Cuenca draws its drinking water from Cajas it is well protected from environmental impacts. South of Cuenca live the indigenous people of **Saraguro ❾**, who have strong cultural pride. Their town has become a center of the indigenous political movement called *Pachacutek* (New Country). Here, men dress formally with short black trousers and women wear decorative shawls closed with a *tupus* (fastening pin). The sleepy town of **Loja** is the gateway to the southern Oriente and the Peruvian border. Quinine, the anti-malaria drug, was first exploited from the forests above the city in the 18th century, which led to their destruction.

Further down the valley, the village of **Vilcabamba ❿** was made famous by the discovery in the 1960s of a large percentage of locals over 100 years old. Visiting doctors have suggested that a mild and stable climate, low stress levels simple and healthy diets, and physical labor on small farms create this happy anomaly. Foreigners have since settled in the region, seeking longevity. Several ecologically and health-minded hostels have sprung up as a result.

Also in the vicinity is **Parque Nacional Podocarpus**, with a highland entrance at **Cajanuma** and rainforest entrance at **Bombascara**. Trails access the park and overnight camping is possible. An active environmental movement in Loja has kept multinational mining companies from moving in and causing deforestation and river poisoning. A spectacular mountain road goes to the town of **Macará** on the Peruvian border. This route to Peru is safer and more beautiful than the coastal crossing at Huaquillas.

The Oriente and the Amazon

The Ecuadorian **Oriente** is the upper Amazon basin east of the Andes, and is nowadays known as "the province of the future". It is a place of endless virgin rainforest cut by fast-flowing rivers and inhabited by jaguars, ocelots, anacondas, monkeys, tapirs, fish-eating bats, piranhas, and more than 450 species of birds. Travel in this region is easier than in neighboring countries, as distances are shorter and transportation quite straightfoward.

The indigenous inhabitants of the Oriente include the Siona, Cofan, Quechua, Quijo, and Huaorani tribes in the basins of the Napo, Aguarico, and Pastazo rivers to the north; and the Shuars, Ashuars, and Saraguros in the south. Colonization and oil development has affected the lifestyles of the tribes, and many traditions have died, such as those of the Shuar, who until the 20th century would shrink the heads of dead

Map on page 198

In February, when apples, pears, and peaches are ripe, young people come to Ambato from as far away as the coast for several days of parades and all-night dancing on the streets at Ecuador's largest festival, the Fiesta of Fruit and Flowers.

BELOW: laden down in Cuenca.

Shrunken head of a Jívaro (former name of the Shuar people).

BELOW: motoring along the Río Napo.

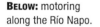

enemies. Until the 20th century the ratio of Shuar men to women was estimated at one to two, due to constant warfare. Some of the Huaorani retain their ancient culture deep in the jungles bordering Peru near the **Río Napo**. They hunt with spears, blowpipes, and poison darts, keep harpie eagles as pets and watch-dogs, and make fire by rubbing sticks together. Most of the Huaorani people do not welcome visitors to their communities, but some are turning to eco-tourism to protect their culture, and it is possible to spend time with the community of the village of Quehueri'ono by prior arrangement.

Several missionaries, including the Bishop of Coca, have been killed for attempting to encroach upon the Huaorani culture. Such disturbances of indigenous life date from 1541, when Francisco de Orellana's expedition departed Quito and stumbled upon the headwaters of the Río Napo. Towns such as Archidona and **Macas** ⓫ were soon established as bases for conquest and for conversion. Many were subsequently abandoned due to repeated attacks from the indigenous people, but the gold prospectors, the Franciscans, and the Jesuits, driven by fierce faith in their gods, gradually pushed back the frontiers.

Oil and tourist booms

The loss of most of the Oriente to Peru following the border war in 1941 stirred the government's attention, which was rewarded in 1967 with the discovery of huge oil deposits near **Lago Agrio** ⓬. The face of the region has changed drastically since then, with towns constructed overnight to provide services for the booming oil industry, which quickly became Ecuador's main money-spinner. In 1989, Lago Agrio was made the capital of Sucumbios, Ecuador's 21st province, while in 1998 the new province of Orellana was created to its south.

Map on page 198

This influx of people has sent wildlife deeper into the forests. In areas on the edge of the Amazon Basin, there is little fauna apart from birds and insects left. For those who are short of time, tours can be organized into the rainforest from the small town of **Misahuallí**. These trips can give a good understanding of how people living in the Oriente have adjusted to these outside influences.

The Napo flows on from Misahuallí to **Coca** ⓭, passing stilt houses with exotic menageries set in rambling banana patches. Farmers load fruit into their dugout canoes until they barely float and then paddle precariously off to market. The oil town of Coca itself has a seedy feel, reminiscent of the frontier towns of the great Wild West. Signs of oil development in the area cannot be ignored. Not too far from Coca however, pure rainforest abounds.

The Río Napo here is ever-widening, bordered on either side by a forest canopy, thickest at the height of approximately 30 meters (100 ft), beneath which grows, in damp dimness, an astonishing assortment of ferns and wild lemon trees with tiny edible ants living inside the stems. Above the canopy, the giant kapok tree stands out, the tallest Amazonian species, which can reach up to 60 meters (200 ft) high and 40 meters (130 ft) around the base of the trunk. Local people on the move seek shelter at night in the hollows between its roots. Its branches are cluttered with bromeliads, strangler vines, and belladona.

Hidden in the forest, just off the River Napo, three hours downriver from Coca, is Sacha Lodge. An elevated boardwalk heads through the forest, arriving at a piranha-infested lagoon in front of the lodge. Resident naturalists and indigenous guides venture into the forest with visitors on nature walks, canoe floats, or up into the 40-meter (130-ft) high observation tower to experience forest life high up in the canopy and maybe spot a sloth lazing atop his tree.

The rewards of a very early morning boat ride to the edge of **Parque Nacional Yasuni** may be the sight of flocks of macaws and parrots descending onto the cliff by the river to feed on the minerals in the soil. Yasuni is a national reserve created to protect and monitor the incredible bio-diversity of this unique rainforest area. The Tiputini River, a tributary of the Napo River, leads to the Tiputini Research Station, where researchers and eco-tourists wake to find groups of monkeys at their cabin window, exotic birds, and always the unnerving chance of a jaguar wandering through their camp.

Coastal Ecuador

The tropical lowland west of the Andes has – along with its inhabitants, who comprise half the nation – been characterized as savage and uncivilized by mountain-dwellers, a place to be exploited. It is the traditional source of Ecuador's wealth, based on bananas, coffee, and cocoa. In late 1997 and early 1998, the effects of the El Niño weather phenomenon caused serious floods and extensive damage.

Coastal Ecuador begins in the north with **San Lorenzo** ⓮ and its neighboring villages, collections of wooden stilt houses suspended in steamy, timeless isolation amid twisting mangrove channels. A new road now connects San Lorenzo to Ibarra in the Sierra, providing more reliable links with the outside world

The Spanish chronicler Cieza de Léon visited the largely ruined Cuenca in 1547 and found fully stocked warehouses, barracks, and houses formerly occupied by "more than two hundred virgins, who were very beautiful, dedicated to the service of the sun."

BELOW: feeding monkeys in a jungle resort.

than the railway. It remains a ramshackle tropical town with a Caribbean feel, pulsating with the beat of Colombian salsa. At **La Tola**, on the edge of the San Lorenzo Archipelago, the coast road begins – a dusty track through mainly uninhabited swamps bursting with vegetation.

Esmeraldas ⓯, strung along the shore of the river of the same name, exemplifies urban coastal culture. This city is loud and vibrant late into the night. Among a population that is chiefly *mestizo* and black, mountain *campesinos* in bowler hats sell fruit, Andean panpipes interrupt Caribbean dance music and techno rhythms, and Chinese restaurants serve sweet-and-sour.

Southwest of Esmeraldas are some of Ecuador's finest beaches. The road passes through **Atacames**, a small resort town that in recent years has become a noisy party town, and on through **Sua**, a beautifully situated, friendly fishing village, finally ending at **Muisne ⓰**, with beaches as remote as they are alluring.

The main road south follows the river through cattle farms and plantations of bananas, palm oil, and rubber, rising 500 meters (1,600 ft) to **Santo Domingo de los Colorados ⓱**. The Colorados, or Zatchila, inhabitants, who live mainly to the south of town, paint black stripes on their faces and wear their hair dyed red with *achiote*, a plant dye, and cut in a bowl shape. They retain their knowledge of natural medicine but dress traditionally only for special occasions.

Perhaps the most scenic of the lowland routes runs from Santo Domingo to **Manta ⓲**, the calmest and prettiest coastal city. On **Tarqui beach**, local fishermen unload their catch of shark, dorado, eel, and the odd tortoise, which are cleaned and sold on the sand amidst an aerial frenzy of seagulls and vultures.

BELOW: crushed ice vendor, Esmeraldas.

Manta is the gateway to the nearby Panama hat villages (*see below*). Fine wickerwork furniture and sisal hammocks are also manufactured here. South of

Map on page 198

Manta is **Parque Nacional Machalilla**, one of the most threatened dry tropical forests in the world. Now with national protection status, it is hoped that this unique forest with its bottle-shaped trees, the skyline dotted with kapok trees and more than 200 species of birds, will survive. The park entrance is just north of **Puerto Lopez** ⑲, a small fishing town. From here the road runs south past Alandaluz Ecological Center, a successful eco-cultural tourist complex with organic gardens, dry compost toilets, and a water recycling system. Cabins are available for US$12 and a restaurant is open to non-guests.

South of the the central coast, all roads lead to **Guayaquil** ⑳, Ecuador's largest and liveliest city, with approximately 2.8 million inhabitants. The Spanish quickly established their regional shipbuilding industry here: enormous 250-ton sailing vessels transported goods from Europe to Lima via Mexico and Panama, and returned laden with gold and silver. New technology and ideas have always come first to Guayaquil: just as it had public streetcars and gas lighting before Quito, so it was the first city to realize independence in 1821, and has long been the bastion of progressive liberal thought. A pleasant walk goes along the extensively refurbished **Malecón Simón Bolívar** past **La Rotonda**, commemorating Bolívar's meeting with San Martín; up to **Las Peñas**, the only extant colonial district, and scenic **Cerro El Carmen**.

Shrunken heads from the Oriente, pre-Inca ceramics, colonial religious paintings, and a changing modern art exhibition fill the **Museo Municipal**. The **Parque del Centenario**, where gymnasts and comedians routinely perform, divides Avenida 9 de Octubre, the city's commercial heart. To escape the frenzy, grab a moment of tranquility in the city's botanical garden, **Parque Bolívar**, and commune with the turtles and iguanas.

Panama hat maker.

BELOW: Panama hats for sale.

ECUADOR'S MOST FAMOUS HAT

Montecristi is the center of production of the Panama hat, a cottage industry that has protected the heads of such notables as Teddy Roosevelt and King Edward VII. The hats are woven from the reed *Carludovica palmata*, cultivated locally and brought on horseback to craftsmen's homes. A top-quality or *superfino* specimen can change hands for up to US$1,000, and should be able to hold water when held upside down. It should also fold up to fit into a top pocket without creasing. Weaving should ideally be done at night or in dull conditions, and the process can take up to three months.

The hats have always been produced in Ecuador, but were shipped worldwide from Panama, hence the misnomer. Made since pre-Columbian times, they caught on among the conquistadors, who were impressed by the headgear of the people of Manabí Province. Soldiers fighting in the Spanish-American War of 1898 wore the hats, and the export market to the US subsequently took off. They caught on in Europe following the 19th-century World Exposition in Paris, as many of Renoir's paintings illustrate. The hats were also a big hit with US Prohibition gangsters, and the market peaked in 1946. Since then demand has fallen, and some say that the production of *superfinos* will not survive much longer.

The Galápagos islands

The first sighting by Europeans of the Galápagos islands was in 1535. It is possible that the ancient Mantan, Incas and even Polynesians visited the islands, which lie 1,000 km (600 miles) off the Pacific coast of Ecuador. From their European discovery until their incorporation into Ecuador in 1832, the islands served as a refuge for European and American pirates, whalers and sealers, where they re-stocked supplies of firewood, water, and giant tortoises for meat, which could remain alive for a year in ships' holds.

Just as the islands were undergoing permanent settlement, the *Beagle* dropped anchor in **San Cristóbal Bay** ㉑ and the 26-year-old naturalist Charles Darwin strode ashore. Previous scientific expeditions had been mounted, but with Darwin's visit, the enormous biological and geological significance of the Galápagos islands was recognized. Although he stayed for only five weeks in 1835, Darwin made many of the observations upon which he based his theories of evolution and the mutability of species. He noticed 13 types of finch, each with a different beak designed to collect its particular food.

The islands' romantic appeal was tarnished over the following century, when a penal colony was established on the island of **Floreana**. Conditions were harsh; administrators gratuitously cruel. The original colonists, some 80 soldiers whose crimes of insurrection had been pardoned, fled the island, leaving the prisoners to their fate. As recently as 1944, a colony was established on **Isabela** to which increasingly hardened criminals were sent. It was dissolved following a riot and mass escape, and in 1959, the islands were declared a national park.

The archipelago was designated a World Heritage Site in 1979 and a UNESCO World Biosphere Reserve in 1985. In an attempt to stop illegal fishing and in

TIP

The Galápagos islands are a national park, and all non-Ecuadorian visitors must pay an entrance fee of US$100 (discounts are available for students with ID and children under 12).

BELOW: cruising around the Galápagos.

Map on page 216

recognition of the conservation issues, in December 2001, UNESCO declared the Marine Reserve around the islands a World Natural Heritage Site. In 1997 the government introduced a law preventing new tourism operations until 2005, and visitor levels have been restricted to 65,000 per annum.

There are 13 major islands, six small islands and 42 islets spread over an area of 80,000 sq. km (30,000 sq. miles). The land consists of lava resting on a basalt base, volcanic refuse produced by successive underwater eruptions which continue today. The islands have never been connected with the mainland, but emerged from the water individually over a million years. The violence of the geological past is most evident on **Isabela** with its chain of five volcanoes as high as 1,700 meters (5,600 ft). One of them, the **Sierra Negra**, has the second-largest crater in the world, measuring 10 km (6 miles) in diameter.

Seeds were transported accidentally by birds and aboard ships. Today the islands support almost 900 plant varieties, the most revered of which is the *palo santo*, found in abundance on **Isla Rábida** ㉒. There are six distinct vegetation zones ranging from low-level desert to the uppermost *pampa*; a walk up to the old sugar mill on San Cristóbal passes most of them.

On **San Bartolomé**, two sparkling horseshoe beaches are separated by a narrow strip of semi-tropical forest. From the island's summit, one of the best vantage-points in the archipelago, the uninhabited volcanic wasteland of **Santiago** stretches away to the west. Within this desert is a freshwater spring. Flamingos dance around the nearby lagoon, and bury each other up to the neck in the coffee-colored sand of **Espumilla Beach**, and, near **Puerto Egas** ㉓ fur seals swim through an underwater tunnel between the open sea and two small, clear pools.

Author Herman Melville had a rather unromantic vision of the Galápagos islands: "Take five-and-twenty heaps of cinders dumped here and there in an outside city lot; imagine some of them magnified into mountains, and the vacant lot the sea..."

BELOW: one of the famous iguanas.

Creatures of the sea

Some of the best snorkeling is done off far-flung islands like **Española** ㉔, the only place in the world in which the endemic waved albatross breeds. In **Gardner Bay**, flapping manta rays probably think you are just another sea lion, but the real sea lions know better, and an aggressive bull should be given right of way. The females and young are playful; they can recognize the 290 varieties of fish in the water, but a pale figure with a mask and flippers is still a curious sight.

The Galápagos are home to the world's only marine iguanas, and the island of **Fernandina** ㉕ holds the largest colony. As inquisitive as the two related land species, they are much more dragon-like with their scaly skin – which turns from black to blue and red during mating season – and the row of spines along their back. Originally land-dwellers, they can submerge for only a few minutes at a time, searching for algae; and upon re-surfacing, snort a salty spray into the air. Watching their antics beneath the smoldering **Volcán La Cumbre**, which erupted in September 1988, is a truly primal experience.

Directly opposite Fernandina is **Urbina Bay**, and one of the few coral reefs in the archipelago. Fish of every color steer clear of the Galápagos penguin, the world's northernmost species. The entrance to nearby **Elizabeth Bay** is protected by a cluster of islands which penguins share with nesting pelicans. En route to Floreana, schools of sperm and killer whales cruise the deep waters, and bottle-nosed dolphins surf the bow waves of boats. At **Devil's Crown** ㉖, named after the jagged, truncated volcanic cone rising from the ocean, sea lions glide along strong currents, which make for adventurous snorkeling.

The beach on **Point Cormorant**, Floreana's most beautiful location, is dotted with olivine crystals, while the adjacent lagoons teem with flamingos.

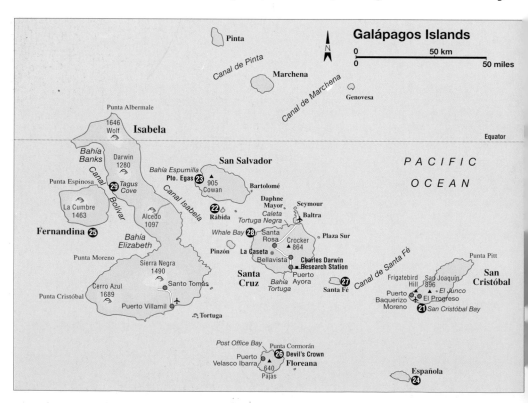

Map on page 216

Around the point is the **Bay of Sharks** – its ring of pristine white sand is popular with nesting tortoises. The name refers to the relatively harmless white-tipped shark, which is found mainly here and off San Bartolomé. It is, along with the enormous and equally docile whale shark, the only kind in these waters. On land, the unchallenged king of the islands is the giant tortoise, which can live for 200 years and weigh up to 300 kg (600 lb). On rocky, sparsely vegetated islands like Isabela and Española, its longer neck and legs and saddle-shaped carapace enable it to reach higher to obtain food. These features are absent from the more cumbersome species inhabiting fertile islands like **Santa Cruz**.

The **Charles Darwin Research Station** was established on Santa Cruz in 1959, on the centenary of the publication of *The Origin of Species*. One of its most important programs is the controlled hatching of tortoise eggs, a necessary step since the introduction by early settlers of feral dogs, cats, goats, pigs, and rats. On **Pinzón**, not one young tortoise has been sighted for nearly 50 years. The feral species also destroy vegetation, but have participated in the evolutionary miracle of the islands in at least one respect: the goats on **Santa Fe** ㉗, in the absence of freshwater, have developed a taste for the sea, and now live on it.

In **Whale Bay** ㉘ on Santa Cruz, ceramic fragments conjure images of the buccaneer Henry Morgan with a blue-footed booby squawking on his shoulder. Pirates and whalers recorded their passage on the cliff faces of **Tagus Cove** ㉙ on Isabela: today the graffiti is seen mainly by flightless cormorants. A more recent ruin is the skeleton of an abandoned 1960s salt mine on Isla Santiago.

The Galápagos islands are one of the few places in the world where animals still live relatively undisturbed, and nowhere are the forces of evolution more clearly displayed. Visitors should leave no scars. ❑

Darwin encountered a "strange Cyclopean scene" on a San Cristóbal beach – two tortoises munching on cactus. One "gave a deep hiss, and drew in its head"; the other "slowly stalked away." Darwin became fascinated with the beasts, noting numerous sub-species.

LEFT: Sally Lightfoot crab.
RIGHT: stairway to heaven.

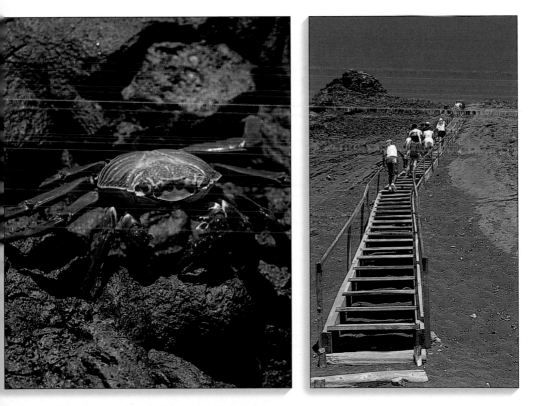

BIRDS OF THE GALAPAGOS ISLANDS

From the marbled godwit to the black-necked stilt, the birdlife on the Galápagos islands, which taught us about evolution, is still rich, rare and rewarding

Where else but on these small islands off the coast of Ecuador will birds come out to greet you? Life with no native predators has made the birds of the Galápagos fearless, which means that many of them are easy to spot. There are 58 resident species, of which 28 are endemic, as well as about 30 migratory birds. The seabirds are the most often seen: in the dry coastal areas you are likely to spot species of the booby family, the waved albatross – only found on the island of Española – and the world's only flightless seabirds, the Galápagos penguin and the flightless cormorant. The best time to come is in winter (October to February) when most migrants are visiting, and birds are reproducing. Then, a serious ornithologist might see 50 species in a week, and even a dilettante should be able to spot two dozen.

There are dangers in paradise, however: the introduction of domestic animals has been bad news. Some prey on the birds, others destroy or compete for their habitats. Farming on the inhabited islands also destroys habitats, and a natural phenomenon, the *El Niño* current, brings mosquito-borne disease and disrupts the food chain.

△ **PEREGRINE FALCON**
The endangered peregrine falcon *(Falco peregrinus)* originates in Canada and the US, and winters in South America. It is frequently seen on the islands of Española, Isabela, Baltra, and Santa Cruz. The world's swiftest bird, this falcon can reach speeds of 320 km/h (199 mph) when it is swooping to attack prey.

◁ **GALÁPAGOS HAWK**
The female Galápagos hawk *(Buteo galapagoensis)* is larger than the male of the species. While the males are monogamous, females will mate with up to seven males per season in order to ensure that breeding will be successful. The female and her males take turns in guarding the nest.

◁ **BLUE-FOOTED BOOBY**
The blue-footed booby *(Sula nebouxii excisa)* has a wonderful courtship ritual in which the male ostentatiously displays his brightly colored feet in order to attract a mate. Two or three eggs are laid and both of the parents share the task of incubating them. Once they have become independent, the young birds leave the islands and do not return to breed until some three years later.

THE SECRET OF DARWIN'S FINCHES

The finches of the Galápagos were vitally important in the development of Charles Darwin's ideas about evolution and the formation of species.

When he set off on his voyage around the world on HMS *Beagle* (1831–36), he believed, like most people of his time, in the fixity of species. But on the Galápagos he observed that 13 different species of the finch had evolved from a single ancestral group, and it was this (together with his observations of the islands' tortoises) which led to his contention that species could evolve over time, with those most suited to their natural environment surviving and passing on their characteristics to the next generation.

The main differences he noted between the finches was the size and shape of their beaks, leading him to conclude that the birds which survived were those whose beaks enabled them to eat the available food.

The 13 species of finch are divided into two groups: ground finches (pictured above is the large ground finch, *Geospiza magnirostris*) and tree finches, of which the mangrove finch, found only in the swamps of Isabela island, is the most rare. You are unlikely to see all of them on a short visit, but it's an enjoyable challenge to see how many you can spot.

◁ **VERMILLION FLYCATCHER**
The vermillion flycatcher *(Pyrocephalus rubinus)* is an attractive little bird and quite unlike any other bird to be seen on the Galápagos islands. It has a high-pitched, musical song and builds a distinctive cup-shaped nest, on which the female incubates the eggs.

△ **FRIGATE BIRDS**
The magnificent frigate bird *(Fregata magnificens magnificens)* and its close relation, the great frigate bird, can be seen near the coasts of many islands. Both males and females have long forked tails and the male is remarkable for the red gular pouch which puffs in the mating season.

◁ **LAVA GULL**
The lava gull *(Larus fuliginosus)* is believed to be the rarest species in the world. It roosts on the shores of saltwater lagoons and builds solitary nests along the coast.

△ **BROWN PELICAN**
The brown pelican *(Pelecanus occidentalis urinator)* is a huge, cumbersome bird, which can often be seen following fishing boats in search of food.

THE TROPICAL GIANT

Laid-back tropical paradise, economic miracle,
or home of the hedonistic carnival – Brazil is
a heady mix of them all

Nearly half the South American sub-continent can be described in one tantalizing word: Brazil. Almost as big as the United States and home to 175 million people, Brazil is a world in itself – a sensuous giant that invariably becomes a part of everyone who experiences its pleasures. Brazil the geographic colossus is also a state of mind, one that loosens up even the most cautious of spirits who venture there. That's the power of the Brazilian *jeito*, or way. Relax, hang loose, improvize, and *nao esquente a cabeça*: don't get hot-headed, come what may.

There is a vibrancy to Brazil unparalleled elsewhere in Latin America; the country's cutting-edge innovations and penchant for fads have led some to call it "the California of South America." But for all its laid-back ethos, Brazil is also a dynamo of economic activity. The world's eighth-largest population produces the planet's tenth-largest economy. Virtually everything one buys in Brazil is made in Brazil. Cars crafted in São Paulo run on lead-free sugar-cane fuel (home-grown, naturally), and their compact-disc players made in the duty-free Amazon port of Manaus play tunes from the recording studios of Rio de Janeiro.

As the major port of entry, Rio *(see page 233)* is where most visitors get their first dazzling impressions of Brazil, with its beautiful beaches, sensuously rounded peaks, and world-famous carnival. But like the iceberg below its tip, there's much more to Brazil than Rio. Nearby is South America's largest metropolis, São Paulo *(see page 238)*. With 13 million people under its towering skyline, this is the country's powerhouse, the center of its massive commercial and industrial output. To the northwest lies Brasília *(see page 239)*, the pristine architectural wonder that sprang up from the wilderness to become the national capital. Beyond the triangle of political, cultural and economic power formed by these three cities are slightly more subdued wonders: the stately colonial cities of Minas Gerais *(see page 241)*, living monument of the gold and diamond booms; the inviting beaches and rich Afro-Brazilian culture of the Northeast *(see page 244)*; the immense rainforests of the Amazon jungle that still cover more than half the country *(see page 254)*; the vast marshlands of the Pantanal, a naturalist's paradise *(see page 252)*; and the enormous waterfalls of Iguaçu *(see page 253)*. ❑

PRECEDING PAGES: coastal splendor, Costa Verde, west of Rio de Janeiro.
LEFT: Christ the Redeemer statue, Rio.

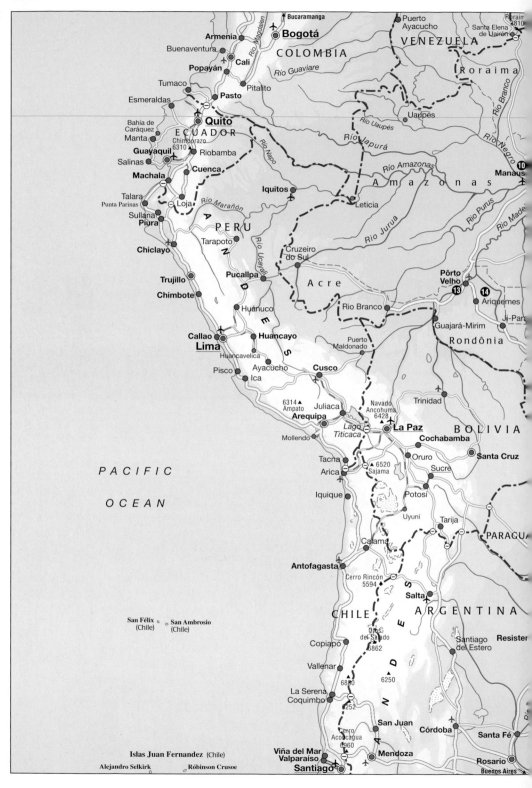

Bucaramanga

Puerto
Ayacucho

Roraim
2810

Santa Elena
de Uairén

VENEZUELA

R o r a i m a

Armenia

Bogotá

Buenaventura

Cali

COLOMBIA

Popayán

Río Guaviare

Río Branco

Tumaco

Pitalito

Esmeraldas

Pasto

Uaupès

Río Uaupés

Río Japurá

Río Magdalena

Quito

E C U A D O R

Río Napo

Río Amazonas

Río Negro

Bahía de
Caráquez

Chimborazo
6310

Manaus

10

Manta

Guayaquil

Riobamba

A m a z o n a s

Salinas

Cuenca

Machala

Iquitos

Talara

Leticia

Río Purus

Punta Parinas

Loja

Río Marañón

Río Juruá

Río Made

Sullana

A

Piura

PERU

Río Ucayali

Cruzeiro
do Sul

Chiclayo

Tarapoto

N

Trujillo

Pucallpa

A c r e

**Pôrto
Velho**

Chimbote

D

Huánuco

Rio Branco

13

Ariquemes

Guajará-Mirim

Ji-Par

E

Puerto
Maldonado

R o n d ô n i a

Callao

Huancayo

S

Lima

Huancavelica

Pisco

Ayacucho

Cusco

Trinidad

Ica

6314 ▲
Ampato

Juliaca

Navado
Ancohuma
6428 ▲

Arequipa

La Paz

B O L I V I A

Mollendo

Lago
Titicaca

Cochabamba

Tacna

Oruro

Sucrè

Santa Cruz

Arica

▲ 6520
Sajama

Potosí

Iquique

Uyuni

Tarija

PARAGU

P A C I F I C

Calama

O C E A N

Antofagasta

Cerro Rincón
5594 ▲

Salta

A R G E N T I N A

San Félix
(Chile)

San Ambrosio
(Chile)

CHILE

Ojos
del Salado
6862

Copiapó

Santiago
del Estero

Resister

Vallenar

▲ 6880

6250

N

La Serena
Coquimbo

6252

Cerro
Aconcagua
6960

San Juan

Córdoba

Santa Fé

Islas Juan Fernández (Chile)

Viña del Mar
Valparaíso

Mendoza

Rosario

Alejandro Selkirk

Róbinson Crusoe

Santiago

Buenos Aires

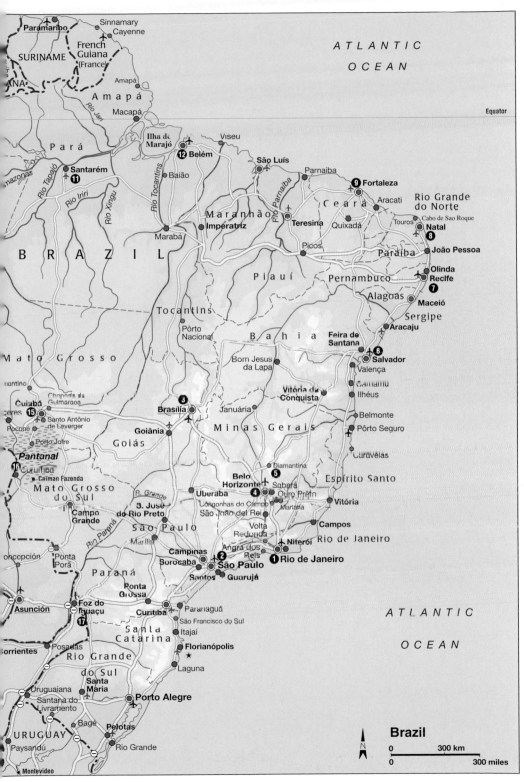

Brazil

ATLANTIC OCEAN

Equator

SURINAME
French Guiana (France)
Paramaribo
Sinnamary
Cayenne
Amapá
Amapá
Macapá
Rio Jari

Pará
Viseu
Ilha de Marajó
Belém
São Luís
Parnaiba
Fortaleza
Rio Grande do Norte

Santarém
Baião
Rio Tapajó
Rio Iriri
Rio Xingu
Rio Tocantins

Maranhão
Imperatriz
Teresina
Ceará
Aracati
Cabo de Sao Roque
Touros
Natal

Marabá
Picos
Piauí
Quixadá
Paraíba
João Pessoa

BRAZIL

Tocantins
Pôrto Nacional

Bahia
Pernambuco
Olinda
Recife
Alagoas
Maceió

Mato Grosso
Bom Jesus da Lapa
Feira de Santana
Sergipe
Aracaju

Chapada dos Guimaraes
Cuiabá
Santo Antônio de Leverger
Poconé
Porto Jofre

Brasília
Januária
Vitória da Conquista
Camamu
Ilhéus
Salvador
Valença

Goiânia
Goiás
Minas Gerais
Belmonte
Pôrto Seguro

Pantanal
Curitiba
Caiman Fazenda
Mato Grosso do Sul

Diamantina
Belo Horizonte
Sabará
Espírito Santo
Curvelos

Campo Grande
R. Grande
Uberaba
Congonhas do Campo
São João del Rei
Ouro Prêto
Mariana
Vitória

oncepción
Ponta Porã
Rio Paraná
S. José do Rio Preto
São Paulo
Marília
Volta Redonda
Campos
Rio de Janeiro

Paraná
Campinas
Sorocaba
Angra dos Reis
Niterói
Rio de Janeiro

Ponta Grossa
São Paulo
Santos
Guarujá

Asunción
Foz do Iguaçu
Paranaguá
Curitiba
São Francisco do Sul

orrientes
Posadas
Santa Catarina
Itajaí
Florianópolis

Rio Grande do Sul
Santa Maria
Laguna

Uruguaiana
Santana do Livramento
Porto Alegre

URUGUAY
Bagé
Pelotas
Rio Grande

Paysandú

Montevideo

ATLANTIC OCEAN

N

Brazil

0 — 300 km

0 — 300 miles

BRAZIL

This vast country pulsates with life, from the rampant fertility of the Amazon to the sensual delights of Rio and the modern sophistication of São Paulo and Brasília

Map on pages 226–7

isitors can only hope to scratch the surface of this huge land, which still has vast unpopulated areas, and reveals its secrets reluctantly. It's worth making the effort, for there is much to discover, from the excitement of Rio de Janeiro and the gastronomic highlights of São Paulo to the majestic forests of the Amazon, scarred red by twisting rivers; and from the abundant wildlife of the Pantanal to the solitude of the arid northeastern "backlands". The past comes to life in the gold towns in the south of Minas Gerais, such as Ouro Preto, Tiradentes, and Congonhas. Harder to get to, but worth the effort, are places like the high plateaux of Bahia State, the Chapada Diamantina, where Brazil's second-highest waterfall tumbles from a mist-clouded plain.

The distance from the Andes to the Atlantic Ocean is almost 4,500 km (2,800 miles), and most of Brazil's attractions are a long way from the big cities, as well as from each other: the Iguaçu Falls is thousands of kilometers from balmy Belém in the north. But traveling around Brazil has become easier and cheaper, due to a price war between the country's airlines.

Travelers looking for warm water, white sand, and tropical beauty will be overwhelmed by the Brazilian coastline – the longest, and perhaps the most beautiful of any country in the world.

PRECEDING PAGES: Sugarloaf Mountain dominates Rio's Guanabara Bay. **LEFT:** exhibitionism at the Rio *Carnaval*. **BELOW:** Ouro Preto.

Conquering the interior

Brazil's interior was first penetrated by Europeans in the late 1600s. The first pioneers were Jesuits proselytizing to indigenous Guaraní, followed by Portuguese immigrants too poor to acquire land in the sugar-cane dominated coastal regions. These settlers pushed into what is now the state of São Paulo to raise cattle and plant subsistence crops. Like the wealthy sugar planters whose labor force was mostly black slaves, these farmers also sought bonded workers, so they organized expeditions to abduct Guaraní who inhabited the region. The Guaraní sought refuge in the Jesuit missions where indigenous peoples lived in educated, highly productive communities.

Despite their barbaric raids, the *bandeirantes* (so named because of the banners they marched under), have gone down in Brazilian folklore as brave pioneers who opened up what has become the country's most productive economic region.

Just when the world market for Brazilian sugar started to go soft around 1700, a new boom shook the country. This time it was gold and diamonds, discovered in the rugged hill country of Minas Gerais. Most of the gold was sent to the Portuguese crown, but enough remained to build the baroque cities of Ouro Preto, São João del Rei, and Sabará. The new treasures were shipped to Europe through Rio de Janeiro,

putting the backwater port on the map, and by 1763 Rio had become so important that the Portuguese crown moved the capital there from the sugarcane and slave entrepôt of Salvador.

Brazilian society showed a penchant for partying from its colonial start. An exasperated 17th-century Jesuit instructor, José de Anchieta, wrote that the country was "relaxing, slothful and melancholic, so that all the time is spent in parties, in singing, and in making merry."

Other booms followed, such as cotton. The biggest and most lasting boom, coffee, started in the late 18th century. The state of São Paulo was covered with coffee plantations as the craze for drinking coffee spread around the world. But coffee prices tumbled in 1930, and with them fell the government. Getulio Vargas, governor of Rio Grande do Sul, then seized the presidency and won Brazilians' hearts with his populist rhetoric and championing of organized labor. He established a corporate state apparently modeled on Mussolini's fascism, losing support after the fall of Hitler and Mussolini. Vargas resigned in 1945.

Eighteen years of constitutional rule and steady economic growth followed, until the early 1960s. With the number of landless peasants increasing dramatically, land reform became an explosive political issue. The military responded to the growing unrest by seizing power in April 1964.

Birth of the "Brazilian Miracle"

The military's crackdown on leftists (many of whom were tortured and killed) and generous fiscal incentives combined to attract a flood of foreign investment. The Brazilian economy boomed, mainly enriching those who were already wealthy. Disenchantment with military rule grew as the economy took a nose-dive in 1980, crippled by enormous bills for imported oil and public works projects, such as a rarely used Amazon highway. The last of a series of military dictator presidents stepped down in March 1985.

BELOW: Emperor Dom Pedro II's summer palace, Petrópolis.

Tancredo Neves, the man chosen to head the new civilian government, was a longtime opponent of the military. But he fell fatally ill on the eve of his inauguration, and his vice-president, José Sarney, was sworn in as president. The Sarney government inherited a foreign debt of more than US$100 billion. Sarney, closely allied with the military, quickly lost political support as inflation, which reached 1,000 percent in 1988, continued to ravage the economy.

Economic woes were accompanied by growing street crime. Such anti-social behavior is relatively recent in Brazil, and is widely considered a product of the huge influx of rural Brazilians into large cities since the 1960s. Some were attracted by jobs, but many arrived as refugees from droughts in the Northeast.

Progress for the poor is often limited by racial discrimination. Although Brazil has been called a racial paradise because of the high number of inter-racial marriages and an absence of open racial conflict, to be black in Brazil almost always means to be poor, and 40 percent of the country's population is black. But whatever their color, there is little chance of a poor Brazilian becoming a rich one.

From bust to boom

Few countries can have changed as much as Brazil since mid-1994, after the election of Fernando Henrique Carduso as president. Inflation, then running at more than 4,000 percent a year, was halted by drastic mea-

Map on pages 226–7

sures, including the introduction of a new currency. This released a huge amount of energy and set off a chain of events that are still transforming the country. Twelve to 15 million Brazilians joined the consumer society for the first time, causing food sales to surge and the demand for many other goods to explode. Credit, absent for three decades, became accessible, and millions went on a shopping spree, particularly for new cars, but as road-building has not kept pace there is chronic congestion. In October 2002, former metal-worker Luis Inácio da Silva, popularly known as Lula, became Brazil's first left-wing president for 40 years. Dubbed the Brazilian Blair for being something of a socialist-capitalist hybrid, President Lula has followed sensible economic policies while not defaulting on the country's US$250 billion public debt. As well as committing to a "Zero Hunger" program – which has brought food to 15 million people – he has continued to meet IMF demands, and secured a series of several hundred billion dollar loans.

The Northeast has progressed rapidly, as factories relocate in search of cheaper labor. Stagnant state capitals such as Fortaleza, Recife, and Salvador, which tend to have more character than the upstart cities of the south, are being given a new lease of life, and long neglected architectural gems are being tastefully restored.

Huge natural resources secure the country's future, but they bring responsibilites toward the environment, particularly in the Amazon region, where destruction has occurred on a massive scale (16 percent of the Amazon forest – an area the size of France – has already been cut down, almost all within the past 40 years). Disturbingly, "Avança Brasil" was announced in 2001. Already underway, the US$40-billion program will include the building of 10,000 km (6,215 miles) of highways, electric dams, and power lines in an attempt to industrialize the area. Indigenous peoples, particularly in the Amazon regions, where their lifestyles have been sus-

Monument to Kubitschek, Brasília.

BELOW: crowded hillside *favela*, Rio

tained over centuries, still suffer daily threats and invasions of their homelands by fire, logging, and from settlers looking for homes away from Brazil's southern cities. Although President Lula has been criticized for his lack of commitment in protecting the rainforest, in June 2004 he announced the designation of four new national forests, covering around 400,000 hectares (1 million acres) of threatened land.

Trouble in the rainforest

This conflict is exemplified in the remote western region of Rondônia *(see page 250)*, where settlers are pushing back the rainforest – and the people who have lived there for centuries. Two factors set off the land rush: first, changes in agriculture in Brazil's prosperous south made many peasants landless in the 1970s. Frequent freezes combined with soaring world prices for soybeans convinced many coffee farmers to cut down their bushes and plant soybeans. Peasants who had sharecropped at the edges of the coffee plantations – assuring growers a stable workforce to harvest the beans – were no longer needed for the mechanized soybean harvest, and were forced to abandon their plots.

Second, the extension of the roadway BR 364 from the coffee regions of São Paulo state to Rondônia, the new Brazilian frontier, put into action the formula for peopling the Amazon enunciated by the Brazilian military, which then governed the country: "A land without people for people without land." Speculators cashed in, buying up enormous tracts for cattle ranches. Such enterprises were subsidized by the Brazilian government until international concerns about the disastrous effect on the ecology forced them to abandon the policy.

BELOW: the glorious church of Glória, downtown Rio.

Brazil has a GDP of over US$900 billion, and nearly 70 percent of its exports are industrial goods – but the gap between rich and poor is still greater than

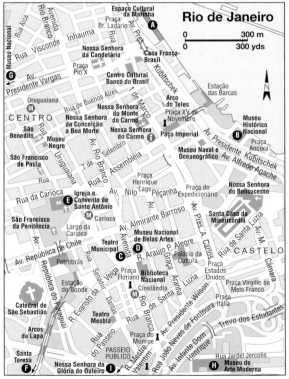

almost anywhere else in the world. In most cities, unemployment has led to rising crime, and muggings are a serious problem. Tourists can be targeted, and caution is needed, but things are not as bad as is often made out. A special police force guards tourists on many of the beaches.

Despite the pace of change, most Brazilians are well aware that the most important things in life are personal relationships, having fun, and making the best of what is available. Visitors will be impressed with their courtesy and friendliness, as well as their unflappable equanimity. Maybe it's because they have so many opportunities to let off steam – in carnival, music, and soccer.

Rio de Janeiro, city of fun

Brazilians call **Rio de Janeiro ❶** *a cidade maravilhosa* – the marvelous city – and they have ample reason to do so. There's the city's stunning setting: flanked to the east by the enormous **Bay of Guanabara** and to the south by the Atlantic Ocean, Rio sprawls around and even up the sides of enormous granite peaks and down to wide sandy beaches. The result of this topsy-turvy topography is a city sculptured around the whims of nature, giving the urban landscape a look that can only be described as sensuous.

The 11 million people who live in and around Rio are known as *cariocas*, and they epitomize the casual, good-natured disposition associated with Brazilians. Part of the *carioca's* sunny outlook may derive from the smug satisfaction of living in a place most people only dream of, where it's possible to join the fun on the beaches for the price of a local bus fare. Another reason for their friendliness could be the open social scene of Rio. Unlike other big cities, where exclusivity heightens the appeal of social gatherings, in Rio people of all classes throng to public places for fun. The beaches are the biggest attraction, followed by soccer stadiums and carnival street parties. In Rio, it's sociable to down a *chopp* (draught beer) and chat with friends on the sidewalk; life is lived in the open air.

Cariocas have a reputation for few inhibitions and tremendous appetites. That image developed in part from the bacchanal bashes of carnival, in part from the tantalizingly tiny beach attire favored by both genders. In Rio, you don't have to be gorgeous to be on display – just uninhibited. *Cariocas* are extremely tolerant (gay men seeking open minds flock to Rio from the rest of Brazil) and anyone can indulge in a little exhibitionism. Pleasure became Rio's main money-maker after 1960, when the seat of government was moved from here to landlocked Brasília. Rio went from being the center of the Brazilian universe to a mere tourist attraction. It took a long time for the city to come to terms with its new identity, but *cariocas* take comfort in knowing that the politicians who moved to Brasília left their hearts in Rio.

From the airport to the city center

Most visitors' first encounter with Rio takes place at the sleek complex of Galeão International Airport. Galeão is located on a purpose-built island north of Rio, and to the west is a massive swampy area known as the Baixada Fluminense, or fluvial lowlands, a poor, featureless

Maps
Area 226–7
City 232

TIP

Tourists can be targets for crime, so try to blend in as much as possible. Dress soberly and keep cameras and valuables out of sight.

BELOW: *carioca* women are renowned for their tiny bikinis.

Guanabara Bay from Sugarloaf Mountain.

BELOW: snorkeling, one of the many outdoor sports available in Rio.

area that is home to two-thirds of the city's inhabitants. The drive into the city from Galeão Airport passes Rio's port and the **Espaço Cultural da Marinha** A (Avenida Alfredo Agache; open Tues–Sun, noon–5pm), one of Rio's principal museums, famous for its finely detailed models of ships. About 500 meters (⅓ mile) southeast is the **Museu Histórico Nacional** Ⓑ (Praça Marechal Ancora; open Tues–Sun), which holds Brazil's national archives.

The main thoroughfare through the heart of the downtown area, **Avenida Rio Branco**, is lined by skyscraping banks, tourist agencies, and the ornate 19th-century buildings of the **Teatro Municipal** Ⓒ (which has a splendid ground-floor café with mosaic tiles). Then there's the **Municipality** (whose steps often serve as seating for evening concerts), and across the street, the **Biblioteca Nacional** (the national library, with neo-classical and Art Nouveau paintings on display) and the **Museu Nacional de Belas Artes** Ⓓ (open Tues–Sun), the country's foremost repository of classic and contemporary Brazilian art holding around 9 million works.

One of the best places to watch the action is on the plaza in front of the Teatro Municipal, an area known as **Cinelândia**. Come nightfall it's like London's Hyde Park, with political campaigners, guerrilla theater, transvestites, and performers of *capoeira* (a stylized fight-dance with its own accompanying rhythms and music). On the other side of the Teatro Municipal is a wide pedestrian mall, **Largo da Carioca**, a favorite haunt of snake-oil vendors and leather artisans.

For a flavor of what Rio was like before the skyscrapers crowded its skyline, wander down the sidestreets off Largo da Carioca. Don't miss the stately Confeiteria Colombo at Rua Gonçalves Dias 32, with a mirror-lined tearoom downstairs and elegant dining room upstairs. *Belle époque* furnishings evoke the late 19th century, when Rio's intelligentsia used to gather here. Stroll down Rua da Carioca for hearty German food and *chopp* at the lively Bar Luiz, a downtown fixture for more than a century.

Rising high above Largo da Carioca to the west is the **Igreja y Convento de Santo Antônio Convent** Ⓔ (open daily), a complex of religious buildings built between 1608 and 1780. Beside the main baroque church is the lovely chapel of **São Francisco de Penitência**. To the south, on the other side of Avenida Republica do Chile, stands Rio's cone-shaped **Catedral de São Sebastião**, finished in 1976.

Interesting neighborhoods

Nearby is the **Arcos da Lapa**, a towering 18th-century aqueduct that now serves as a bridge for the picturesque trolley cars, or *bondes* (pronounced "bon-jees") – so called because the system was funded by foreign bonds. The trolleys shuttle from a station by the cathedral to the steep streets of **Santa Teresa** Ⓕ, to the west of the center. Known for its precipitous topography and grand views, Santa Teresa is one of the most bohemian of Rio's neighborhoods; many of its residents are artists and musicians. Be sure to see the **Chácara do Ceu** (open Wed–Mon) on Rua Martinho Nobre. This small museum has splendid views of the city and a great collection of Brazilian and European paintings, including works by Picasso, Braque, and Matisse. Take a detour to the northern suburb of Quinta da Boa Vista to the **Museu Nacional**

Map on page 232

G (open Tues–Sun), which is in the palace of the emperors of Brazil. A throne room and reception rooms remain among an eclectic ethnographic and natural history collection.

Going south

Much of the shoreline between downtown Rio and the Bay of Botafogo, including Santos Dumont airport, is the result of *aterro* (landfill). Toward the airport, international and Brazilian modern art is also on display in the exciting **Museu de Arte Moderna** **H** (open Tues–Sun), which stands in grounds landscaped by Robert Burle Marx, off Avenida Infante Dom Henrique.

South of the museum in the Parque do Flamengo is a tall stone monument built to honor Brazilians who died in World War II. There is a beach here but the polluted state of Guanabara Bay makes the water less than inviting. Across the road, on a cliff, is the baroque **Igreja de Nossa Senhora da Glória** **I** and adjacent museum. The next bay going south is **Botafogo**, a lovely expanse with a marina and several movie theaters near the beach.

Emerging like a gigantic granite knee 400 meters (1,300 ft) from the waters of the entrance to Guanabara Bay is **Pão de Açúcar** (Sugarloaf Mountain). Cable cars leave **Praia Vermelha** station every half hour to sweep visitors up the mountain via the Morro da Urca, with restaurant and amphitheater. To the west of Sugarloaf begin Rio's legendary beaches. The first wide arc spans the neighborhoods of Leme to the east and Copacabana to the west, with a naval station at the western point. **Leme** is mostly residential and quiet. Rua Princesa Isabel, which divides Leme from Copacabana, is a favorite with prostitutes, and nightlife in the area tends toward the seedy side. **Copacabana**, with 350,000 residents, is Rio's most

The best way to see the elegant 19th-century homes of Santa Teresa is to take one of the yellow streetcars that leave from the cathedral. Leave valuables behind, since the open-sided cars are vulnerable to pickpockets.

BELOW: garlic for sale in a Rio market.

Carnaval!

Nothing else merits more preparation, more prolonged and devout attention, and a more lavish outpouring of private resources than the annual convulsion that has come to symbolize Brazil, for better or for worse. Extravagance, self-indulgence, exhibitionism, and a kind of gleeful innocence are the basic elements – qualities that color life in Brazil, albeit less intensely, the rest of the year. Streets normally clogged with vehicles are reclaimed by revelers on foot; macho men lasciviously parade in drag; laborers masquerade as 18th-century royalty; mothers dress up like babies; the wealthy watch the poor perform; people stay up all night and sleep all day.

Carnaval arrived with the Portuguese, a reinvention of the winter festivities of Europe. The celebrations are ostensibly the last shot at merry-making before the 40 days of fasting that precede Easter (the name is believed to be a derivation of the Italian *carne vale,* or

farewell to meat). *Carnaval* in Brazil began as an aggressive spree of throwing water, mud and flour at passers-by. This still characterizes *Carnaval* in Bolivia and Argentina, but was banned in Brazil in the 19th century.

But the *Carnaval* that Brazil is renowned for did not become a tradition until the 1930s, when neighborhood groups began to compete. Samba *(see page 57)* has become the signature music of *Carnaval.* Today the competition between samba schools is akin to the rivalry between top sports teams. Most of the members come from the humblest of Rio's neighborhoods. Samba schools hold practice sessions for months before *Carnaval,* which are often open to the public. The moment of glory comes at the gates of Rio's mammoth samba stadium, the Sambódromo, designed by Oscar Niemeyer. Some 85,000 spectators can be seated along this kilometer-long parade strip to watch the samba schools go dancing by. If you can't get a ticket, you can see the schools line up outside on Avenida Presidente Vargas.

The best street dancing is in Salvador, where carousing hordes follow deafening sound systems. As is the case everywhere during *Carnaval,* it's best to dress minimally (shorts or bathing suits) to blend into the crowds and not attract thieves. Many travelers prefer *Carnaval* in the Northeast. In Recife the preeminent *Carnaval* music is *frevo,* which ignites passions, while Bahian *Carnaval* features *afoxé,* monotonous music often sung in African languages by subdued participants in flowing satin robes.

Less frenetic *Carnavales* are held in the cities of Olinda and Ouro Preto, and in Rio's outlying suburbs. Class lines dissolve as revelers hop down the streets in camaraderie fueled by generous amounts of beer and *cachaça* (sugar-cane brandy). *Carnaval* has moved off the streets and into the clubs recently, and this is where the most intense debauchery and exhibitionism goes on.

Not everyone in Brazil is wild about *Carnaval.* Many intellectuals sneer at the kitsch, wanton drinking and lewdness. But for outsiders, there is probably no better time to see the Brazil of everyone's fantasies. ❑

LEFT: clothes serve a purely decorative purpose at Rio de Janeiro's *Carnaval.*

Map on page 232

densely populated neighborhood, and can be quite hectic. But it's a lively place to enjoy street celebrations during *Carnaval* and New Year's Eve. Although aged and somewhat the worse for wear, the **Praia de Copacabana** beach is magnificent, and stretches out almost a block to the water. It's floodlit at night, but stay close to the crowds on the sidewalk to avoid getting mugged. Tourists wandering by the water are considered "papaya with sugar" by petty thieves.

After Copacabana comes **Praia de Ipanema**, which connects at its western end with another beach, called **Leblon**. Both Ipanema and Leblon are much more attractive neighbourhoods than faded Copacabana, and altogether more pleasant areas for tourists to stay. Behind them to the north is the freshwater **Lagoa Rodrigo de Freitas**, a large natural lagoon surrounded by highrises and restaurants.

South to the most unspoiled beaches

North of the lagoon are the **Jockey Club** race track and the **Jardím Botánico** on the street of the same name. Some 5,000 species of Brazilian plants cover the garden's 100 hectares (250 acres), and though some of the grounds have gone to seed, a visit is still a pleasure. Another natural adventure is the ride up the proverbially hunchbacked **Corcovado Mountain** on the impressive steep cog railway that leaves from Cosme Velho. A newly installed escalator takes passengers from the station to the summit, where there is a café. At the top, 710 meters (2,330 ft) above the ocean, towers Rio's trademark statue of **Cristo Redentor** (Christ the Redeemer). The road down from the statue wends through the **Parque Nacional da Tijuca**, a tropical reserve that includes 100 km (60 miles) of narrow, two-lane roads winding through the forest's thick vegetation, and with several breathtaking look-out points.

Trendy boutiques with artistic signs like this are plentiful in Brazil's many coastal resorts.

BELOW: flying down to Rio.

South of the sands of Leblon, sprawling up the sides of granite slopes, are two *favelas* or hillside shantytowns – **Vidigal** and **Rocinha** (the latter is the largest in South America). Their residents, who number hundreds of thousands, often endure precarious circumstances in order to live close to their jobs on the south side of the city.

Further to the south is **São Conrado**, a fast-growing beachside suburb still free of the congestion that's endemic to the rest of Rio. Hang-gliders swoop down from the slopes above to wide sandy expanses below. The cleanest beaches lie even further south beyond the primordial plains of **Barra de Guaratiba**. These are the areas not yet fully conquered by "the marvelous city". To see them is to understand the awesome beauty that gives Rio its enduring magic.

São Paulo: Brazil's workhorse

The first thing that strikes most visitors to the city of **São Paulo** ❷ is its sheer enormity. Home to 18 million *paulistanos*, as the city's natives call themselves, São Paulo's phenomenal growth shows no signs of abating. Already the city covers nearly 2,600 sq. km (1,000 sq. miles), and it is ringed by mushrooming suburbs. São Paulo is a center of trade and industry. Two-thirds of the country's industrial goods are produced here, including nine out of 10 automobiles. "São Paulo works so that the rest of Brazil can play," *paulistanos* will tell you. Since its foundation in 1554, the city has always attracted self-reliant individualists – it was Brazil's equivalent of the Old West, and today proudly honors its old pioneers, the *bandeirantes*. Those who followed came from all over the world, especially in the 19th century, bringing industrious work habits. More recent immigrants have come from the drought-stricken states of northeastern Brazil. Poorly educated and unskilled, they often end up in the festering slums that house half the city's population.

Colonial Parati, on the Costa Verde between São Paulo and Rio de Janeiro.

BELOW: São Paulo.

São Paulo is not a place to spend your whole vacation, but it is well worth a visit. Its restaurants are as diverse as they are numerous – a reflection of the city's varied ethnic makeup. The predominant cuisine is Italian, but there are also Japanese, German, Lebanese, and French restaurants.

Paulistanos consider themselves trailblazers in the arts as well as industry. The pride and joy of the city is the MASP, the **Museu de Arte de São Paulo** (Avenida Paulista 1578; open Tues–Sun 11am–6pm; free), with nearly 1,000 pieces originating from both Ancient Greece and contemporary Brazil, along with changing temporary exhibitions.

Beneath the chaos

Perhaps the best way to explore São Paulo is by its clean, fast subway network. Stop off at **Liberdade**, home to the largest ethnic-Japanese community outside Japan. There are many inexpensive sushi bars in this area, and on Sundays there's a food and crafts fair at **Praça Liberdade**. Neighborhoods such as **Jardim Paulista** or **Jardim America** have tree-lined streets and mansions that provide respite from the downtown rush. Another favorite oasis is the lovely **Parque do Ibirapuera**, with curving pavilions designed by Oscar Niemeyer. Every odd-numbered

Map on pages 226–7

year, São Paulo hosts one of the world's largest international art shows, the prestigious Biennial, in a pavilion here. Linked to the pavilion by an undulating walkway is the **Museu de Arte Moderna** (open Tues–Sun), exhibiting work by Brazil's 21st-century sculptors and painters.

Not far away, on Rua do Horto, is the **Horto Florestal** (open daily), founded in 1896. A pleasant place to spend an afternoon, the park has a playground, picnic areas and the Pedra Grande viewpoint, offering a beautiful view of the north of São Paulo city. Inside the park is the **Museu Florestal Octvio Vecchi**, displaying a huge variety of native wood samples.

Whether you like snakes or not, the **Butantã Snake Farm** should not be missed. Some 80,000 snakes there are milked for venom daily, and serum is prepared for distribution throughout Brazil. There is a museum as well, located at Avenida Dr Vital Brasil 1500, in the Pinheiros district.

At night, São Paulo has a wide variety of clubs and cafés to while away the hours. Live music is even more plentiful here than in Rio. There's also a counter-culture quarter, the **Bela Vista** (popularly known as **Bixiga**), centered on Rua 13 de Maio. There are few old buildings left in the city, but the **Teatro Municipal**, which has resident opera and dance companies, evokes the elegant days of 19th-century coffee barons. The city frequently hosts world-class performers – *paulistanos* may be workaholics, but they demand the best when they knock off for some play.

Medical researcher and friend, Butantã snake farm.

Brasília: futuristic capital

Rising out of the great scrubby expanses of Brazil's central *cerrado*, **Brasília** ❸ looks more like a gleaming extra-terrestrial settlement than Brazil's national

BELOW: Butantã snake farm.

capital. Absent are the red-tile roofs, intimate passageways, and panache of pastel hues typical of Brazilian cities. Brasília is a cool, regimented architectural wonder, a "city of the future" that Brazilians are still trying to reconcile with the present. At 1,150 meters (3,773 ft) above sea level and more than 800 km (500 miles) from the coast, Brasília was built precisely because of its isolation from the great coastal cities. When Juscelino Kubitschek was elected president in 1955, he vowed that before he left office Brazil would have a new capital in its unpopulated interior, and he firmly believed that this capital would be a magnet to pull Brazilians away from their beloved coastline.

By 1956, work had already begun on Brasília. The city plan, drawn up by urban planner Lucio Costa, consisted of a central line of government buildings crossed by a curved arc of residential buildings – a layout that resembled the shape of an airliner. The architect chosen to design the structures was the Brazilian Oscar Niemeyer, a one-time student of the great modern Swiss architect Le Corbusier with whom he collaborated in the design of the United Nations Headquarters building in New York. The project of Brasilia was to incorporate all that was new in materials and design. Work proceeded at a furious pace, and by its inauguration in April 1960, Brasília already had 100,000 inhabitants.

At this time, Brazil's automobile industry was quickly expanding, so Brasília was designed with the certainty that everybody would get around in cars in the future. Wide thoroughfares sweep through the city, oblivious to the needs of pedestrians. With no sidewalks and few cross-walks, Brasília has the country's highest pedestrian mortality rate. Its grassy knolls are crisscrossed by red earth paths created by Brazilians who still depend on their feet to get around.

According to a popular joke, there are three great things about Brasília: its cool air, its enormous sky, and its air shuttle to Rio.

BELOW: Brasília's Foreign Ministry.

Modern wonder

Brasília is characterized by the graceful, pristine architecture of its public buildings. Down the hill past the main bus terminal, the Eixo Monument (the Monumental Axis) opens onto the **Esplanada dos Ministérios** (Ministries Esplanade). Flanking the end of the Esplanade are Niemeyer's two finest buildings, the **Palácio Itamaratí**, housing the Foreign Ministry, which floats in splendid isolation in the midst of a reflecting pool; and the **Palácio da Justiça** (Ministry of Justice), whose six curtains of falling water on the exterior echo the natural waterfalls around Brasília. At the eastern end of the esplanade is the **Praça dos Três Poderes** (Three Powers Plaza) – a dense forest of political symbols: the **Palácio do Planalto**, the **Supremo Tribunal Federal** (Supreme Court), and the twin towers and offset domes of the **Congresso Nacional** – the building whose silhouette is the signature of Brasília. On the plaza proper is the small **Museu Histórico de Brasília** (open daily). Inside is a series of panels outlining the history of Brasília and the most memorable sayings of Kubitschek, whose powers of hyperbole must have rivaled his talent for construction.

In front of the supreme court is a blindfolded figure of Justice, sculpted by Alfredo Ceschiatti. Facing the Palácio do Planalto are the figures of *The Warriors* by Bruno Giorgi, a tribute to the thousands of workers who built Brasília. A note of whimsy is added to the plaza by Niemeyer's pigeon house, the **Pombal**.

The most recent addition to the plaza is the **Pantheon Tancredo Neves** – a tribute to the founding father of the New Republic, who died in April 1985 before he could be sworn in as president. Inside the darkened interior is Brasília's most extraordinary and disturbing artwork. The mural, by João Camara, depicts the story of an uprising in the 18th century led by Brazil's best-known revolutionary, Tiradentes (Joaquim José da Silva Xavier). Painted in seven black and white panels (rather like Picasso's *Guernica*), it is heavy with masonic symbolism.

The **Catedral Metropolitana da Nossa Senhora Aparecida**, at the western end of the Esplanada dos Ministérios, is a unique concrete building with a spectacular stained-glass domed roof. Three hundred meters (330 yards) away, on the northern side of the Eixo Monument near the Rodoviária, is the pyramid-shaped **Teatro Nacional** (open daily), where art shows and other exhibitions are held.

Minas Gerais: treasure trove of the Portuguese

Nestled in the steep hills north of Rio de Janeiro are some of Brazil's most beautiful colonial-era cities, in the large state of **Minas Gerais**, a mining region. In the 18th century it was the world's principal source of gold and today more than half the country's minerals and nearly all its iron ore come from here.

Belo Horizonte ❹, today's capital city of Minas Gerais, is neatly planned and a good base from which to explore the region. A hundred kilometers (60 miles) to the south lies the most prized creation of Brazil's Golden Age, the beautifully preserved city of **Ouro Preto**. Its name comes from the gold encrusted with

Congress building, Brasília.

BELOW: Brasília, a monument to mid-20th century urban planning

Watching the world go by, Ouro Preto.

LEFT: colonial church, Minas Gerais.
RIGHT: sculpture by Aleijadinho, Congonhas do Campo.

black iron oxide that was discovered nearby, early in the 18th century.

The find set off a gold rush, and Ouro Preto soon became the colonial capital of Minas Gerais. The gold lasted more than a century, during which time Ouro Preto and several nearby cities acquired sumptuous baroque churches and mansions, the only lasting heritage of 1,200 tons of gold extracted during that era. Thanks to the Brazilian government's decision to declare the entire city a national monument in 1933, many of its colonial treasures are intact, and it has been made a World Heritage Site by UNESCO. Cobbled streets wend through hilly quarters lined by well-kept colonial homes. Thirteen baroque churches gild the city of 25,000, many displaying the genius of the sculptor and architect Antônio Francisco Lisboa, better known as *Aleijadinho*, or Little Cripple. Afflicted as an adult by a crippling disease, Aleijadinho sculpted some of Brazil's most beautiful and expressive statuary – with his hammer and chisel strapped to his wrists.

The self-taught artist almost single-handedly shifted the esthetics of the Golden Age from the boxish forms of mannerism to the sensuous curves of baroque. The most striking example is the exterior of the church of **Nossa Senhora do Rosario dos Prêtos**, built by black slaves (there were insufficient funds to complete the interior). Nearby is the church of **Nossa Senhora do Pilar**, whose interior is a profusion of baroque carved angels and gilded walls. At the center of town is the recently restored **Praça Tiradentes**, fronted by the imposing **Museu da Inconfidência**. Just off the square is the church of **São Francisco de Assis**, an exquisite example of Aleijadinho's artistry and a repository of some of his most moving wood and soapstone figures. More of Aleijadinho's work can be viewed at the impressive **Nossa Senhora do Carmo**

Map
on pages
226–7

church (open Tues–Sun), also on the plaza , and at the sacred art collection in the nearby **Museu do Oratório** (openTues–Sun).

Ouro Preto has an important mining school, the sprawling **Escola de Minas**, which incorporates a mineralogy museum (open Tues–Sun), and there is an interesting gem museum in the imposing **Governor's Palace** nearby.

Treasures of stone

The colonial town of **Mariana**, just east of Ouro Preto, is another treasure left by gold barons who expressed gratitude for their good fortune by building extravagant churches. Work by Aleijadinho and Athayde can be found here, as well as a former beating post for slaves marked by a stone monument to Justice.

Some 30 km (20 miles) west of Ouro Preto is **Congonhas do Campo**, the site of Aleijadinho's greatest feat: his hauntingly beautiful soapstone carvings of twelve Old Testament prophets outside the majestic church of **Bom Jesus do Matozinho**, a shrine for pilgrims. There are also 66 expressive carvings in cedarwood of Christ's Passion by Aleijadinho and his students.

Located 100 km (60 miles) to the south, **São João del Rei** is a colonial city of 60,000 with three striking 18th-century churches. There is also beautiful pewterware made at a local factory. The railway station has been turned into a gleaming museum, the **Museu Ferroviário** (open Tues–Sat), a fascinating reminder of old-fashioned rail travel. Nearby is the silversmith village of **Tiradentes**, named after the man who agitated for independence from Portugal and was hanged in Ouro Preto. **Sabará**, 22 km (14 miles) east of Belo Horizonte, has fine examples of Aleijadinho's work in its church, as well as Oriental influences, brought by Portuguese Jesuits.

BELOW: the colonial charm of Ouro Preto.

The least commercialized of all the colonial towns is the World Heritage Site of **Diamantina** , 284 km (175 miles) north of Belo Horizonte. Once the center of a diamond boom, Diamantina was the birthplace of President Kubitschek, founder of Brasília. The colorful **Nossa Senhora do Rosário** church was built entirely by slaves, and the woodcarvings of the saints are black. The informative **Museu do Diamante** (Diamond Museum; open Tues–Sun) has a back room in which grisly implements of torture used against slaves are kept.

Baiana girl.

Salvador and the Northeast

Brazil's Northeast is quite different from its prosperous south. The accent is different, the people are different, the food is more fiery, and the barren *sertão* (scrubland) is more like an African desert than tropical Brazil. For the essence of the Brazilian mystique, one must go to where it all began: **Bahia**, the state where Pedro Alvares Cabral established contact between Portuguese and native cultures in 1500. **São Salvador da Bahia de Todos os Santos**  is Brazil's first capital and is still the richest source of the country's cultural identity. Salvador – also known as Bahia, the name of the state – is where much of the food, religion, dance, and music that characterize Brazil originated, where Catholic Portuguese culture blended with the beliefs and esthetics of the slaves who were brought from West Africa.

The 2.6 million inhabitants of Salvador, known as *baianos* (pronounced bye-*ah*-nooz) are known throughout Brazil for their laid-back, festive temperament. The city is convulsed by street celebrations most months of the year. *Carnaval* is the biggest – it officially begins a day before carnival in the rest of the country. Salvador's carnival is entirely participatory – frenzied hordes of dancers

revel behind *trios elétricos* – floats laden with live bands and deafening sound systems. It is not for the faint-hearted, as the crowds often get unruly.

Rich heritage

The backdrop for all this revelry is a city with a rich heritage and a beautiful natural setting. Salvador is built mostly on a high escarpment overlooking a bay; the upper level of the city, where almost all the ancient buildings are found, is known as **Cidade Alta**. The **Terreiro de Jesus** square is home to three of Salvador's most famous churches, the largest of which is the **Catedral Basílica**. Rising majestically from the adjoining square, **Praça Anchieta**, is one of the world's most opulent baroque churches, **São Francisco**. To the north side of Terreiro de Jesus, the **Museu Afro-Brasileiro** (open Mon–Fri) in the old medical faculty highlights the strong African influence on Bahian culture.

The **Pelourinho** neighborhood is full of pastel-hued 17th- and 18th-century colonial buildings, considered by UNESCO the best examples in the New World. Here you'll find practitioners of *capoeira*, a kind of foot-fighting martial art originally brought by slaves from Angola, performed to the rhythm of a tambourine and the throbbing sound of a *berimbau*, whose single steel string stretched across a bowed stick resonates in a hollowed gourd. *Capoeiristas* perform on the street for donations, but they also give shows during the evening at a cookery school and restaurant called SENAC (open Tues–Sat) on Pelourinho's plaza. It's best to visit Pelourinho in daylight, or in groups, since street crime flourishes after dark. Visitors will notice numerous women street vendors wearing flowing white lace dresses. They are known as Baianas, and they sell the spicy and sweet specialties of Bahian cuisine.

TIP

Bahian cooking is considerably more spicy than elsewhere in Brazil, and generous amounts of coconut oil – *dêndé* – are used. Seafood predominates, and is often prepared in succulent stews called *moquecas*.

BELOW: *Baiana* lace dresses, Salvador.

A famous Art Deco elevator called the Elevador Lacerda whisks you down from near the Praça Municipal to the **Cidade Baixa**, which has a big handicrafts marketplace called the **Mercado Modelo**. The white, lace-decorated garments sold here are typically Bahian and the market is a lively microcosm of Bahian life. Left from the market is the church of **Nossa Senhora de Conceição de Praia**, which houses the image of Bahia's patron saint and is the site of the annual religious procession held on December 8, one of the most important feast days in Salvador's Catholic calendar.

About 10 km (6 miles) in the opposite direction stands the famous church of **Nosso Senhor do Bonfim** and another market, the **Mercado São Joaquim**, fascinating but rather run-down and dirty.

Cidade Baixa is the departure point for schooners taking tourists around the bay, and for passenger boats to small towns in the vicinity, as well as the island of **Itaparica**, where Club Med built its first installation in Brazil. Most of the island's 20,000 inhabitants make their living fishing, and the simple restaurants serve delicious seafood. Be sure to try the marinated fresh oysters.

Pristine beaches

Like Rio, Salvador is a city that lives at its beautiful beaches. The most accessible from downtown is **Barra**, small but extremely popular. Bars near the beach are often jammed, and the fun continues long after sundown. Barra is at the tip of a long scalloped shoreline of beaches, most of them shaded by palms and with grassy areas. The best are the farthest out from the city, **Itapoán** and **Piatã**. It's best to hit these beaches on weekends when there are crowds, both for safety and because there will inevitably be live music performed at local *al fresco* bars.

Porto Seguro is the home of the sensual lambada *dance, which is taught by curvaceous women at a host of waterfront bars.*

BELOW: the blood of a slaughtered chicken drips on an initiate's head during a *Macumba* ritual.

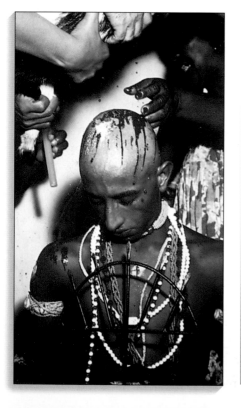

RELIGIOUS SPIRIT

Street intersections and meeting halls are places where you may see *Macumba*, rituals practiced with variations throughout the country. *Macumba* came with the West African slaves, and its phalanx of deities belongs to the traditions of the Yoruba-speaking peoples. The imposition of Christianity simply resulted in each of the saints taking a corresponding identity with a Yoruba deity.

Because street intersections form a cross, they are thought to be centers of power. Visitors are usually welcome to watch *Macumba* rites, although photography is forbidden. *Candomblé* is the kind of *Macumba* practiced around Salvador, where slaves first disembarked. Drumming is always an element and its hypnotic rhythms frequently plunge participants into wild gyrating trances. This happens at the sacred meeting places called *terreiros*. Devotees wear white to honor Oxalá, *Candomblé*'s equivalent to Christ and the highest of the deities.

In southern Brazil, another kind of *Macumba* flourishes – *Umbanda*. It is a kind of white magic – good deeds and generosity are asked of the gods. It blends Catholicism, *Candomblé*, and "Spiritism", a cult which started in France in the mid-19th century. People are believed to be visited by the spirits of deities during *Umbanda* sessions.

Some 80 km (50 miles) north of Salvador is **Praia do Forte**, a 11-km (7-mile) stretch of white-sand beach, bordered by 100,000 coconut palms, that has become increasingly popular with tourists. Also around 80 km (50 miles) north of Salvador, the **Costa do Sauipe** complex, opened in January 2001 at a cost of US$100 million, a luxury hotel complex, closed to non-residents.

Ilheus, a coastal city 390 km (240 miles) south of Salvador, is a mixture of modern and ancient architecture. The city is renowned for its lively carnival and the lovely beaches nearby, and is the center for 95 percent of Brazil's cocoa production. Further south down the coast is **Porto Seguro**, a tourist hub, where Cabral and his explorers first set foot in Brazil.

Inland from Salvador begins the enormous scrub region called the *sertão*, frequently parched by drought and a tableau of human misery. The *sertanejos* who live there are often forced to leave to avoid starvation.

Beyond Salvador

Bahia is the southernmost part of a nine-state region collectively known as the Northeast, home to a third of Brazil's population. The *nordestinos* have, until very recently, benefited least from Brazil's material progress. Those who live along the coastal regions of Bahia are predominantly of African descent, while those living inland and to the north are a Portuguese/Amerindian mixture.

The Northeast has wonderful white-sand beaches where you can still find fishermen using *jangadas,* an ancient precursor to the windsurfer. The city of **Maceió** has the most spectacular beaches nearby. North of Maceió is **Recife** ❼, the principal city of the Northeast, with 1.4 million inhabitants. Recife's beaches are protected by coral reefs, and the most popular is in the well-to-do **Boa**

Map
on pages
226–7

Hammock room only on the deck class of an Amazon steamer.

BELOW: sunset over the River Amazon.

BELOW: opera in the jungle: Teatro Amazonas.

Viagem sector of the city. Located just to the north is **Olinda,** a beautifully conserved colonial gem designated a World Cultural Monument by UNESCO.

Further up the coastline is **João Pessoa**, the Americas' easternmost city. It's very pleasant and brightly painted, with a wealth of baroque churches. Huge sand dunes distinguish the beaches of **Natal** ❽, capital of the state of Rio Grande do Norte. Outside the city are other oceanside enclaves, such as delightful **Touros** (95 km/60 miles to the north), shaded by coconut groves.

Fortaleza ❾, the capital of Ceara, once drab and utilitarian, has benefited from the huge amount of capital that has flowed into the region in the past few years, using some of it to completely rebuild the seafront area, which now rivals Recife's Boa Viagem for elegance and liveliness. The city has become a very popular destination for international tourists.

The river ports: Manaus to Belém

The last thing you might expect in the middle of the Amazon jungle, 1,600 km (1,000 miles) from the sea, is a thriving port city. But **Manaus** ❿ was cut from the wilderness in the 19th century: where mad conquistadors once searched in vain for gold, Brazilians found a modern El Dorado of rubber. Today, this strange outpost is enjoying a new boom as a tourist destination and one of the duty-free capitals of South America. Arriving in Manaus by boat is dramatic, not because of the city, which is spread out on low bluffs – but because it is the meeting place of two Amazon tributaries at an 8-km (5-mile) wide junction. The dark River Negro, which looks like fizzy cola when riverboats churn it up, hits the yellowish River Solimoes, and the two vast currents run together, side by side without mingling their differently colored waters.

The chaotic bustle of modern Manaus is a dim reflection of its past glory. In 1888 the pneumatic tire was invented, and Amazon rubber suddenly became very valuable. For a brief, dazzling period, Manaus became the richest city in the world. Pioneers flooded into the jungle, creating the boom town of fast fortunes and grand gestures portrayed in Werner Herzog's film *Fitzcarraldo*.

Thousands of rubber tappers collected latex from isolated trees found deep in the jungle, working as virtual slaves along the sinuous waterways of the Amazon, and the newly rich rubber barons, quaffing champagne and lighting their cigars with US$100 bills, earned Manaus a name for extravagance and decadence. When the rubber boom collapsed, Manaus fell into a torpor that was only broken in 1967, when it became a duty-free zone.

The most famous and bizarre monument to the boom days is the grand opera house, the **Teatro Amazonas** (open for tours Mon–Sat). Materials for this temple of art in the jungle were wholly imported from Europe: white marble from Italy, iron pillars from England, and polished wood from France.The original house curtain remains, painted with Grecian nymphs lolling in the Amazon River. In its heyday, the opera house, attracted such greats as the Italian tenor Caruso and today, fully restored, it can still pull in international names.

The old **port area** of Manaus is thriving. Wooden riverboats dump exotic cargoes while overhead circle black urubu birds. Ramshackle houses have been thrown up around the port on precarious stilts. A more imposing construction is the stone **Alfândega** (Customs House), dating from 1906.

Toucan in the Amazon.

For a glimpse of the lost Amerindian cultures of the area, head for the **Museu do Homem do Norte** (open Mon–Fri), on Avenida Sete de Setembro 1385, which gives a good idea of traditional lifestyles. There is even a "beach" near

BELOW: sunset over Manaus dockside.

SLOWLY DOWN THE AMAZON

Nothing quite matches the romance of taking a slow boat down the world's greatest river. This vast waterway is still plied by hundreds of vessels: from ocean-going cargo ships to passenger boats. Your best bet is to take a half-day trip from Manaus or Belém. Longer voyages are not really geared for tourists and are just a means of getting from A to B. Smaller, wooden vessels known as *gaiolas*, or "birdcages", after the crowded mid-deck levels where passengers pile over one another in hammocks, still work the smaller tributaries from Manaus to Benjamin Constant, on the border of Colombia, then onward into Iquitos in Peru, and back. Finding one of these boats is largely a matter of patience and luck. The smaller companies have no fixed schedules, and the only way to arrange a booking is to wander around the port, talk to people and check out the boats for yourself. You'll no doubt be approached by skippers or agents offering you space on their boats. These can be relatively comfortable or crowded, noisy and somewhat unhygienic. Food is basic, and bottled water should be taken. Stops are made at jungle villages, where the whole population turns out to watch the boat unload beer, pass out a few letters and take on a cargo of bananas.

Anaconda crossing!

the **Hotel Tropical**, where braver swimmers can prove that the river is free of piranhas and electric eels which can so spoil a holiday.

Many tour companies head deeper into the jungle, but need a few days to get past the disordered "development" before finding virgin territory with animals. Jungle lodge stays are also on offer, with nature-watching canoe trips.

Beyond Manaus

Further down the Amazon is the port of **Santarém ⓫**, at the confluence with the Tapajós River. Once a colonial fortress, Santarém today is a kind of Dodge City for half a million jungle gold prospectors, or *garimpeiros*. On the south side of the mouth of the Amazon stands proud, stately **Belém ⓬**, 145 km (90 miles) from open ocean. A city of more than a million inhabitants, Belém retains some of the graceful airs of its rubber-boom heyday. Its old town has colonial-era homes and churches and there's a fort nearby commandeered by Círculo Militar.

Belém's striking **Catedral de Nossa Senhora da Graça**, built in 1617, contains artworks in Carrara marble and paintings by the Italian de Angelis. Not far away is the dockside municipal market **Ver-o-Peso** (Check out the Weight), where fishermen bring their catches. Another landmark is the **Emilio Goeldi Museum**, with exhibits of native crafts from nearby **Marajó Island**. An interesting new addition to the town is the Estação das Docas – imaginatively restored warehouses with tourist facilities and restaurants.

Rondônia: Brazil's Wild West

BELOW: rough and ready in Rondônia.

If you thought the days of the Wild West were over, consider **Rondônia**. At the beginning of the 1970s this Brazilian state was tree-tangled wilderness on the southern flank of the Amazon jungle, bordering Bolivia. It was home to just a few thousand hardy rubber tappers. Today, settlers have pushed their way pell-mell into almost every corner of Rondônia, hacking down the jungle and frequently enforcing their land claims with the squeeze of a trigger. In the 1980s, nearly one-quarter of the Rondônian rainforest was destroyed, mostly by burning, to clear land for planting and cattle pastures. In the dry season, from May to October, a blanket of smoke hangs over the state as forests are incinerated. With the extension of roadway BR 364 from São Paulo to the capital of Rondônia, the riverport of **Porto Velho ⓭**, express buses carried peasant migrants directly to the new frontier. A ride up the highway in one of the local buses that ply the route provides a revealing view both of frontier life and rainforest devastation. Along the highway are vast pastures cluttered with charred stumps and tall naked trunks of once mighty rainforest trees. On the horizon looms the high dense wall of jungle that used to cover the pastures.

A boom town called **Ariquemes ⓮** along BR 364 gives a taste of the free-for-all world of the frontier. At the bus station, or *rodoviária*, sleek buses pull in from the south, discharging loads of dazed migrants clutching their possessions. Some are met by relatives. A shop at the station sells T-shirts proclaiming "Rondônia – you have to see it to believe it."

In town, the dusty streets are lined by weather-beaten storefronts and filled with homesteaders shopping for provisions. Many have blond hair and blue eyes, legacies of their German forebears who settled in Brazil's south. Snake-oil vendors compete with bible-thumping evangelists for attention. Inside noisy bars, men shoot pool and talk about the latest confrontations between squatters and well-armed land barons.

Determined settlers

Despite endemic malaria, periodic shoot-outs, and poor soils, few of these people ever have second thoughts about having left the south behind. They are proud of their tenacity and are determined to make it on this quickly expanding frontier. Discussions about ecological destruction fail to move them; short-term survival is their top priority. Those who occupied the rainforest before the land rush – the rubber tappers and the indigenous Amerindians – have been forced further west as the frontier encroaches on their way of life.

Rubber tapping has all but been abandoned in Rondônia as the trees have disappeared, despite laws enacted for their protection. Some 300,000 Brazilians still survive collecting the fruits of the forest – wild rubber, Brazil nuts, and resin. They now live mostly in the state of Acre, west of Rondônia on the borders of Bolivia and Peru. Key to their survival is their isolation and international pressures to protect their benign co-existence with the rainforest. Some protected areas called "extractive reserves" have been established for these jungle harvesters. But as Brazil's population continues to grow faster than the new jobs, the pressures to clear the forest that have transformed Rondônia are likely to keep moving westward.

Ilha de Maracá, near Boa Vista.

LEFT: snappy sunbathers.
RIGHT: a red-necked Tuiuiú

*Unfortunate
piranhas, Pantanal.*

The Pantanal: bird paradise

An enormous marsh called the **Pantanal** is perhaps the most exquisite gallery of all for observing Brazilian fauna. Comprising 230,000 sq. km (89,000 sq. miles) of seasonally flooded swampland east of the Paraguay River on Brazil's western border with Bolivia, the Pantanal is home to more than 600 species of birds, 350 kinds of fish, and an abundance of reptiles and animals. There are white ibises, egrets, blue herons, green parakeets, pheasants, and the 2-meter (7-ft) tall white Jabirú or Tuiuiú stork.

During the rainy months (October to April) when waters are high in the north, the birds feed on fish in the southern sector. From May until September, they move to the shallower waters in the north. The best time to visit is in the winter months of June, July, and August; January and February are infernally hot and humid. When the waters recede from the northern Pantanal, wide sandy riverbanks are exposed and large alligators, called jacarés, like to sun on the sand. There are also ocelots, pumas, wild boar, jaguars, red lake deer, tapirs, and a large furry rodent, the capivara.

Exploring the swamps

Access to the Pantanal's edge is quite easy, but getting around inside is another matter. **Cuiabá ⑮**, capital of Mato Grosso, is an attractive city that once enjoyed a gold boom, though it gets intensely hot here. Some 70 km (45 miles) northeast of Cuiabá there are cool waterfalls at **Chapada de Guimarães**, the source of much of the water that enters the northern part of the swamp. Just south of Cuiabá is **Santo Antônio de Leverger**, on the edge of the marshland. From here it's possible to fly to hotels and cattle ranches, or *fazendas*, within the Pan-

BELOW: wildlife-watching at the Caiman Ecological Refuge, Pantanal.

tanal. You can obtain ground transport, boats, flights, even hot-air balloon rides at these lodges, for observing the wildlife. Fishing is permitted – piranhas are prized for their supposed aphrodisiacal powers – but hunting emphatically is not. The main attraction is **Baia Chacorore**, a huge shallow water basin flocked with roseate spoonbills. Its banks literally crawl with alligators.

You can drive into the Pantanal along the partially completed **Trans-Pantaneira Highway**, which starts just outside the small town of **Poconé**, 102 km (63 miles) from Cuiabá. Vehicles can be hired here. The road is often rough and sometimes floods, but it crosses many rivers (there are 126 bridges) and provides a close-up view of wildlife. The road ends 145 km (90 miles) into the Pantanal at Porto Jofre. Accommodation is available en route and at the port.

Although the Pantanal reaches up to the city limits of **Corumbá ⓰**, a border town on the southwest flank, local tours reveal little much of the wildlife has fled to more remote areas. The best way to see the swamp is to arrange passage on cattle boats that penetrate more deeply into the area.

Iguaçu Falls and the Itaipú Dam

Armadillo, caught for the cameras only.

The famous falls, which link the Brazil, Paraguay, and Argentine borders, are described fully in the Argentina chapter *(see page 336)*. The closest Brazilian city to the falls is **Foz do Iguaçu ⓱**, near the junction of the Paraná and Iguaçu rivers. This frontier town has grown phenomenally in the past decades, due to the construction of the world's largest hydroelectric dam, the **Itaipú** (Guaraní for "Singing Rock"). It is well worth visiting, and is only possible on a guided tour. Built jointly by Brazil and Paraguay, it is powered by the waters of the Paraná River, which divides the two countries. ❑

BELOW: twilight flight, Pantanal

THE RICHES OF THE AMAZON RIVER

The world's greatest river and largest rainforest, in the heart of Brazil, is estimated to contain one-tenth of the plant and insect species on earth

The Amazon River is one of the greatest symbols of Brazil. It rises in the snows of the Peruvian Andes just a short distance from the Pacific Ocean. It then travels across the heart of South America – a distance of 6,570 km (4,080 miles) – before it flows out into the Atlantic Ocean at the equator. It has about 15,000 tributaries, some of which, like the Araguaia and the Madeira, are mighty rivers in themselves. Just past Manaus, one of the most spectacular river sights is the meeting of the "black waters" of the Negro river with the "white waters" of the Solimoes river, two other Amazon tributaries. The Amazon has a heavier flow than any other river, depositing in the ocean each year about one-fifth of the world's fresh water.

At its mouth the Amazon is 300 km (185 miles) wide, a labyrinth of channels and islands, one of which has a greater landmass than Switzerland. The water flows with such force that it is still fresh 180 km (110 miles) out into the ocean.

RAINFOREST AND AMERINDIANS

The Amazon's network of dark, dense jungles has often been referred to as The Great Green Hell. In the west of the Amazon basin, it is still possible to fly for several hours and see nothing below but a carpet of tropical forest, broken only by rivers snaking their way through the trees. The Amazon has remained virtually unchanged for the past 100 million years, for it did not pass through the same ice ages that altered other parts of the world's landscapes. Some areas are still inhabited by indigenous groups who have survived through the centuries and have never had contact with the world outside their own jungle.

△ **AMAZON CRUISES**
A river trip along the legendary Amazon, taking in the sights, sounds, and smells of the verdant jungle, is one of the highlights for many visitors to Brazil.

▷ **BLACK SPIDER MONKEY**
This delightful animal uses its tail to swing from branch to branch in the forest.

◁ **POISON ARROW FROG**
The poison from this brightly colored frog used to be extracted by the Amerindians to use on the tip of arrows.

△ **RIO MADEIRA**
Though just a tributary of the Amazon, the Madeira river itself flows over a distance of more than 1,600 km (1,000 miles).

DEFORESTATION IN THE AMAZON

Over 51 million hectares (126 million acres) of the forest have been destroyed. Despite reforestation programs, the rate of growth is still far exceeded by the rate of destruction and only about two-thirds of the original forest remain. In the 1960s and 1970s, in the east of the basin, the government built a vast network of roads, and cattle companies moved in, burning the forest to sow pasture. But ranching was not successful, for the soil, once denuded of the protective forest cover, quickly became barren.

Foreign timber companies demand the Amazon's hardwoods, now that the rest of the world's hardwood forests have been destroyed; and big grain farmers, cultivating genetically engineered soybeans, are moving in here from the south of Brazil.

△ JUNGLE LODGING
At the eco-friendly Ariau Hotel guests can hear the bewitching sounds of the tropical forest at night.

▽ VICTORIA REGINA
The indigenous water lily has enormous, circular leaves that can be up to 2 meters (6 ft) across.

◁ URUCU BERRIES
Amazonian Amerindians treasure the Urucu tree. Its berries contain a red-colored dye that they use to paint their bodies and faces.

△ RUBBER TAPPING
Thousands of families, living deep in the rainforest, still tap rubber trees for the latex.

▷ TOUCAN
This striking bird, a recognizable image of the Amazon forest, uses its huge yellow bill to crush the seeds it feeds on.

THE SOUTHERN CONE

*Often considered the most European part of South America,
this region contains some of its most cosmopolitan
cities and starkly stunning scenery*

El cono sur – the "southern cone" of Paraguay, Argentina, Uruguay, and Chile – makes up a geological and cultural unit quite apart from the rest of South America. Sparsely populated in pre-Columbian days by nomadic tribes, these countries today form the most ethnically and climatically European part of the continent.

European settlement came late to the south, with many areas unexplored until the late 19th century. The newcomers were from many places besides Spain, Portugal, and Italy. Small colonies remain here of Germans, Boers, Britons, and Swiss, all descendants of these pioneers. The attraction was the prospect of sudden wealth: several decades ago these countries were relatively affluent, riding on booms of agriculture and minerals.

Isolated Paraguay *(see page 265)* has no access to the sea, but its capital, Asunción, has become a bustling duty-free center – although horse-drawn carts still clatter through its streets, beneath statues of long forgotten generals. Most of the country is made up of the vast, sparsely populated Chaco lands *(see page 272)*.

Squeezed between the Pacific Ocean and the Andes mountains, ultra-narrow Chile *(see page 279)* covers a huge range of latitudes. Heading south from the northern Atacama Desert – one of the driest in the world – you pass through the moderate climate of the capital, Santiago *(see page 281)*, with its surrounding vineyards *(see page 284)*, to the snow-covered forests of the Lake District *(see page 290)*. Beyond that are the glaciers, peaks, and windswept fishing villages of Chilean Patagonia *(see page 295)*.

The republic of Uruguay *(see page 311)*, once dubbed "the Switzerland of South America" for its progressive political tradition, had enough money from beef to build a powerful social welfare state. Today, the country seems frozen in the 1920s. The capital, Montevideo *(see page 313)*, is a quaint city where hand-cranked automobiles still groan through the streets, while the country's beautiful beaches are mostly used by the wealthy from elsewhere in the world.

The second-largest country on the sub-continent, Argentina *(see page 321)* was at the beginning of the 20th century its richest by far. Things haven't gone quite as expected since then, and the elegant capital Buenos Aires *(see page 325)* is crowded with the crumbling Parisian relics of the boom days. Argentina sprawls over every climatic zone, with arid northern plains where *gauchos* still ride *(see page 338)*, the sub-tropical province of Misiones *(see page 336)*, lush forests around Bariloche *(see page 339)*, the windswept, sheep-strewn plains of Patagonia *(see page 341)*, and at the southern tip of the continent, the chilly, mountainous island of Tierra del Fuego *(see page 344)*. ❏

PRECEDING PAGES: huge chunks of ice broken from the glacier melt in the Canal de los Tempanos (Channel of the Icebergs) at Glacier National Park, Argentina.
LEFT: traditional chaps: *gauchos* of northwest Argentina.

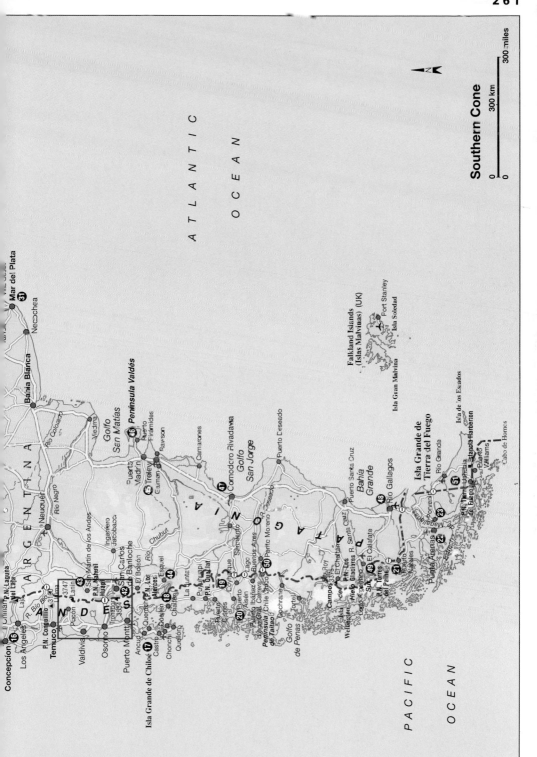

Southern Cone

PARAGUAY

Map
on pages
260–1

*One of the continent's most intriguing nations, this is a land of
Utopias and experimental communities, where the language of the
original inhabitants shares pre-eminence with that of their colonists*

Surrounded by Bolivia, Brazil, and Argentina, the small subtropical nation
of Paraguay lies at the heart of South America. The River Paraguay divides
the country into two distinct halves: the lush, fertile east, where most of the
population lives, and the barren Chaco tablelands to the west, home to a few
scattered settlements, Mennonite farmers, and nomadic Amerindians. The River
Paraguay eventually feeds into the River Plate, linking the country historically
and geographically to the other River Plate nations of Uruguay and Argentina.

"An island surrounded by land" is how exiled Paraguayan novelist Augusto
Roa Bastos has described his landlocked native country. The phrase refers not
only to Paraguay's physical remoteness but to a kind of psychic solitude brought
about by wars, dictatorships, and a profound sense of ethnic unity. A visitor to
the capital, Asunción, can't help noticing the profusion of monuments commemorating military rulers, crushing defeats, and Pyrrhic victories. Yet one is
also struck by the tropical prettiness of the colonial city, and by the soft-spoken,
gentle manners of Paraguayans, reminders that the Spaniards who first settled
this region dreamed not of plunder but of founding an earthly paradise.

In a country where almost everyone is of part Guaraní descent, schoolbooks
devote considerable space to pre-Columbian Paraguay. The Guaraní were the
original inhabitants of what is now Asunción. Mainly
farmers, they were also accomplished warriors who
bore suffering stoically. Early Spanish chroniclers
reported with horror that the Guaraní were cannibals,
although this custom was apparently limited to the
ritual eating of prisoners of war. Their language, in the
words of one Spanish priest, was "one of the most
copious and elegant on the globe", and it was used as
a *lingua franca* throughout the region.

Arrival of the Spanish

Asunción was founded on August 15, 1537, by
Domingo de Irala, a man of letters who came seeking
refuge from the miseries of the settlement at Buenos
Aires and the rigors of the conquest. The Guaraní,
who were also anxious for Inca gold, were eager to
form an alliance with the Spaniards and gave them
their daughters as tokens of good faith. The discovery
that the Incas had already been conquered and plundered by Pizarro, and the lush life in Asunción, far
from the sea and the watchful eye of the Spanish
crown, induced Irala and his men to stay. The colonial
farms were organized in a feudal manner, although
intermarriage evened out the social hierarchy.

Fulgencio Yegros declared Paraguay's independence on May 14, 1811, and ruled along with a
civilian lawyer named Doctor José Gaspar Rodríguez
de Francia. Soon after independence Francia seized

PRECEDING PAGES:
the Itaipú Dam.
LEFT: guards at the
Panteón de los
Héroes, Asunción.
BELOW: young
Paraguayans.

Steam train waiting to depart from Asunción station.

BELOW: 19th-century etching of General Urquiza's Palace, San José.

power, and Congress named him supreme dictator for life in 1816. To protect Paraguay from the danger of annexation by Argentina or Brazil, Dr Francia closed the borders: no one was allowed in or out during his 24-year reign.

"El Supremo", as Francia was called, ruled by absolute decree. A learned man, initially a frugal and honest ruler, he grew deranged by power and isolation. At one point he ordered all the dogs in the country killed; he also decreed that none of his subjects could look at him in the street. At his death in 1840, no Paraguayan priest was willing to say a funeral Mass, and a priest was finally imported from Argentina. Paraguay was plunged into political chaos until the next dictator, Carlos Antonio López, was proclaimed in 1844.

López was an enlightened despot who re-opened the country to progress and sent students to Europe to study. But his son and designated successor, Francisco Solano López, was a weak and spoilt young man. Feeling that Paraguay's neighbors did not take his country seriously, he intervened in Uruguay's civil war, and quickly found himself at war with Brazil and Argentina as well. The ensuing War of the Triple Alliance was disastrous for Paraguay. The country was further ravaged by cholera, and López, at this point seriously unhinged, ordered the execution of hundreds of people, including his two brothers and scores of officers. Abetted by his Irish mistress, Elisa Lynch, he also executed his childhood sweetheart and other society ladies who had snubbed Madame Lynch. On March 1, 1870, he was shot by one of his own generals after refusing to surrender. "I die with Paraguay," he exclaimed, which was almost literally true. After the war, more than half the population of 525,000 were dead; of the survivors, only 29,000 were adult males. Paraguay was rebuilt mostly by women, who resigned themselves to a polygamous society as the Catholic Church looked the other way.

Between the fall of Solano López and Paraguay's bloody Chaco War with Bolivia, the country changed presidents 32 times and endured two assassinations of presidents, six *coups d'état*, two revolutions and eight attempted revolutions. Paraguay won the Chaco War of 1932–1935, fought over a piece of barren land that was believed to contain oil and other mineral deposits *(see page 38)*, but once again the male population was devastated. A succession of dictators followed, until in 1954 the son of a German brewmeister, Alfredo Stroessner, seized power and ruled with an iron fist for nearly 35 years.

Winds of change

Stroessner played off one political faction against another while providing a sanctuary for fleeing Nazis and exiling, imprisoning, torturing, and killing rivals and opponents. In the all-pervading climate of corruption, Paraguay became notorious as a haven for smuggling, much of it in narcotics. Human rights activists and some of the country's artists and writers, notably the novelist and poet Augusto Roa Bastos and the artist Carlos Colombino, provided a moral center for resistance. Stroessner's regime brought some notable innovations, but in 35 years these developments may well have occurred without him. In the 1970s, the construction of a Brazilian-Paraguayan hydroelectric dam at Itaipú in eastern Paraguay stimulated land investment, expanded financial services, and provided thousands of jobs. The giant Paraguayan-Argentine hydroelectric project at Yacryeta, proposed in 1973, began operating in 1997.

On February 3, 1989, Stroessner was overthrown by General Andrés Rodríguez, his right-hand man and father of his daughter-in-law. Rodríguez promised a free press and a gradual return to democracy after the coup and his Colorado Party was elected into office in 1991. Gleeful Paraguayans took down the photographs of Stroessner, exiled to Brazil, that graced every shop window, changed the names of streets and towns, and decapitated statues of the former president. Since then Paraguay has been experiencing a process of democratic transition, marked by a new constitution, political and press freedoms, and regular elections. Paraguay has also joined the Mercosur common market, a development that upsets some of the more extreme nationalists but which has opened the country to foreign investors.

Offsetting these achievements are continuing wide disparities in wealth and an absence of land reform, not to speak of a pervasive military presence in national politics that surfaced in May 1996 in an attempted coup by the popular General Lino Oviedo. Despite these blemishes, democracy in Paraguay seems to be here to stay. Luís Gonzales Macchi was elected in 1999, representing the first coalition government in decades, and the ruling Colorado Party won the presidency again in April 2003, with Nicanor Duarte Frutos extending their run to over half a century.

Asunción: elegance and neon lights

Today, **Asunción ❶** matches the dynamism of most South American cities while retaining a sleepy elegance, with elegant colonial mansions rubbing shoulders with luxury boutiques, duty-free shops, and neon

Map on pages 260–1

The atmosphere of rather seedy militarism of the Stroessner years is brilliantly captured in Graham Greene's novel Travels With My Aunt.

BELOW: musicians perform with the traditional Guaraní harp.

A Bilingual Land

Spanish explorers in Paraguay, unlike other colonies, did not clash with the local population but blended to form a homogeneous, bilingual society. This was possible mainly because the local Guaraní had nothing the Spanish conquistadors wanted to steal. What the Guaraní did have to offer was a peaceful life in a fertile country.

It is difficult to say how much the notorious Guaraní "harems" kept by the Spaniards were fact and how much exaggeration for the benefit of their miserable compatriots in Buenos Aires, but it was true that a great deal of social mobility was achieved by intermarriage, and that the *mestizo* offspring were not considered marginal citizens.

Sociologists also cite the relatively high position of women in Guaraní society as a factor in the continuing status of the mother tongue. But perhaps the most decisive element in Paraguayan bilingualism was the missionary work of the Jesuits. Although the

Jesuits imposed Spanish on the Amerindians, they were impressed by the complexity and musicality of Guaraní, and produced catechisms and hymns in the native language. Ironically, as a result, the Guaraní neglected much of their original music. Nevertheless, Guaraní music still has a distinctive sound.

In 1624, the Jesuit priest Antonio Ruiz de Montoya created the first Guaraní dictionary and grammar, giving the language a written form and thus a better chance of survival.

During the dictatorship of Doctor Francia (1814–40), marriage between Paraguayans of pure Spanish descent was forbidden. This attempt to dilute the country's ruling class increased contact between the two cultures and their languages. Guaraní was considered a sort of homely argot rather than the speech of educated people, but its use became widespread during the War of the Triple Alliance, as a symbol of national pride and unity. On the battlefields of the Chaco War (1932–35) Spanish was banned and Guaraní was spoken, as a secret language. As a result, many older Paraguayans with little or no indigenous heritage speak Guaraní more fluently than Spanish.

In urban areas today, more than 70 percent of the population is completely bilingual; less than 12 percent speak only Spanish. In rural areas, the use of Guaraní still supersedes that of Spanish; 60 percent of the population speak only Guaraní. Before the 1970s it was rare for teachers to use Guaraní in the classroom, but changing ideas about bilingual education have made the new generation not only fluent but literate in Guaraní.

Novels and poetry are published in Guaraní translations; there are also theater productions, and television and radio shows in the language. The influence of Guaraní on the language of the conquistadors is notable even to those who don't understand Guaraní: the musical tones, the penchant for modesty and understatement – none of which are characteristics of Spanish.

But despite ever-present Guaraní melodies, and the 1981 Law of Native Communities guaranteeing Amerindians' rights over their lands and cultures, the social status of full-blooded Guaraní remains inferior.   ❑

LEFT: a Guaraní woman sells handicrafts outside the Guaraní Hotel in Asunción.

Map
on pages
260–1

lights. The **Plaza de los Héroes** is bright with butterflies and birds of paradise. Many passers-by seem to have come directly from central casting: fruit vendors with baskets on their heads, furtive black-market money-changers, the cluster of helmeted military police investigating a broken water pipe.

Gone are the bright yellow electric streetcars that Stroessner revived after the oil crisis of the 1970s. Gone too is the neon sign that flashed STROESSNER: PEACE, WORK, AND WELL BEING over the square, but its focal point is still the ornate **Pantéon Nacional de los Héroes**, which was built as a copy of Les Invalides in Paris. Inside are the tombs of the two López presidents, of two unknown soldiers, and a small urn containing what remains of the dictator Francia. It's said that his bones were dug up and flung into the river by an angry mob.

But no matter how Paraguayans feel about their military governments, this is a country that reveres soldiers; it's not at all unusual for passers-by to stop at this shrine and make the sign of the cross before the heroes' crypts. Diagonally across from the pantheon are shop windows that display Chaco War memorabilia. West of the Plaza de los Héroes, on Presidente Franco, is the **Casa de la Independencia**, where independence was declared in 1811 and which nowadays houses a museum with relics from the revolution (open daily; free).

The historic old town

The oldest part of the city can be reached by following Calle Chile down toward the River Paraguay. On a small bluff is the pastel **Palacio del Gobierno**. It was built in the style of the Louvre by Francisco Solano López, who imported much of the building's beautiful interiors and furniture from Paris. He did not have much time to enjoy the palace, since its construction was interrupted by the

The Palacio del Gobierno was designed by a British architect, Alonso Taylor. Having fallen out with his patron, Taylor was tortured in the palace basement but escaped with his life, unlike numerous other victims of El Mariscal.

BELOW: stormy sky over Asunción.

War of the Triple Alliance. Further along El Paraguayo Independiente are the tree-lined **Plaza Constitucion**, the **Congressional Palace**, and the **Cathedral**, which has an excellent museum of religious objects. Opposite the Palacio is the 18th-century **Manzana de la Rivera**, or Casa Viola. Once the headquarters for Stroessner's élite forces, it is now an innovative cultural center incorporating a museum of the history of the city, an art gallery, library, and bar. The Spanish Government paid for its renovation to mark the 500th anniversary of the "discovery" of America. A short distance further on are the **Aduana** (Customs House), the port buildings and the barracks, naval headquarters and old fortifications that provide eloquent testimony to the one-time status of Asunción as a frontier city with only the river separating its inhabitants from the wild lands of the Chaco. From a pier by the palace a tiny ferry takes passengers across to the island of **Chaco-i**.

Parks and plazas

East of the Plaza de los Héroes is another large and pleasant square, the **Plaza Uruguaya**, which was once the site of a famous convent and was renamed in tribute to the Uruguayan government when they returned Paraguayan flags captured in the War of the Triple Alliance. There are two interesting bookshops in pavilions in the plaza, which also has stalls selling leather work, paintings, and other crafts. Handicrafts made by the indigenous Macá people in their settlements on the outskirts of the city can be bought here.

A short distance away is the **Estación San Francisco**, a relic of the López years which was designed by Alonso Taylor. Restored courtesy of the Spanish government, the building is a Victorian gem, built largely of wood, but with cast-iron supports and a tower that was once the home of the station master. The station used to be the terminus for the British-run track to Encarnarción in southern Paraguay that ultimately linked to Buenos Aires. Nowadays occasional trains run to nearby Areguá on Lake Ypacaraí, pulled by wood-burning locomotives.

The Itaipú hydroelectric dam has given Paraguay the cheapest electricity in South America. World Bank loans for the project also enriched some Paraguayans beyond their wildest dreams. Some of their splendid houses can be seen if you take a trip along Avenida España. There are also some beautiful old colonial houses with wide verandahs and gardens of bottle-brush and banana trees on this road, as well as the American Embassy, the library, and Stroessner's former home, now a museum.

Parque Carlos Antonio López, on the Avenida of the same name, provides a good view of the city from the Antonio López and Río Gallegos intersection. The **Jardin Botánico**, 7 km (4 miles) outside Asunción, which has its own zoo, is well worth a visit, as are the nearby **Museo de Historia Natural** and the **Museo Indigentista**, both former residences of the two López presidents.

A reservation of the Macá people, who were brought here from their home in the Chaco as a tourist attraction, is located across the river. They live in rather dismal conditions. Ironically, the best handicrafts are to be found in the middle-class suburb of **San Lorenzo**,

BELOW: Guaraní woman selling *chipas*, small cakes made from maize, in an Asunción market.

along the eastern highway, where the shop of the **Museo Boggiani** offers authentic and very beautiful artifacts made by the indigenous people of the Chaco.

Map on pages 260–1

Traveling east

The Mariscal Estigarribia Highway crosses Paraguay to the Brazilian border town of Ciudad del Este, formerly Ciudad Presidente Stroessner. By express bus the trip takes about four hours, but there are interesting stops along the first half of the journey. About 20 km (14 miles) east of Asunción is **Capiatá**, which was first settled by the Jesuits in 1640. It has an interesting church, which contains a 17th-century sculpture made by the Guaraní under Jesuit instruction. Some 10 km (6 miles) east is **Itagua**, famous for its production of *ñandutí*, or spiderweb lace, which is woven by hand into handkerchiefs, tablecloths, and hammocks and displayed by the weavers in stalls along Route 2. There is a museum and an annual festival in July.

The resort town of **San Bernardino**, 55 km (35 miles) from Asunción on **Lake Ypacaraí**, is a favorite retreat of prosperous Paraguayans and a center for watersports. The lake, immortalized in a hauntingly beautiful Guaraní song, measures 5 by 24 km (3 by 15 miles) and is an idyllic spot, surrounded by tropical vegetation. The resort town of **Areguá**, on the southern shore of the lake and terminus for the short steam train journey from Asunción, has many shops and stalls selling earthernware. **Caacupé ❷**, 24 km (15 miles) down the road from San Bernardino, is another popular resort and religious shrine. On December 8, pilgrims come to this town from all over Paraguay carrying heavy stones on their heads as penance. Nearby are the villages of **Tobatí**, which has pottery and woodcarvings, and **Piribebuy**, which has a fine church and an interesting museum. There are some lovely small resorts in the hilly, verdant countryside between Piribebuy and Paraguari near **Chololó**, where bathing is possible in refreshing streams.

Ciudad del Este ❸, on the Brazilian border, has been called South America's biggest late-night shopping center. It's a bustling, rather unattractive city with a makeshift boomtown air. Brazilians arrive by the busload to buy electronics, watches, and other imported goods in the huge air-conditioned malls. The city is also a magnet for con artists, who hawk everything from imitation perfume to "musical" condoms. More impressive is the nearby **Itaipú Dam**, the world's largest hydroelectric project. Ciudad del Este is connected to the Brazilian counterpart city of **Foz do Iguaçú** *(see page 253)* by the **Puente de la Amistad** (Friendship Bridge), and is a portal to the famous falls of Iguazú *(see page 336)*. There are tours and public transport to Iguazú and Itaipú, but the Salto Monday Falls, 10 km (6 miles) out of town, are only accessible by taxi.

On the trail of the Jesuits

Most of the Jesuit *reducciones* were set up in the fertile High Paraná, southeast of Asunción along Route 1. In **Yaguarón**, 48 km (30 miles) south of the capital, there is a Franciscan mission, built in 1640. The church is a jewel of the Hispano-Guaraní baroque.

A Paraguayan witticism has it that every sentence starts in Spanish and finishes in Guaraní. Another saying is that Spanish is the language of the head and Guaraní of the heart.

BELOW: shop till you drop in Ciudad del Este, Paraguay's consumer capital.

A Jesuit Utopia

In colonial times Paraguay encompassed parts of what are now Bolivia, Brazil, and Argentina. Within this vast area the Jesuit order created an administrative unit or province that achieved a semi-independent status. Like the Franciscans who preceded them, the Jesuits' primary mission was conversion. They insisted on the human value and dignity of the indigenous peoples and offered an alternative to the Spanish *encomienda* system *(see page 28)* that sought only to exploit their labor.

The Jesuits' first efforts at conversion started in 1587, one of the fathers being Thomas Fields, an Irishman from Limerick. The decision to gather the native population into settlements was made at a synod in 1603 and confirmed by Philip II of Spain in 1609. The following year, small parties of Jesuits began to travel into what was still largely unknown territory to Europeans. In the wild lands of the Chaco the Jesuits did no

better than the Spanish military expeditions that occasionally sallied forth from Asunción. With the Guaraní to the south and east of the city, they succeeded.

In the early years the Jesuit *reducciones* (missions) were threatened by the *mamelucos* or *bandeirantes*, slave raiders from Brazil. In 1629 thousands of Guaraní were forced to flee from the upper Paraná, but 12 years later a Jesuit-led army, drawn from the missions, put the *mamelucos* to flight. The missions then flourished. Ultimately the Jesuits gathered in around 150,000 Guaraní to 30 missions in a broad belt of territory on either side of the River Paraná, living by theocratic-socialist principles.

By the early 18th century the missions were flourishing and were acquiring a reputation amongst European travelers as micro-Utopias. The Guaraní were farmers, herding cattle and sheep, and cultivating crops such as *yerba maté* (herbs for maté tea – *see page 315)*. Some developed skills as fine craftsmen and sculptors. The Jesuit priests also found the Guaraní to be highly musical and introduced them to European idioms, to the harp and the guitar.

But the grand experiment in communal living was not to last. The Jesuits always had their enemies, and by the mid-18th century these included royal advisers in far away Madrid. In 1767 the Jesuits were expelled from the country and the Guaraní were left to fend for themselves, at the mercy of the slave raiders or absorbed into the *encomienda* system. Most of the greatest Jesuit churches were destroyed or fell into ruin, but the remains of the missions (some still in ruins and some restored) bear testimony to the achievements of the Jesuits in this region. This whole historic episode has also been powerfully reconstructed in the movie *The Mission*, starring Jeremy Irons and Robert de Niro.

Eight of the Jesuit missions were in what is now southern Paraguay, with the rest in the neighboring Argentine province of Misiones *(see page 336)* and Brazil. The missions are accessible from Asunción by Route 1 running southeast to Encarnación. ❑

LEFT: the imposing remains of a Jesuit mission in Southern Paraguay.

Map on pages 260–1

Nearby is a museum dedicated to Doctor Francia. The first Jesuit ruins are at **San Ignacio Guazú ❹**, at Km 226. The **Museo Jesuitico** houses a fine collection of indigenous art from the missionary period. Another museum has some interesting exhibits on the Chaco War. Route 4 runs west to **Pilar** and ultimately to **Humaitá**, near the junctions of the rivers Paraná and Paraguay, and whose garrison held out for three years during the War of the Triple Alliance.

To the northeast of San Ignacio is **Santa María de Fé**, established in 1669. It has a modern church and a museum that houses dozens of Guaraní-made carvings of saints and apostles. Sixteen kilometers (10 miles) south is **Santa Rosa**, founded in 1698. The church was destroyed by fire in 1883, but wooden carvings, a tower, and frescoes remain. These include a figure of the Annunciation, which is one of the great works of the Hispanic-American baroque. To reach the Jesuit ruins of **San Cosmé y Damian**, turn off Route 1 at Km 306 and travel 30 km (20 miles) south. Of particular interest is the sundial, which is all that remains of what was once a world-renowned astronomy center, built by Father Buenaventura Suarez and Guaraní laborers.

The city of **Encarnación ❺** was founded by the Jesuits on what is now the Argentinian (southern) bank of the River Paraná, and transferred to the present site on the northern bank in 1621. There is nothing left of the original Jesuit mission of Itapúa. The city, which is close to the **Yacyretá dam**, is a good center for exploring the Jesuit missions at Trinidad and Jesús de Tavarangue. Nearby are Japanese colonies which produce soybeans, vegetables, timber, maté, and cotton. About 30 km (20 miles) northeast of Encarnación is Paraguay's most splendid ruin, **Trinidad**. The sheer size of the mission, which has been declared a world heritage site by UNESCO, gives some idea of the scope of the Jesuit project in the New World. It was founded in 1706, relatively late in the Jesuit era, and the church was only finished in 1760, a few years before the expulsion of the Jesuits. There are many interesting features including a pulpit, carved in great detail. In addition to churches, Amerindian houses and crypts, there is a baptismal font and an impressive carving of the Holy Trinity, which was hollowed at the back so that a priest could hide inside and give an echoing rendition of the voice of God. Ten kilometers (6 miles) along a road north of Route 6 is **Jesús de Tavarangue**, founded by the Jesuits in 1685. Much of the site remains unfinished, as the Jesuits embarked on a massive building program seven years before their expulsion. The most remarkable surviving features are the three arched doorways built by Catalan architects in the Spanish *mudéjar* style.

Traveling northeast

Less frequently visited than the populous eastern region, the northeast of Paraguay has a number of interesting and remote places to explore. Accessible by taking Route 2 from Asunción to Coronel Oviedo, then heading northward by Routes 3 and 5, is **Pedro Juan Caballero ❻**, a town located on the Brazilian border. Here travelers can cross into Brazil, or travel southwest to **Parque Nacional Cerro Corá**, scene of the last battle in the War of the Triple Alliance and the

BELOW: detail of Jesuit architecture.

death of "El Mariscal" López. There are monuments to him in the national park, as well as some caves with intriguing pre-Columbian petroglyphs.

The River Paraguay provides an important route to the north. Some 300 km (200 miles) upstream from Asunción is **Concepción**, which is a significant port for trading with Brazil and has a good market. There is boat traffic further upstream which, depending on river conditions, may be used to reach some of the more remote places. Some of these places are also accessible by four-wheel drive from the Chaco. The ports on these stretches of the river, such as Puerto Casado and Fuerte Olimpo, can be reached by air or boat, and a ship, *Paraguay Cruise,* allows visitors to explore the **Pantanal** and the **Swamp of Nembucu**. Travelers on a tighter budget should ask for accommodation upon arrival if they wish to visit these intriguing but isolated small towns.

The vast expanses of the Chaco

This desolate region, which is extremely hot in summer and waterless for months at a time, covers 60 percent of Paraguayan territory but holds only four percent of the population. It was once the preserve of indigenous groups, including the Nivaclé and Lengua people, who now share the region with military personnel, Mennonite colonists, and other assorted migrants. There are a number of Catholic missions and large *estancias* (ranches), for this is cattle-rearing country. Unlike most of the Chaco, the Mennonite areas have good roads and facilities, and hotel accommodation is available in the towns. It is also possible to camp in the Chaco, as long as you take everything with you – especially water. The Chaco is a paradise for ornithologists, with immense gatherings of birds after the rains.

BELOW: Mennonite furniture shop.

The **Low Chaco**, the region nearest Asunción, is a primeval terrain of marsh

NEW SOCIETIES

The Chaco, like many remote regions, has attracted a number of unusual immigrant communities. Best known are the Mennonites, a strict Protestant Anabaptist sect, who began to arrive from 1927 onwards. They run their own banks, schools, and hospitals, and subsist on a co-operative farming system, and they can often be seen in 19th-century dress at markets in Asunción. Most speak a variety of old German known as Platt Deutsch.

Less well known is the settlement of Nueva Germania, north of Coronel Oviedo. This was the site of a very different experimental community founded in 1886 by Elisabeth Nietzsche, the fanatic sister of the philosopher Nietzsche, and her equally fanatical anti-semite husband. Their plan was to found a pure Aryan colony, but the venture foundered as the colonists came up against the unforgiving realities of dense vegetation, intense heat, and torrential rains combined with a perplexing absence of ground water. Undaunted either by the rage of the duped colonists or by the suicide of her husband, Elisabeth returned to Germany where eventually she was able to greet Hitler as her true leader. The bizarre story is told in the book *Forgotten Fatherland: The Search for Elisabeth Nietzsche* by Ben Macintyre.

Map
on pages
260–1

and palm forest, and is used for cattle ranching. It is easily accessible by traveling over the river bridge from Asunción and then up the first few kilometers of the Trans-Chaco Highway to **Villa Hayes**. This small town is named after the 19th-century American president Rutherford B. Hayes, who arbitrated in Paraguay's favor in a territorial dispute after the War of the Triple Alliance.

At about Km 250 is **Pirahu**, which is a good place to stop and find out about road conditions. About 20 km (12 miles) further on is **Pozo Colorado**, the turning for Concepción, and at Km 415, **Cruce de los Pioneros**. All these places have restaurants and service stations, and Cruce also has a supermarket and a good hotel with an excellent restaurant.

About 50 km (30 miles) further along the highway, and off to the right, is **Loma Plata**, largest of the Mennonite towns. Further on, and also off to the right, is the Mennonite town of **Filadelfia** ❼, capital of the **Central Chaco**. Further north along the Trans-Chaco Highway, at Km 540, is **Mariscal Estigarribia**, a military post with facilities for the traveler. The paved road stops here. Further on, conditions can be very difficult, although the road does go all the way to Santa Cruz in Bolivia. It is possible to travel from Asunción to Bolivia by bus, especially in winter when road conditions tend to improve.

Further north is the **High Chaco**, a desert of thorn forests and military outposts. The roads are unpaved, and the land is rich with wildlife: jaguars, pumas, tapirs, and poisonous snakes, as well as a kind of wild hog, discovered in 1975, which was thought to have become extinct in the Pleistocene Era. The large, remote **Parque Nacional Defensores del Chaco** is difficult to reach and to travel around – enquiries should be made to the Dirección de Parques Nacionales in Asunción. ❑

BELOW: puma on the prowl in the High Chaco.

CHILE

This is a geographically diverse land, where you can experience the blistering heat of the Atacama Desert and chilling Patagonian winds, as well as beaches, lakes, mountains, and city delights

Map on pages 260–1

Snaking down the Pacific coast of South America from latitude 18 to 56, Chile covers a huge range of temperatures and landscapes. Squeezed between the Andes and the Pacific, never more than 180 km (110 miles) wide, this spaghetti-like strip of land extends over 4,300 km (2,700 miles) of coastline. Within its borders are the world's driest desert, lush expanses of forest and a spectacular array of glaciers and fiords. Stretched directly along the Pacific "ring of fire," Chile also has some 2,085 volcanoes, of which 55 are active. In parts of the country, earth tremors are an almost weekly occurrence.

In the north of the country is the arid and mysterious Atacama Desert, rising to more than 4,500 meters (14,760 ft) above sea level as it meets the Bolivian *altiplano*. The northwest coast is distinguished by a range of expansive Pacific beaches and resorts. Chile's eastern boundary runs along the Cordillera de los Andes, which provides a mountain setting for Santiago, the capital city, placed right in the middle of the strip. South of Santiago the land becomes cooler, greener and more "alpine". Chile's Lake District has 12 great lakes and most of the country's active volcanoes. Further south, the coastline breaks up into islands, the largest being Chiloé, a rainy location steeped in regional folklore. In the far south of the country lie the remote territories of Chilean Patagonia, the glaciers and mountains of Torres del Paine National Park, and the subarctic regions of Tierra del Fuego.

PRECEDING PAGES: Torres del Paine National Park. **LEFT:** harvest time in the Lake District. **BELOW:** Santiago's business center.

The wild geography hasn't stopped Chile from becoming one of the continent's most developed nations. Travelers are often surprised by the efficiency of Chile's banking system, public transport, and services, though beneath the affluent surface are social and economic imbalances waiting to be redressed.

Chileans are renowned among Latin Americans for an unusual creative flair: Chilean folk musicians, poets, painters, and theater groups are followed in every country on the continent. And their reputation for legalizing (new laws are hawked in the streets of Santiago alongside chocolates and newspapers) and business acumen has earned Chileans the somewhat facetious label as "the English of South America."

The traditional hospitality of Chileans, noted by travelers from the 18th century on, is even more evident today. After years of dictatorship, Chileans have welcomed the influx of foreigners as a sign of support for their democracy.

Socialism to Fascism

Chile made few headlines on the world stage until 1970, when the country's first ever elected socialist government came to power under Salvador Allende, in spite of efforts by the right and the United States to subvert the process. The narrow margin of victory lim-

ited Allende's power, but his reforms to improve the standard of living for the poor initially worked: wages increased, land was redistributed, and jobs were created. But opposition mounted from the middle and upper classes, terrified of revolution, and from the left, who considered Allende too soft on the middle class. Fearing nationalization, local and foreign capital fled. Production declined while demand increased, spurring rampant inflation. The right and the US government plotted to oust Allende, financing a 1972 truckers' strike. The truckers were soon joined by shopkeepers and professionals. But Allende's Unidad Popular won 44 percent of the seats in the March 1973 congressional elections.

In the early hours of September 11, 1973, the Allende government fell in a bloody storm as troops surrounded the presidential palace, congress, newspapers and party headquarters. Some working-class *barrios* were strafed. The air force bombed the Presidential Palace, killing Allende. Thousands of "subversives" were herded into concentration camps, and a four-man military junta took over, declaring a state of siege and declaring that Marxism would be eradicated from Chile. At least 2,500 people (some estimates say 10,000) were killed.

Museo de Bellas Artes, Santiago.

The leader of the coup, General Augusto Pinochet Ugarte, ruthlessly crushed the opposition; dissidents – and many innocents – were imprisoned, tortured, exiled, or murdered. But in 1988 the tide finally began to turn against Pinochet; a referendum on his presidency was announced for October 5. Voters were registered, exile was abolished, and a state of emergency in effect since 1973 was lifted. The majority of the seven million Chileans voted "No", resulting in a resounding defeat. Pinochet accepted his fate, announcing that elections would be held in 1989.

BELOW:
General Pinochet.

The new government took office on March 11, 1990, but Pinochet kept cronies in eight seats in the Senate and remained head of the army. Confidence

Map
on pages
260–1

and democracy slowly returned, helped by an "economic miracle", which made debt and hyper-inflation seem like problems of the past. Events came full circle in 1993 when the center-left Democratic Coalition's Eduardo Frei, son of the 1960s president, was elected president. In March 1998, Pinochet retired as head of the army but, as a former president, he was entitled to a life seat in the Senate, which he took up amid a wave of street protests. Pinochet was under house arrest in the UK for over a year pending his extradition to Spain to face charges of torture. In 1999, Frei faced right-wing protests at Pinochet's treatment and rising unemployment, but his achievements included a program of small business loans to farmers and road modernization, and, in November 1999, he signed an agreement giving Peru access to the port at Arica, thereby ending decades of tension.

Early in 2000 Pinochet was returned to Chile because of ill health and was eventually found unfit to stand trial. In the same year, Ricardo Lagos, representing a coalition between Christian Democrats, Socialists, and other smaller parties, was elected president. Lagos aimed to combine economic growth with greater social justice, but his government has been overshadowed by high unemployment, forcing it to concentrate on short-term relief, rather than long-term social reform. In 2002 all charges against Pinochet were dropped on the grounds that he was mentally unfit to stand trial. He resigned from his life Senate seat and retired from public life. Limited progress has been made in investigating the dictator's human rights abuses.

Santiago, Chile's sophisticated center

The conquistador Pedro de Valdivia is said to have forgotten his tortuous journey to Chile from Peru when he gazed upon the valley at the point where the

LEFT: colonial reflections, Santiago.
RIGHT: shoeshine break, Plaza de Armas, Santiago.

Fortunes for sale, Santiago.

BELOW: statue of the Virgin, Cerro San Cristóbal, Santiago.

Mapocho and Maipo rivers descend from the Andes on their journey to the Pacific Ocean. Surrounded in all four directions by peaks rivaling the Alps, Valdivia knew he had found the right place for a settlement. Today, the conquistadors might not recognize **Santiago ❽**, the smoggy home to 5 million of Chile's 15 million people, but it has a charm unmatched in South America.

Valdivia marked the center of Santiago with the **Plaza de Armas** (1541). It served as a market and a place of public hangings. Today, this clean, tree-lined square, is a haven for old men, shoe shiners, vagrants and lovers. The pink **Correo Central** (1882), which houses the most efficient postal service in South America, has an impressive iron skylight that illuminates the central corridor. Next door, the excellent **Museo Histórico Nacional** in the Palacio de la Real Audiencia traces Chile's history from its pre-Columbian roots to the present. On the west side of the square is the country's largest church, the **Cathedral** (1748–89), with an impressive baroque interior.

Two blocks away on Calle Catedral is the **Congreso Nacional** (1876), a neoclassical structure that was home to Chile's legislative branch until it was closed in 1973. The federal courts are across the street. The imposing **Palacio de la Moneda** (1805) is four blocks south on Calle Morandé. It originally served as the mint, but later became the presidential palace, where President Allende was killed in the 1973 military coup; bullet holes are still visible on the buildings opposite.

Paseo Ahumada, a pedestrian mall linking Plaza de Armas to the **Avenida Libertador Bernardo O'Higgins**, is the heart of Santiago, offering a human collage of business people, street vendors and money changers. Across the Alameda, the city's major east–west artery, is the imposing, chalky-red **Iglesia San Francisco** (1586). The church has interesting touches of Arab influence remnants of the Spanish. Alongside is **Barrio París-Londres**, where mansions from the 1920s border sinuous streets. Uptown from Ahumada, three blocks along Calle Augustinas, and past the 17th-century church of San Augustín is the **Municipal Theater**, built in 1857 and one of the finest on the sub-continent. Plays, concerts, and other cultural events are held around the small, dimly lit **Plaza Mulato Gil**.

Green spaces beneath the Andes

Santiago's founders were careful to include green spaces. Valdivia founded the city while standing atop one of its present-day parks, **Santa Lucía**, a small hill topped with terraces and a replica castle, which offers a view of the downtown area. **Parque Forestal** (1891) follows the course of the Mapocho River (corresponding to metro stations from Mapocho to Salvador). Banana trees line winding footpaths which betray the park's narrow confines. The **Museo de Bellas Artes** is here, a copy of the Petit Palais in Paris, with a fine collection of works by Chilean artists.

The **Parque Metropolitano** covers four hills towering 800 meters (2,600 ft) over Santiago. A tram goes to a terrace on the peak, commanding a view of the whole city when the smog is not too thick. There is a statue of the Virgin Mary, two pools, a zoo, a botanical garden, and a wine-tasting center that offers the best of Chile's vineyards. A cable car descends half

the length of the mountain, to Calle Pedro de Valdivia in the *barrio alto*. Strolls or horseback rides around the expansive **Parque O'Higgins** (Metro Line 2) became stylish for city dwellers when it opened in the late 1800s. **El Pueblito** is a replica of a typical southern village.

Bellavista is the cultural heart of Santiago, the night-time haunt of artists, writers and people who go to see and be seen. Dimly lit streets are sprinkled with raucous cafés, art galleries, and restaurants, while roving theater troupes, musicians, and hippies peddle their work. At night, tables spill from bars along **Calle Pío Nono**, Bellavista's main street. On the side streets, quaint homes with flowering gardens, eccentric details, and sculpted balconies weave an intriguing architectural quilt. The house where poet Pablo Neruda created many of his greatest works is on Calle A. Márquez de la Plata.

Mercado Franklin (four blocks east of Metro Franklin) is a weekend flea market that winds for several blocks through an abandoned slaughterhouse. Six blocks north of the Plaza de Armas along the Mapocho River is the colorful fresh food center **Mercado Central**.

High fashion is also available in Santiago at a reasonable cost. Uptown, the **Los Leones** area on Calle Providencia (Metro Los Leones), is an affluent neighborhood with several chic boutiques and swanky stores. **Parque Arauco** (Avenida Kennedy 5413) and **Apumanque** (Avenida Apoquindo/Manquehue) are fashion malls on the upper-east side of the city.

Around Santiago

The lofty Andes, the tranquility of rural valley communities, and the cool breezes of the coast are all within a few hours of the capital by car or bus. On

Map on pages 260–1

BELOW: vineyard harvest.

Wine Country

The conquistadors introduced vineyards in Chile in the 16th century to supply the symbol of Christ's blood for the Catholic communion. Small wineries were nurtured on *haciendas* in the Maipo Valley throughout the colonial period by patrons doing their bit for the church. Today wine is one of Chile's finest products – its purpose rarely spiritual – and an increasingly popular export even to wine-soaked Europe.

The first commercial vineyard was established in 1851 when Silvestre Ochagavía brought French vine stock to the Maipo valley. Mining magnates built extensive irrigation projects, and the vineyards spread further from the river banks. The valley's lime-heavy soil, elevation, and dry climate were ideal for producing world-class wines. Chileans boast that when French vines were destroyed by a fungus in the late 19th century, their vines were rushed across the Atlantic to replenish the stricken vineyards. The larger labels out-

grew the confines of the valley in the early 1900s and new wineries sprung up near Los Andes and Rancagua. Today, the finest reserves carry the mark of *Cajón del Maipo*, near Santiago. The Maipo Valley comes alive in March during the *vendímia* (harvest), when grapes are transported to the presses. Several wineries are open to the public, with informative tours and generous tastings.

The grounds of the Viña Cousiño Macul, on Avenida Quilin on the eastern outskirts of Santiago, are themselves a work of art, with a central lagoon stocked with waterfowl from around the world. It has been in the hands of the same family since 1856. Bottles can be bought from the grand stone cellars and tours are available Monday to Friday. However, air pollution is driving the company out of Santiago, and most of the land will soon be given over to a housing development.

Viña Santa Carolina, founded in the Ñuñoa neighborhood in Santiago (near the Estadio Nacional) in 1875, is named after the owner's wife. Though the vines have been transplanted to Molina and San Fernando, the stately colonial Casa Patronal remains, with the cellars nearby.

An hour's drive south of Santiago at Pirque, near to Puente Alto, is Viña Concha y Toro. Melchor Concha y Toro founded the winery in 1883, and it is now the largest in Chile with more than 10 vineyards in Maipo, San Fernando, and Rancagua. A visit to the original vineyard and cellars could be included in a weekend trip to the mountains.

About 32 km (20 miles) southwest from Santiago, at Santa Ana, is Viña Undurraga, founded in 1885 by Francisco Ramón Undurraga, who imported vines from France and, a first for Chile, German stock from the Rhine Valley. Undurraga built his cellars and a magnificent colonial mansion to entertain guests, including royalty. The public is welcome, but reservations are necessary.

In 1927, José Canepa acquired choice parcels of wine country, and planted Cabernet Sauvignon, Sauvignon Blanc, and Riesling vines in the Maipo Valley, Curicó, and Lontué. Now the most modern winery in South America, its plant on Camino Lo Sierra is open to the public. ❑

LEFT: vats in a Chilean wine *bodega*.

the eastern end of the city at the foot of the Andean mountains is **El Pueblito de los Domínicos**. A creek meanders through the small village, around a cluster of adobe huts with thatched roofs. The sounds of craftsmen at work drift from the workshops where they produce leather, ceramics, and metals. In nearby **Lo Barnechea**, people still ride horses around the village, and each weekend vendors set up an antique fair in the shadow of the town's adobe church.

Above Lo Barnechea, **El Arrayán** has become a refuge for city dwellers who have built comfortable and breezy homes on the Arrayán River valley. The **Santuario de la Naturaleza** park follows the narrow Arrayán canyon.

Santiaguinos venture to the **Cajón del Maipo** on weekends to take afternoon tea, nibble on *empanadas* and *kuchen* (strudel) and relax in little towns and trails along the 60-km (40-mile) canyon. The valley has distinct characteristics. A sinuous road leads from **Puente Alto** southeast, against the current of Maipo and its tributaries, to finally reach its source near the 5,000-meter (16,600-ft) extinct volcano **El Morado**. Arid peaks with names like **Punta Negra**, **Peladero**, **Lomo del Diablo**, and **Yerba Buena** meld with the changing day's sun, turning from green and brown in the day, to blue, pink, orange, and red before disappearing at dusk. The narrow valley floor is lush and intensively cultivated with vineyards and pasture land. Hiking, swimming, camping, and climbing are practiced in the area, and there are many picnic areas close to the road.

San José de Maipo, 25 km (15 miles) from Puente Alto, was founded in 1791 when miners discovered silver in the surrounding hills. Its adobe homes and central square pay homage to the past. At **San Alfonso** (Km 40) there is hiking and camping at **Cascada de las Ánimas** facing the canyon wall. The road forks at **San Gabriel** (Km 47) where the mountains darken and the air grows

Map on pages 260–1

Enjoying a beer at the rodeo.

LEFT: mud baths near the Argentine border.
RIGHT: skiing, Valle Nevada.

thinner. **Lo Valdés** (Km 70) is on the southern fork of the road, a veritable oasis on the semi-arid slopes of the Morado volcano. The Refugio Alemán is a pleasant inn near extensive trails for exploring the snow-capped peaks surrounding the area. Nearby, **Baños de Colina** are natural hot springs in a small valley with magnificent views of the Andes and the valley below.

South of Puente Alto across the boulder-strewn Maipo River ravine is **Pirque**, birthplace of Chile's best wines *(see page 284)*. The **Reserva Nacional Río Clarillo** is in the midst of a semi-arid area where the best of indigenous cacti and flora flourish. In colonial times, Spanish aristocrats used to take vacations on the sandy shores of **Laguna de Aculeo**. The lake fills a valley 60 km (37 miles) from the capital, in a wooded mountain setting. There are camping facilities, hotels, and several restaurants along the shore. Twenty years ago the government built a dam where the **Tinguiririca** and **Cachapoal rivers** meet, forming the nation's largest man-made lake. **Rapel Lake** provides waterskiing, swimming, and fishing.

Fit and healthy in Arica.

BELOW: dry vineyards, Valle Elqui.

Skiing in the Andes

The omnipresence of dizzying Andean peaks makes Chile one of the finest ski centers in the world, with challenging runs that can be enjoyed from June to September. Four resorts are within sight of Santiago. Farellones-Colorado and La Parva are ski villages above El Arrayán, just 50 km (30 miles) from Santiago along a sinuous road with 50 hairpin bends (access is controlled in winter and drivers are only allowed to head up there until noon). Valle Nevado, set in a remote valley above Farellones, is a posh resort built in 1988 by the owners of Les Alpes in France. There is a four-star hotel, and eight lifts to slopes as high as 3,350 meters (11,000 ft) above sea level. Portillo is one of the most famous resorts in South America, 2,745 meters (9,000 ft) above sea level in an Andean pass 7 km (4 miles) from the Argentine border at Mendoza.

Pomaire, 60 km (35 miles) southwest of Santiago, has become a part of nearly every Chilean household. Dark clay scraped from Mallarauco Mountains is hand-shaped into pottery and sculpture, and fired in large rustic stone ovens to be sold in the dozens of adobe homes along the town's dusty main street.

The Pacific coast

Algarrobo, 110 km (70 miles) west of Santiago, became a resort in the late 1800s and is known for its calm seas and elegant vacation homes. It has also become an important yachting center, hosting international competitions. Nearby **El Quisco** is a tranquil town with wide beaches complementing a small fishing port and yacht club. **Isla Negra**, 4 km (2½ miles) to the south, is hidden within a cool pine forest, its rocky coast battered by great swells. Poet Pablo Neruda's home, the inspiration for many of his works, is on a bluff above the sea. It is now a museum (open Tues–Sun; tours arranged through the Neruda Foundation in Santiago, tel: 777-8741, or at Isla Negra, tel: 35 461284, or it can be visited independently).

The port of **Valparaíso ⑨**, 120 km (75 miles) north of Santiago, is an enchanting town where a map is unnecessary and wandering is bliss. It is split between the geographically flat port area and 17 *cerros* (hills) that tower above the bay. The picturesque port is host to a strange brew of sailors, prostitutes, vagabonds, and tourists. The *cerros* are an impressive maze of colorful homes, winding streets, narrow alleys, rickety *ascensores* (funiculars), hidden plazas, and treacherous stairways that cling delicately to the precipitous slopes. **Muelle Prat**, dating from the 16th-century, is the oldest part of Valparaíso's port. To the west, at **Caleta El Membrillo**, fishermen unload their catch near weathered *picadas*, small shacks where the freshest seafood in the city is served. Nearby **Cerro Santo Domingo** is a delightful maze of streets and stately homes built by the emigrant merchants who founded Valparaíso.

Map on pages 260–1

Rickety rides

Valparaíso's *ascensores* are the best guide to the upper city. For a few pesos, these romantic wooden carriages make harrowing ascents to the neighborhoods high on the *cerros*. Ascensor Artillería (1893) first ran on coal, and goes to Avenida 21 de Mayo, providing a fantastic view of the bay. **Paseo Yugoslavo** is a promenade that winds along Cerro Alegre, among homes and gardens dating back to the early 1900s. Alegre is reached by the Ascensor El Peral.

Ascensor Concepción (1833) is the oldest elevator, reaching a neighborhood dating to the 19th century. Homes along **Paseo Atkinson** are simple wooden structures that creep up the mountainside. **Iglesia Anglicana San Pablo** (1858) was built by British immigrants. Ascensor Barón serves the panoramic **Mirador Diego Portales** on the west side of the bay. **Convento and Iglesia San Francisco** (1845) was also used as a lighthouse to guide ships into the port.

A road along seaside cliffs leads 18 km (11 miles) south to **Laguna Verde**, a

BELOW: traveling in style, Viña del Mar.

small fishing village set in a cove, with a long, unspoiled white beach. **Quintay**, 45 km (28 miles) from Valparaíso, is a fishing port surrounded by rocky cliffs. It has an expansive beach, with fine white sand and provisions for camping.

Viña del Mar, the garden city, is a cosmopolitan Pacific resort, with a spicy mix of beaches, lush gardens, and nightlife. Viña is taken over in the summer by Chileans and Argentines who crowd the expensive nightspots and bask on its golden, albeit polluted beaches. A century ago Viña was the retreat for affluent *porteños* (people from the port area) from Valparaíso. They built mansions with large gardens that later became the city's parks.

The **Quinta Vergara** is Viña's most elegant park, filled with exotic plants from around the world. The **Palacio Vergara** (1908) was built by Viña's founders and today houses the **Museo de Bellas Artes**. The **Anfiteatro** hosts the International Festival of Song in February. **La Plaza** is the palm-filled center of old Viña with the neo-classic **Club de Viña** (1910), **Teatro Municipal** (1930), **Hotel O'Higgins** (1935), and the **Casa Subercaseaux** on its borders.

Pedestrian precinct **Calle Valparaíso** is a magnet in summer, with cafés, shopping malls, and an artisan fair. At the end of the street is **Cerro Castillo**, a hill sprinkled with late 19th-century mansions and terraces overlooking the bay. Calle Alamos winds up the hill, past Castillo Brunet and the presidential palace. Avenida Peru is a misty promenade following the shore north of the hill. The **Casino Municipal** is the premier gambling house on the Pacific side of the continent, where the rich play for high stakes. The promenade continues along Avenida San Martín, bordering long beaches mobbed by tourists in the summer.

Reñaca, 8 km (5 miles) north, is the chic place to be in the season. Its mile-long beach lies below rocky mountains speckled with fashionable apartments and smart hotels, which are accessible by little trams and stairways. The sleepy fishing village of **Horcón** is the center of Chile's counter culture. It is set on a rocky peninsula 90 km (55 miles) north of Viña del Mar, in the midst of a eucalyptus forest, with a small wharf and colorful skiffs towed in and out of the water by teams of horses.

Northern deserts

Northern Chile has a mysticism that sets it apart. The 1,900 km (1,100 miles) from Santiago to Arica seem silent, a landscape sprinkled with whitewashed adobe villages marooned in the **Atacama Desert**. Tradition bends the rules of Catholicism, and visits by extra-terrestrials find their way into the folklore.

Arica 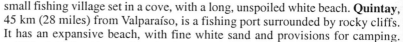, in the far north, is right on the threshold of Peru. The streets are filled with markets and stores catering to Peruvian and Bolivian smugglers. Arica is also known for its beautiful beaches and nightlife. **Plaza Aduana** provides cool respite from the desert sun. Nearby is **Iglesia de San Marco** (1876), a wrought-iron sanctuary designed by Gustave Eiffel. The **Morro de Arica** is a huge mountain with magnificient views of the city, the Pacific, and the desert. A museum in an old fortress recalls the battle for Arica during the War of the Pacific (1879), when the city was won from Peru. Several travel firms offer day trips east to **Lago Chungará**, near Bolivia, a mag-

TIP

On a visit to El Tatio Geysers, bring aspirin with you and lots of water to drink to ease the effects of altitude – headaches and nausea are common at this height. At the geysers, take great care not to tread on thin ground.

BELOW: Arica.

nificent if harrowing journey to 4,400 meters (14,500 ft). The emerald lake is surrounded by snowy peaks that rise high above the shoreline. The town of Chungará is located in **Parque Nacional Lauca**, where alpacas, *vicuñas* (deer-like llamas), *vizcachas* (large hares) and white geese with black-tipped wings perambulate along the road.

Map on pages 260–1

Spectacular landscape

Calama ⓫, south of Arica, is a mining center servicing the massive Chuquicamata copper mine, 16 km (10 miles) away. Wisps of sulfur vapor from the mine linger among its bars, cheap hotels, and restaurants. Tours of the open-pit mine are available. Three hours on the sinuous road to Bolivia is **Géiser del Tatío**, an impressive field of scalding geysers at an altitude of 4,500 meters (14,764 ft). The geysers are at their most exuberant at sunrise.

The pleasant village oasis of **San Pedro de Atacama ⓬**, 93 km (58 miles) southeast of Calama, was the most populated Atacamanian town in pre-Columbian times. It was conquered by the Incas in 1450, and by Pedro de Valdivia in 1540. The beautiful **Iglesia de San Pedro** (1641) is constructed of the same white adobe as most of the town. Next door is the impressive **Museo Arqueológico** (open daily; small entrance fee), with a fine collection of pottery, mummies, and ancient Amerindian vestments. Nearby is **Pukara de Quitor**, a mountainside stone fortress built by the Atacamanians during the Inca siege.

Colonial tower, Lauca National Park.

In the distance are lofty snowcapped volcanoes, including **Licancábur**, at 5,600 meters (19,300 ft) the highest in South America. Not far from the village is the enormous **Salar de Atacama** salt basin, as well as the **Valle de la Luna** (32 km/20 miles on a very bumpy road), a mysterious desert valley endowed

BELOW: Valle de la Luna.

Church mural depicting conquistadors as Roman centurions, Parinacota, Lauca National Park.

BELOW: wooden house, Lake District.

with supernatural qualities and ringed by jagged, white peaks which contrast with the ochre valley floor. At twilight its formations turn brilliant colors while salt crystals shimmer in the moonlight.

West of **Copiapó ⑬** are **Caldera** and **Bahía Inglesa**, which comprise three successive bays with long, unspoiled beaches and year-round warm water. **La Serena ⑭**, a colonial city founded in 1543 as a trade link en route between Santiago and Lima, Peru, is known for its 30 distinctive churches. Remodeled in the 1950s, it is now one of the most attractive towns in Chile. The **Iglesia San Francisco** (1627) on Calle Balmaceda has a baroque facade, with interior mudejar details. The **Mercado La Recova** has a good selection of regional crafts.

Tongoy (61 km/38 miles south of La Serena) is a summer resort on a high peninsula overlooking the Pacific, with expansive, white beaches. Along the Elqui River is the narrow, serpentine **Valle del Elqui**. This lush refuge is famous for its clear blue skies, dry mountain air, steep arid mountains, and intensely cultivated pastures and vineyards that are the source of the national liquor, pisco. **Monte Grande ⑮**, a small village along the river, is where the Nobel Prize-winning poet Gabriela Mistral spent her infancy. Her tomb is on the road to Cochiguaz and her birthplace in **Vicuña** is now a **museum** (open daily). There are a number of communes in the area whose inhabitants practice meditation in what is considered to be a focal point of mystical energy.

South to the Lake District

The Lake District is a land of extreme beauty, a seemingly endless succession of lush alpine valleys, low Andean hills and snow-covered volcanoes. The outstanding scenery is reflected in the bitter-cold waters of the lakes, which were

formed by the abrasive retreat of glaciers that once covered the region. Roughly half of the region's population lives in the cities, making a visit to the area a euphoric escape from the bustle of urban life. It's hard to believe that this natural paradise was once forbidden to outsiders. The Mapuche people wiped out every foreign settlement south of the **Río Bío Bío** at the end of the 16th century, and remained undefeated until the 1880s.

Concepción , Chile's second-largest city (pop. 368,000), on the banks of the mighty Bío Bío, was little more than a garrison town until 1818, when Bernardo O'Higgins declared Chile's independence there. The downtown area is best explored on foot on the streets near the plaza. Four blocks south is **Parque Ecuador**, which winds up **Cerro Caracol** (Snail Hill) for a good view of the city. North is the **Universidad de Concepción**, founded in 1919.

About 29 km (18 miles) east of Los Angeles, deep within a wooded Andes valley, the town of **Salto del Laja** is the gateway to the Lake District. The frigid waters of the Laja River slice through some of the most beautiful scenery in Chile, before plunging 35 meters (115 ft) into a deep, rocky canyon, which is eternally bathed in a foggy mist. Within sight of the valley are four volcanoes that rise high above the forest.

The road east snakes through huge pine forests, nearing the mountains as the valley narrows and the terrain becomes semi-arid. Huge lava fields lie nearby, flanked by mountain cypress. **Parque Nacional Laguna del Laja** is located in a narrow valley. In the center is a 200-meter (650-ft) high volcanic cone that holds **Laja Lagoon**, and to the right is the desolate cone of **Laja Volcano**. Three of the four lakes in **Parque Nacional Conguillío** (110 km/70 miles east of Temuco) were formed by the depressions in lava fields spewed out by the

Map on pages 260–1

BELOW: Villarrica Volcano.

Llaima Volcano (3,100 meters/10,170 ft) within the past 50 years. The narrow valley is covered with arucaurias up to 1,200 years old, plus oaks and cypresses.

Turbulent landscape

Villarrica **Ⓐ** is a major resort on the shore of the 1,140-sq. km (440-sq. mile) **Lago Villarrica**. Its blue waters change hue as the sun falls, reflecting the perfect cone of the Villarrica volcano. The lake is scarred by eruptions from the still-active volcano, which glows like the end of a giant cigar at night. The first European colony at Villarrica was beseiged by the Mapuche in 1598, and collapsed without survivors in 1602. The colony was not re-established until 1882. There is a Mapuche museum near the tourist office at Villarrica. The resort village of **Pucón Ⓑ**, on the other side of the lake, is a summer haven for affluent Chileans, and its dirt roads are filled with bungalows and hostels run by the German immigrants who have settled in the area. **Parque Nacional Villarrica**, on the steep slopes of the volcano, is a bizarre mix of untouched forest and barren lava fields that seared through the woods during an eruption.

Slender **Lago Caburga Ⓒ**, 24 km (15 miles) to the east, was formed when lava flows were blocked by the precipitous, densely wooded valley. Foot trails lead to the **Eagle's Nest Falls**, which are surrounded by lush ferns that thrive on the mist. Three pristine lagoons are hidden in the small valley, and several hot springs, fed by volcanoes, gush from the ground.

Lakes Calafquén, Panguipulli, Pellaifa, Neltume, Riñihue, Pirehueico, and, in Argentina, Lacar, are collectively known as the **Seven Lakes**. This little-known area wasn't really settled until the late 1800s, due to its remote setting and harsh winters. **Lican-Ray Ⓓ** was built for tourists on a wooded peninsula overlook-

TIP

It is possible to hike to the 1,900-meter (6,500-ft) peak of Villarrica Volcano and peer into the steamy crater, but take care, as the weather can turn stormy at a moment's notice.

BELOW: street musicians, Valdivia.

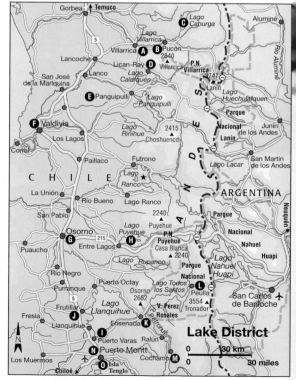

Map on page 292

ing Calafquén Lake. It is said to have the nicest beach in the area and is a magnet for vacationing Chileans in summer. **Panguipulli ❺**, a small, picturesque town on the banks of the lake, has an interesting Capuchin mission and church. A road leads to the tip of a wooded peninsula, with sandy beaches on the lake. Nearby, **Salto del Huilo Huilo**, the highest waterfall in Chile, crashes down a deep vine-covered gorge into the River Fuy, producing an eternal rainbow.

German settlements

One of the first Spanish settlements in Chile was **Valdivia ❻**, located at the confluence of several waterways in the Valdivia Estuary. The streets follow the sinuous rivers, and **Calle General Lagos** near the waterfront and lively port still has remnants of the architecture that German immigrants brought with them in the 19th century. The **Austral Museum** (open Tues–Sun) on **Teja Island**, chronicles the German migration. Nearby is the **Austral University**, with a large campus. Valdivia was heavily fortified by the Spanish after 1600 to guard against Mapuche invasions. Tours are available to see the forts along the river.

The nearby city of **Osorno ❼**, 880 km (550 miles) south of Santiago, is the center of a cattle region. It lies east to west across the Rahue River, surrounded by azure-green pasturelands nourished by abundant rainfall. The city was settled by German farmers, its shingled wooden homes and streets with names like Buschman, Amthauer, and Matthei reminiscent of a distant past. **Calle Bulnes** has good river views. Try to catch the morning **Feria Ganadera**, Chile's largest cattle market, where burly *campesinos* haggle over animals.

Lago Puyehue ❽ (60 km/37 miles east) is a popular fishing and camping spot. The **Casablanca, Puyehue, Puntiagudo**, and immense **Osorno** volcanoes

BELOW: Lago Negro.

Wooden boat and fishermen's houses, Puerto Montt.

are all within sight of the lake's waters. Near the eastern shore are the **Puyehue Hot Springs**, known for their therapeutic qualities. On the road to the Casablanca Volcano, through lush virgin forest, is **Aguas Calientes** (hot springs).

Picturesque towns creep up to the edge of **Lago Llanquihue** and the perfect cone of the snow-capped Osorno Volcano is eternally reflected in its frigid waters. **Puerto Varas ❶**, 19 km (12 miles) to the south, is an immaculate town created in 1854 to handle lake commerce to Puerto Montt. Today it is a thriving stop-off point for tourists who like to gamble in the casino at **Gran Hotel Puerto Varas** on the shore. **Frutillar ❶**, on the northern lakeshore, is filled with interesting German homes with meticulous gardens, and has a peculiar claim to fame: the world's southernmost palm tree. In February it hosts the **Semanas Musicales de Frutillar**, a music festival renowned throughout the sub-continent.

On the eastern shore is **Ensenada ❶**, a tiny village set in the shadow of the Osorno Volcano and surrounded by lush forest cut by lava flows. About 16 km (10 miles) east, the rapids of the **Río Petrohué** are broken by strange lava formations comprised of thousands of black volcanic stones, reminders of an ancient eruption. The Petrohué feeds into **Lago Todos Los Santos**. There are daily boat excursions along the length of the lake to **Peulla ❶**, a magnificent journey along shoreline mountains covered in dense virgin forest.

The unkempt gravel road south from Puerto Varas to Cochamó is a journey through an area of great wilderness beauty. **Cochamó ❶** is a tiny village on the estuary, a branch off to the Pacific through spectacular fiords that rise up to 1,500 meters (4,900 ft) straight out of the water. At Cochamó you can hire fishermen to give you a tour of the estuary in a skiff, where it's easy to spot seals, 30 kg (70 lb) groupers, and even whales.

BELOW: fishing boats, Puerto Montt.

Puerto Montt was founded in 1853 by the adventurer Vincente Pérez Rosales, with a handful of German immigrants intent on settling Llanquihue province. The area mushroomed when the railroad arrived, 60 years later. Today the city is a grimy port, gateway to Chiloé and the Patagonia frontier. Despite its size, Puerto Montt has a small-town feeling, with many homes of northern Germanic design: wooden, with pitched roofs, ornate balconies, and shingles well weathered by the region's eternal drizzle. The cathedral in the central square is the city's oldest building, made of redwood. Puerto Montt faces the Reloncaví Sound, and a walk along the waterfront is a good introduction to the city.

Angelmó, a contiguous fishing port, is a jewel of indigenous maritime activity. Shacks on the pier offer fresh *erizos*, *locos*, and other cold-water seafood, and burly fishermen mend their nets by the skiffs on the shore. The pier is lined with artisan shops that sell a wide selection of woolen goods and wood carvings. Young boys will row you across to Isla Tenglo , where you can walk around its fishing communities.

The rugged south: Chilean Patagonia

South of Puerto Montt, the land and sea become one as the country breaks into a maze of islands, fiords, rivers with myriad tributaries, lakes, and wooded mountains with trees a thousand years old. Chilean Patagonia is a place of forbidding, intense beauty that has escaped the ravages of man.

The island of Chiloé ⑰ emerges just out of sight of Puerto Montt, a romantic place filled with picturesque villages, a hundred tiny enchanted islets, misty waterways, and little wooden homes. Chiloé is steeped in fishing tradition, and the magic of its culture attracts trekkers in search of the customs, legends, and

Maps on pages 260 & 292

Traditional wood-tiled church, Chiloé.

BELOW: chopping wood, Chiloé.

folklore of its friendly people. It is home to lively dances like the *cueca* and *vals*, local dishes like *curanto*, drinks like *chicha de manzana*, and myriad legends, festivals, and rituals all its own. Somehow it has held on to its oldest traditions.

The island is known for its 150 wooden *capillas* (chapels) with distinctive shingled steeples, porticos, glass-paned windows, and three doors. Sixteen of these are UNESCO World Heritage Sites as they are the only Latin American example of a rare form of ecclesiastical wooden architecture. Many of the chapels are in poor shape, but in early 2004, the Inter American Development Bank authorized a grant of US$2.8 million for their repair. Although the island erupts several times a year with the largest religious festivals in Chile, Chiloé's people cling to paradoxical legends: *el trauco*, a mysterious old man who leaves young women pregnant during the night; or *caleuche*, a magical ship of endless party cheer that seduces fisherman who are lost forever on the high seas.

Ancud is Chiloé's largest town, with narrow streets packed with wooden commercial buildings from its heyday as a bustling port. The **Museo Azul de las Islas de Chiloé** (open Jan and Feb daily; Mar–Dec Tues–Sun; entrance fee), in an old fortress near the water, contains exhibits on Chilote culture and mythology. The road south to **Quemchi** snakes past an interesting coastal area settled by European families.

Castro (founded in 1567), on the shores of a protected fiord, is one of the oldest cities in Chile. The **Iglesia San Francisco de Castro** is an unusual wooden cathedral on the plaza. The **Museo Municipal Etnológico** (open Tues–Sun) explains the island traditions. On the outskirts of Castro, the **Museo de Arte Moderno** (open Nov–Feb Tues–Sun) shows some of Chile's best contemporary art in a prizewinning farmhouse conversion. In February the **Festival Cos-**

Quellón is famous for its soft, gray ponchos, which are very resistant to the rain because the wool used for making them is raw and still full of natural oils.

LEFT: *guanacos,* Paine National Park. **RIGHT:** Chinook salmon.

tumbrista Chilote is a marvelous display of island culture. At the waterside, fishermen park their skiffs beside rows of *palafitos*, houses on stilts.

Nearby **Dalcahue** is famous for its Sunday artisan fair, where fine woolen sweaters can be found. **Chonchi** (26 km/16 miles south of Castro) is built on a cliff face overlooking the water. There is a nice church among several colorful large houses with well-kept gardens. Heading northward, **Queilén** is a picturesque town on a narrow peninsula with beaches at each end, and elegant old homes dating back to its founding as an immigrant colony in 1900. Ferries leave from **Quellón** (not to be confused with Queilen), the southernmost port.

South to the end of the world

South of Chiloé lies the remote Region Aisén del General Ibáñez del Campo, where visits still give the sensation of penetrating a new frontier. The Carretera Austral winds through the largely uninhabited archipelago in the far south for more than 1,000 km (600 miles). The region is still largely untouched by humans, save a few fishermen and farmers. It is an amazing landscape where rocky cliffs drop into lush river valleys and dense jungles are bordered by glaciers. **Chaitén** ⓲ is a coastal town with food, lodging, and good ocean and mountain views, which is accessible by a six-hour ferry journey from Chonchi or by road (56 km/35 miles). **Santa Bárbara**, 11 km (7 miles) north, is a picturesque fishing village with a wide beach.

The south is a contrasting mix of lush forest, waterfalls emerging from icy cliffs, glaciers, and valleys flanked by the icy slopes of the Andes. From Santa Lucía the road follows the Río Frío along a wooded valley, reaching **La Junta** at the confluence of three rivers, from where there are excursions to the

Map
on pages
260–1

Visit the park, get the badge.

BELOW: wild scenery at the end of the world.

LEFT: a cargo boat in the Southern Ocean.
RIGHT: produce for sale, Punta Arenas.

picturesque **Lago Rossellot**, and **Lago Verde**. The road continues to **Lago Risopatrón** and **Termas de Puyuhuapi**. Nearby **Parque Nacional Queulat** has amazing views of the *ventisqueros* (glaciers). **Puerto Cisne** to the south, is a small beachside village that was colonized by Germans and Italians in the late 19th century. Heading inland, **Coyhaique** ⑲ is a large town, and a good jumping-off point for exploring the region. Founded in 1929, it is largely a government and military center. The **Museo Regional de la Patagonia** (open Mon–Fri; small entrance fee) is a good introduction to the region's history. South of the city the land turns rugged, with trees giving way to weathered scrub. Steppe grasses begin to appear, buffeted by incessant winds. The area was settled by ranchers who made their fortunes with enormous *fundos* (ranches).

Puerto Aisén ⑳, to the south, is a beautifully kept town, founded to service the ranches in 1914. In the region is **Laguna San Rafael**, a pristine lake which is only accessible after a journey through fiords and archipelagos. The lake is enclosed by the **San Valentine Glacier**, which sends huge blocks of 20,000-year-old ice crashing into the water as it makes its way to the sea. A few firms offer cruises there from Puerto Montt. About 95 km (60 miles) south of Puerto Aisén is **Lago General Carrera**, South America's second-largest lake. It juts into Argentina, with views of the vast pampa to the east. On the Chilean side it is bordered by barren, rocky mountains eroded by glaciers. Several towns have lodgings along the shore, including **Puerto Ibáñez**, **Chile Chico** and **Cochrane**.

Torres del Paine

Down at the far south of the Andes mountain chain, **Torres del Paine National Park** is one of the newest nature reserves in South America, a 1,630-sq. km

Map on pages 260–1

(630-sq. mile) uninhabited wilderness. Aficionados agree that the unique physical formations of the Paine (pronounced *pie-nay*), crowded with glaciers, lakes, and animals, offer the most magnificent walking in the world. The best time to be there is between December and April.

The jumping-off point for the National Park is **Puerto Natales ㉑**, a small, sleepy town set beside the Ultimo Esperanza Gulf, with a couple of hotels, and restaurants serving the local specialty, king crab. Tour boats head out from Natales to nearby glaciers. Not far away is a huge cave where a prehistoric Milodon sloth was found frozen several years ago.

But most people visit Puerto Natales to arrange a trip to the Paine. Several times a week (every morning in summer), vans and buses make the three-hour drive along a rough dirt road to the park. The trail winds through mountain passes before descending to the foot of the Andes, providing the first view of the **Cuernos del Paine** (Horns of the Paine): twisted pillars of grey granite dusted with snow, invariably surrounded by billowing clouds. As everywhere else this far south, weather in the Paine can be unpredictable, even in summer. The famous **Torres del Paine** (towers) are even more spectacular than the Cuernos, but are often obscured by the harsh, incessantly windy weather. Accommodation can be found at the Hostería Pehoe on a lake and the Posada Rio Serrano, an eccentricly converted *estancia* (farm estate).

Several day trips can be made from these bases, as well as more ambitious walks. The park has over 250 km (150 miles) of tracks, including a seven-day circuit. Along the way are *refugios* or shelters, often scanty wood and corrugated iron structures that barely keep out the elements – sleeping bags and cooking gear are essential. Those who complete the full seven-day circuit may be reward-

Freshly caught centolla, *king crab.*

BELOW: tree bent in submission to the Patagonian wind.

Map
on pages
260–1

*Bowsprit of the
Lonsdale, wrecked
near Punta Arenas.*

BELOW: Fuerte
Bulnes, near Punta
Arenas.
RIGHT: *guanacos* in
Torres del Paine
National Park

ed with extraordinary views of snow-covered peaks, turquoise lakes, and lush valleys. The trails are lined with orange, red, and purple flowers. Much of the park is lushly forested, although a worm plague killed many trees in the late 1990s. Walks pass the accessible **Grey** and **Dickman glaciers**.

Most routes allow walkers to see plenty of animals, most commonly the guanacos: unlike camelids in other parts of South America, they appear unafraid of people and can be easily photographed from up close. Although the weather can turn from fair to foul and back again within minutes, the memories of the park will last well after your clothes have dried. Many people who go for a day end up staying a week: the liberating sensation of being in one of the most remote and untouched wilderness areas on earth is worth savoring.

The remote Magallanes

The southernmost province of Magallanes is a solitary place with towns called Porvenir (Future) and Ultimo Esperanza (Last Hope) that try to shake the feeling that you have reached the end of the world. This is where the tip of South America has crumbled into myriad islands as the land, sea, and ice mingle. The forbidding nature of the territory is reflected in the names of some of the islands, which include Madre de Dios and Isla Desolación.

Punta Arenas ㉒ is a port city on the rolling hills above the barren, windswept steppe on the Straits of Magellan. This is a peculiar part of the world: the sky looks bigger here, and people seem distant and less open to outsiders, while the sun glares through the torn ozone layer. Punta Arenas is known for its monuments to the Yugoslav settlers and ranchers who pioneered the region. The **Museo Regional de Magallanes** (open Nov–Apr Mon–Sat 10.30am– 5pm, Sun til 2pm; May–Oct daily 10.30am–2pm; entrance fee except Sun), provides a fascinating trip back to the days before the Panama Canal opened, when the city boomed as ships called in on their journeys round the cape. **Cerro La Cruz** has good views of the city and across the straits to Tierra del Fuego.

Tierra del Fuego, an island of inhospitable terrain across the straits from Punta Arenas, was discovered as Magellan struggled to make the passage to the Pacific in 1520. In the late 19th century the land was settled by a few immigrants from Yugoslavia and England who came to start sheep ranches, and cash in on the 1881 gold rush. The wooded mountains and swamps on the western side are cold and snowy in the long winter; the rainforests to the east are warmer and wetter; and the wind never ceases on the treeless pampas facing Punta Arenas.

Porvenir ㉓, settled primarily by Yugoslavs, is the largest town on the island. The **Provincial Museum** (open Mon–Fri) is recommended. You can take a ferry across the straits from Punta Arenas to Porvenir docks, where a sign gives the distance to every port of Chile, as well as to Belgrade.

The town itself is quiet and sleepy, little changed since the late 19th century. A road continues to the Argentine side of the island *(see page 344)* and the icy waters of Cape Horn passing the southernmost piece of inhabited land on earth. ❑

EASTER ISLAND

*Visiting this tiny Pacific outpost means a long flight from Chile,
yet each year many visitors make the journey to wonder
at its mysterious monolithic figures*

Hidden in the endless wastes of the Pacific, nearly 4,000 km (2,500 miles) from the coast of Chile, the small remnant of volcanic rock named Easter Island was once the most isolated place to live on earth. But in recent decades the Polynesian culture that left behind huge and inexplicable statues has drawn increasing attention from around the world. Where once only one ship a year made the visit to the island, today flights arrive regularly from Santiago. This tiny triangular south seas outpost measuring just 24 km (15 miles) across has a population of around 2,500, but there is a lot to explore. Easter Island has a wonderful raw, unspoiled beauty with windswept coastlines, gentle, treeless hills and a lush interior. Golden beaches and coconut palms are in short supply.

Archeologists now believe that Easter Island may have been first populated as long ago as 400 AD. The Norwegian adventurer and archeologist Thor Heyerdahl argued in his famous book *Aku-Aku* that the inhabitants came from South America, noting resemblances between the island culture and that of Tiahuanaco in Bolivia *(see page 181)*. But most academics today agree that the first settlers came from Polynesia, bringing sweet potato, sugar cane, and bananas to the fertile ground of the island. Left in total isolation for centuries, the settlement prospered and spread. Its people created not only the remarkable stone *moai*, but also the *rongo rongo* script, the only writing system known in all Polynesia and the Americas.

The first Europeans arrived on Easter Sunday in 1722, giving the island its name. Dutch Admiral Roggeveen spent a day ashore, recording (unlike later accounts) that the statues were upright, the lands were neatly cultivated and "whole tracts of woodland" were visible. The population may have been as large as 12,000.

Turbulent times

The picture changes in later descriptions. European explorers in the late 18th century noted that many of the statues had tumbled, little land was under cultivation and there were only a thousand people. The most likely explanation for the island's decline is that the population of Easter Island had outgrown its resources; the food supply failed, the forests were felled and soil began to erode. Without wood for canoes to escape from the island, fighting and cannibalism broke out, and the *moai* were toppled.

The people of Easter Island were to endure further suffering in the 19th century, when whalers and slave traders came to call. Of one thousand islanders taken as slaves to the guano islands off Peru in 1862, only a hundred were released alive, of whom only 15 survived the return journey, bringing smallpox to wreak further havoc in the community. By 1871, only 175 islanders remained. Today over

LEFT: one of many *moai* statues.
BELOW: *moai* in the old volcanic quarry of Ranu Raraku.

*Young Easter
Island man in
traditional dress.*

BELOW: the *moai*
of Ahu Akiví.

3,500 people live on the island, but about a quarter were born on the mainland, of Chilean ancestry. The airfield, opened in 1967, increased tourism, and in 1988 the airstrip was extended to become an emergency landing strip for the space shuttle, thrusting the island into the technological age. In the early 1990s Kevin Costner brought a Hollywood film crew to the island to produce the historically creative film *Rapa Nui*. Despite being a monumental flop, the film brought a surge of tourist traffic to the island in its wake. Rapu Nui is the indigenous name of the island, the whole of which is a national park and a World Heritage Site.

The mysterious *moai*

No one knows the true story behind the *moai,* but they are thought to have been symbols of gods and ancestors. They were carved from around 900 AD, out of the soft volcanic tufa of **Rano Raraku**, where some 400 incomplete pieces remain, many as high as 5.5 meters (18 ft) – the largest is 21 meters (69 ft) tall. Each probably took a year to complete. Once finished, the *moai* was cut out of the quarry and transported to a family burial platform called an *ahu,* some being given red stone "topknots." The family dead were usually placed in a vault beneath the *moai*, which was probably believed to transmit *mana*, or power, to the living family chief. All of the standing *ahu moai* that can be seen now have been re-erected in modern times. In the period of the tribal wars, all the *moai* were toppled, presumably to break the *mana* of the family chief they protected.

The most famous of the *moai* are the standing sentinels embedded in the ground on the southern slope of Rano Raraku. These haughty-looking statues

remain eyeless: *moai* were only given coral eyes once they were raised on *ahus*, at which time the *mana* began to work. Most of the sites can be reached on foot if you're happy to put in a couple of hours' walking through marvelous countryside, but make sure you bring water with you.

The "Bird Man" cult

The most geologically spectacular place on Easter Island is the volcano **Rano Kao**, with its steep crater and multicolored lake. The ruined village of **Orongo**, sitting on steep cliffs above the crashing sea and three foam-washed islands, is surrounded by rocks with "Bird Man" carvings: a man's body is drawn with a bird's head, often holding an egg in one hand. Fortunately we know quite a lot about the Bird Man cult, as it continued up to 1862. It involved a strange rite that probably began in the period of the wars. The basis of the cult was finding the first egg laid by the *Manu Tara*, or sacred bird, each spring.

The chief of each tribe on the island sent one chosen servant to Moto Nui, the largest of the islets below Orongo. Swimming across the dangerous waters, the servants or *hopus* spent a month looking for the first egg. On finding the egg, the successful *hopu* plunged into the swirling waters with the egg strapped to his forehead, swam to the mainland, and climbed the cliffs to Orongo. The *hopu's* master, named Bird Man for the year, would be given special powers and privileges. Today there are more than 150 Bird Man carvings in the area, overlaid with fertility symbols. Nearby are markings and stones that have been interpreted as forming part of a solar observatory, where on the summer solstice the sun can be seen rising over Poike peninsula – one more mysterious attraction on this beautiful and fascinating island in the Pacific. ❑

Map on page 303

TIP

Motorbikes, jeeps and horses can be rented. Guided tours by four-wheel drive are highly recommended. You won't cover every single site in just one day's tour, but you'll see the most important ones.

BELOW: Easter Island women.

JUAN FERNÁNDEZ ISLANDS

The location of the true story that inspired the fictional Robinson Crusoe, these little-known Pacific islands are also home to some fascinating and unique species of plants and animals

Named after Spanish navigator Juan Fernández, who discovered them in 1574, the Juan Fernández Islands owe their notoriety to a classic novel written by Daniel Defoe. Their place in history was set when Scottish mariner Alexander Selkirk was marooned on Isla Mas a Tierra, now officially known as Isla Robinson Crusoe, for four years in 1704. His experience provided the inspiration for Daniel Defoe's classic tale, *Robinson Crusoe*.

The three Juan Fernández islands – Isla Robinson Crusoe, Isla Alejandro Selkirk, and Isla Santa Clara – lie 650 km (400 miles) off the Chilean mainland. The whole archipeligo is a national park and World Biosphere Reserve. Reaching them today can seem as complicated as it was for Selkirk to get off them 300 years ago. Unless you travel on a pre-arranged tour, flights to the islands from Santiago are irregular, to say the least. Winter rains flood the dirt runway, limiting air traffic to the months of October through April.

The flight to Isla Robinson Crusoe is followed by a one-and-a-half hour journey in an open fishing boat to the township of **San Juan Bautista**. On a fine day, the water is clear and blue, with schools of fish zigzagging below and the obese Juan Fernández seals sunning themselves by the shore. The boatmen often smoke succulent lumps of freshly caught cod and share them around with bread and water. The township of San Juan Bautista, where almost all of the archipelago's 500 inhabitants live, is located roughly where Selkirk spent his enforced leisure time. Set beneath forest-covered fists of stone with their peaks always lost in the gray mist, it consists of a few unpaved streets, a bar, a soccer field, and a small cemetery with ship's anchors above many of the graves. With just a handful of automobiles, the only noise is the never-ending howl of the wind.

BELOW: the fictional Robinson Crusoe.

In Selkirk's footsteps

The classic hike from town follows Selkirk's path to **El Mirador** – the lookout used by the marooned sailor every day to scan the horizon on both sides of the island. Start early, at about 8am, to arrive before the mists roll in. The path runs through crops of introduced eucalyptus into higher forests of indigenous trees. It also passes the remains of an old Spanish fort, as well as a turnoff to a rock bearing sailor's graffiti from 1866 – a ship and a giant fish.

The trail becomes a corridor through rainforest before revealing a knife-shaped peak. In the saddle of the mountain is the only place to see both sides of the island: lush, green Juan Bautista to the west; dry, brown swirls and jagged peaks on the northern side of the mountain. A plaque was erected here by a British warship in the 19th century commemorating Selkirk's ordeal. It has more recently been joined by a small memorial from one of the mariner's descendents from Largo in Scotland. On the return journey, call in at the **Caves of the Patriots**, where 300 pro-Spanish soldiers fled in 1814 after Chile's declaration of independence. Unlike Selkirk, they couldn't stand the wind and rain in their huge, damp caves, so gave themselves up. Back on shore, a number of other caves vie for the title of Selkirk's home, although for most of the time the mariner lived in his own handmade huts.

Within the town is CONAF, the island's national park service, financed mostly by European funds. The center operates to protect the unique flora and fauna of the area that put the island on the UNESCO World Heritage list. The plant life is unusually varied on the island, with 101 endemic varieties including a range of enormous ferns, many of which look as if they would be at home in Dr Seuss books. Of the unique animals, the red hummingbird is the most famous for its needle-fine black beak and silken feather coverage. CONAF spends most of its time trying to eradicate threats introduced by humans: everything from mulberry bushes to the wild goats and feral cats descended from Selkirk's days. Rabbits were once a problem, but have been controlled by the simple solution of paying a trapper to catch and sell the animals on a daily basis (the islanders thought this a more humane solution than introducing the disease myxomatosis).

Biologists on the islands regularly turn up new finds: recently, a fern called *Dendroseries macranta* that had not been sighted since 1907 was found in a remote corner of the island.

But one of the real pleasures of any visit is just taking a seat by the wharf and watching the world go by, sipping on a beer and chatting with the islanders. Prepare to eat your fill of the local lobster too, as there may be little else on the menu – delicious for the first few days but palling by the end of your stay. ❏

The local delicacy is langosta de Juan Fernández – *a clawless lobster, which is also shipped to the Chilean mainland.*

BELOW: Isla Santa Clara.

URUGUAY

This tiny nation, wedged in between Argentina and Brazil, was once a pioneer of social reform. It retains flavors of colonial opulence and rural frontier life, as well as elegant beach resorts

Map
on pages
260–1

L ong known as the Switzerland of South America, owing to its size, its democratic tradition and its dependence on the banking sector, Uruguay and its capital, Montevideo, are often seen virtually as one. This is not so surprising, given that the country covers an area of just 186,000 sq. km (72,000 sq. miles) and that more than half of its population of 3.5 million is located in Montevideo, the rest being spread among attractive coastal towns and the interior of the country, dedicated to cattle, sheep, rice, and fruit production.

Successive colonial wars decimated Uruguay's indigenous Charrua population; the population today is made up principally of the descendants of Italian and Spanish immigrants who arrived in the late 19th and early 20th century, as well as a black or mixed-race minority descended from former slaves and Brazilian immigrants. Usually seen as less formal than the Argentines, the Uruguayans are of similar ancestry, though as a small and family-based society they are also less open in their social relations, in particular with foreign visitors.

Although Uruguayans tend to use Argentina as a reference point (they call themselves *Orientales*, or Easterners, as opposed to the Argentines to the west), there are some marked differences between Montevideo and Buenos Aires. One is Montevideo's racial mixture. In the 19th century, rumors of fair treatment attracted emancipated slaves from Brazil and Argentina. The army offered them a familiar regimented life, and many joined the infantry, which considerably reduced their numbers. Uruguayans claim to have no racial prejudice, but blacks tend to occupy the bottom rungs of the economic ladder.

Another difference from Argentina is Uruguay's strong secular tradition. The Catholic church plays no role in government, and holidays all have secular names: Christmas is Family Day and Easter or Holy Week is Tourism Week.

Uruguay claims to host the world's longest Carnival, held in Tourism Week (Easter) – it may be a little more sedate than the Rio version, but it is a good place to see *Candomblé*, which evolved from rituals and traditions brought by African slaves. The country also has a long tradition of tango, with many tango stars born in the country. Tango week is in October.

PRECEDING PAGES:
house of the painter
Paez Vilaró, Punta
del Este.
LEFT: *gaucho* with
maté gourd.
BELOW: Colonia del
Sacramento.

Building a nation

The Portuguese were the first Europeans to settle the region, founding the city of Colonia in 1680. In 1726, Spain established a colony in Montevideo; the two countries battled over the area until Spain won possession in 1726. In 1815, José Gervasio Artigas led Uruguay to independence, becoming leader of the Uruguayan nation, but wars with Brazil postponed full independence for 10 years *(see page 31)*. Artigas was eventually forced into exile in Paraguay. For the

next 50 years, civil wars raged between two political forces: the Blancos (whites) and Colorados (reds). Initially feuding factions, they would eventually evolve into Uruguay's major political parties. In 1872, in the interest of beef exports, peace was established by ceding the Blancos' influence to the countryside and the Colorados' to the city, a division that remains to this day.

Montevideo is said to be a corruption of a Galician sailor's cry: "Monte vi eu!" (I saw a hill!).

The social revolution

José Batlle y Ordóñez is usually credited with forging the model of civic order that Uruguay became during the first half of the 20th century. Batlle (pronounced *Ba-zhay*) studied in Paris, and returned to Uruguay full of enlightened ideas. He became a political journalist, fearlessly attacking the country's dictators, founded his own newspaper, *El Dia*, in 1886, and gradually made his way into politics. He was elected president for the first time in 1903.

On a four-year sojourn in Europe between presidential terms, Batlle was impressed with the Swiss social legislation and state-operated industries. In his second term, he legalized divorce, abolished the death penalty, and established an eight-hour workday. He also forbade naming public buildings after saints. His 1918 Constitution provided complete freedom of the press, the prohibition of arbitrary arrest, and decreed that prisons were for reform, rather than punishment.

After his death in 1929, Batlle's reforms had succeeded in liberalizing both parties. The widespread peace and prosperity of the past decades prevented even the conservative moneyed classes from objecting to the advance of social security and workers' rights. A coup d'état in 1933 temporarily halted progress, but a 1942 Constitution provided explicitly for universal health, accident, and unemployment insurance, and gave illegitimate children the right to inherit.

BELOW: an early 19th-century view of Montevideo harbor.

End of the welfare state

The collapse of Uruguay's wool and beef economic base in the late 1950s produced a crisis in the country's welfare system and a boom in poverty and unemployment. This in turn facilitated the rise of the guerrilla group Tupamaros in the 1960s and, in 1973, the rise of a repressive military government. During 12 years of dictatorship, one in every 50 Uruguayans was arrested at some point for presumed subversive activity. One in every 500 was sentenced to six years or more in prison, and some 400,000 fled into exile. Following the return to civilian government in 1985, Uruguay enjoyed comparatively high living standards and a relatively equitable distribution of wealth. But the country's banking system has become increasingly uncompetitive, and no industry has yet arisen to replace the declining demand for wool and beef exports, despite Uruguay's membership of the Southern Cone trade organization Mercosur, where it is overshadowed by Argentina and Brazil. Some opening of the state monopolies of oil, energy and communications, and foreign investment may mark the road to growth in the largely stagnant economy. Elections are held every five years, and voting is compulsory. Jorge Batlle of the center-right Colorado Party was elected as head of state and government in March 2000. Tax increases, among other measures, were implemented in May 2002 in an effort to prevent neighboring Argentina's financial crisis from entering Paraguay, and in August of that year the Government closed banks for almost a week to prevent mass withdrawal of savings. A general strike was held in protest.

Map on pages 260–1

Uruguay has a median age of 47 – much older than in other Latin American countries. This is due partly to traditionally small families, but is also a result of the mass exodus of young people during the years of military government.

Montevideo and the coast

To visitors it can seem as if all roads in Uruguay lead to the beach – not so surprising given that the country has one of the most attractive coastlines in the continent. Even the capital, **Montevideo ㉔**, is noted for its long beaches, and virtually all the country's principal tourist destinations are on the coast, linked by the *ruta interbalnearia* (inter-beach route) running from Montevideo to Chuy, on the Brazilian border. Visitors who have had enough of the beach may want to head into the country and enjoy a slice of rural Uruguayan life on an *estancia* (ranch), sampling Uruguay's famous beef and wine. Rural activities range from horseback riding to wild boar hunting.

The most pleasant way to travel to Uruguay is to cross the River Plate from Buenos Aires. There is a choice of hydrofoil, catamaran, or ferry bus, taking between three and four hours. From the decks, the low hill that gave Montevideo its name comes slowly into view. Landing in Montevideo harbor and walking through the musty customs office may give you the sensation of going back in time. Old British Leyland buses and electric trolleys make their way down cobbled streets jammed with scooters, cyclists and pedestrians. Uruguay's high import duty on automobiles has filled Montevideo's streets with vehicles that would be considered antiques elsewhere. (Uruguayan auto mechanics are said to be among the best in the world.) The rural air is reinforced every August with a farm show, held in the **Parque Prado**.

With a population of nearly 2 million, Montevideo is the only town of any size in Uruguay. Economic

BELOW: make do and mend in Montevideo.

*Colorful hand-woven
landscape.*

hard times have given it an elegantly shabby look, although ceremonial occasions such as afternoon tea are as important as they are in Buenos Aires, as is the perpetual ritual of *maté (see page 315)* – you'll see people with their *maté* gourd and thermos of hot water on buses and in bank lines.

The best place to begin a tour of Montevideo is at the **Plaza Cagancha** (also called Plaza Libertad) on the main thoroughfare, Avenida 18 de Julio, named after the day in 1829 when Uruguay was finally freed of Argentine and Brazilian control. You'll find the main tourist office on Plaza Cagancha, offering brochures and free city maps. Avenida 18 de Julio runs downhill, past the **Gaucho Museum** at No 998 (open Mon–Sat), with its eclectic collection. The street leads to the city's main square, **Plaza Independencia**. To the left is an unattractive skyscraper known as the **Palacio Salvo**, which is, mysteriously, a beloved landmark for Montevideans. To the right is the Art Deco **Hotel Victoria**, now owned by Sun Myung Moon's Unification Church. In the middle of the square is the subterranean tomb and equestrian statue of General José Artigas. Also worth visiting are the cream-colored **Government House**, now used only for ceremonial purposes, and the jewel-like **Teatro Solís**, an exact copy of the Teatro María Guerrero in Madrid. Recently renovated, the theater was established in 1856 and is still operating, making it one of the oldest theaters in the Americas.

Into the Old Town

BELOW: Plaza de la
Independencia,
Montevideo.

The archway at the west end of Plaza Independencia is part of the city wall that once protected Montevideo against its many invaders. It marks the entrance to the **Ciudad Vieja**, or Old Town, a neighborhood of narrow, winding streets

and early 20th-century buildings. The heart of the Old Town is **Plaza Constitución**. Here is the old *cabildo*, or town hall. Like the **Cathedral**, also in the square, it's been renovated but retains its colonial appearance. The cathedral dates from the beginning of the 19th century and is the oldest building in the city. The *cabildo* has a good **Museo de Historia** dedicated to the history of the city, containing clocks, furniture, and portraits. **La Bolsa** (the Stock Exchange), the **Banco de la Republica**, and the imposing **Aduana** (Customs House) are all north of the plaza and worth a look. Also intriguing is the **Palacio Taranco**, on the Plaza Zabala, the former home of a wealthy merchant who imported every stick of furniture and even the marble floors from France.

Following Calle Piedras down to the waterfront leads to the **Mercado del Puerto**, a lively market with a series of open-air restaurants at one end. The market is only open in the afternoons; it's as much about atmosphere as the produce on sale, and Saturdays are particularly lively.

From the old town there is a view across the port to the **Cerro**, the 139-meter (456-ft) hill that gave the city its name, topped with a lighthouse and fort.

A city of beautiful beaches

If the weather is good, try to visit one of the city's clean white-sand beaches. It also has two lovely parks of historical interest. The **Prado** is located northwest of downtown (follow Agraciada north from 18 de Julio) in a neighborhood where some of Uruguay's grand old houses still stand. It was once the property of a 19th-century financier named José Buschental, who built a 40-hectare (100-acre) estate here and married the niece of Emperor Dom Pedro II of Brazil. He brought fish from Asia as well as exotic plants and animals from around the

In 1939 the great German battleship Graf Spee was sunk a couple of kilometers off Montevideo; its anchor can be seen in the port. The city stadium was built using metal plates from the leviathan's salvaged bulkheads.

BELOW: enjoying a cup of *maté* in the traditional way,

A CUP OF MATÉ

Everything stops for *maté* in Uruguay – in fact, so important is this stimulating brew that many Uruguayans carry their own DIY *maté* kit around with them at all times. This usually consists of a drinking gourd known as a *culha* or *maté*, sometimes decorated with silver, containing *yerba* (dried leaves); a *bombilla* (drinking tube), which has a strainer at one end; and a hot water flask.

Maté, or *yerba maté*, is brewed from the leaves of an evergreen plant, *Ilex paraguariensis*, which is related to the holly and grows wild in Paraguay and southern Brazil. The drink was popular with the Guaraní people in pre-Columbian times, and the leaves were first cultivated on a large scale by the Jesuits.

Maté is now an integral part of the culture of Uruguay, Paraguay, Argentina, and Brazil, with the cup sometimes shared between friends or family. Each guest drinks from the cup and passes it back to the host to be refilled in turn.

Maté is usually drunk plain, but sometimes lemon juice, sugar, or even milk are added. Iced *maté* is also very popular. *Yerba maté* has diuretic and anti-rheumatic properties, and *maté* teabags are available in many northern hemisphere health shops.

world. This area has a statue of Buschental, as well as 800 varieties of roses. **Parque Rodó**, just behind the city's **Playa Ramirez** beach, is resplendent with palms, eucalyptus, and native *ombú* trees. It was named after José Enrique Rodó, one of the most prominent 19th-century South American writers, whose most famous work, *Ariel*, influenced a generation of intellectuals.

Promenades and smart hotels

In summer, many Buenos Aires political news articles are datelined Punta del Este – Argentina's movers and shakers are all at the beach. The family of Paraguay's dictator Stroessner was vacationing at "Punta" when he was overthrown in 1989.

BELOW: an *asado* (barbecue) at the port markets.

The metropolitan beaches stretch east as far as **Carrasco**, a fashionable suburb with streets shaded by big trees and houses that belong to the few well-to-do people left in Uruguay. This old casino still opens every season, though its glory days are long past. Montevideo's international airport lies just beyond Carrasco, 14 km (9 miles) from the city center.

Beyond Carrasco, the highway turns inland, but smaller roads branch off to the beaches. At Km 42, shortly before Atlántida, is the **Fortín de Santa Rosa**, an 18th-century fortress converted into a hotel with a virtually private beach and an excellent restaurant. **Atlántida**, 45 km (28 miles) from Montevideo, is surrounded by a windbreak of cypress and eucalyptus. The beach also has a casino, golf course and tearoom. Just beyond Atlántida is **Piriápolis**, a pretty town on a curving bay with an old-fashioned promenade dominated by the imposing Argentino Hotel, a 1920s spa with mineral baths, stained-glass windows, and an elegant solarium where you may sip the curative sulfur-flavored water.

The most famous beach on the Uruguayan coast is **Punta del Este** **㉕**, a jet-set-studded peninsula that attracts well-heeled Argentines as well as a fair share of international celebrities and European royalty. Prices at "Punta" make this primarily *porteño* resort an exclusive one. The peninsula has two long and beautiful beaches: the Atlantic one is more windswept than the tranquil bay side. Those who don't share the Argentine herd instinct might find Punta more attractive off-season, when hotel rates go down and cool autumn breezes clear the sand of body-to-body sunbathers.

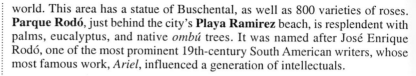

North of Punta del Este, the Uruguayan Atlantic coast is rich with gorgeous seascapes and deserted white-sand beaches. Along the coastal highway toward Brazil, it's worth stopping at the 18th-century Portuguese fortresses of **Santa Teresa** **㉖** and **San Miguel** **㉗**, now beautiful national parks and popular bird sanctuaries, and **Punta del Diablo**, an attractive fishing village with a number of small restaurants offering excellent seafood.

European communities

West of Montevideo are some interesting European settlements. **Colonia Valdense** was settled by Waldensians from the Piedmontese Alps, and **Colonia Suiza** is a small Swiss enclave, also known as **Nueva Helvecia**. Some 50 km (31 miles) west of Colonia Valdense is the 17th-century Portuguese town of **Colonia del Sacramento** **㉘**. Colonia retains more of its original flavor than most cities in the region, partly because little has happened here since the Portuguese founded it as a rival to Buenos Aires in 1680. With a population of little more than 10,000, Colonia can have the air of an Iberian ghost town.

Sights to see in the old quarter include the **Museo Español**, in a restored 18th-century viceroy's mansion; the **parochial church**; and the **Museo Portugues**, which has an excellent collection of mahogany and Cordoban furniture, and military uniforms. Narrow cobbled streets lead toward the river, where you can walk along the promenade to the remains of the colonial fortifications. A couple of miles further out stands a grandiose bullring, not used since Uruguay outlawed bullfighting at the beginning of the 20th century. A hydrofoil connects Colonia with Buenos Aires; there is also the slower but more nausea-proof ferry.

North along the River Uruguay

For Uruguayans, a trip up the River Uruguay is the patriotic equivalent of an American tourist's pilgrimage to New England. The small, tidy villages where nothing appears to be happening were at one time the crucibles of Uruguayan independence. About 30 km (18 miles) up the river from Colonia is **La Agraciada**, where the famous "Thirty-three Orientales" *(see page 31)* landed from Argentina and organized a battalion to expel the Portuguese from Uruguayan soil. A statue to General Lavalleja, the patriots' leader, is on the beach.

The port of **Fray Bentos** commemorates revolution of a different kind in its **Museo de la Revolución Industrial**. Fray Bentos was the site of the country's first meat extract factory. **Paysandú ㉙**, further upriver, is the town where Artigas led his followers when they fled Spanish rule in Montevideo. Today it's a popular spot for stalking the delicious *pez dorado* game fish. It's also where **Artigas Bridge** crosses the Uruguay River to Argentina. North of Paysanú are the remedial hot mineral springs of **Termas de Daymán** and **Arapey**. ❑

Map on pages 260–1

Browsing for bargains at the Sunday Tristan Narvaja fair.

BELOW: the fashionable Parque Hotel, Montevideo, *circa* 1920.

ARGENTINA

*Despite the current political and economic strife, it is still
possible to travel throughout Argentina, from its stimulating capital,
Buenos Aires, to the furthest reaches of its mighty territory*

Map
on pages
260–1

The second-largest country in South America and the eighth-largest in the
world, geographical magnitude is not the only grand aspect of Argentina. The
country is characterized by large cities, large ranches, large open spaces,
even large steaks. In the mid-20th century, Argentina was one of the richest nations
on earth and seemed set to become the Texas of South America. But instead, the
country became notorious for political drama and military dictatorships.

Argentina has always been heavily oriented toward its capital, Buenos Aires,
with the city sometimes described as a giant's head on a dwarf's body. Most of
the country's economic, political, financial, and industrial activity is focused on
the Buenos Aires area, implying that the distribution of wealth and resources is
extremely skewed. Until the most recent economic crisis, which has driven
much of the population into poverty, Argentina's people lived well, enjoying
restaurants, museums, and theaters. Throughout the country, the urban middle
class had its nearby beach, lakeside resort, ski center, or mountain village retreat.

Argentina covers a range of latitudes, from the sub-tropical northeast, with
Jesuit ruins and the imposing Iguazú Falls, to the Andean northwest, changing
abruptly from barren mountains to lush greenery, with the colonial architecture of Salta and the sugar-producing province of Tucumán. Central Argentina
is characterized by spectacular mountain scenery,
vineyards and impeccable urban planning in Mendoza; green mountains and lakes in Córdoba; and
attractive beach resorts in Buenos Aires province. In
the south, bleak oil towns co-exist with Welsh communities, pseudo-Tyrolean architecture, pretty towns
surrounded by snow-capped mountains and lakes, and
magnificent glaciers in the far south. All have a highly
developed tourist industry with good transport links,
accommodation, and food.

PRECEDING PAGES:
late afternoon on
the pampa.
LEFT: pedestrian
mall of Lavalle,
Buenos Aires.
BELOW: tango hero
Carlos Gardel.

The people of Argentina

Argentines are known for strong localist tendencies
and a capacity to disdain those from the rest of the
sub-continent, tempered by a genuine instinct to be
hospitable. While the *porteños* (inhabitants of Buenos
Aires – literally "people of the port") see their city as
more sophisticated and cosmopolitan than the rest of
the country, many provincial cities – Tucumán, Mendoza, and Córdoba – have large populations of
second- and third-generation descendants of European and Arab immigrants, and are far enough away
from the capital to have developed an exciting cultural, artistic, and academic life of their own.

Very few indigenous peoples remain, with small
groups of Guaraní, Colla and Toba (or Witchi) in the
far north and Mapuche in the south, marginalized by
the so-called "European" culture of Argentina.

Porteños, gauchos and caudillos

In the 18th century, when Buenos Aires was thriving as a smuggling center, fortunes began to be made in cattle hides and mule-breeding, and indigenous people were forced back from the pampas. Huge tracts of land were set aside for a few Spanish families, whose names would recur again and again as the power-brokers of Argentina. For 70 years after independence in 1816, civil wars raged, with Buenos Aires trying to impose central rule over local strongmen *(caudillos)*, and their armies of *gauchos* – *mestizo* horsemen from the pampa *(see page 338)*. The most famous *caudillo* was Juan Manuel de Rosas, who rose from the chaos of civil war in 1829 to become governor of Buenos Aires province and *de facto* ruler of Argentina. Rosas is remembered for his reign of terror, enforced by secret police, and his nationalist policies, enabling Argentine goods to compete against foreign trade. After 23 years, he was thrown out and his supporters massacred. His protective tariffs were dismantled, and the country was flooded with foreign goods, while the civil wars resumed.

It was not until 1886 that the final step toward nationhood was made, when Buenos Aires was separated from its province and declared the capital of Argentina. The country's leaders were eager to appear cultured and urbane, notably Domingo Sarmiento, who divided the world into "civilization" – represented by all things European – and "barbarity": the *caudillos*, *gauchos*, and Amerindians. Codes were introduced to control the *gauchos*. General Julio Roca embarked on a "Conquest of the Wilderness" in the 1880s to open up the pampas and Patagonia. Any indigenous person in his path was killed, the rest herded into reservations. Cultivation of the pampas exploded to keep up with the new demand for beef. Railways were laid and Argentina was soon outstripping its rivals, Australia and Canada, in agricultural advances.

BELOW: a 19th-century painting of a *gaucho* and his *china*.

The immigrants arrive

Thousands of laborers were needed to keep the boom going. Before 1880, only a trickle of foreign workers stayed in Argentina. Overnight they became a flood. Most were poor peasants from northern Italy, with the next largest group coming from Spain. But Argentina's boom wealth was not shared among these new arrivals, and Argentina remained the property of around 200 close-knit families known as "the oligarchy". The result was a distortion in ownership that has stunted the country's growth and political life.

As the economy expanded, the new-found importance of Buenos Aires allowed it to shed the Hispanic colonial atmosphere and become an expression of all things French. The 16th-century street plan was cast aside and streets widened into grand avenues lined with marble footpaths, cafés, and jacaranda trees. But political and economic inequalities began rising to the surface. Protest movements against the oligarchs' grip produced the middle-class Unión Cívica Radical, forerunner of today's party of the same name. While tensions grew in the 1920s, Buenos Aires became the cultural mecca of Latin America. The rich indulged in tango parties and balls rather than worry about social ills. Then the Great Depression hit. Nobody was surprised when, on Sep-

Map on pages 260–1

tember 6, 1930, the Argentine military marched into the Presidential Palace to take power under General José Uriburu. It was the first of many interventions.

The age of Perón

The military handed over to a series of conservative governments in the 1930s, allowing the oligarchy to run the country as if nothing had changed in 40 years. Then, in 1943, a group of young army officers staged a successful coup. One of the figures in the new government was a man who even today has a personality cult that dominates Argentine politics: Juan Domingo Perón. Perón joined the Army at 16, and became an ardent admirer of Mussolini while serving as military attaché in Italy. Perón took the post of Secretary of Labor and started to organize trade unions and to champion disenfranchised and unprotected workers. He was joined by the beautiful actress, Eva Duarte. The daughter of a peasant, Evita shocked high society but was worshiped by the working class for her passionate, if occasionally incoherent, speeches on their behalf. Thanks to her, women got the vote and a public health service was developed.

Perón became president, nationalized industries and started social welfare programs, while Eva toured Europe in jewels and couture dresses as if she were royalty. She died of cancer in 1952 at the age of 33, but the Vatican resisted calls for her canonization. The Perón magic quickly began to wear off: the cost of living was rising, government spending was out of control, and corruption rife. When it was rumored that Perón would distribute arms to the trade unions, the military struck, bombing the Presidential Palace and forcing Perón to flee on a Paraguayan gunboat. His supporters were purged from every level of government, and even mentioning Perón's name in public was banned.

BELOW: Eva and Juan Perón.

Lighthouse, Buenos Aires harbor.

The "dirty war" and war with Britain

Despite the repression, Perónism lived on through 18 years of incompetent military and civilian rule. When full democratic elections were allowed in 1973, Perónist candidates won easily – and invited the aging founder back from exile in Spain to become president once again. Returning in triumph to Buenos Aires, Perón promptly died, leaving the presidency to his third wife, a cabaret dancer known as Isabelita. Argentina's economy nose-dived again, guerilla fighting began in the mountains in Tucumán, and terrorists began letting off bombs and kidnapping prominent figures. The military let the situation drag on until they had popular support for a coup in 1976. Then they began a "dirty war" to purge Argentine society of everyone suspected of left-wing sympathies. As many as 30,000 people were kidnapped, tortured, and secretly executed in the campaign.

But in 1982, with inflation reaching record levels and poverty growing, President Galtieri decided to distract attention by taking the Falkland Islands (Las Malvinas to the Argentines; *see page 350)*. The possession of these windswept rocks had been contentious since the British annexed them in 1833. After a brief, bloody war during which British Prime Minister Margaret Thatcher rejuvenated her electoral prospects on the back of her zeal to counter-attack while the UN was still negotiating a peaceful solution, the Argentines were defeated and the humiliated military were forced to call democratic elections in 1983.

Radical candidate Raúl Alfonsin unexpectedly won the presidency and guided the country into a new democratic era. In 1989 the Judicialist (Perónist) party's candidate Carlos Menem won the presidential elections by a landslide. Menem imposed a series of draconian economic reforms and reformed the constitution to allow for his re-election.

BELOW: jubilant Argentines took to the streets on the return of democracy in 1983 after seven years of military rule.

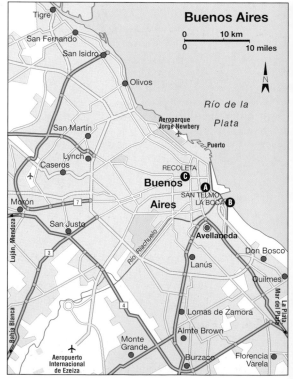

Recession and poverty

In 1998, Menem proposed further reforms to allow himself a third term, despite repeated allegations of corruption, but in October 1999 his 10-year tenure as president ended when Fernando de la Rúa, representing the Radical Civic Union, was elected with 49 percent of the vote. Splits within his coalition government over continuing high-level corruption led to the resignation of vice-president Carlos Alvarez a year later. The recession rapidly worsened and poverty and unemployment rose sharply, with jobless rates at 25 percent and around half the population below the poverty line. One in four children was suffering from malnutrition – in a country capable of feeding 10 times its population.

The country was on the verge of imploding financially, politically, and socially. Bank accounts were frozen, and in December 2001 President Fernando de la Rúa resigned after 27 people died in food riots, and three days later Adolfo Rodriguez Saa was named interim president; he resigned a week later. On January 1 2002, Congress elected Peronist senator Eduardo Duhalde as caretaker-president. Days later, the government devalued the peso, ending 10 years of parity with the US dollar. Three months later, banking and foreign exchange activity were suspended.

In November of 2002, the country defaulted on a US$800m debt repayment to the World Bank, after failing to secure IMF aid. Peronist governor Nestor Kirchner won the presidential run-off vote in May 2003 when his rival, former President Carlos Menem, withdrew from the race. During Kirchner's first year in office, the country's economy has expanded 12 percent and the President has made serious attempts to address human rights issues.

Buenos Aires: a sophisticated city

Few countries are so gripped by their capital cities as Argentina is by **Buenos Aires** ③⓪. Everyone and everything that passes through Argentina must at some stage come to "the Paris of South America." Sprawling over the flat, empty pampas, by the shores of the muddy Río de la Plata (River Plate), Buenos Aires flaunts its European heritage. It is a city of immigrants who always intended to return home, but still find themselves, somewhat uncertainly, in a remote land. But it is also a city with a creative energy that can put New York to shame. Despite the current political and economic woes, you can still see people of all ages enjoying a meal in a restaurant, lining up for a movie theater session or in deep discussion in a café.

Porteños are a special breed, renowned for their contradictions. Obsessed with style, they turn their city into an open-air fashion parade. They are in love with the theater, public debate, and the spectacle of politics. Privately, the dramas of the mind exert an endless fascination: Buenos Aires has more psychiatrists per head of the population than Manhattan.

A slice of Europe

Buenos Aires was founded more than 400 years ago, but it was virtually re-created at the end of the 19th century. Riding the beef boom of the 1880s, the city's

Maps,
Area 260–1
City 324

BELOW: the Obelisk on Avenida 9 de Julio, the widest street in the world.

Beef and Red Wine

L ong before arriving, you will have heard that Argentina is a carnivore's paradise. Although it is exported to many parts of the world, the best beef is consumed at home with an almost religious reverence. Until recently Argentina's fine wine was one of the country's best-kept secrets, with very little being imported overseas, despite being the world's fifth-largest producer. Today Argentine wines are being appreciated on dinner tables worldwide. Taken together, a cut of beef with a bottle of red are both a simple meal and part of a gastronomic ritual that goes to the heart of the country's traditions.

Steak preparation is regarded as an art, and the *parrillas* (steak houses) on every corner in Buenos Aires can seem more like temples to beef than restaurants. The most extravagant have meat in their windows being cooked in traditional *gaucho* fashion, with whole carcasses crucified on metal crosses around a mound of coals. Others have

stuffed cows flanking the doorways, and over the tables are posters illustrating the cuts. The most expensive and leanest cut is the *bife de lomo*, roughly equivalent to a sirloin steak in other countries. The popular *bife de chorizo* is cut from the rib near the rump, while a *bife de costilla* is a T-bone.

In a class of its own is the *tira de asado*, which is a strip of rib roast usually large enough to feed two. The *parrillada* is a portable grill of mixed cuts, including plenty of offal and sausages – for the most committed carnivores. *Vacio* comprises of the bottom part of what in the US is designated as sirloin, porterhouse and the flank, and is the juiciest of all cuts. *Matambre* is shaped like a Swiss roll with a vegetable and hard-boiled egg filling. Often served cold, it can be an appetizer, or eaten inside French bread.

If you like your beef rare, order it *jugoso*; medium, *a punto*; and well done, *bien hecho*.

Steaks at an Argentine restaurant are unlikely to be sullied by vegetables, gravy, or sauces. The most common accompaniment is a salad, which can vary from lettuce and tomato to a giant mixed extravaganza with artichokes and eggs. For those whose taste buds require a little more than salt and flesh, order the *salsa chimichuri*. This oregano and spice mix is traditionally a *gaucho's* favorite. The flavor is considered so strong that asking for it often gets a grunt of respect from the most sombre waiter – although the spices are unlikely to surprise most foreign palates.

Argentina is the sixth-largest consumer of wine in the world. Grown near Mendoza and the drier stretches of the north near Salta, wines are both absurdly cheap and amazingly good. *Vino común*, served in jugs, is at the rougher end, but you will appreciate any of the inexpensive bottled *vino fino* on the wine list. There are around 50 varieties, and though many European grapes are used, Malbec and Torrentes are a local specialty. One positive thing to come out of the economic collapse is an increase in exports from the country's chief wine-growing region – Mendoza. And the USA is one of the biggest foreign consumers. ❑

LEFT: meat is rarely off the menu in the restaurants of Buenos Aires.

Map on page 324

Hispanic colonial buildings were leveled and replaced in the image of Paris. It was a time of tremendous wealth: Buenos Aires was a world center of fashion and high art, the cultural mecca of the Americas. But cracks were already appearing, and no sooner was the city built than the decline began. This sense of faded grandeur makes it a fascinating place to wander through. Buenos Aires is not so much a city of sights as of atmospheres, where the main pleasure is to stroll through the neighborhoods, stop for a coffee, stroll on again and absorb the everyday flavor of a city that seems to exist in a world of its own.

El Centro

The center is carved up by wide avenues, lined by jacaranda trees and magnificent buildings that nobody has ever had the money either to knock down or restore. Bulbous cupolas protrude from roofs, windows are framed by statues of Greek gods, and hidden inside are chandeliers and marble stairways.

The natural spot to start is at the pedestrian walkway of **Florida**, which is crammed at every hour of the day with *porteños* trying to catch glimpses of themselves in window reflections as they pass. It is lined with boutiques selling Argentina's famous leather goods, although shoppers should control themselves until reaching the cheaper **Avenida Santa Fe** at the **Plaza San Martín**, where a dramatic statue commemorates one of the only heroes in Argentine history who commands universal respect. The better shops in Florida are also at this end, between Avenida Córdoba and Santa Fé. Intersecting Florida is another pedestrian mall, **Lavalle**, with movie theaters, bingo and video game halls, restaurants, and bargain stores, and which can clog with people at night.

The presidential palace is called the **Casa Rosada** (Pink House), for the tint of its masonry. It stands in the **Plaza de Mayo**, where guards in blue uniforms strut and parade, surrounded by schoolchildren. Since 1980 an alternative procession has been mounted every Thursday by the white-scarfed Madres de la Plaza de Mayo, who still demand information on the whereabouts of their "disappeared" children.

On the port side of the Casa Rosada are the recycled 19th-century brick warehouses of the old port of Buenos Aires, now the smart area for working and eating out. An oasis of sun and silence at the edge of the bustle of the banking district, the **Puerto Madero** dockland development is an ideal place for a late afternoon drink on the promenade overlooking the water. At the other end of the plaza is one of Buenos Aires' few colonial buildings, the **cabildo** or municipal palace. Inside this whitewashed edifice, which now houses a museum, the city's independence from Spain was declared in 1810. Next door is the **Catedral Metropolitana**, where General José San Martín is buried. The grand **Avenida de Mayo** stretches from here to the **Palacio del Congreso**, which looks like the White House in Washington DC. On the way, it crosses the **Avenida 9 de Julio**, which despite being the widest avenue in the world, manages to be clogged with traffic at most hours of the day. The street's crowning glory is the **Obelisco**, a rather tasteless phallic object around which the city revolves.

The colorful houses of La Boca, Buenos Aires.

BELOW: presidential guards on parade, Buenos Aires.

TIP

San Telmo's major event is the Sunday antique market in the main square. Here you can scour hundreds of stalls for unique memorabilia of Argentina's past while live jazz is played in nearby cafés and buskers tango in the streets.

The nearby **Avenida Corrientes** is the showbusiness heart of Buenos Aires, lined with bright lights, Art Deco theaters and movie theater palaces from the 1920s. Argentines prefer to eat dinner very late, and the restaurants along this street can be packed until 2am, while on Saturday night, the last movie session does not even begin until 1.30am. Corrientes is also noted for its dozens of bookstores, which are crowded with browsers until the early hours of the morning. The **San Martín Cultural Center** hosts art exhibitions, film festivals, and photographic displays.

A few blocks northeast, on Plaza Lavalle, is the sumptuous **Teatro Colón**, one of the world's great opera houses. A performance here should not be missed, if only for the experience of sitting back in wooden armchairs with plush velvet padding, looking out over six gilded tiers and gallery boxes. Guided tours are given daily of the theater's three floors of underground workshops and the small museum commemorating appearances by such greats as Melba, Nijinsky, Pavlova, and Caruso.

Café society

To understand Buenos Aires, try to do as the *porteños* do: spend as much time as is humanly possible in the *confiterías* or cafés of the city, watching the world go by. To the *porteño*, Buenos Aires is mapped out not by streets, landmarks, or *barrios*, but by key places to sit, write, think, and observe.

Two of the city's oldest and most venerable *confiterías* are located within walking distance of this area. The Ideal, on Suipacha, near Corrientes, was where the once sizable British community in Buenos Aires met for high tea every afternoon. These days you can still have tea and cakes surrounded by pol-

BELOW: looking for a gramophone? Try San Telmo.

Map on page 324

ished wood, brass, and marble pillars while being serenaded with waltzes played on an ancient electric organ. Possibly the most famous of the *confiterías* is the Tortoni, on Avenida de Mayo and Piedras. In the 1920s it was the hangout of bohemians such as the writer Jorge Luis Borges, listening to tangos, experimenting with cocaine and debating politics. Its red leather chairs, sparkling mirrors, and chandeliers have changed little since that time, and every Friday night older patrons gather in a back room to hear the tango again.

Remnants of the colonial city

For a taste of Buenos Aires as it used to be, head for the artistic *barrio* of **San Telmo** Ⓐ, south of the Plaza de Mayo. During the 1700s it was the riverside hub of the city, with one third of its population black. Its cobbled streets are lined by low buildings, tango bars, and antique shops.

Colonial streetlight.

The most surprising thing about the working-class suburb of **La Boca** Ⓑ is the sudden splash of color in the otherwise reserved city. Coming to life in the mid-19th century as the home for Genovese dock workers, this *barrio* by the river is famous for its houses of corrugated iron, all painted in different dazzling tones. The 20th-century Argentine painter Benito Quinquela Martin was a leading influence in the suburb's use of color, and his home has been turned into a gallery for his paintings of dock workers. By night, La Boca has a series of gaudy restaurants where bands play renditions of kitsch classics.

The city's upper crust fled to the **Barrio Norte** in the 1870s when yellow fever hit Buenos Aires. Today it is the most elegant and refined of *barrios*, where old ladies in minks sit under oak trees in outdoor cafés and businessmen in European suits arrogantly order waiters about. The neighborhood is

BELOW: a night at the opera – the opulent Teatro Colón.

Dance of Passion

L oneliness and despair, jealousy, and homesickness – all are themes of tango, Argentina's most famous musical tradition. The accompanying dance is a demonstration of strutting Latin *machismo*: passionate, erotic, and flamboyant. So closely associated with the history of Argentina, tango is said to be a distillation of the national character. Where Brazil has the exuberant *samba*, *porteños* listen to the melancholy tango. True or not, the tango lingers throughout Buenos Aires like a perfume from another age.

The origins of tango can be traced to the slums of Buenos Aires at the end of the 19th century, where cultures from around the world were meeting – discharged soldiers from Argentina's civil wars, descendants of African slaves and boatloads of Italian and Spanish immigrants. Overwhelmingly male, the new arrivals gathered in the bars and brothels. They shared the loneliness of exiles, mixing their national music to create the haunting

tango sound. The dance was invented before lyrics were introduced, usually performed by two males waiting in line at the local bordello.

Before long, the tango was gaining popularity amongst the *porteño* working class. By the early 20th century, the wheezing sound of the *bandoneon* (concertina) had been added to the guitar, flute, violin, and piano of tango ensembles. Writers even began putting their names to tangos. Only the snobbish upper classes kept aloof from the new rhythm, preferring to keep to their waltzes and polkas.

When the tango reached Europe, mothers in Edwardian England tried in vain to stem the popularity of the sensual dance, with its thrusting hip movements and intertwined limbs. Kaiser Wilhelm of Germany banned his staff from performing it. But for the rest of Europe, tango was the rage. And once the dance had succeeded in the salons of Europe, the Argentine upper crust accepted it wholeheartedly, agreeing with the French that it must be the very essence of Latin style.

In 1917, the little-known singer Carlos Gardel recorded the tango *Mi Noche Triste*. Almost overnight, the handsome figure became the first great tango star whose voice was heard around the world. Although arguments continue as to whether Gardel was born in France or Uruguay, he is remembered in Argentina as *El Pibe del Abasto* – the kid from the Abasto district of Buenos Aires. He became a movie star in Argentina, his place in the local pantheon assured when he was killed in an airplane accident in 1935 – as though Gardel were living out a tango himself. Today, new techniques are used to improve his old recordings, and in Buenos Aires they say: "Every day he sings better."

Tango fell into a lull in the 1950s until it was pushed in new directions by *tanguistas* like Astor Piazzola. Trained in classical and jazz music, he led a revival with his new, energetic arrangements. In the 21st century tango is enjoying an extraordinary renaissance. In the beginning of the 1990s, it was only danced by aging locals in half-empty venues. Today, it is an exciting, fashionable pastime, practiced by trendy youths in steamy, underground dance-halls. ❏

LEFT: singing tango on the street, San Telmo.

built around a giant walled cemetery, the **Recoleta** . Hundreds of ornate marble crypts contain the remains of the city's wealthiest families, with giant angels and grim reapers adding to the unsettling effect. The *barrio* is also home to the city's range of *albergues transitorios* – hotels rented out by the hour – where, overlooking the Recoleta necropolis, local denizens can steal a few tense hours of sensory gratification.

Maps
Area 260
City 324

When the urban rush becomes too much and you feel the need for a view and fresh air, head for the **Costanera Norte**. A promenade runs along the brown Río de la Plata, where on a clear day you may be able to pick out the coast of Uruguay in the distance. Fashionable *parrillas* (grillhouses) line the road on the other side of the walkway, for when the exercise loses its charm. In October or November, a classic day can be spent at the polo by heading out to **Palermo** playing fields. An alternative day trip venue is the **Tigre Delta**, a weekend refuge for *porteños* of all ages for more than a century. Trains leave regularly from the cast-iron **Retiro** station in central Buenos Aires, taking passengers to the quiet, tree-lined rivers and canals within an hour. Wooden ferries leave for destinations further into the delta, where modern French restaurants and guest houses retain the atmosphere of the 1930s.

To the disgust of the Argentine old wealth, the Recoleta's most famous occupant is the daughter of a provincial nobody, Evita Perón. Thousands visit her tomb every year, in a crypt of black marble which has a single rose before it.

Beaches, lakes, and mountains

About five hours' drive from Buenos Aires are the Atlantic coastal resorts of Mar del Plata, Villa Gesell, and Pinamar. **Mar del Plata** ㉛ is also accessible by air in about 30 minutes from Buenos Aires. By far the largest of the country's seaside towns, it has an enormous quantity of hotels at all prices, all of which fill up from mid-December to mid-February.

BELOW: Mar del Plata.

This very attractive city is the country's most attractive resort, and has a long *rambla* (pedestrian area) along the coast, beginning at its famous casino. The beach becomes heavily overpopulated in summer, but suburban areas are reasonably peaceful throughout the year. There are many *confiterías* and restaurants serving excellent seafood, and a good variety of movie theaters and nightclubs. Further north on the coast, **Villa Gesell** and **Pinamar** are much smaller and more peaceful. Both towns have more open spaces and wooded areas, in addition to their beaches, Pinamar being the more exclusive of the two, with more nightlife.

West to the land of wine and sun

The city of **Córdoba** ㉜, some 700 km (435 miles) northwest of Buenos Aires, is one of the country's cultural and religious centers, known for the number of lawyers and seminaries it houses. The university is one of the oldest and most distinguished in Argentina, and the city offers both well-preserved colonial architecture – especially in religious buildings – and an active modern urban life.

The lakeside resort of **Villa Carlos Paz**, a former German enclave which still slightly resembles a Bavarian village, lies 36 km (22 miles) west, in the green sierras of Córdoba. Villa Carlos Paz is often crowded in summer, but has a wide range of hotels and restaurants, as well as beautiful scenery and access to the Sierra. To the north are **Cosquín**, a smaller town which hosts the National Folklore Festival in January, and **Rio Ceballos**, a quiet place to enjoy the mountains and rivers, and to walk in the Córdoba range, which is less rugged than the Andes. All these towns are easily reached by excursions from Córdoba city. Southwest of Córdoba, on the Chilean border, **Mendoza** ㉝ is more a tribute to hard work and ingenuity than to Argentina's natural scenery. An arid province at the foot of the Andes, Mendoza attracted Italian and French settlers in the late 19th century who, with encouragement from the progressive provincial government, installed irrigation methods that allowed the province to become one of Argentina's principal agricultural zones. Known as "the land of sun and good wine," Mendoza is the country's principal area of wine production and vineyards, although its prosperity is also based on its significant oil reserves.

Mendoza is not as architecturally interesting as cities like Córdoba, due to earthquake devastation. However, it is by far the cleanest and tidiest city in Argentina, and full of trees planted to dispel the desert image. To the west of the city is the huge **Parque San Martín**, with hillside views of the city, a lake, horsedrawn carriage rides, the local university, and a monument to San Martín, whose famous Andes crossing to Chile began at Mendoza. Public buses and organized tours go to the wine *bodegas*.

From the central plaza an attractive pedestrian precinct leads past the provincial legislature to **San Martín**, the main street, where the tourist office is located. The attractive **Plaza España** was donated to the city by the Franco government in the 1940s and displays a beautiful collection of Spanish tiles, as well as an example of the Mendozan obsession with foun-

BELOW: ceiling of Córdoba Cathedral.

tains, lawns, and trees. Mendoza is the base for a number of outdoor activities, including pony trekking and skiing, though the most exclusive center for skiing is the **Las Leñas** resort, roughly 400 km (250 miles) southwest of Mendoza.

Northern traditions

The north is the only part of the country where indigenous people still survive in significant numbers. The region gives visitors a fascinating glimpse into Argentina's colonial past and the Andean countries just across the border. It was here that the first Franciscan monks settled, coming south from Peru and building whitewashed chapels in the desert.

Tucumán , 90 minutes from Buenos Aires by air or about 16 hours by bus, is known as the "cradle of independence," because Argentina's independence was declared in the **Casa de la Independencia** in 1816. Nightly *son et lumière* shows are held here. On the **Plaza Independencia** is the neo-French style government house and the **Cathedral**. Nearby are the churches of **San Francisco** and the **Virgen del Rosario**. Near the main plaza, on and around Avenida 24 de Septiembre, are various craft shops and a number of restaurants offering excellent regional specialties. The tourist office and the **Museo Folk-lórico** (open daily) are also on Avenida 24 de Septiembre.

Leaving Tucumán by bus or car for Tafí del Valle, the road winds through mountainous terrain with sub-tropical foliage, rivers, and waterfalls, as well as the El Cadillal reservoir near Tafí, an attractive mountain village favored by Tucumános for summer holidays. To the north of Tafí, the mountains become dry and moonlike before arriving at Quilmes, the well-preserved remains of an 18th-century Amerindian village (open daily 9am–5pm). Some 20 km (12

Jesuit church tower, Alta Gracia.

BELOW: Argentina's arid north.

miles) further north is Amaicha del Valle, the only village in Argentina where indigenous people hold the title to their ancestral lands. The Fiesta de la Pachamama (Mother Earth Festival) is held here in February. Santa María, 10 km (6 miles) away, is an attractive place turned boomtown by the nearby Bajo La Alumbrera gold and copper mine. About an hour beyond Santa María is Cafayate, a pretty town surrounded by wineries. The scenery between Tucumán and Cafayate (about a six-hour drive) is among the most breathtaking and varied in Argentina.

Colonial churches and markets

Salta ㉟ is an open, relaxed town that can be used as a base to explore the surrounding provinces. Neo-colonial buildings line the straight streets that head toward the mountains, often little more than outlines obscured by dust. The center of town is an unexpectedly green plaza with well-preserved Spanish and Italian-style buildings. Most of the city's best colonial buildings are on La Florida and Calle Caseros, which has the **Casa Uriburu**, housing a colonial-era museum (open Tues–Sun); the Iglesia de San Francisco; the Convento de San Bernardo; and the **Cabildo** (City Hall), housing the **Museo Histórico del Norte** (open Tues–Sun). Most of the rooms are devoted to European-Argentine heroes from the Wars of Independence, with paintings of their deeds alongside medals, vests and gloves. The Amerindian section, covering the Incas and their customs, contains a dry and poorly explained collection of pots and pans. For an altogether different view of the city, take the cable car up to Cerro San Bernardo.

The north of Argentina is saturated by religion but visitors to Salta may be surprised by the number of churches and statues dedicated to San Francisco. The **Cathedral** contains the town's pride and joy: the Virgin and Cristo del Milagro, statues carved in the 16th century and credited with miraculous powers. The ship carrying them from Spain was wrecked, but the figures were washed up on the Peruvian shore. Then in 1692, an earthquake in Salta was dramatically halted when the statues were paraded in the streets. The simple, almost childlike figures are almost lost in the huge baroque altar. Across the aisle, the faithful pray before a life-sized effigy of Christ fresh from the cross, complete with vast holes in his chest and a virtual fountain of fake blood. Depictions of suffering in colonial religious art had to be horrific if they were to impress indigenous people as worse than their own lives.

For a change of pace, one of the most exciting trips from Salta is to take *El Tren a las Nubes* – the Train to the Clouds. Due to the height at which the train travels it is quite common to see clouds under its bridges. Fully equipped with a dining car, this poetically named service leaves Salta once a week for a spectacular journey through nearby mountains. It climbs through the barren **Quebrada del Toro** across steel span bridges to the small town of **San Antonio de los Cobres** at 4,000 meters (13,000 ft) in the Andes, to its highest point at **Abra Chorrillos** (4,475 meters/14,680 ft) and then to the Chilean frontier at **Socompa** ㊱. The whole trip takes almost 15 hours, crossing 29 bridges and 13 viaducts in all.

BELOW: corn on the cob for sale.

Toward the Bolivian frontier

A highway heads north from Salta to **Jujuy** ③. The population becomes more indigenous the closer you get to the Bolivian border, while the road gets rougher, the houses poorer, and the religious imagery stranger. Tiny chapels can be seen in the most remote villages. One of the most curious, in **Uquaia**, contains the *Angeles Caballeros*: a painting of angels dressed as 17th-century musketeers.

The road climbs to over 3,000 meters (9,800 ft) and the countryside dries out completely along the *quebrada* (gorge) of the **Rio Grande**. Odd land formations appear: some mountains are sharp triangles, others seem to spill like molten lava, while others look like decayed ants' nests. The small, poor town of **Humahuaca** ③ is almost in Bolivia. In early afternoon it becomes an empty dust bowl, with winds sweeping from the valleys to cover everything with orange powder. The only sound comes from the 16th-century church. The town has several guest houses and restaurants, and is not far from the extensive archeological site of **Coctaca**, whose mysteries are still being unraveled.

Humahuaca is dominated by a huge iron monument to Argentina's 19th-century war of independence. An artistic sleight-of-hand has given the fierce figures staring down over Humahuaca Amerindian faces, brushing over the memory of newly liberated European settlers who spent the rest of the 19th century wiping out the indigenous population in the rest of the country. The local sense of history is also revealed by the old schoolhouse, which is emblazoned with the sign "Republic of Bolivia." Ask any of the students why and they look at the sign as if for the first time. The school masters are no more helpful. It was a long time ago, they might tell you, perhaps even a century.

"But I only teach European history," they will smile, and walk away.

Map on pages 260–1

BELOW: Jesuit ruins, San Ignacio Miní.

Misiones and the Jesuit ruins

Sticking out like a crooked finger from the northeast of Argentina, the subtropical province of **Misiones** boasts some unexpected associations. Graham Greene used its wet and steamy towns as the setting for his novel *The Honorary Consul,* where expatriate Britons and South American revolutionaries accidentally meet. More recently, the award-winning movie *The Mission,* which was shot in the area, publicized the province's 18th-century Jesuit empire.

A visit to the region usually begins in the provincial capital of **Posadas** ㊲, which is accessible from Buenos Aires by daily flights. The town has a Paraguayan handicrafts market and several museums. A highway escapes north from the town into the rich green countryside, kept lush by regular downpours. The road follows the flood-prone **Río Paraná**.

It was in this same region in the 1600s that the teams of Jesuit priests began setting up their mission stations *(see page 271).* At their height in the 18th century, they housed 100,000 of the local Guaraní people, studying, growing grain, and carving musical instruments which became renowned in the finest courts of Europe. Today, the ruins of the greatest Jesuit mission at **San Ignacio Miní** ㊵ (open Mon–Fri, 7am–7pm, with a nightly *son et lumière* show), just a two-hour drive from Posadas, are announced by the unfortunate marriage of a piece of Jesuit art caught in a concrete military bridge, designed by a former province governor. The grounds themselves are more tastefully kept. Busloads of visitors wander among the old Jesuit living quarters and cathedral, decorated with indigenous carvings of celestial beings and stars. Outside, the priests' gravestones bear simple messages: "Here Lies Father Juan, a good man." Other Jesuit ruins can be found nearby, mostly overgrown by jungle. Sitting amongst these shattered relics of their religious empire, it is difficult to contemplate the experiment that flourished here for over 150 years. While indigenous people in the rest of South America were being brutally exploited on plantations, here they were working and learning in a system that has earned the praise of many modern socialist writers. The Jesuit priests distributed grain according to need, and arranged indigenous armies to keep out slave traders.

Only when the Jesuits were expelled was the fatal flaw of the system revealed. The priests had ruled a paternalistic order, never training the Amerindians to run it themselves. With the Jesuits in exile, slave traders were more successful, the crops failed and the Guaraní people fled back into the jungle. Today, their descendants have returned to the ruins – selling plastic flutes and feathers to tourists.

Iguazú Falls

The other great attraction of Misiones is a few hours further up the highway to the border with Brazil: the magnificent **Cataratas del Iguazú** ㊶. The falls can be reached from the commercial center of **Puerto Iguazú**. This spectacle is one of South America's most extraordinary sights. Vast torrents of water thunder over the various cascades with such force that most visitors wear waterproof raincoats for protection from the violent spray. The falls are divided between Brazil

A linguistic note: we have used the Spanish spelling Iguazú here; but it is Iguaçu in Portuguese and Iguassu – usually – in English.

BELOW: Jesuit ruins, San Ignacio.

and Argentina – while the Brazilian side is most spectacular, the Argentine side is more pleasant to explore – but to see them properly one must visit both sides. If attempting to do so in a day (which is possible, with some effort – and don't forget your passport), it's best to start out on the Brazilian side. Though more removed from the falling waters, the Brazilian vantage point gives a much more panoramic view of the immense cascade. The light there is best in the morning for photographers.

This side also gives one the best views of the most spectacular section of the falls, the roaring **Devil's Throat**. Fourteen falls combine forces in their 100-meter (330-ft) fall, pounding the water below with such force that there is constantly a huge rainbow-spanned cloud of spray hovering above them. Swallows make their nests under the roaring waterfalls. A catwalk on the Brazilian side, reached by a winding foot trail and an elevator, gives more intimate views. Helicopter rides are also available but disturb local wildlife.

A stop at the Argentine interpretive center can provide much useful information about the falls and surrounding flora and fauna. A train service takes visitors to the start of two walking trails, which explore the Argentine falls, including one that takes visitors over the water rushing into **Devil's Gorge**. It's also possible to climb down a series of trails and stairways to the river below, where a short (recommended) boat trip takes visitors to the island of San Martín, making a pass close to one of the falls. The climb back up is strenuous, and should be attempted only by those in good shape.

The Argentines have created a national park adjacent to the falls, where there is a jungle trail posted with information, and a bird hide overlooking a swamp. A trek through the park can take most of the day. In the evening, catch a bus to

Map on pages 260–1

Cacique birds' nests.

BELOW:
Iguazú Falls.

The Gaucho

Scattered through the *estancias* of the Argentine hinterland are horsemen wearing a uniform from the country's distant past: black Spanish hats, woven Amerindian shawls, baggy pants known as *bombachas,* and carrying deadly knives called *facónes*. They are the last descendants of a breed of South American cowboys, the *gauchos*.

From the early days of Spanish settlement, individuals disappeared to the countryside and mixed with the local population. Fleeing criminals, escaped slaves, and deserting militiamen lived at the fringes of society and were known as *la gente perdida:* the lost people. They developed their own harsh, nomadic lifestyle on the pampas, taming wild horses to ride and slaughtering escaped cattle, while learning how to hunt with the skillful use of lassoes and the *boleadores*: three balls connected by ropes that could wrap around the legs of any running target. Soon known as

gauchos – the name may have derived from the local word for "orphan" – they had a growing reputation for gambling, horsemanship, and knife-fighting. Women, called *chinas*, played a subsidiary role in this macho lifestyle. Often kidnapped from settlements, they raised children in small huts indistinguishable from those of the indigenous population.

But in the late 18th century, large tracts of pampas land was distributed to prominent *porteños*. Fences were put up in the grasslands and *gauchos* were seen as little better than cattle thieves. Many grudgingly signed up as ranch hands, working for subsistence wages on the lands they once roamed.

When the British took Buenos Aires in 1806, many *gauchos* were pressed into the army. After independence, they joined up with the private armies of provincial *caudillos*, who allowed them to indulge in their usual drinking, gambling, and knife-fighting for several decades without undue molestation. But as the era of civil wars drew to a close, the days of the *gaucho* were numbered. New codes were introduced to regulate their movements, dress, drinking habits, and diet. Thousands were pressed into military service.

Soon the *gaucho* was a symbol of the backward, chaotic Argentina that the statesmen of Buenos Aires wanted to destroy. *Gauchos* were described by Domingo Sarmiento as "biped animals of the most perverse stripe" whose carcasses were only good to fertilize the earth. Barbed wire fences hindered their movements still further – the *gaucho* was being eliminated as a distinct social grouping.

As this was happening in the 1870s, José Hernandez wrote in two parts his classic epic poem, *The Gaucho Martin Fierro*, which lamented the passing of the wild frontier past.

By 1926, when the second great literary work on *gauchos* appeared, *Don Segundo Sombra* by Ricardo Guiraldes, the *gaucho* was nothing more than a literary memory. This does not mean to say that there are not glimpses of the lost *gaucho* culture in the Argentina of today. In the furthest reaches of the country, on remote farms in Salta and Patagonia, hands still wear traditional *gaucho* dress – even if they are as likely to be driving a Land-Rover as riding a horse. ❏

LEFT: *gaucho* on a Buenos Aires *estancia*.

Puerto Canoas, where the day's dying light heightens the beauty of Devil's Gorge as swallows dive into their nests in the walls behind the tumbling water.

Iguazú Falls are best visited in fall and spring – summers are intensely hot and the busiest time for tourists, while the water level drops considerably in winter. There are hotels on both the Brazilian and Argentine sides. Near the falls a marker shows the point at which Paraguay, Brazil, and Argentina all converge.

The only sight capable of crowning the Iguazú experience is **Moconá Falls**, where the River Uruguay falls into itself in a fault more than a kilometer long, not far from the Brazilian town of **Tenente Portela**. For a panoramic view, take a ferry to Brazil from the Argentine town of **El Soberbio**. Boat trips are on offer in the same town for those craving a close-up white-water view.

Bariloche: Switzerland in the Andes

Strategically placed between the towering Andes and the plains of Patagonia, for six months of the year **San Carlos de Bariloche** ⓬ is a booming holiday resort with a unique alpine flavor. Summer brings hordes of travelers enjoying walks amongst the lush forests, spectacular glaciers, and mountains of the surrounding Lake District. Later, the winter snows bring South America's select set of affluent skiers to the Andean slopes, filling Bariloche's restaurants by night with raucous fireside carousing. The remaining neglected months of the year are perhaps even more delightful: in spring, the valleys of the Lake District are filled with flowers and greenery, while fall brings the slow shift of the forest colors to red, orange, cinnamon, and ochre.

The alpine atmosphere attracted Swiss, German, and Austrian settlers at the end of the 19th century. Today the town itself is a reproduction of a Tyrolean skiing village. Many of the buildings are designed like chalets, while the streets are full of chocolate shops and restaurants offering Swiss fondue, trout, and roast venison. But the real attraction is the surrounding countryside. Bariloche's setting, by the shores of **Lake Nahuel Huapi**, surrounded by jagged brown mountains, is spectacular. In the distance you can spot the towering **Mount Tronador**, the highest peak in the region at 3,554 meters (11,660 ft).

Begin your visit by going to the **Patagonian Museum** near the **Civic Center**. It relates the region's history from the days when indigenous nomads roamed the countryside, covered from head to toe in animal grease for warmth, to the arrival of the first white pioneers. Outside in the square is a statue of General Roca, leader of the desert campaign which led to the virtual extermination of local tribes.

Dozens of tour companies offer visits to the surrounding attractions – alternatively, you can hire a car in Bariloche to explore the dirt roads and byways of this magnificent region on the border of Chile. The *circuito chico* or "short circuit" runs out along Lake Nahuel Huapi to the Hotel Llao Llao. Refurbished and reopened after years of neglect, it reflects the glory of its heyday in the 1940s. Boats run from the docks of Bariloche to **Isla Victoria**, whose myrtle forests are said to have inspired some of Walt Disney's advisers when drawing backgrounds for *Bambi*.

Map on pages 260–1

Iguazú means Great Waters in Guaraní – a fitting name for the most spectacular waterfalls in the western hemisphere. Taller than Niagara Falls by 20 meters (65 ft) and twice as wide, Iguazú Falls consists of 275 cascades over a gulf of nearly 3 km (2 miles).

BELOW: St Bernard dogs in front of the Centro Cívico, Bariloche.

Ski school plaque, Bariloche.

Continuing around the circuit is the path to **Cerro Lopez**. In summer, the peak can be climbed to a refuge run by Club Andino, where hikers can stay overnight. On a clear day the summit offers spectacular views over the lakes and mountains of the region to Chile. Day trips can also be taken from Bariloche to **Cerro Tronador**, **Cerro Catedral**, **Cerro Otto**, and the waterfalls of **Los Cesares**. The region is world-famous for its trout fishing from November to March, and in summer there is sailing and windsurfing on the lakes.

Exploring the wild countryside

Also passing through some of the world's most magnificent scenery is the so-called route of the seven lakes, which winds along the border with Chile. It leads to the small town of **San Martín de los Andes** ❸, a more upmarket tourist destination than Bariloche, often used as a base for hikes, camping trips, and skiing. The return trip over the **Córdoba Pass** runs through the lower regions of Neuquen province, much drier and closer to the Patagonian wastes. Fingers of stone protrude from thorny expanses, in what one English traveler in 1920 compared to the prehistoric *Lost World* imagined by Scottish novelist Sir Arthur Conan Doyle. Many of the *estancias* or ranches of the region are still English-run and worked by Chilean *peons* (farmhands) or weather-beaten *gauchos*, whose ponchos, knives, and *bombachas* are definitely not worn just for tourists.

For a longer excursion, an overnight trip can be made to **El Bolsón**, once a hippy refuge of the 1960s, now a tourist and fishing resort with a twice-weekly handicrafts market. Further south, a road cuts through the serene **Cholila Valley** to **Esquel** ❹. First settled by the Welsh, it is now the base for visiting **Parque Nacional Los Alerces** and the gateway to the **Chubut Valley**. The National

BELOW: Lake Nahuel Huapi and Cerro López.

Park, dotted with lakes and crossed by streams, features walking trails and horseback riding opportunities. Standing by the shores of the lake is **Estancia Nahuel Huapi**, founded by a Texan cowboy named Jared Jones in 1889. The house, which is still standing, was a refuge for Butch Cassidy and the Sundance Kid, on the run from the Argentine authorities, having brought their Wild West ways to the new frontier of Patagonia in the early 1900s.

Map
on pages
260–1

Wild, windswept Patagonia

Way down at the chilly southern end of South America, Patagonia has for centuries been a byword for the remote and the strange. But today Patagonia is linked to Buenos Aires with daily flights, and by bus for those with enough time to fully appreciate the size of this flat, empty plain that takes up one-third of the country's landmass. Heading south, the rich cattle country dries out and becomes divided into sheep stations. As recently as the 19th century some of these ranches were bigger than small European countries, with their owners ruling like royalty. Many are still run by the descendants of the original British owners, who continue to speak English in preference to Spanish.

First stop is the city of **Trelew** ⑤, surrounded by dry bluffs and dusty scrub. Thousands of Welsh colonists came here after 1865, fleeing their homeland, where their culture and language was being repressed by the English, to set up a "Little Wales" in the middle of nowhere. Despite some early disasters, the colony began to succeed. The Welsh used their irrigation skills to make the desert bloom, and soon Patagonian wheat was winning prizes at international shows. Welsh was spoken in the streets and taught in the schools. But by the beginning of the 20th century, things were going awry in Trelew. The Argentine

LEFT: inhabitant from the Welsh colony of Chubut.
RIGHT: a Patagonian *peon* (farm laborer).

government had imposed its authority on the town and many Spanish-speaking immigrants, attracted by the Welsh success, had arrived with their families. Floods devastated the area's crops. Many settlers left for Canada or Australia, but the core of the community stayed on, their Welsh nationalism slowly being diluted by intermarriage with Spanish speakers.

Today, Trelew looks much like other provincial Argentine towns, although the street signs are still in Welsh. Echoes of its origins can be found in the old Hotel Touring Club, with cracked windows and an antique wooden bar full of old men playing chess on quiet afternoons. Many of the town's elders still speak in their native Welsh to one another, using Spanish when necessary. For a taste of the Welsh colony as it once was, take a half-hour bus ride to the village of **Gaiman**. Built around the irrigation canals that converted the desert into an oasis, Gaiman has a number of Welsh tea houses serving up Welsh cream pastries to passing visitors. A small museum located in the old railway station is well worth a visit.

The Portuguese explorer Fernando Magellan, the first European to see Patagonia, reported it to be full of dog-headed monsters and natives with steaming heads.

Whales and frontier towns

Easily reached from Trelew is the famous **Península Valdés** ④, which contains some of the world's most spectacular wildlife. Charles Darwin spent weeks here on his famous journey in the *Beagle*, and today tourists come to watch the sea lions yawning by the rocky shore and hundreds of penguins wandering in lines to the sea. During September and October, enormous right whales can be seen throwing up their tail fins as they mate dramatically off shore.

Flying south from Trelew, the Patagonian plain below looks increasingly desolate. Towns like **Comodoro Rivadavia** ④, once center of a brief oil boom, and

BELOW: rounding up sheep, Patagonia.

Río Gallegos ㊽ 3,000 km (2,000 miles) south of Buenos Aires, are devoid of rural charm. Unfortunately, because most flights pass through here, many travelers end up spending a night. Nothing much has happened since 1905, when Butch Cassidy and the Sundance Kid held up a bank on the main street

Changing to a small propeller-driven plane in Río Gallegos, a one-hour flight cuts west across the plains to the foothills of the Andes and some of the most magnificent scenery in South America. The village of **El Calafate** ㊾ is surrounded by snowcapped mountain peaks and sits next to **Lago Argentino**, which seems to be full of turquoise milk rather than water. This remote village is enjoying a boom as the stepping-off point to the huge blue glaciers wedged in the forest-covered countryside nearby.

The most famous is **Perito Moreno** ㊿, in a national park of the same name, a 50-meter (160-ft) high wall of ice which cuts through a lake. It cracks and growls throughout the day, with enormous chunks of ice regularly falling from its side to send waves of water thundering to the shore. The glacier is still advancing in four-year cycles. Blocking off part of the lake, the water level rises until the glacial wall collapses in a spectacular scene lasting several hours.

From Calafate you can visit the sheep *estancias* of Argentina's deep south, where the occasional *gaucho* figure still works. Sheep-raising is a key industry in Patagonia, and between October and January, traveling teams of workers arrive for the shearing season. **La Anita** became notorious in 1921, when the whole of Patagonia was paralyzed by a strike of farmhands, known as *peones*. The organizer was a young Spanish anarchist named Antonio Soto, who had wandered through the Buenos Aires stage to Patagonia. The mostly British

Map on pages 260–1

Steaks for an asado.

BELOW: the Perito Moreno glacier.

estancieros called on the government for help, and the army ended the strike, with bouts of shooting followed by mass executions. One of the biggest of these was at La Anita – although it has since changed hands, and hardly anybody remembers where the 200 or so workers are even buried.

Located a few hours from Calafate is the **Parque Nacional Fitzroy**, where you can pass from the windswept plains to lush and wet forest amongst the snowcapped Andes. Hikes through the park cross mountain streams and landscapes reminiscent of Scottish moors. Clouds are constantly billowing overhead, but on a good day you can often catch a glimpse of Mount Fitzroy, a sheer knife of granite that is a favorite with fearless mountaineers.

Tierra del Fuego: last stop before Antarctica

It is the forbidding image of Tierra del Fuego that paradoxically lures travelers to the southernmost tip of South America. It was named "land of fire" by Magellan, who saw mysterious fires in the darkness when first passing the island.

For centuries afterwards, Tierra del Fuego was feared by sailors for the icy Antarctic winds that blew their ships toward jagged rocks. Few of them considered **Ushuaia** ❺, the world's most southerly town, an attractive refuge from the storms. Over the years it progressed from a primitive whaling station to a prison colony where Russian anarchists eked out their last days. Today, the land at the end of the world can be reached by daily flights from Buenos Aires. Ushuaia is no longer the wild outpost it once was, but an odd blend of modern tourist center, Klondike-style boomtown, and the gateway to one of the world's last great wilderness areas.

BELOW: penguin colony at Punto Tombo, near Trelew.

The northern half of the island is flat sheep farming land – much like the rest

of Patagonia – but the south is rugged and thickly forested. Approaching Ushuaia by plane is suitably dramatic, since the town is surrounded by snow-capped claws of granite. The dominating peak, **Mount Olivia**, would suit a Walt Disney wicked witch for its mist-shrouded and vaguely evil appearance. The weather lives up to Tierra del Fuego's reputation: even during the 20 or more hours of summer daylight, it shifts erratically from cold drizzle to perfectly cloudless skies, with the only constant being a gusty southern wind.

Ushuaia itself is far from being a picturesque pioneering town. It is home to a large naval base, government offices, and stores for imported goods. Houses with decorative cornices built by prisoners are still scattered in the older part of town and have a somewhat Russian flavor. They are intermingled with modern concrete structures, imported Swedish prefabs, and hundreds of small, wooden shanties. Usable land is in short supply in the area hemmed in by mountain and sea; new houses climb the mountainsides and many people live in poor conditions. Nevertheless, subsidized building and improvements are going on everywhere. The main street is like an open-air department store, with duty-free electronic goods being offered. One of the town's claims to fame is the Bank of Tierra del Fuego, which is the world's first financial institution to have a branch in Antarctica.

Housed in a former prison, the **Museo Marítimo** and **Museo del Presilio** provide an interesting glimpse into the town's role as a penal colony. The **Beagle Channel**, on which the town sits, was named after the boat that carried Charles Darwin here in the 1830s for his famous wildlife studies. Boat trips can be taken on the channel past mountains dropping sheer into the water, circling islands populated by penguins or sea lions.

Map on pages 260–1

BELOW: Ushuaia, the world's south-ernmost town.

Map on pages 260–1

At one time Argentina had 80 million sheep and was one of the world's largest wool producers. Today only 30 million remain.

BELOW: a group of Ona Amerindians, before they were wiped out by settlers.
RIGHT: sleepy elephant seal.

Windswept wilderness

Parque Nacional Tierra del Fuego is the main attraction of Ushuaia because of its easily accessible wilderness area. The walking here is simply magnificent, following the spectacular coastline to lakes and glaciers. The park preserves the sense of being at the end of the world, with paths that wind around spongy moss oozing cold water, past tough shrubs and thorny bushes and trees that the wind has bent 45 degrees. The path to **Bahia Ensenada** passes an encouraging altar to the Virgin of Lujan, Argentina's patron saint of travelers. There is a camping ground at the rocky beach, where you can breakfast on sweet calafate berries. Stepping stones lead to **Bahia Lapataia,** where you can pick fresh mussels from the sea. A picturesque narrow-gauge train will take you into the Tierra del Fuego National Park along a route formerly used to transport prison inmates to cut timber for houses.

Just three hours' drive from Ushuaia along a winding dirt road is **Harberton** *(see below),* the first *estancia* on Tierra del Fuego. Founded by the Rev. Thomas Bridges in 1888, it is open to tourists, with guides in English and Spanish. Harberton is worth visiting not just for its history but for the beauty of its setting. Surrounded by trees and flowers, perched above the blue Beagle Channel, it seems like the calmest place on earth.

Back in Ushuaia, shops are full of books on the local Ona people, but they are dull, anthropological works written as if they were still wandering around the countryside. The rumors of murders are denied or forgotten, with only a few scraps suggesting the contrary: a ledger showing that only women and children were brought back from raids; a photo in a Liverpool newspaper showing a mass grave found by police. The final certainty of the destruction of these tribes is that the only fires now burning in Tierra del Fuego are from the oil rigs off its coast. ❑

A GRISLY PAST

The good Reverend Thomas Bridges spent much of his time in Harberton in the late 19th century working with the Ona people and writing a dictionary of their complex Yaghan language. To his dismay, he could see before his death that the lists of words would soon be the only monument to those who spoke them. As the British writer Bruce Chatwin noted, Darwin's theory of "survival of the fittest" was put into brutal practice in the 1890s. The indigenous people of the area, who had lit the fires that Magellan saw, occasionally killed and ate the sheep brought onto their land by European settlers. The newcomers decided to remove this "pest" en masse. Official records show that most of these people died of disease, but the folk memory persists of active resistance, battles, and massacres.

The most grisly tale is of white bounty hunters being paid £1 sterling per pair of Amerindian ears. Old-timers tell of such gruesome characters as the Scotsman Alex MacLennan, nicknamed the Red Pig, famous for his drunken ravings about killing indigenous folk. The Englishman Sam Hyslop, who is credited with gunning down 80 people of the Ona tribe, was caught by Amerindians and flung from a cliff.

THE FALKLAND ISLANDS

These tiny, windswept islands in the South Atlantic were at the center of a violent international conflict in the 1980s. Now peace has returned to the sheep pastures and penguin colonies

Some 500 km (300 miles) off the coast of Argentina, the Falkland Islands (Las Malvinas to Argentines) offer the type of treeless, windswept, austerely beautiful landscapes similar to the Orkney and Shetland Islands in Scotland. Attempts have been made to plant trees with little success. Like Scotland, the islands offer four seasons in one day, with sun, wind, and rain coming and going in a matter of minutes; also similar to Scotland are the hills and valleys uncharacteristic of flat Patagonia. There are southern desert-like landscapes, tall grass, and wild flowers, though in places the scenery is marred by signs warning of minefields left over from the 1982 war (some 17,000 mines remain in certain areas hidden beneath sandy beaches).

With a total area of some 12,000 sq. km (4,633 sq. miles), the islands have a population of around 3,500 *kelpers* (residents, universally of British origin), with 500,000 sheep, plus five species of penguin, geese, whales, elephant seals and sea lions for company. Some 1,500 *kelpers* live in the capital, **Port Stanley**, known as Puerto Argentino to the Argentines who claim sovereignty over the islands. The few hundred youngsters who live outside the capital attend school by radio; teachers visit for two weeks each year. There is a monthly mail, to and from England.

PRECEDING PAGES: windswept solitude in the Falkland Islands.
BELOW: Magellanic penguins.

Disputed territory

The Falklands and South Georgia Islands have been in British hands since 1833, although Argentina has been firm in demanding sovereignty for over a century, on the grounds that the islands were taken from Spain by the British and that after Argentine independence from Spain, they should technically have reverted to Argentine territory. Claims by various European powers had always been doubtful and frequently shifting since the first reported sightings of the uninhabited islands in the late 16th century, although since its independence Argentina has never wavered from its claim that "*las Malvinas son Argentinas*." The area became strategically important to the rest of the world only in the latter part of the 20th century, with the realization that the islands offer a claim both to Antarctic territory and to offshore oil deposits that have become increasingly exploitable with modern technology.

The 1982 war between the UK and Argentina followed an invasion first of South Georgia and then of the Falklands by troops sent by alcoholic Argentine dictator Leopoldo Galtieri. The war brought about the deaths of 655 Argentines, many of them conscripts, and 255 British soldiers. Thereafter, the attitude of the *kelpers* to Argentine sovereignty claims hardened still further, not unnaturally, with distrust of Argentine politicians reaching new heights. Communications with Argentina were cut off, and it was not until July 2000 that a Joint Declaration between the Argentine and British governments was enforced, permitting Argentines to visit the islands. Prior to this, only relatives of the fallen soldiers were allowed occasional visits to Darwin Cemetery, near the site of the battle of Goose Green, where the remains of an Argentine fighter plane lie.

Despite the traumatic experience of the invasion and the emphatic rejection of post-war Argentine overtures by the *kelpers*, the economic life of the islands improved after the war, not just because of oil exploration. A permanent garrison of some 2,000 troops has been based in Mount Pleasant since that time, a new airport, hospital, and secondary school have been installed, and average annual income is now around US$20,000, a 700 percent increase over pre-war levels. Economic life centers on fishing; this includes fishing licenses to foreign ships operating in the islands' 240-km (150-mile) exclusion zone, agriculture, and services, especially tourism, which benefits from the spectacular wildlife. Agricultural lands were sub-divided and sold by the Falkland Islands Development Corporation after the war, and are now in the hands of local farmers.

Direct travel between Argentina and the islands is still limited but flights are available in Chile. Cruises are also available from Uruguay in spring and summer. Port Stanley is a picturesque town noted for its Englishness, with neatly painted houses framed by lawns and flowerbeds, and three churches. Port Stanley has various types of accommodation to offer visitors, including two hotels, and a few guesthouses, lodges, and self-catering cottages. There are restaurants and bars, but no theaters. It also has virtually the only trees in the islands, brought from abroad and laboriously protected from the winds which constantly batter the islands. The port, with its windbreak hill backdrop, steadfastly faces the treacherous Southern Ocean and the still visible wreckage of old fishing vessels.   ❑

The islands took their English name from the Falkland Sound, named after a British peer in 1690. Seventeenth-century French seafarers named the islands Les Isles Maloulnes ("Malvinas" in Spanish) after their St Malo home.

BELOW: Carcass Island settlement, Falklands.
OVERLEAF: heading for home, Ecuador.

✲® INSIGHT GUIDES

TRAVEL TIPS

CONTENTS

Getting Acquainted

Climate

In South America, temperature depends greatly on altitude above sea-level, and temperate climates can be found among mountain landscapes away from the coast. Hot temperatures tend to prevail throughout the year in the lowlands, mainly along the coast. The **Colombian highlands**, for example, has moderate weather all year round, while the coast is tropical. The only seasons here are wet and dry, varying by region.

Venezuela has a tropical climate with average temperatures of 27°C (80°F). Four climatic zones are represented within its boundaries: hot, mild, cool and cold.

The rainy season lasts from mid-May until the end of October, but showers may fall in December or January. In Caracas, the January average temperature is 18.6°C (65°F), rising to 21°C (70°F) in July.

Peru's coastline has average temperatures of 14–27°C (58–80°F), while in the highlands – or sierra – it is normally cold, sunny and dry for much of the year, with temperatures ranging from 9–18°C (48–65°F). The rainy season in the sierra is from December to May. The jungle is hot and humid with temperatures ranging from 25–28°C (77–82°F).

Lima alone suffers from the climatic condition the Peruvians call *garua* – a thick wet fog that covers the city without respite throughout the winter.

Ecuador's regions each have a distinct climate. The coast is hottest and wettest from January to April. The mountains are driest and clearest between June and

September, and in December. The Oriente is usually inundated with rain between June and August, followed by a drier season until December. As on the coast, however, a torrential downpour is never out of the question.

In **Bolivia**, the average temperature in the highlands – the most popular area to visit – is 10°C (50°F). Rain falls heavily from November to March here, but May to November is very dry. The average temperatures in La Paz are 6–21°C (42–70°F) during summer and 0–17°C (32–63°F) in winter.

In **Brazil**'s jungle region, the climate is humid equatorial, with high temperatures and humidity, and heavy rainfall all year round. The eastern Atlantic coast of Brazil, from Rio Grande do Norte to the state of São Paulo, has a humid tropical climate, also hot, but with slightly less rainfall than in the north and with summer and winter seasons. Most of Brazil's interior has a semi-humid tropical climate, with a hot, rainy summer from December to March and a drier, cooler winter (June to August).

Part of the interior of the northeast has a tropical semi-arid climate – hot with sparse rainfall. Most of the rain falls during three months, usually March–May. The average temperature in the northeast is 24–27°C (75–80°F).

Brazil's south, below the Tropic of Capricorn, has a humid subtropical climate. Rainfall is distributed regularly throughout the year and temperatures vary from 0–10°C (32–40°F) in winter, with occasional frosts and snowfall (but the latter is rare) to 21–32°C (70–80°F) in summer.

Paraguay has a subtropical climate. Summers (December to February) are very hot and humid; spring and fall are milder. In winter (June to August) temperatures can drop to 5°C (41°F) but it never snows.

Chile's central valley (Santiago, Valparaíso, Viña del Mar) has a Mediterranean climate with summer (January and February) averaging 28°C (82°F), and winter 10°C (50°F).

Evenings are cool and it rains in winter but the weather is generally pleasant.

On the coast, it is humid, cloudy and windy, so it feels colder than inland. The lake district has a pleasant temperate climate, but winds can be chilly. The mountains are cold and it rains a lot. Patagonia is almost always cold. Fog, rain and high winds are not uncommon even in the summer.

In **Uruguay** fertile grasslands alternate with wooded hill country and lush river valleys. The climate is temperate. June, July and August can be quite cold and damp. Spring (September through November) and fall (March through May) are pleasant; summers (December through February) are hot but tempered by the cool Atlantic breezes.

Most of **Argentina** lies within the temperate zone of the southern hemisphere. The northeastern part is very humid and subtropical but has mild winters. The pampas are temperate while the southern part of the country has colder temperatures and rain most of the year.

Rainfall varies in the humid pampas (which comprises the province of Buenos Aires, and some of the Córdoba and La Pampa provinces) from 99 cm (39 inches) in the eastern parts to about 51 cm (20 inches) near the Andes.

Health

Consult your local public health service before leaving home and be sure to get a certificate for any vaccination you have. The most common illnesses are picked up from contaminated food and water, so you should pay particular attention to what you eat and drink.

The quality of tap **water** in much of South America is unreliable.You are advised to drink only bottled water, or to take purifying tablets.

Hepatitis, picked up from contaminated food and water, is common, and all travelers should get immunized against the disease.

Malaria occurs in jungle areas of South America, so you should take anti-malaria tablets if you are visiting any part of the Amazon.

Yellow fever, transmitted to humans by mosquitoes, is prevalent in the whole of South America except Chile, Argentina and Uruguay. You are therefore advised to seek immunization. A yellow fever shot protects you for 10 years, but is effective only after 10 days, so plan ahead. You may be asked to show your yellow fever vaccination certificate if arriving from a country where yellow fever is endemic.

Your physician or, in the UK, the Medical Advisory Service for Travellers Abroad (MASTA), tel: 0906 8224100, will advise you about other tropical diseases that may be endemic in the area you are visiting – such as dengue fever and Chaga's disease. All travelers should check that they are inoculated against tetanus, typhoid and polio.

You should take some form of remedy for **stomach upsets** and **diarrhea**, which is likely to be the main complaint of most travelers. Immodium is a popular travel companion, but note that this medication treats the symptoms and not the cause.

The other main cause of illness in the **heat**. Have respect for the power of the tropical sun: wear a hat and be sure to drink plenty of fluids.

Travelers planning to spend time in the Andes should be aware of the dangers of **altitude sickness** (*soroche*). Anyone arriving by air in La Paz, for example, is likely to need several days to acclimatize.

Acute mountain sickness (called *puno*) is totally unpredictable – even the fittest people can be affected – and the only solution is to go back to a lower altitude as fast as you can. If you must continue, rest for a few days, drink lots of fluids but do not smoke or consume any alcohol.

Security and Crime

The crime rate is generally high in South America, although risks can be minimized by taking a few basic precautions. Jewelry should not be worn and large amounts of money and expensive watches should be kept out of sight. Wear a money belt when traveling. Keep an eye on your possessions at all times and make use of hotel safes whenever possible (but always take a verified list of what you have deposited). Do not leave valuables in cars. Avoid walking alone and in deserted areas after dark. Never carry packages for other people without checking the contents.

Colombia is part of a major drug-smuggling route, so it is particularly important that you do not carry packages for other people. Be guided by advice before you leave home about which areas are safe.

The crime rate in **Venezuela**, particularly in Caracas, is high. You should not walk alone in narrow streets in downtown Caracas after dark and it is strongly recommended that you do not travel by car at night, particularly in the countryside where, should you have an accident or breakdown, the risk of robbery and other crimes is much greater.

Petty crime is rife in the urban centers of **Peru**. Pickpockets and thieves are common in Lima and Cusco and are amazingly adept at slitting open shoulder bags, camera cases and knapsacks. Officials also warn against dealing with anyone approaching you in the hotel lobby or on the street, allegedly representing a travel agency or specialty shop.

A special security service for tourists has been created by Peru's Civil Guard. They are recognizable by a white braid across the shoulder of their uniforms and can be found all over Lima, especially in downtown areas. In Cusco, all police have tourism training. The tourist police office in Lima is in the Museo de la Nación, Av. Javier Prado Este 2465, San Borja, tel: 476 7708. In Cusco: Calle Saphi in the Delegación de Policía, two blocks from the Plaza, tel: 249652.

Traveling alone and after dusk is not advisable. Don't hitch-hike. For journeys overland choose well-known and established bus companies. Carry your passport at all times. For specific inquiries, contact your embassy.

Photography

Film is much more expensive than in the US and UK, so stock up before you go. If you need to buy some once traveling, check the expiry date first.

Note that it is forbidden for military sites (including ports, transport terminals and bridges) to be photographed. It is best to ask permission if you are unsure.

Many people, particularly from indigenous cultures, are sensitive about having their portraits taken, so always ask permission first.

The US State Department and the British Foreign Office both publish detailed information on all South American countries and offer advice to travelers. Their websites are, respectively:
US: http://travel.state.gov
UK: www.fco.gov.uk

Money Matters

Travelers' checks in US dollars are the safest and most convenient form of currency, acceptable all over South America. Sterling and other currencies are not worth bringing (except if you are visiting French Guiana, whose currency is the euro, or the Falkland Islands, where sterling is used).

Changing money You can change money in banks, *casas de cambio* (exchange bureaux) and larger hotels; *casas de cambio* usually give the best rate of exchange. Take checks and cash in a variety of large and small denominations since exchange rates in some countries can change dramatically overnight; and bring only notes in optimum condition as some exchange bureaus can be sniffy about old notes. It is worth bringing a pocket calculator as some rates of exchange run into the thousands.

Cash You will always need to carry some cash with you, of course, and should think ahead if you are traveling into a rural area for some time. But try not to exceed the amount covered in your insurance policy.

Credit and debit cards are also widely accepted, with ATMs (cash machines) located in most cities. Before leaving home, memorize your PIN number, and check handling fees and cover in the event of loss or robbery. Many establishments also add their own supplementary charges.

See the separate Money section under each country for more details.

Finally, it is worth remembering the much-quoted advice: pack half the clothes you think you'll need, but twice the money.

Shopping

Much of South America's best bargains are still to be found in the local markets, particularly in the Andean countries, where prices are low and the choice of goods extensive. Jewelry, textiles, jumpers, ponchos and leather goods are all widely produced. A certain amount of haggling is expected but be careful not to go too far. Only too often you hear tales of people stomping off in a huff because a trader refused to cut the price of an item by the equivalent of US$1.

Venezuela's craftsmen hold a prestigious position because of the variety and quality of their workmanship. Outstanding Quibor ceramics have pre-Hispanic origins, molded using styles and techniques handed down through the generations. Baskets, hammocks, hats and other products made from vegetable fibers can be found in the towns and villages along the Easter Coast. Beautifully woven ponchos, colorful blankets and caps are sold by the Andean people while craftsmen of the *llanos* (prairies) sell four-string guitar-like musical instruments called *cuatros* as well as harps and mandolins.

Bolivia likewise produces a wide range of craft work, including tapestries, woolen clothing and wooden sculptures. And **Peru** is also known for the quality of its

handicrafts, as well as its bargain gold, copper and silver items. A good range can be found in the *artesanías* markets in Lima.

Colombia specializes in emeralds and leather goods, but if you're looking for a number of different gemstones, **Brazil**'s tremendous variety is unmatched, and prices are low. If you're not an expert gemologist, it's wise to buy from a reliable jeweler. The three leading jewelers operating nationwide are H. Stern, Amsterdam Sauer and Roditi, but there are other reliable smaller chains. The top jewelers have shops in the airports, shopping centers and in most hotels. Leather goods are another good buy in Brazil; the finest leather comes from the south.

Chile's open, import-oriented free market economy offers a selection of just about anything you want to buy, but also produces some fine copper ornaments and lapis lazuli jewelry.

Ecuador is renowned as the home of the Panama hat and also for its colorful balsawood carvings, as well as tapestries, leather goods and embroidered textiles from Otovalo market and other outlets; while **Paraguay** is famous for its *ñandutí* (*guaraní* for cobweb) lace, used to decorate bedcovers, tablecloths, mantillas, etc. Other good buys are guitars and harps, gold and silver filigree jewelry, tooled leather, and ponchos of cotton and wool.

Be careful when buying wool as *vicuña* are an endangered species and selling *vicuña* wool is against international law.

Planning the Trip

Getting There

BY AIR

Argentina
From Europe: Aerolíneas Argentinas, Air France, Alitalia, Avianca, British Airways, Iberia, Lufthansa, Varig.
From/via US: American Airlines, United Airlines, Varig.
From Australasia: Aerolíneas Argentinas.

Bolivia
From Europe: Aerolíneas Argentinas, British Airways, Grupo TACA, LanChile, Varig.
From/via US: American Airlines.
Within South America: LanChile.

Brazil
From Europe: Aerolíneas Argentinas, Air France, Alitalia, Avianca, British Airways, Continental Airlines, Cubana, Grupo TACA, Iberia, LanChile, Pluna, TAM, TAP, Transbrasil, Varig.
From/via US: American Airlines, Continental Airlines, Delta, LAB, Transbrasil, United Airlines, Varig.

Chile
From Europe: Aerolíneas Argentinas, Air France, Avianca, British Airways, Iberia, Grupo TACA, LanChile, Lufthansa, Varig.
From/via US: American Airlines, Continental Airlines, LanChile, United Airlines.
From Australasia: Aerolíneas Argentinas, LanChile.

Colombia
From Europe: Air France, Alitalia, British Airways, Continental Airlines, Iberia, Varig.

Air Passes

If you are planning to cover large distances and time is short, consider buying one of the air passes that most Latin American airlines offer, covering one or a combination of countries. These passes usually work out cheaper than buying individual flights locally. They must be bought outside the country concerned, in conjunction with your transatlantic flight. Airpasses are currently available for Argentina (Aerolíneas Argentinas), Bolivia (Aerosur), Brazil (Transbrasil, Varig, Vasp), Chile (LanChile, Ladeco), Colombia (Avianca), Peru (Aeroperu) and Venezuela (Avensa/Servivensa).

From/via US: American Airlines, Avianca, Continental Airlines, United.

Ecuador
From Europe: Air France, Avianca, British Airways, Continental Airlines, Cubana, Grupo TACA, Iberia, LanChile, Lufthansa.
From/via US: American Airlines, Continental Airlines.

French Guiana
From Europe: Air France.
From/via US: Air France.

Guyana
From Europe and US: British West Indian Airlines (connecting with British Airways or Virgin).

Paraguay
From Europe: Aerolíneas Argentinas, Air France, Iberia.
From/via USA: American Airlines, LanChile, Pluna, Varig.

Peru
From Europe: Aeroflot, Aerolíneas Argentinas, Avianca, Air France, Alitalia, Continental, Iberia, Grupo TACA, LanChile, Lufthansa, Varig.
From/via US: Aerolíneas Argentinas, American Airlines, Avianca, Continental Airlines, Grupo TACA, LanChile, United Airlines, Varig.

Suriname
From Europe: Surinamair.
From/via US: Surinamair.

Uruguay
From Europe: Aerolíneas Argentinas, Iberia, LanChile, Pluna, Varig
From/via US: American Airlines, United Airlines.

Venezuela
From Europe: Air France, Alitalia, Avianca, British Airways, Iberia, KLM, TAP.
From/via the US: American Airlines, Continental Airlines, United Airlines.

Tour Operators

In the United Kingdom
Encounter Overland, adventure group tours. 2002 Camp Green, Debenham, Stowmarket, Suffolk, IP14 6LA, tel: 01728 862222, fax: 01728 861127, www.encounter.co.uk
Exodus, adventure group tours. Grange Mills, Weir Road, London SW12 0NE, tel: 0870 240 5550 (admin/reservations), 020 8673 0859 (brochures/trip notes), fax: 020 8673 0779, www.exodus.co.uk
Explore Worldwide, adventure group tours. 1 Frederick St, Aldershot, Hants GU11 1LQ, tel: 01252 760000, fax: 01252 760001, www.explore.co.uk
Journey Latin America, flights, tailor-made itineraries, escorted tours, and adventure trips. 12/13 Heathfield Terrace, Chiswick, London W4 4JE, tel: 020 8747 3108 (flights), 0208 747 8315

Arriving by Boat

An unusual alternative to flying is to join a cargo ship in England and travel by sea. For further information contact Strand Travel, Charing Cross Shopping Concourse, London WC2N 4HZ, tel: 020 7836 6363, fax: 020 7497 0078, www.strandtravel.co.uk

(tours), fax: 020 8742 1312; www.journeylatinamerica.co.uk
South American Experience, flights and tailor-made itineraries. 47 Causton Street, London SW1P 4AT, tel: 020 7976 5511, fax: 020 7976 6908, www.southamerican experience.co.uk
STA, specialists in student and under-26 fares, tours and hotels, with 400 branches worldwide. Tel: 08701 600599; www.statravel.co.uk
Trailfinders, longhaul and transatlantic flights. Tel: 020 7292 1888, www.trailfinder.com
Trips Worldwide, specialists in tours to the Guianas. 14 Frederick Place, Bristol BS8 1AS, UK, tel: 0117 311 4400, fax: 0117 311 4401, www.tripsworldwide.co.uk.

In the United States
South American Explorers' Club
Tel: 607 277 0488, fax: 607 277 6122, www.samexplo.org/

What to Pack

Take light summer clothes if you are heading for tropical zones. Note that shorts and very skimpy tops are frowned upon in churches. In the highlands, a sweater should suffice in the evenings. Take a thick raincoat and woolen clothing if you are heading up into high mountain areas.

Pack some high-factor sunscreen and remember to take a hat. A money belt may also be useful.

Rechargeable batteries and a recharger are useful for electrical equipment.

Argentina A – Z

Getting Acquainted

Area 2,780,400 sq. km (1,074,000 sq. miles)
Capital Buenos Aires
Population 38 million
Language Spanish
Currency Peso ($)
Weights & measures Metric
Electricity 220 volts
Time zone GMT -3hrs, EST +2hrs
Dialing code 54 (Buenos Aires +11)

Government & Economy

The Republic of Argentina has a federal system, with 24 provinces and a strong central government, headed by a president.

Argentina was once one of the world's richest farming economies with agriculture and livestock

Embassies/Consulates

The following are in Buenos Aires:
Australia: Calle Villanueva 1400, tel: 4779 3500, fax: 4779 3581.
Canada: Calle Tagle 2828, tel: 4808-1000, fax: 4808-1111, www.dfait-maeci.gc.ca. Mailing address: Casilla de Correo 1598, C1000WAP Correo Central, Buenos Aires.
Ireland: Avda del Libertador 1068, 6th floor, tel: 5787 0801, fax: 5787 0802.
UK: Calle Dr Luis Agote 2412/52, tel: 4808 2200, fax: 4808 2274, www.britishembassy.gov.uk.
US: Avda Colombia 4300, tel: 5777 4533, fax: 5777 4240, http://usembassy.state.gov/buenosaires.

Public Holidays

- **January** 1
- **March/April** Maundy Thursday and Good Friday
- **May** 1, 25
- **June** 10, 20
- **July** 9
- **August** 17
- **October** 12
- **December** 8, 25

providing 50 percent of export earnings, and the country is virtually self-sufficient in oil. However, Argentina suffered a severe economic decline in 1998, which, together with high-level political corruption, poverty and unemployment brought the country to the verge of imploding financially, politically and socially by 2002. In November of that year Argentina defaulted on an US$800m debt owed to the World Bank, having failed to secure IMF aid. In 2003 the IMF agreed to provide a US$3.1bn rescue package, and in April 2004 economic growth rose, after a deep four-year recession.

Visas

Tourists coming to Argentina must have a valid passport; a visa is not necessary for citizens of the US and Western Hemisphere countries (excluding Cuba) and Japan, who can stay for three months. In some cases a tourist card is all that is needed; this must be verified with a travel agent.

Money

In the present political and economic turmoil, restrictions may be imposed on withdrawing money from banks and *casas de cambio*. It is important to take alternative means of payment, e.g. credit cards (which are widely accepted) and US dollars in cash, in small denominations.

Religious Services

St Andrew's Presbyterian Church at the corner of Belgrano and Peru has an English service at 10am. The community church in Acassuso also has an English service at 10.30am. A free bus leaves downtown at 9.30am from outside the Methodist Church at Corrientes and Maipú (opposite Telefónica).

Getting Around

From the Airport
Ezeiza International Airport (EZE) is the arrival point for all foreign travelers. It is about 40 minutes from downtown Buenos Aires. There are buses to the center of the city every 30 minutes, and plenty of taxis, as well as the **Manuel Tienda** minibus service.

By Air
Traveling by air within Argentina is via the local airlines, which are Austral, Aerolíneas Argentinas, Lineas Aereas del Estado (LADE), serving mostly Patagonian destinations, Dinar, ARG, Southern Winds, and Linea Aereas Privadas Argentinas (LAPA).

Jorge Newberry Airport, also known as Aereoparque, is used for flights within Argentina and bordering countries.

For tourists who wish to visit several cities, the Aerolíneas Argentinas (www.aerolineas.com.ar) 30-day "Visit Argentina" ticket can be used to stop off in various towns, although there have been complaints about this airline's baggage handlers stealing from passengers' luggage, so it may be wise to carry valuables with hand luggage.

The "Visit Argentina" ticket is made up of four flight coupons which can be added to make up eight in total. Austral sells similar tickets. They cost around US$450 (US$100 for extra coupons), and must be purchased outside Argentina in conjunction with an international flight ticket. Confirmation 24 hours before the time of your flight is strongly recommended. There is a departure tax of around $15 to be paid on leaving the country.

By Sea

Few **cruise ships** call at Buenos Aires. Traveling to Uruguay on the ferry is a pleasant and inexpensive trip. Contact **Ferrytur**, Calle Córdoba 699, tel: 4315 6800. There are boat connections between Uruguay and Argentina: Tigre to Carmelo and Montevideo to Carmelo. Ferry services run to Colonia from Daraena Sur and a hydrofoil service runs between Montevideo and Colonia four times a day during the summer. The English-language daily, *Duenos Aires Herald*, has listings of all sailings to Argentina.

By Bus

Buses are an excellent way to get around Buenos Aires, which is a very large city. They are usually prompt and inexpensive, but try not to use one during the rush hour as the lines are very long. Bus stops are located throughout the whole city. The number and destination are clearly marked. Long-distance travel on buses is also available. A huge, modern bus terminal is located in Retiro. Information on destinations can be obtained there from the different companies.

Bus services are available from Chile, Bolivia, Paraguay, Uruguay and Brazil. Large air-conditioned buses are usually used for long-distance overland travel, but travelers must remember to be vigilant to ensure personal safety.

By Rail

All international train services were suspended after 1994, when the government withdrew funding from Ferrocarriles Argentinos, and domestic services have been increasingly marginalized. For up-to-date information contact:

Ferrocarril Nacional Roca (southern) tel: 319 3900;
Ferrocarril Nacional Urquiza (north-eastern) tel: 553 7038;
Ferrocarriles Argentinos, tel: 306 1010.

Trains do run to the suburbs of Buenos Aires, however. There are four main rail terminals in the city:
Retiro: tel: 4311 8074/4317 4000. To Delta Tigre, Capilla del Señor and Bartolomé Mitre.
Constitución: tel: 4304 0031. Local trains.
Federico Lacroze: tel: 4553 5213. Excursions on a 1888 Scottish Neilson steam engine.
Once: tel: 4317 4407. Buenos Aires province. The ride from Olivos to Tigre along the coast offers excellent views of the River Plate.
Tren de la Costa: tel: 4315 7778.

By Road

Traveling by car is possible. Most of the roads are paved but cautious driving is absolutely essential. Speed limits are posted and should be followed closely.

The Automobile Club of Argentina in Buenos Aires on Avda Libertador 1850, tel: 802 6061/7061, is very helpful and can provide maps and useful information.

By Taxi

These can be easily recognized in Buenos Aires – black with a yellow roof – and are readily available 24 hours a day. The meter registers the fare. A bit of advice: be careful when

Media

The main local papers are *La Nación* and *Clarín*. The English paper is the *Herald* and there's a free tourist information paper, the *Buenos Aires Times*. There are newspaper and magazine stands throughout Buenos Aires, where these and some foreign papers, as well as many international magazines, may be found.

There are five TV channels, and cable TV is available. Most of the programs are brought in from the US and some from Europe. Many drama series are locally made.

Radio stations carry a variety of programs. The BBC runs from 5pm to about 12.30am. A number of stations play international hits, tango music and talk programs.

Remise Taxis

Remise taxis are private cars that can be rented, with a driver, by the hour, day or any other time period. Fares normally work out much cheaper than those charged by ordinary taxis.

A list of *remise* offices can be found in the telephone directory, and staff in your hotel should be able to provide information too.

paying and make sure the correct change is given; quick exchanges of incorrect bills have been known to take place, especially with the tourist who doesn't know the language or the currency. A small tip *(propina)* is expected.

By Subway

The subway system, better known as the **Subte**, is the fastest and cheapest way to get around Buenos Aires, and is the oldest in South America, built in 1913. Trains run daily from 5.30am to 10.15pm and tickets cost 50¢ flat fare per journey. The rides take no more than 25 minutes, and the waiting is between three to five minutes. The artwork at some of the stations is unique and has an interesting history: many of these painted tiles were baked by artisans in Spain and France at the beginning of the 20th century and around the 1930s

Medical Services

Healthcare in Argentina is good. Hospitals have trained personnel who have studied at home and abroad. There are excellent specialists in most of the medical fields, who make a point of attending international medical congresses to learn about recent advances in medical science and to bring them to Argentina.

Medical equipment is very costly, but all efforts are coordinated in order to maximize benefits. In some sections of the country, the hospitals may not have up-to-date equipment, but what is available is adequate for an emergency situation.

Emergency Numbers

For general emergencies, dial **101** for the **Police**, who can advise about other emergency services in the area. For the **ambulance** service, dial **107**. For medical emergencies in the Buenos Aires area, you can contact the following: **British Hospital**, Calle Perdriel 74, tel: 4309 6400.
Children's Hospital Pedro Elizalde, Calle M.Oca 40, tel: 4300 2115 **Ricardo Gutierrez**, Calle Gallo 1330, tel: 962 9280.
Hospital de Clinicas, Calle Córdoba 2351, tel: 961 6001.

Business Hours

Offices open Mon–Fri 9am–6pm, and banking hours are Mon–Fri 10am–3pm. Stores normally open Mon–Fri 9am–8pm, but you'll often find that they close for several hours in the middle of the day.

All government agencies and banks close on public holidays.

Postal Services

The main post office is located on Calle Sarmiento 189, and operates Mon–Fri, 8am–8pm. Other small post offices are found throughout the city. Hotels are the best source of stamps.

Telecommunications

Telephone services are run by *Telecom* in the north and *Telefónica Argentina* in the south. Phone cards are available. Domestic calls can be made from public telephone boxes using coins or cards. In main cities the **Centros de Llamadas** offer good telephone and fax services. International public phones have a DDI sign. Many telephone offices send international faxes. In Buenos Aires you can make international calls and send faxes from the communications office on Avda Corrientes 705. Open 24 hours.

E-mail and **Internet** can be accessed at The Internet Center, Calle Maipú 24, tel: 343 1500; fax: 334 6283.

Travel Agencies

ASATEJ, Calle Florida 835, 3rd floor, Office 315, Buenos Aires, tel: 4311-6953, fax: 4311-6840. Primarily aimed at students, but there's no age limit. Bright and cheerful office with noticeboard brimming with items for sale, travel news, travelers seeking companions.
Cosmopolitan Travel, Calle L. Alem 986, 7th floor, Buenos Aires, tel: 4311-6684/6695. 24-hour service available and many languages spoken.
Eurotur, Calle Viamonte 486, Buenos Aires, tel: 4312 6070, fax: 4311 9010, www.eurotur.com. Tours, transport and accommodation for individuals and groups throughout Argentina. English spoken; highly professional and recommended.
Eves Tourismo, Calle Tucumán 702, Buenos Aires, tel: 4393-6151. Helpful and efficient for travel in Argentina and abroad.
Kallpa Tour, Calle Roque Saenz Pena 811, 1st floor, Office D, Buenos Aires, tel: 4394-1830/1860, fax: 4326-2500; www.kallpatour.com. Specialists in trekking, horseback riding and cultural tours.

Useful websites include: www.grippo.com.ar (in Spanish) www.liveargentina.com (in six languages, and easy to use).

Useful Addresses

There are *casas de turismo* (tourist offices) in most big towns in Argentina. Buenos Aires has the following offices and services:

The **National Tourist Office** is at: Calle Santa Fe 883, tel: 4312 2232, fax: 313 6834, www.turismo.gov.ar. Open Mon–Fri 8.30am–10pm, Sat 9am–7pm. Other tourist information centers are: Calle Sarmiento 1551, 5th floor 1042, tel: 4476 3612, Diagonal Norte/Florida, Gallerias Pacifico, Retiro Bus Station, Ezeiza International Airport, and Jorge Newbery Airport. In these booths travelers can obtain maps of the city and a bilingual (Spanish and English) tourist information newspaper, the *Buenos Aires Times*; it offers complete listings of what is happening in the city. *Where*, a booklet listing shopping, dining and entertainment, can be obtained in most hotels.

The provinces of Argentina have offices in Buenos Aires where tourists can obtain information. Pamphlets about special events, attractions, hotels, restaurants, etc. are readily available. All the offices are located in the center of town and can be easily located. Look in the phone book.

Where to Stay

Buenos Aires

Carsson, Calle Viamonte 650, tel: 4322 3551. Faded, charming elegance. **$$$**
Claridge Hotel, Calle Tucumán 535, tel: 4314 7700; fax: 4314 8022, www.claridge-hotel.com. Old-fashioned British style. **$$$**
Gran Hotel Colón, Calle Carlos Pellegrini 507, tel: 4320 3500, fax: 4320 3507, www.colon-hotel.com.ar. Rooftop pool. **$$$**
Gran Hotel Hispano, Avda de Mayo 861, tel: 4345 2020. Housed in a colonial building and popular with budget travelers. **$$**
Libertador Hotel, corner of Calle Córboda & Maipu, tel: 4322 8800; fax: 4322 9703. Modern and central. **$$$**
Marriot Plaza Hotel, Calle Florida 1005, tel: 4318 3000, fax: 4315 3008, www.marriottplaza.com.ar. For the rich and famous with renowned Plaza Grill. **$$$**
Orly Hotel, Calle Paraguay 474, tel: 4312 5344. Basic rooms, good location. **$**

Hotel Price Guide

Prices for a double room including continental breakfast.
$ = US$30 – inexpensive
$$ = US$30–50 – moderate
$$$ = US$50 plus – expensive

A Rural Haven

Estancia Getaway: Visitors to Buenos Aires have the chance to get away from the buzz of the city, in the small town of San Antonio de Areco, about 110 km (70 miles) away. In this peaceful location, with beautiful scenery, the Aldao family has converted the Estancia La Bamba into a country inn, with all the facilities to make a stay comfortable and memorable. For more information tel: 392 0394 or 392 9707.

Phoenix, Calle San Martín 780, tel: 4312 4845; fax: 4311 2846. Faded old-world charm, fabulous large rooms, friendly staff, and a central location. **$$**
Sheraton Buenos Aires Hotel & Towers, Calle San Martín 1225, tel: 4318 9000; fax: 4318 9353. Magnificent view over the river and port. **$$$**
Waldorf Hotel, Calle Paraguay 450, tel: 4312 2071; fax: 4312 2079, www.waldorfhotel.com.ar. Modern, near shopping streets. **$**

Puerto Iguazú
Hotel International de Iguazú, Reservations in Buenos Aires, tel: 4311 4259; fax: 4312 0488. Located in the National Park where the falls are, offering a magnificent view of its spectacular cascades. Very modern and with all facilities including golf course. **$$$**
Las Orquideas, Ruta 12 at Km 5, tel: 420 472. Comfortable and inexpensive, outside the city in a beautiful location. **$–$$**
Hotel Salta, Calle Buenos Aires 1, tel: 4211 011; fax: 4310 740. Good hotel in the main square. **$$**

Mendoza
Hotel Aconcagua, Calle San Lorenzo 545, tel: 520 0500, fax: 420 2083. A few blocks from the main shopping area, with modern architecture, pool and air-conditioned rooms. **$$$**
Plaza Hotel, Calle Chile 1124, tel: 423 3000. Traditional establishment, in front of a

beautiful plaza, with lovely antique furnishings. **$$$**
Hosteria Puente del Inca, Ruta 7, Las Heras, tel: 4380 480; fax: 4380 477. Secluded, within sight of Aconcagua. **$$**

Bariloche
Edelweiss Hotel, Avda San Martín 232, tel/fax: 426 165. A large hotel with sauna, fitness rooms and a good restaurant. **$$$**
Hotel Tronador, Ruta 237, Km 19, Bariloche, tel: 468 127. Small lodge-type hotel with excellent food, fishing, horseback riding, hiking and beautiful surroundings. In front of the Mascardi Lake, southwest of Bariloche. Open Nov–April. **$$**

Carlos Paz
El Ciervo de Oro, Calle Hipólito Yrigoyen 995, tel: 422 498. Lovely, cozy lodge-type hotel right on the lake, with pool. Excellent food. **$$**

Tucuman
Hotel Garden, Calle Crisóstomo Alvarez 627, tel: 081 4311 246. Clean and comfortable with reasonable rates. **$**
Grand Hotel, Avda de los Proceres 380, tel: (0381) 450 2250. The only 5-star hotel in Tucumán. Comfortable and central, with all facilities. **$$$+**

Ushuaia
Cabo de Hornos, Calle San Martín y Rosas, tel: 422 487. Clean and comfortable. **$$**
Del Glaciar, Camino Glaciar Martial Km 3.5, tel: (2901) 430 640, fax: 439 638. Four-star hotel above the city. **$$$**
Las Hayas Resort Hotel, Camino Glaciar Martial Km 3, tel: 430 710 18, www.tierradelfuego.org.ar/lashayas. Five-star hotel set on a hill with great views, spa and minibus to the city.

Calafate (Lago Argentina)
Hotel La Loma, Calle B Roca and 15 Febrero, tel: 4910 16. In the National Glacier Park, with 27 rooms, centrally located with lovely views. Open Oct–April. Several languages spoken. **$**

What to Eat

Hotel breakfasts are rarely exceptional, and you'll do better to head for a local *confitería* or bar. A traditional breakfast includes *café con leche* (white coffee) and *medias lunas* (croissants, smaller and denser than the French variety). Other types of pastry *(facturas)* are usually also available. Good *confiterías* in the center of Buenos Aires include the Florida Garden (Calle Florida and Paraguay) and the wood panelled Richmond (Calle Florida near Corrientes). Breakfast is usually available from 8am.

Argentina is well known for its beef. The typical meal will begin with *empanadas* (meat pastries, although the filling will vary according to the region), *chorizos* (pork and paprika sausages) or *morcilla* (pork blood sausages), and an assortment of *achuras* (sweetbreads). For the main course, excellent meat dishes such as *bife de chorizo* (T-bone steak), or *tira de asado* (roast) are the most popular choices, accompanied by various salads. To finish off, try a *flan* (custard), topped with *dulce de leche* and some whipped cream.

Restaurant Guide

Prices for a three-course meal for two, including house wine.
$ = US$30 – inexpensive
$$ = US$30–50 – moderate
$$$ = US$50 plus – expensive

Eating in Buenos Aires

The scope of this guidebook does not allow a listing of restaurants from all parts of Argentina, so the list below focuses just on Buenos Aires, where there is a vast choice. It is possible to eat out every day of the year and still not savor the cuisine of all the recommendable restaurants in the city. Dining out in Buenos Aires is a delightful experience. Food, wine and service are usually excellent.

Eating out is a favorite pastime of the locals (porteños), but the menu is not the only attraction. Restaurants are a place to socialize, to see and be seen, and share a bottle of wine until the early hours of the morning. Nevertheless, porteños take eating seriously. A list of recommended eateries follows, but don't be afraid to try any clean, well-lit place that catches your fancy. The food is almost always fresh and well-prepared in a simple Southern European style.

Restaurants in Buenos Aires open for lunch at noon, and for dinner around 8pm. But no one dines out in the evening before 9pm, with restaurants really coming alive between 10pm and 11pm. At weekends, restaurants stay busy long after midnight.

Regional Argentine

El Ceibal, Calle Güemes 3402, tel: 4823 5807; Cabildo 1421, tel: 4784 2444. Great place to try specialties from Northern Argentina, including locro (corn chowder), humitas (tamales) and empanadas. **$$**.

Parrillas (Steakhouses)

El Mirasol, Calle Davila 202, tel: 4315 6277. Upscale parrilla in posh Puerto Madero district, elegant atmosphere, reservations recommended. **$$$**
El Palacio de la Papa Frita, Calle Lavalle 735, tel: 4393 5849. Inexpensive and popular. **$$**
La Chacra, Avda Córdoba 941, tel: 4322 1409. Huge portions. **$$$**
La Estancia, Calle Lavalle 941, tel: 4326 0330. Classic grillhouse in the heart of the city. **$$**
La Veda, Calle Florida 1, tel: 4331 6442. Dark wood paneling, excellent peppered steak, tango dinner show most evenings. Reservations recommended. **$$$**.
Los Troncos, Calle Suipacha 732, tel: 322 1295. Excellent meat and fruity wines at bargain prices. **$$**
Munich Recoleta, Calle R.M. Ortíz 1879, tel: 4804 3981. Popular for nearly 40 years, for the lively atmosphere and great steak. Reservations are not accepted. **$$**

Popular Eateries

Bárbaro, Calle Tres Sargentos 415, tel: 4311 6856. A BA landmark, a charming, old-world version of the hole-in-the-wall bar, a great place for a simple midday meal or for music, beer and bar food in the evening. **$**
La Casa de Esteban de Luca, Calle Defensa and Carlos Calvo. In the heart of San Telmo, in a colonial-style building, popular Sunday lunch after the San Telmo fair. **$**
Pippo, Calle Montevideo 345. No frills but great atmosphere and unbeatable prices. Try a bife de chorizo (T-bone steak), or a bowl of vermicelli mixto (pasta noodles with pesto and bolognaise sauce), washed down with the house red and soda water. **$**
Restaurant Dora, Calle L. Alem 1016, tel: 4311 2891. An upscale version of a popular eatery with rave reviews on the enormous steaks and simple seafood dishes, a downtown "don't miss." **$$**
Te Mataré Ramirez, Calle Paraguay 4062, tel: 4832 7030 . An excellent, original, international assortment of dishes, located in Palermo. Ideal for either a romantic evening or a business dinner. Specializes in dishes with aphrodisiac qualities. **$$–$$$**

Attractions

The Argentine people are extremely cultured and sport-loving. A wide range of activities are available, from the Buenos Aires Opera, to skiing in Bariloche. Museums, galleries, theaters, bookstores and libraries are among the places to be visited. See the Places section of this book for descriptions of the most popular places in Buenos Aires and around the country.

Theaters & Concerts

The theater season in Buenos Aires usually opens in March, with a large number and variety of plays on offer. There is always something worth seeing. Check the local paper or with your hotel for the current and best ones available. Recitals and concerts are promoted by the Secretary of Culture in an effort to bring culture to the people. The public responds enthusiastically by attending all events. Open-air concerts are very popular on hot summer evenings and are held in any of the city's numerous parks.

Teatro Colón: Most of the world's renowned performers are well acquainted with this magnificent theater. The building is in the Italian Renaissance style with some French and Greek influence. It has a capacity for 3,500 people, with about 1,000 standing. The acoustics are considered to be nearly perfect. Opera is one of the favorite programs for the season. Ballets are another favorite, performed in the past by greats such as Nureyev, Godunov and the Bolshoi Ballet. The local company is very good and many of its members go on to become international figures. The Colón also has a magnificent museum, where the theater's history and mementos are stored. A guided tour of the theater and the museum can be arranged by calling 4378 7132. Tours: Mon–Fri 11am–3pm, Sat 9am, 11am and noon. Tickets are for sale at the box office on Calle Tucumán. Closed Jan and Feb.

San Martín Theatre: Calle Sarmiento 1551, tel: 4371 0111, offers a variety of plays and musicals, and free music performances and exhibitions in the foyer. Check the local paper for performances.

Nightlife

The nightlife in Buenos Aires is more lively than in many major cities of the world. Argentinians enjoy staying up late. People wander the streets care-free into the small hours, even though crime is on the rise.

Discos, nightclubs, cabarets and bars can be found in most of the capital. Hear the latest hits from around the world and dance into the morning at, for example, **Cemento** on Calle Estados Unidos 700, or for a more formal crowd, dance at **Le Club** on Calle Quintana 111, or at **Hippopotamus**, Junin 1787. Other possibilities include: **Roxy**, Calle Rivadavia 1900; reggae and rock; **New York City**, Avda Alvarez Thomas 1391, tel: 552 4141; popular with older clubbers; **El Dorado**, Calle Hipólito Yrigogen and 9 de Julio; young, interesting crowd.

Tango Shows

A good tango show can be found almost everywhere, but the best shows are in Buenos Aires. Reservations are suggested for the following:
Casablanca, Calle Balcarce 688, tel: 4331 4621. Excellent show, prices include drinks.
La Ventana, Calle Balcarce 425, tel: 4331 0217. Small, atmospheric venue, with good food and excellent show, featuring both tango and folk music from around South America. Inclusive show and meal, with pick up and drop off from your hotel
Michelango, Calle Balcarce 4332, tel: 4331 8689. Mixed repertoire of tango and folk music and dance, in atmospheric former monastery.

Sports

Trekking
There are many tour operators in Las Heras, Mendoza, which specialize in climbing and trekking tours. One of the best is
Servicios Especiales Mendoza, Calle Amigovena 65, 5500 Mendoza, tel/fax: 4244 721.

Skiing
The main ski resorts in Argentina are the **Cerro Catedral Complex**, located near Bariloche; **Valle de las Leñas**, in the south of Mendoza Province; **Los Penitentes**, a small resort near the town of Mendoza.
There are also a number of small facilities located throughout the southern provinces, including one in Tierra del Fuego and another near Esquel. Package tours tend to keep down the costs of a ski vacation.

Horseback Riding
A weekend in the Pampa makes a relaxing excursion. Within a couple of hours' drive are many *estancias* (ranches) that offer horseback riding, *asados* (barbecues) and displays of *gaucho* (cowboy) skills. Some also have rooms and offer inclusive packages
Estancia La Bamba in San Antonio de Areco (115 km/70 miles from Buenos Aires) offers comfort and tranquility. Tel: 4392 9707.
Estancia El Carmen de Sierra is an historical building in Arrecifes, 170 km (106 miles) from Buenos Aires, offering accommodation, horseback riding and a swimming pool. Tel: 036646 41083.
Estancia Los Patricios, on Ruta 41 near San Antonio de Areco, is a beautiful ivy-covered *estancia* with riding, golf, swimming pool, local music and folk dancing, barbecues in a barn, and accommodation. Tel: 03326 3823.

Shopping in Buenos Aires

The best-known, and the most touristy, shopping street in the Argentinian capital is Florida, with Avenida Santa Fé coming a close second. You'll find the most expensive boutiques in Recoleta, the most exclusive part of Buenos Aires – primarily along Avda Alvear, Quintana, Ayacucho and small side streets.
The city's finest jewelry stores are located at the beginning of Florida and on Avda Alvear. Also, Sterns is located in the lobby of the Sheraton Hotel. The garment district is known as Once, and is accessible by taxi.
For antiques, try the historic *barrio* of San Telmo. Every Sunday the San Telmo Fair takes place. The plaza is surrounded by stalls, which sell an array of objects, from cheap to outrageously expensive. Around the plaza are many antique stores.
Buenos Aires also has a number of factory outlets (far from the city center), where a large selection of good-quality merchandise is available at low prices.

Bolivia
A – Z

Getting Acquainted

Area 1,100,000 sq. km (424,200 sq. miles)
Capital Sucre is the legal capital but La Paz is the effective capital.
Population 8.6 million. Seventy percent live in and around La Paz, Oruro and Lake Titicaca. About two-thirds are of pure indigenous stock, most of the rest are *mestizos*, or mixed Spanish and local descent, locally referred to as *cholos* and *cholas*. About 1 percent are of African heritage, and a fraction of pure European and Japanese descent.
Language Quechua, Aymará, Spanish and Guarani
Currency Boliviano = 100 centavos
Weights & measures Metric
Electricity 110 volts in La Paz, 220 volts elsewhere. Check first.
Time zone GMT 4hrs, EST 1hr
Dialing code 591 (La Paz +2)

Government & Economy

The president is elected by popular vote every four years under the 1967 constitution. The country is divided into nine departments, each controlled by a delegate appointed by the president. Millionaire Gonzalo Sanchez de Lozada was forced to resign as president in October 2003 after violent street protests. He was replaced by Carlos Mesa.
La Paz is the seat of the government and congress, although the supreme court sits in the small city of Sucre, the legal capital.
Bolivia is the poorest country in South America. More than half the population subsist on agriculture.

Until the collapse of prices in 1985, tin was the major export earner for the country. Today, Bolivia still mines gold, silver and zinc. Natural gas is exported. The biggest money-spinner is coca growing, which the government hopes to curb – it employs thousands of peasants and contributes an undetermined but significant sum to the official economy.

Visas

Citizens of the United States and most European countries do not need visas; Australians, New Zealanders and most Asians do. At the border, the guards will grant entry for between 30 and 90 days. The immigration office for visa extensions: Avda González 240. On departure, a US$20 tax is levied.

Money

Exchange your money in either banks or hotels as there is a lot of false currency in circulation. Ask for low-value Bolivian banknotes and only carry small amounts with you. Credit cards are not always accepted outside of major hotels and restaurants. Visa cash advances are possible from the Banco de La Paz in the capital.

Getting Around

From the Airport
El Alto, at some 4,060 meters (13,320 ft) above sea-level on the

Tour Agencies

Most tour companies offer trips all over the country. For information on trekking and lists of recommended mountaineering guides, contact: **Club Andino Boliviano**, Calle México 1638, tel: 2312 875.

For organized trekking and adventure tours, **Andes Expediciones**, Avda Camacho 1377, Edificio Saenz, 3rd floor, Oficina 1, La Paz, tel: 2319-655 is one specialist agency.

altiplano above La Paz, is the highest international airport in the world. Taxis to the center take about 30 minutes and cost US$8. **Cotranstur** minibuses also go to various points downtown, for about US50¢ (but allow about 1 hour because of all the drop-offs).

By Air
Domestic airlines LAB, TAM and AeroSur cover routes between most major towns and cities. Fares are comparatively cheap and, if time is short, it can be worthwhile to avoid a back-breaking bus journey, especially from La Paz to Potosí (on this route, it is necessary to fly to Sucre then take the four-hour bus journey to Potosí). **Crillon Tours** offers a comfortable minibus connection that can be arranged in La Paz – their office is at Avda Camacho 1223, tel: 236 1990.

By Bus
The bus network in Bolivia is well-developed, being the main form of public transportation for most Bolivians. The quality of service, however, depends on the conditions of roads (of which only some 5 percent are paved), and the terrain covered. Luxury services run between La Paz, Cochabamba and Santa Cruz; there are quite rough services to Potosí. A wide choice of services are available to Coroico and Copacabana. Toilet stops are few and far between, and the facilities very basic.

Most travelers enter Bolivia via Lake Titicaca in Peru. Many firms offer minibus connections between Puno and La Paz. Crillon Tours (see address above) offers a luxury hydrofoil service both ways across the lake, allowing a stopover on the Island of the Sun, a meal in Copacabana and drinks on the water – as well as a visit to the Museum of the Altiplano, with audio-visual displays, which gives an excellent introduction to Bolivia. If you are taking this route, make quite sure that you don't need to change buses at the border.

It is also possible to travel from Argentina by land, crossing the

Truck Transport

To really get off the beaten track, trucks are the standard transport in the Andes. These are usually dilapidated, high-sided vehicles, with only a tarpaulin to protect you from the elements. They are often used by locals going to market, so you are likely to share your space with sacks of fruit and vegetables, or livestock (and in some cases slaughtered carcasses too). Most trucks leave early in the morning, from the market areas; timetables are unreliable and fares highly variable (though usually about half the equivalent bus fare); best to ask locally. A Bolivian truck journey may not be the fastest, but will be an authentic experience to remember.

frontier at La Quiaca and continuing by bus or train – a slow but fascinating journey.

By Train
Trains run from La Paz to Oruro and Potosí. This is a long journey, so worth paying for a pullman seat if available. Tickets can be bought in advance but schedules change frequently and delays are common.

From Brazil, the so-called **Tren de la Muerte** (Death Train) comes up from Corumbá on the edge of the Pantanal to Santa Cruz. Tickets can be up to 50 percent cheaper at the station than from a travel agent, despite agents' scare tactics. It is advisable to get on the train as soon as it is possible to do so. The train is not particularly comfortable and can take anything from 12–40 hours to reach its destination.

There are train and bus links to and from Chile.

By Taxi
For longer distances within La Paz, taxis are probably the best way to get around, either privately to go anywhere in the city for about US$1.40, or caught as colectivos, sharing with passengers along a fixed route for about US25¢ each.

Medical Services

Make sure you have medical insurance that will provide you with private medical cover.

Major hotels have doctors on call. The **Clínica Alemana** in La Paz (Calle 6 de Agosto 2821, tel: 242 2302), and the **Clínica Americana**, Avda 14 de Septiembre, Obrajes, tel: 278 3500, are competent and well-run.

Business Hours

Most businesses function Mon–Fri 9am–noon and 2–6pm; banks generally close at 4.30pm.

Embassies/Consulates

Canada: Avda 20 de Octubre 2475, tel: 241 5021, www. boliviaembassy.ca
UK: (also representing New Zealand): Avda Arce Casi Campos 2732, tel: 243 3424, fax: 243 1073, www.britishembassy. gov.uk/bolivia
US: Avda Arce 2780, Consulate on Avda Potosí, tel: 243 0120, fax: 243 3900, lapaz.usembassy.gov.

Newspapers

In La Paz, you can choose from the conservative daily *El Diario*, the independent dailies *Hoy, Los Tiempos, Ultima Hora*, or *La Razon*, or the weekly, English-language publication the *Bolivia Times*. Other cities have their own local papers.

Postal Services

The main post office in La Paz is at Avda Mariscal Santa Cruz and Oruro, open Mon–Sat 8am–10pm, Sun 9am–noon. The outbound mail is quite efficient. The *poste restante (lista de correos)* keeps letters for three months.

Communications

Telephones
Telephone calls can be made by satellite to the United States and Europe. You can call from your hotel, which is the most expensive option, or the Entel offices in La Paz, Edificio Libertad, Calle Potosí and Ayacucho 267. Public telephones, found in all major cities, are the cheapest option. Phone cards can be bought in various denominations. All telephone numbers dialled nationally must be prefixed with the local dialling code: 2 (La Paz and Potosí); 3 (Santa Cruz and Panolo); or 4 (Cochabamba and Central region).

Internet
Internet access is widespread, although not always reliable. **Useful websites** include: www.bolivia.com, comprehensive information, in Spanish only. www.boliviaweb.com, tourist information in English. www.titicaca.com, created by Crillon tours; information in 4 languages.

Hotel Price Guide

Prices for a double room including continental breakfast.
$ = US$50 – inexpensive
$$ = US$50–100 – moderate
$$$ = US$100 plus – expensive

Where to Stay

La Paz
Presidente, Calle Potosí 920 and Sanjines, tel: 2367 193, fax: 2354 013. Situated downtown. Heated indoor pool, solarium, gymnasium, sauna, beauty parlour, conference facilities. **$$**
Radisson Plaza Hotel, Avda Arce 2177, tel: 244 1111, fax: 244 0402, www.radisson.com. North American hotel chain; traditional. **$$$**
Residencial Rosario, Calle Illampu 704, tel: 245 1658, fax: 245 1991, www.hotelrosario.com. Highly recommended; lovely colonial building, with a café and its own travel agency, running local tours and bus connections to Puno, Peru and Chile (*Turisbus*, tel: 245 1341, fax: 245 1911). **$**

Potosí
Hostal Colonial, Calle Hoyos 8, tel: 6224 809. Not great, but the best on offer. **$**
Hotel El Turista, Calle Lanza 19, tel: 6222 492. **$**

Sucre
Hostal Libertad, Calle Anicato Arce 99, tel: 6453 101. **$**
Colonial, Plaza 25 de Mayo 3, tel: 6454 709. **$**

Copacabana
La Capula, Calle Michel Pérez 1 3, tel: 862 2029, www.hotelcapula. com. Lovely hotel with a friendly atmosphere and distinctive Moorish-style architecture. **$**
Hotel Rosario del Lago, Calle Rigoberto Paredes/Avda Costanera, tel: 862 2141. Right on the lake and very attractive. **$**

What to Eat

Bolivian food varies by region. Lunch is the main meal of the day and many restaurants offer an *almuerzo completo* or three-course fixed menu. Staple foods of the highlands are potatoes, bread and rice. Meats are highly spiced. Trout from Lake Titicaca is excellent.

Where to Eat

La Paz
Casa del Corregidor, Calle Murillo 1040, tel: 363 633. International and local dishes. Folk music. **$$**
El Arriero, Avda 6 de Agosto 2535, tel: 232 2708. Claims to serve the best meat in the world. **$$$**
Los Escudos, Edificio Club de la Paz, tel: 322 028. Local food and live music. **$$**

Restaurant Guide

Prices for a three-course meal for two, including house wine.
$ = US$50 – inexpensive
$$ = US$50–100 – moderate
$$$ = US$100 plus – expensive

Hare Krishna, Pasaje Jauregui, 2262. Reasonably priced vegetarian food. Popular with travelers. **$**
Wagamama's, Pasaje Pinilla 2557, tel: 2434 911. Fish and sushi and other Japanese specialties. **$**

Potosí
El Mesón, Plaza 10 de Noviembre, tel: 6223 807. Historic restaurant, with wide-ranging menu. **$**

Sucre
Restaurant Sanga, Calle Tarapaca 161, tel: 64 22547. Recommended vegetarian food. **$**

Drinking Notes

The usual tea, coffee and soft drinks are readily available in restaurants and cafés, as is the *mate de coca* in tea bags.

Bolivian beer, brewed under German supervision, is surprisingly good. The favorite drink of everyday Bolivians is *chicha*, the potent maize liquor produced near Cochabamba. Keep in mind that altitude intensifies the effects of alcohol – both the intoxication and the hangover. Also remember that most Bolivians drink to get drunk.

Nightlife

La Paz has several *peñas* (folk clubs). Try the most popular, **Peña Naira**, on Calle Sagárnaga, tel: 2325 736, just above Plaza San Francisco, open every night, with a US$5 cover charge. Others are at the **Casa del Corregidor** and **Los Escudos** (*see Where to Eat section above*).

Where to Shop

The artisans' market in La Paz is on Calle Sagarnaga, between Mariscal Santa Cruz and Isaac Tamayo, and has a vast selection of craftwork. Most shopping takes place in markets. Vendors give a price and if buyers are not happy with it they are expected to offer an alternative.

Brazil
A – Z

Getting Acquainted

Area 8,512,000 sq. km (3,285,600 sq. miles)
Capital Brasília
Population 176 million. Over half the population are white or near-white, 11 percent are Afro-Brazilians and the rest are of mixed race.
Language Portuguese
Currency Real (plural, reais*)*
Weights & measures Metric
Electricity Mostly 127 volts; 220 volts in Brasília, Florianópolis, Fortaleza, Recife and São Luís; 110 volts in Manaus.
Time zone Major cities and eastern half of country GMT -3hrs (EST +2hrs); Mato Grosso and the north GMT -4hrs (EST +1hr); Acre and western Amazonas GMT -5hrs (EST).
Dialing code 55 (Brasília +61, Rio de Janeiro +21)

Government & Economy

Brazil is a federal republic with 27 states, each with its own legislature. The federal government exercises enormous control over the economy. The head of government is the president, who has extensive powers and exercises more control over the nation than the American president does over the USA. Luiz Inacio Lula da Silva became the country's first left-wing president for 40 years in 2002.

Brazil is almost self-sufficient in food production and is the world's largest producer of coffee. It has huge reserves of metals and minerals and has seen expansion in technology-based industries in recent decades. The gap between rich and poor is huge.

Visas

If Brazilians need a visa in advance to visit your country, you will need a visa in advance to visit Brazil. US citizens need to apply for a visa in advance; European Union citizens do not. Your airline or travel agent will be able to tell you if you need a visa; or contact a Brazilian consulate or embassy.

If you do not need a visa in advance, your passport will be stamped with a tourist visa upon entry. This usually permits you to remain in the country for 90 days. If you apply for a visa in advance, you have up to 90 days after the issue date to enter Brazil. Upon entry, you will get a tourist visa allowing you to stay in Brazil for up to 90 days.

Customs

You will be given a declaration form to fill out on the plane before arrival. Customs officials spot check half "nothing to declare" arrivals.

Money

ATM machines are found throughout Brazil, and major shopping areas usually accept Visa and MasterCard/ Cirrus cards. The two major banks that provide this service are HSBC and Banco do Brasil. Using ATMs is the easiest way to obtain foreign currency. You can exchange foreign currency at accredited banks, hotels and tourist agencies. If you can't find one of these, some travel agencies will exchange your currency, although this is, strictly speaking, an illegal transaction. The few hotels that exchange travelers' checks give a poor rate.

Boat Trips

Short sightseeing or day-long boat tours are available in cities located on the coast or on major rivers. Many towns have local ferry services across bays and rivers and to islands. Schooners and yachts, complete with crew, may be rented for an outing.

Banks will not exchange *reais* or travelers' checks into foreign currency. The only exception is the Banco do Brasil. You cannot get travelers' checks cashed into dollars.

Most hotels will accept travelers' checks and/or most major credit cards. Many restaurants and shops take credit cards. You can also pay with US dollars.

Holidays

January 1 New Year's Day (national holiday); Good Lord Jesus of the Seafarers (four-day celebration in Salvador da Bahía).
January 6 Epiphany (regional, mostly in the northeast).
January (3rd Sunday) *Festa do Bonfim* (Salvador da Bahía).
February 2 Iemanjá Festival in Salvador.
February/March (movable) Carnival (national holiday; celebrated all over Brazil on the four days leading up to Ash Wednesday. Most spectacular in Rio, Salvador and Recife/Olinda).
March/April (movable) Easter (Good Friday is a national holiday; Colonial Ouro Prêto puts on a colorful procession; passion play staged at Nova Jerusalem).
April 21 Tiradentes Day (national holiday in honor of the martyred hero of Brazil's independence – celebrations in his native Minas Gerais, especially Ouro Prêto).
May 1 Labor Day (national holiday).
May/June Corpus Christi (national holiday).
June/July *Festas Juninas* (a series of street festivals in honor of Saints John, Peter and Anthony, featuring bonfires, dancing and mock marriages).
June 15–30 Amazon Folk Festival (held in Manaus).
June/July *Bumba-Meu-Boi* (processions and street dancing in Maranhao).
September 7 Independence Day (national holiday)
October *Oktoberfest* in Blumenau (put on by descendants of German immigrants).
October 12 *Nossa Senhora de Aparecida* (national holiday honoring Brazil's patron saint).

November 2 All Souls' Day (national holiday).
November 15 Day of the Republic (national holiday, also election day).
December 25 Christmas Day (national holiday).
December 31 New Year's Eve (on Rio de Janeiro beaches, gifts are offered to Iemanjá).

Getting Around

From the Airport
Most visitors arrive at **Galeão International Airport** in Rio. There are official airport taxis, for which you pay a fixed rate in advance according to your destination (approximately US$35 to Copacabana, for instance). If you take a regular taxi, check out the fares posted for the official taxis so that you will have an idea of what is a normal rate. There are also regular air-conditioned **Alvoradas** buses, which leave from the 1st floor of the arrivals building, stopping at the city bus station and all central districts. A tax of US$36, paid in local currency, is levied on international flights.

By Air
Brazil has a good network of domestic flights. Recent deregulation means that as well as established companies such as Varig, TAM, Rio-Sul, Transbrasil, and Vasp, there are also budget airlines such as Gol, BRA and Trip. Rio-Sul and Nordeste are both part of Varig. All of the larger lines fly extensive routes throughout the country and have ticket counters at the airports and ticket offices in most cities. At smaller airports in the more remote cities, these may only be manned shortly before a flight.

There is a 30 percent discount for night flights *(vôo econômico or vôo noturno)* with departures between 10pm and 6am.

Transbrasil, Vasp and Varig also offer air passes which must be bought outside Brazil. Ask your travel agent about these – they are a good deal if you plan to travel extensively within Brazil.

The large airlines also cooperate

in a shuttle service between Rio and São Paulo (with flights every half hour), Rio and Brasília (flights every hour) and Rio and Belo Horizonte (usually about 10 flights per day). Although you may be lucky, a reservation is a good idea.

By Bus
Comfortable and punctual bus services are available between all major cities, and to several other South American cities, including Asunción (Paraguay), Buenos Aires (Argentina), Montevideo (Uruguay) and Santiago (Chile). While it is a good way to see the countryside, distances are huge, you sit in a bus for several days and nights, and the landscape is not continuously fascinating. Nevertheless, buses on longer routes will stop for meals at regular intervals. Also, some luxury *(leito)* overnight services are available between large cities that include on-board service and blankets. On some routes, there may be just one bus per day (such as the Rio–Belém route, a 52-hour trip) or just one or two per week.

By City Bus
The larger cities have special air-conditioned buses connecting residential areas to the central business district, including routes from airports and bus stations, that pass by many of the larger hotels. You will be handed a ticket as you get on. Take a seat and an attendant will come around to collect your fare.

Regular city buses are entered through the back door (often quite a high step up) and after paying the *cobrador*, who will give you change, you move through the turnstile.

Theft is common on crowded buses, particularly in Rio and São Paulo, even in daylight. Avoid the rush hour when passengers are packed tight. Don't carry valuables, keep shoulder bags in front of you and your camera inside a bag. Avoid attracting attention by speaking loudly in a foreign language.

City Rio has three bus routes aimed specifically to help visitors. Color coded – blue, orange and lilac

– the air-conditioned tourist buses cover most of the city's main attractions and points of interest, and tourists can get on and off the bus as many times as they like. Tickets valid for 24 hours can be purchased.

By Subway

Rio and Sâo Paul both have good, although not extensive, subway services. Lines radiate from the city centers and are extended by bus links. Maps in the station mean you can find your way without needing Portuguese.

By Boat

Local boat tours and excursions are available in coastal and riverside cities. There are also options for longer trips.

Amazon River boat trips last from a day up to a week or more. These range from luxury floating hotels to more rustic accommodations. Boat trips can be taken on the São Francisco River in the northeast and in the Pantanal marshlands of Mato Grosso, popular for wildlife safaris and for angling. The Blue Star Line will take passengers on its freighters which call at several Atlantic coast ports. Linea C and Oremar have cruises out of Rio which stop along the Brazilian coast on the way down to Buenos Aires or up to the Caribbean. Book well in advance for the longer trips.

By Rail

Except for crowded urban commuter railways, trains are not a major form of transportation in Brazil and rail links are minimal. There are a few train trips, which are tourist attractions in themselves, either because they are so scenic or because they run on antique steam-powered equipment.

In the southern state of Paraná, the Curitiba–Paranaguá railroad is famous for spectacular mountain scenery. A return trip can be done in a day. Bear in mind that you may not see much on a cloudy day.

In Minas Gerais, antique steam locomotives haul passengers between São João del Rei and Tiradentes on Friday, weekends and holidays. In the state of Rio de Janeiro, the Mountain Steam Train runs between Miguel Pereira and Conrado every Sunday.

By Taxi

Taxis are the best way for visitors to get around. Radio taxis are slightly more expensive, but safer and more comfortable. In major cities, there are two metered rates. Rate 2 is higher and charged after 9pm and on weekends. Make sure the driver puts the meter on and charges the right rate. Some drivers try to make money from tourists by refusing to put the meter on. If a driver tries to agree a fixed fare, he is proably overcharging you. Insist on the meter being used, or take another cab.

By Car

Car rental facilities are available in the larger cities. Both **Avis** and **Hertz** operate in Brazil; www.avis.com, tel: 0800 198 456 or www.hertz.com, tel: 0800 701 7300 toll-free. The two largest Brazilian national chains are: **Localiza**, www.localiza.com.br; and **Nobre**, www.nobre.com.br. There are also good local companies. You can rent a car with your regular driver's license. For a relatively modest additional fee you can hire a driver with the car.

If you plan to drive a lot in Brazil, buy the excellent *Quatro Rodas* (Four Wheels) *Guia Brasil*, complete with road maps, city and regional itineraries, and hotel and restaurant listings (in Portuguese), available at most newsstands.

Speeding fines can be huge (several hundred dollars).

Medical Services

If you need a doctor while you are in Brazil, the hotel you are staying at should be able to recommend reliable professionals. Many of the better hotels even have a doctor on duty. Your consulate will be able to supply you with a list of physicians who speak your language. In Rio de Janeiro, the English-speaking **Rio**

Health Collective, Avda das Américas 4430, Sala 303, Tijucate, tel: 021 325 9300, Extension 44, runs a 24-hour referral service.

Check with your health insurance company before traveling – some insurance plans will cover any medical service that you may require while abroad.

Business Hours

Business hours for offices in most cities are Mon–Fri 9am–6pm. Lunch time closures may last hours.

Banks open Mon–Fri 10am–3pm. Currency exchange houses usually operate 9am–5.30pm.

Media

The *Miami Herald*, the Latin America edition of the *International Herald Tribune* and the *Wall Street Journal* are available on many newsstands in the big cities, as are a selection of international weekly magazines.

Postal Services

Post offices generally open Mon–Fri 9am–5pm, Sat 9am–1pm. In large cities, some branch offices stay open until later. The post office in the Rio de Janeiro International Airport is open 7am–8pm.

Communications

Telephones

Pay phones in Brazil use phone cards *(cartão de telefone)*, which are sold at newsstands, bars or shops.

An orange sidewalk *telefone público* is for local or collect calls; blue is for direct-dial long-distance calls within Brazil.

All standard telephone numbers in the country are changing from seven to eight digits. This process has been completed in Rio, but will continue in the rest of the country until 2005. Your hotel or a tourist office should be able to clarify matters for you.

Internet

Brazil is very well connected with Internet services, and Internet cafés are found throughout the country. Connections tend to be slower and more expensive away from major cities. While much of the web content on Brazil is in Portuguese, major websites offer pages in English.

Useful Websites

In Brazilian only:
Brazilian Government
www.brazil.gov.br
Estado de Sâo Paulo
(newspaper/links)
www.estado.com.br
O Globo (newspaper/links)
www.oglobo.com.br

Tourist Information

Brazil's national tourism board, Embratur, has offices all over the world. To obtain information, contact Rua Mariz e Barros 13, Rio de Janeiro, 20270, Brazil, tel: 021 273 2212, fax: 021 273 9290, www.embratur.gov.br.

Each state has its own tourism bureau. The principal offices are:
Manaus: Emamtur, Rua Tarumã 379, tel: 092 234 5642, www.visitamazonas.com.br. Information Center: Airport.
Rio de Janeiro: Riotur, Rua da Assembleia 10, 8–9th floors, tel: 021 297 7117/242 8000; Flumitur, Rua da Assembleia 10, 8th floor, tel: 021 398 4077, www.rioconventionbureau.com.br. Information Centers: International Airport, Bus Station, Corcovado, Sugar Loaf, Cinelândia Subway Station, Marina da Gloria.
Salvador: Bahiatursa, Loteamento Jardim Armação, Centro de Convenção da Bahia, tel: 071 371 1522/230 3159, www.bahia.com.br. Information Centers: Airport, Bus Station, Mercado Modelo, Porto da Barra.
São Paulo: Anhembi Centro de Feiras e Congressos, Avda Olvavo Fontoura, 1209, tel: 011 267 2122. Cebitur, Avda Brigadeiro Faria Lima 1323, São Paulo, www.spcvb.com.br. Information Centers: Praça da República; Praça da Liberdade; Praça Ramos de Azevedo; Avda Paulista, corner of Rua Augusta; Shopping Center Morumbi; Shopping Center Ibirapuera.

Embassies/Consulates

Canada: Brasília: SES, Avda das Nações Unidas 16, Quadra 803, Lote 16, s1. 130, tel: 061 321 2171. São Paulo: Avda das Nações Unidas 12901, 16th floor, Torre Norte, tel: 550 94321.
UK: Brasília: SES, Sector de Embaixadas Sul, Quadra 801 Conjunto K, tel: 061 225 2710. Rio de Janeiro: Praia do Flamengo 284, 2nd floor, tel: 021 2555 9600. São Paulo: Rua Ferreira de Araújo 741, 2nd floor, Pinheiros, tel: 011 3816 2303. Also see www.reinounido.org.br/
US: Brasília: Avda das Nações Unidas, Quadra 801, Lote 3, tel: 061 312 7000. Rio de Janeiro: Avda Pres. Wilson, 147, tel: 024 2292 7117. São Paulo: Rua Padre João Manoel 933 (Jardim America), tel: 011 3081 6511, www.embaixada-americana.org.br.

Where to Stay

Tourist offices provide comprehensive lists of hotels. This listing features mainly upscale hotels.

Rio de Janeiro (City)

Caesar Park, Avda Vieira Souto 460, Ipanema, tel: 2525 2525, www.caesarpark-rio.com. Slick and well located in Ipanema. **$$$**
Copacabana Palace, Avda Atlântica 1702, Copacabana, tel: 2548 7070, fax: 2235 7330, www. copacabanapalace.com.br. Exquisite 1920s hotel; the best in town. **$$$**
Intercontinental Rio, Rua Perfeito Mendes de Morais, São Conrado, tel: 3323 2200, fax: 3322 5500. Polished and upmarket. **$$$**
Ipanema Inn, Rua Maria Quitéria 27, Ipanema, tel: 2523 6092, fax: 2511 5092. Great location; mid-range. **$$**
Meridien, Avda Atlântica 1020, Leme, tel: 3873 8888, fax: 3873 8777, www.meridien-br.com. Smart, international option. **$$$**

Hotel Price Guide

Prices for a double room including continental breakfast.
$ = US$50 – inexpensive
$$ = US$50–100 – moderate
$$$ = US$100 plus – expensive

São Paulo (City)

Caesar Park, Rua Augusta 1508/20, Cerqueira Cesar, tel: 3371 3000, fax: 3287 1123, www.caesarpark.com.br. Executive hotel. **$$$**
Maksoud Plaza, Alameda Campinas 150, Bela Vista, tel: 3145 8000, www.maksoud.com.br. One of the best hotels in the city. **$$$**
San Michel, Largo do Arouche 200, tel: 3223 4433, fax: 3221 5131. Recommended budget hotel. **$**

Brasília

Brasília Carlton, Setor Hoteleiro Sul, Quadra 5, Bloco G, tel: 224 8819, fax: 226 8109, www. carltonhotelbrasilia.com.br. Good facilities. **$$$**
Hotel Diplomat, Setor Hoteleiro Norte, Quadra 2, Bloco L, tel/fax: 326 2010. Good value. **$$**

Belo Horizonte

Belo Horizonte Othon Palace, Avda Afonso Pena, 1050, Centro, tel: 3273 3844, fax: 3212 2318, www.othon.com.br. Spacious rooms; overlooks the park in the center of town. **$$$**

Salvador da Bahia

Bahia Othon Palace, Avda Oceânica 2456, Ondina, tel: 071 203 2000, fax: 071 245 4877, www.othon. com.br.. One of the best hotels in town. **$$**
Hotel Palace, Rua Chile 20, tel: 071 322 1155, fax: 071 243 1109. Comfortable and good value. **$$**
Mercure, Rua Fonte do Boi 215, tel: 330 8200. Newly opened in Rio Vermelho. **$$**

Olinda

Pousada dos Quatro Cantos, Rua Prudente de Morais 441, tel: 081 3429 0220, fax: 081 3429 1845. Beautiful old building. **$$**

Recife

Hotel do Sol, Avda Boa Viagem 978, Tel: 081 3091 0991, www.hsol.com.br. Reasonable prices; located on the beach. **$$**

Recife Palace Lucsim, Avda Boa Viagem 4070, tel: 3465 6688, fax: 3465 6767, www.lucsimhotels.com.br. Luxurious, with sea views. **$$$**

Manaus

Ana Cássia Palace, Rua dos Andradas 14, Centro, tel: 622 3637, fax: 622 4812. Swimming pool and sauna. **$$$**

Manaós, Avda Eduardo Ribeiro 881, Centro, tel: 092 633 5744, fax: 092 232 4443. Next to Teatro Amazonas. **$$**

Tropical Manaus, Praia de Ponta Negra, tel: 659 5000, fax: 658 5026. Reservations, tel: 0800 150 006. Great situation in private park 12km (7 miles) from center. **$$$**

What to Eat

A country as diverse as Brazil naturally has regional specialties, a result of varying geography, climate and immigration patterns. In parts of the south, the cuisine reflects the influence of a German community, while Italian and Japanese immigrants brought their skills to São Paulo. Some of the most traditional dishes are adapted from African or Portuguese foods.

Brazil's National Dish

Considered to be Brazil's national dish (although not found in all parts of the country), *feijoada* consists of black beans simmered with a variety of dried, salted and smoked meats. Originally made out of odds and ends to feed slaves, nowadays the tail, ears, feet, etc. of a pig are thrown in. *Feijoada* for lunch on Saturday has become somewhat of an institution in Rio de Janeiro, where it is served complete with white rice, finely shredded *couve* (kale), *farofa* (manioc root meal toasted with butter) and sliced oranges.

The staples for many Brazilians, however, are rice, beans and manioc. Although not a great variety of herbs is used, Brazilian food is tastily seasoned. Many Brazilians enjoy hot pepper *(pimenta)*, and the local *malagueta* chilis can be infernally fiery or pleasantly nippy, depending on how they're prepared.

The most unusual Brazilian food is found in Bahia, where a distinct African influence can be tasted in the *dendê* palm oil and coconut milk. The Bahianos are fond of pepper, and many dishes call for ground raw peanuts or cashew nuts and dried shrimp. Two of the most famous Bahian dishes are *vatapá* (fresh and dried shrimp, fish, ground raw peanuts, coconut milk, *dendê* oil and seasonings thickened with bread into a creamy mush); and *moqueca* (seafood in a *dendê* oil and coconut milk sauce). Although delicious, note that the palm oil as well as the coconut milk can be a rich mixture to digest.

Popular all over Brazil is the *churrasco* or barbecue. Most *churrascarias* offer a *rodizio* option: for a set price diners eat all they can of a variety of meats.

Dishes found in the Amazon include those prepared with *tucupi* (made from manioc leaves and having a slightly numbing effect on the tongue), especially *pato no tucupi* (duck) and *tacacá* broth. There are also many varieties of fruit that are found nowhere else. The rivers produce many fish, including piranha.

Drinking Notes

Brazilians are great social drinkers and love to sit for hours talking and often singing with friends over drinks. Brazilian beers are really very good (note that *cerveja* usually refers to bottled beer; draft beer is *chope*).

Brazil's own unique brew is *cachaça*, a strong liquor distilled from sugar cane, a type of rum, but with its own distinct flavor. Each region has its locally produced *cachaça*, also called *pinga*, *cana* or *aguardente*. Some delightful mixed drinks are concocted with *cachaça*. Tops is the popular *caipirinha*. It's

Coffee Stop

Café is roasted dark, ground fine, prepared strong and taken with plenty of sugar. Coffee mixed with hot milk (*café com leite*) is the traditional breakfast beverage throughout Brazil. Other than at breakfast, it is served black in tiny *demitasse* cups (there are even little stand-up bars that serve only these small coffees, *cafezinho*).

really a simple concoction of *cachaça*, crushed lime – peel included – and sugar topped with plenty of ice. Some bars and restaurants mix their *caipirinhas* sweeter than you may want – order yours *com pouco açucar* (with a small amount of sugar) or even *sem açucar* (without sugar).

Where to Eat

Lunchtime is usually noon–3 pm, although some restaurants stay open all afternoon. For locals, this is the heaviest meal of the day. Dinner is 7pm–midnight (locals tend to eat late), but some restaurants stay open until 1 or 2am. Many restaurants in Brazil are closed Sunday evening and/or Monday, so check before setting out. At the more expensive restaurants, it is advisable to make reservations.

A portion is usually for two people. It is perfectly acceptable to ask for a doggy bag.

Comida a kilo restaurants (literally meaning food by weight) are great, cheap places to get a wide choice of usually good quality dishes. Because you help yourself you can sample foods you would not otherwise order and you are not limited by your level of Portuguese. *Lanchonetes* are snack bars.

The following is a small selection of places to eat in the main cities.

Rio de Janeiro

Casa da Feijoada, Rua Prudente de Morais 10, Loja B, Ipanema, tel: 2247 2776. Specializes in Brazil's favorite dish. **$$**

Contemporâneo, Rua Paul Redfern 37, Ipanema; tel: 2512 9494. Eclectic, contemporary cuisine. **$$**

Confeitaria Colombo, Rua Gonçalves Dias 32 (Center), tel: 2232 2300. Worth a visit for the fantastic art nouveau decor. Afternoon teas a specialty. **$**

Grottamare, Rua Gomes Carneiro 132, Ipanema, tel: 2523 1596. Popular and busy seafood restaurant. Mon–Fri dinner only, Sat–Sun lunch and dinner. **$$**

São Paulo
Arabia, Rua Haddock Lobo 1397, tel: 3061 2203. Wonderful Lebanese food. **$$**

Cheiro Verde, Rua Peixoto Gomide 1413, tel: 289 6853. Cheap and cheerful vegetarian restaurant. **$**

Fasano, Rua Vittorio Fasano 88, tel: 3896 4000. One of the best Italian restaurants in South America. **$$$**

Koyama, Rua 13 de Maio 1050, Bela Vista, tel: 283 1833. Excellent Japanese food in traditional surroundings. **$$**

Brasília
Antigamente, Setor de Clubes Esportivos Sul Trecho 4, Conjunto 5, tel: 316 6967. Open daily for lunch, except Monday. Typical Brazilian food in a beautiful building that is also a cultural and antiques center. **$$**

Vila Borghese, Comércio Local Sul, Quadra, 201, Bloco A, lj.33, tel: 226 5650. Open daily for good Italian food. **$$**

Salvador
Barbacoa, Avda Tancredo Neves 909, Pituba, tel: 342 4666. Open daily. One of the best barbecue houses in Salvador. **$.**

Trapiche Adelaide, Praça dos Tupinambas 2, Avda do Contorno,

Restaurant Guide

Prices for a three-course meal for two, including house wine.
$ = US$50 – inexpensive
$$ = US$50–100 – moderate
$$$ = US$100 plus – expensive

tel: 326 2211. International cuisine in a wonderful location right by the main bay. **$$$**

Recife
Bargaço, Avda Boa Viagem 670, tel: 3465 1847. On the sea front; seafood a specialty. **$$$**

Oficina do Sabor, Rua do Amparo 355, tel: 3429 3331. Award-winning and one of the best in town. **$$$**

Belem
Lá em Casa/O Outro
Avda Governador José Malcher 247, Nazaré, tel: 223 1212. Delicious Amazonian specialties, including ice cream made from tropical fruits. **$$**

Manaus
Paramazon, Rua Santa Isabel 1176 (Cachoeirinha), tel: 233 7768. Typical Amazonian dishes. **$$**

Music and Dance

Brazil is famous internationally for its music, and has exerted great influence on musical styles abroad, especially jazz. It is easy to buy Brazilian music abroad, but there is much more to discover on-the-spot.

A huge variety of musical forms have developed in different parts of the country, many with accompanying forms of dance. **Bossa nova**, **samba**, **choro** and **seresta** are popular in Rio and São Paulo, for example. And if you are visiting at Carnival, you'll see and hear plenty of music and dancing in the streets, mostly samba in Rio and *frevo* in the northeast. There are also shows all year long designed to give tourists a taste of Brazilian folk music and dance.

The classical music and dance season runs from Carnival through mid-December. Major Brazilian cities (mainly Rio, São Paulo and Brasília) are included in world concert tours by international performers. One of the most important classical music festivals in South America takes place in July each year in Campos do Jordáo in the state of São Paulo.

Chile
A – Z

Getting Acquainted

Area 756,626 sq. km (292,134 sq. miles)
Capital Santiago de Chile
Population 16 million, 90 percent of whom are *mestizo*.
Language Spanish
Currency Peso
Weights & measures Metric
Electricity 220 volts
Time zone GMT -4hrs, EST +1hr
Dialing code 56 (Santiago +2)

Government & Economy

Chile had a military dictatorship with an horrendous human rights record until 1990, when a peaceful transfer of power to a civilian government took place. Socialist Party leader Ricardo Lagos was elected president in 2000.

Chile is a stable country with a solid free-market economy. Main exports are copper, fish, fruit, paper, and chemicals.

Visas

Passports and tourist cards only are required by citizens of Australia, Canada, Ireland, South Africa, the UK, and the USA. Citizens of New Zealand need a visa. Tourist cards valid for 90 days are issued upon arrival (Australian and North American nationals will be charged for this), and can be renewed for a further 90 days for a small fee at the immigration office on Calle Moneda in Santiago. To stay longer than 180 days, go to a border country and return – a quicker method than the bureaucratic application procedure.

Embassies/Consulates

Australia: Calle Gertrudis Echenique 420, tel: 228 5065.
Canada: Calle Nueva Tajamar 481, Torre Sur, 12th floor, Santiago, tel: 362-9660, fax: 362-9665, www.maeci.gc.ca.
New Zealand: El Golf 99, Office 703. Tel: 290 9802.
South Africa: Avda 11 de Septiembre 2353, 17th floor, tel: 231 2862, www.embajada-sudafrica.cl.
UK: El Bosque Norte 0125, 3rd floor, Santiago, tel: 370 4100, fax: 3335 5988, www.britemb.cl.
US: Avda Andrés Bello 2800, Santiago, tel 232-2600, fax: 330-3710, www. usembassy.cl.

Customs

Bags may be searched for agricultural products that may harbor disease, so food should be eaten or disposed of.

Clearance at border posts inland can be a bit more cumbersome: bags here are thoroughly searched for agricultural products, and contraband searches are more frequent. Still, delays are not that long.

Money

Changing money on the streets is not advisable anywhere.

ATMs, called *Redbanc*, are prolific, even in quite small towns. They accept some major credit cards and some bank cards, although not in remote areas. Hotels, restaurants and shops generally take most credit cards. Major banks, bureaux de change and hotels will change dollar travelers' checks, and some shops and restaurants also accept them, albeit for a large fee.

US dollars are the most easily exchanged unit of currency throughout Chile.

Getting Around

From the Airport

Santiago's main airport for international and domestic flights is

Arturo Merino Benítez Airport, at Pudahuel, 17 km (11 miles) from the city. It is relatively small and customs procedures are quick and easy. There are frequent buses from the airport for about US$1.30; and the "Delfos" shuttle bus, which costs around US$12. A taxi should cost about US$30 to the center of town, but agree a price before starting your journey.

A tax of around US$20 is charged on arrival in Chile by air. If you fly out of the country you must pay an exit tax of about US$18.25. Domestic flights charge around US$8 tax.

By Air

Flying long distances in Chile can be very cheap if you take advantage of last-minute offers. **LanChile** and its subsidiary **LanExpress**, as well as Peru's **Aero Continente**, operate domestic flights. LanChile has a **national booking service** (tel: 526 2000 from Santiago; tel: 600 526 2000 from the rest of the country). For Aero Continente, call 242 4242 from Santiago or 02 242 4242 from the rest of the country.

By Bus

Chile's private intercity bus service is excellent and inexpensive. Roads are well maintained and buses are new, comfortable, and run on time. In Santiago, do check carefully which terminal your bus leaves from, as there are several, all on the main underground line. Bus termini are: Buses Norte: Amunategui 920, tel: 671 2141; Los Héroes: Roberto Pretot 21, tel: 696 9250; Santiago: Avda L. Bernardo O'Higgins 3800, tel: 779 1385; Alameda: Avda L Bernardo O'Higgins 3794, tel: 776 1023. During off-peak times, you can bargain for a cheaper fare; always ask before you pay full fare.

Santiago's chaotic bus system is privately owned. Fares are cheap, but the system is difficult to use. The best way to find your bus is to look for the street on the marquee in the terminal or ask the driver.

To and from Argentina: a number of bus companies go to Argentina from Antofagasta, Santiago,

Osorno, and Punta Arenas. The main services are Cata, Tas-Choapa and El Rápido. A single ticket from Santiago to Mendoza costs around US$14 and Santiago to Buenos Aires around US$45. Pluma buses operate throughout Brazil.

By Train

Chile has a passenger rail network stretching from Ollagüe (and on to Bolivia) in the north to its southern railhead in Puerto Montt. Most of the system is state owned, trains are fairly punctual, fares are reasonably priced (with some student discounts), but meals on board are expensive. Train timetables can be obtained and bookings made at Estación Central, Alameda 3170, tel: 376 8500; Estación Metro Universidad de Chile, Local 10, tel: 688 3284; Providencia Agencia de Turismo Traveller Zone, Paseo Las Palmas 2229, local 18, tel: 946 1835

International routes: there are four lines linking with neighboring countries: two to La Paz, Bolivia – via Arica or from Antofagasta via Calama; one from Arica to Tacna, Peru; and one from Antofagasta to Salta, Argentina.

Santiago Metro: three lines cross the city and provide fast, safe and inexpensive access to most places of interest. Trains run Mon–Sat 6.30am–10.30pm, and Sun and holidays 8am–10.30pm. Fares vary according to the time of day; the simplest option is to buy a *boleto valor* – a low-cost charge card, which deducts the fare for each journey automatically.

Public Holidays

- **January** 1 (New Year's Day)
- **March/April** Easter
- **May** 1, 21 (Navy Day)
- **June** 25
- **July** 2
- **August** 15 (Assumption)
- **September** 3, 11, 18 and 19 (Independence Day)
- **October** 12 (Columbus Day), 15
- **November** 1 (All Saints' Day)
- **December** 8 (Immaculate Conception), 25 (Christmas Day)

Hitchhiking

Hitchhiking in Chile is relatively safe, except for women on their own, and relatively easy. Truckers will pick you up sometimes, but motorists are reluctant to stop, so don't depend on it. Traffic is sparse in isolated regions.

By Taxi

Black taxis with yellow roofs can be found at taxi ranks or can be flagged down in the street, and all run on meters. Tipping the driver is not customary.

Collective taxis (colectivos) have a fixed route similar to buses and may carry up to five passengers. The fare is displayed on the windshield. Tourist taxis are blue, but while in better condition than regular taxis, are more expensive and do not run on a meter. They can be found in front of hotels.

Emergencies

The police (carabineros) patrol regularly. They are friendly, generally helpful and do not expect to receive money for their assistance.

Call 133 for police, 131 for Ambulance, 132 for Fire Brigade.

There are several good hospitals in Santiago, such as Clínica Las Condes, Calle Lo Fontecilla 441, emergency tel: 800 211800/ 2105150, Clínica Santa María, Avda Santa María 0410, tel: 461 3000; and Clínica Aleman, Avda Vitacura 5951, tel: 212 9700. Contact your embassy for a list of physicians.

Business Hours

Business hours change from city to city. In Santiago: they are as follows: Mon–Fri. 9am–1.30pm, 2.30–6.30pm. Banks open Mon–Fri 9am–2pm. Exchange houses generally open Mon–Fri 9am–6pm, and Sat am.

Newspapers

There are several independent dailies such as El Mercurio, La Tercera and La Segunda. For business and finance read Diario Financiero and Estrategia. International newspapers are readily available.

Postal Services

Most post offices open Mon–Fri 9am–5pm, and Sat until noon. The system is fairly reliable. Poste Restante (Lista de Correos) in Santiago is in the main post office in the Plaza de Armas.

Telephones

Coin-operated public phones for local and international calls are prolific in the cities, and some take credit cards. The main phone companies have offices in most cities. Buy a pre-paid card so you can call from any phone booth.

Where to Stay

There is a high standard of hotels in Chile, especially in the main cities. Recommended places in the major tourist areas include:

Santiago

Hotel Caribe, Calle San Martin 851, tel: 696 6681. Friendly; high-ceilinged rooms; clean communal showers. $
Hotel Carrera, Calle Teatinos 180, tel: 698 2011, fax: 672 1083, www.carrera.cl. Santiago's most traditional luxury hotel, overlooking the presidential palace. $$$
Hotel Foresta, Calle Victor Subercaseaux 353, tel: 639 6261, fax: 632 2996. A beautiful place overlooking Santa Lucía Park. $
Hotel Los Españoles, Calle Los Españoles 2539, tel: 232 1824, fax: 233 1048. Classy, quiet establishment, near shopping and restaurant district. $$
Residencial Londres, Calle Londres 54, tel: 633 9192, fax: 638 2215. Good atmosphere. Single rooms available. $
Hotel Santa Lucía, Calle Huérfanos 779, 4th floor, tel: 639 8201, fax: 633 1844. Cheap, clean and cheerful. $

Santiago Hostelling International, Calle Cienfuegos 151, tel: 671 8532, fax: 672 8880, near the Los Héroes underground station. $
Vegas Hotel, Calle Londres 49, tel: 632 2498, fax: 632 5084. Colonial charm in a clean and friendly place with large rooms. $

Viña del Mar

Cap Ducal, Avda Marina 51, tel: 626 655, fax: 665 478. The best seafront view, with an excellent but expensive restaurant. $$
Hotel Español, Plaza Vergara 191, tel: 685 145, fax: 685 146. Reasonable-value hotel. $$
Garden Hotel, Calle Serrano 501, tel: 252 777. Decent rooms.$$
Hotel O'Higgins, Plaza Vergara s/n, tel: 882 016, fax: 883 537. Viña's famous grand hotel. $$
Residencial Victoria, Calle Valparaíso 40, tel: 977 370. Large and characterful place, opposite the railway station. $$

Valparaíso

Hotel Brighton, Pasaje Atkinson 151, tel: 223 513, fax: 598 802. Overlooking the bay. Excellent value, but booking is essential, as the hotel only has 6 rooms. $$

Arica

Hotel Americano, Calle General Lagos 571, tel: 257 752, fax: 252 150, www.hotel-americano.cl. Popular with business travelers. $$
Hotel El Paso, Calle General Velásquez 1109, tel/fax: 231 965. Quiet, with swimming pool and tennis courts. $$
Hotel Lynch, Calle Patricio Lynch 589, tel: 251 959, fax: 231 581. Inexpensive. $
Residencial La Blanquita, Calle Maipú 472, tel: 232 064. Basic, but with clean rooms and good hot showers. $.

Hotel Price Guide

Prices for a double room including continental breakfast.
$ = US$50 – inexpensive
$$ = US$50–100 – moderate
$$$ = US$100 plus – expensive

Savona, Calle Yungay 380, tel: 232 319, fax: 231 606. Quiet and comfortable and it has a laundry. **$**.

Puerto Montt
Colón Apart Hotel, Calle Pedro Montt 65, tel: 264 290, fax: 264 293. Modern seafront hotel with self-catering suites. **$$**
Hotel Montt, Calle Antonio Varas 301, tel: 253 651, fax: 253 652. **$$**.
Hotel Vientosur, Calle Ejército 200, tel/fax: 258 701. **$$**.
Hotel Vicente Pérez Rosales, Calle Antonio Varas 447, tel: 252 571, fax: 255 473. **$$**

Castro
Hotel Unicornio Azul, Avda Pedro Montt 228, tel: 632 359, fax: 632 808. Don't miss this delightful and inexpensive hotel. A good base to see the best of Chiloé Island. **$**

Easter Island
Hotel Hanga Roa, Avda Pont, tel: 100 299. Expensive, as are nearly all on the island, but the most luxurious. **$$$**
Rapa Nui Inn, Avda Atamu Tekena s/n, tel: 100 228. Comfortable, with local hospitality. **$$**

What to Eat

It's not unusual to have three or four meals a day in Chile. Lunch is the main meal, and restaurants have lunch menus for as little as US$4. It starts with a simple salad, followed by a hot bowl of *cazuela* or soup with meat, chicken or seafood, or *empanadas* (pastries stuffed with meat, onions, a boiled egg and a couple of olives). In summer don't miss *humitas*, seasoned puréed corn wrapped in corn leaves, or *pastel de choclo*, a corn and meat pie. Seafood is a

Restaurant Guide

Prices for a three-course meal for two, including house wine.
$ = US$20 – inexpensive
$$ = US$20–50 – moderate
$$$ = US$50–70 – expensive

Drinking Notes

Wine is by far the best alcoholic drink in Chile. *Undurraga, Concha y Toro, Carmen, Santa Rita*, and *Pirque San Pedro* are among the more famous names. They are all worth sampling and most are inexpensive *(see page 284 for more details)*.

favorite in Chile. Try *jaiva* (crab) or *locos* (abalone). The main course usually consists of rice and chicken, meat or fried fish. Dessert is followed by a cup of instant coffee.

At night, sandwiches are popular fare: Chile is famous for its *churrasco* (steak sandwich with avocado), *chacarero* (steak with green beans), or *completos* (hot dogs with tomatoes, avocado and mayonnaise).

Where to Eat

Santiago
For good, inexpensive eating, try the Bellavista neighborhood, where there are numerous places along Calles Pio Nono, Constitución and Antonio López de Bello. Watch your belongings.
Aquí Está Coco, Calle La Concepción 236, tel: 235 8649. Not cheap, but by far the best place in Santiago to sample Chile's wonderful fish. **$$$**
Café del Patio, Avda Providencia 1640-A, Local 8, tel: 236 1251. Organic vegetarian café that also serves drinks until 2am. **$**
El Caramaño, Calle Purísima 257, tel: 737 7043. Traditional Chilean dishes at very reasonable prices. **$**
El Huerto, Calle Orrego Luco 054, tel: 233 2690. Excellent vegetarian food. **$**
El Otro Sitio, Calle Antonia López de Bello 53, tel: 777 3059. Some of the most reliable Peruvian food available in Santiago. **$$**
El Parrón, Calle Providencia 1184, tel: 251 8911. One of the most traditional places to eat barbecued meat. **$$**

La Tasca Mediterránea, Calle Purísima 141, tel: 735 3901. Reasonably priced Spanish seafood in a Mediterranean atmosphere. **$**
Mikado, Calle Francisco Bilbao 1933, tel: 225 2947. High-class Japanese restaurant. **$$$**
Rivoli, Calle Nueva de Lyon 77, tel: 231 7969. Good, well-priced Italian food. Outdoor seating in summer. **$**
If you are near the downtown Mercado Central at lunchtime, go to **Donde Augusto** for fish and shellfish and lots of atmosphere. **$**

Valparaíso
El Bote Salvavidas, Muelle Prat (overlooking the port) for *caldillo de congrio* or other typical seafood dishes.
Café Turri, Calle Templeman 147, Cerro Concepción, with its marvellous view over the bay, is best reached by the Ascensor Concepción.

Viña del Mar
For cheap meals, it is best to eat sandwiches and *platos del día* at Viña's innumerable cafés. **Cap Ducal**, the city's most famous waterfront restaurant, serves excellent seafood. For a reasonable lunch, try the daily menu at **Club de Viña** on the plaza. North of Viña, the coastal stretch between **Montemar** and **Cochoa** is a happy hunting ground for small restaurants, serving local seafood: **El Pacífico** is particularly well known.

Culture in Santiago

There are over 100 theaters in Santiago, putting on classical, modern or avant-garde plays by Chilean and other playwrights. The best-equipped and most reliable theaters are:
Teatro La Comedia, Calle Merced 349, tel: 639 1523. The home of one of Chile's best theater groups.
Teatro Antonio Varas, Calle Morandé 25, tel: 698 1200.
The best of the city's multi-screen cinema complexes,

Art in Santiago

There are several art galleries along Santiago's Avda Nueva Costanera, including the A.M.S. Marlborough, Tomás Andreu and Plástica Nueva. On Calle Alameda, try Arte Actual in the Centro de Extensión of the Universidad Católica.

Cinemark 12, is in Alto Las Condes shopping mall, while the nearby mall houses another complex, **Showcase Cinemas Parque Arauco**.

Nightlife

Santiago

Nightlife starts late in the capital – around midnight. Check out the cafés and bars along Calle Constitución and in Bellavista for a bohemian crowd. In Calle Providencia, people gather in **Brannigan's** and other pubs along Suecia and Generál Holley. Near Manuel Montt on Providencia is the English-style **Phone Box Club** and **Café del Patio**. There is a choice of pubs and discos along Paseo San Damián in Las Condes.

La Casa en el Aire Arte, Calle Antonia López de Bello 0125, Bellavista, has live music every night. For salsa, go to **La Habana Vieja**, Calle Tarapacá 755. **Confitería Torres**, Avda B. O'Higgins 1570, is the haunt of tango lovers. Good food and a great atmosphere.

Where to Shop

For the latest fashions, visit the department stores and boutiques on Providencia near Los Leones and Manuel Montt.

Stores open Mon–Fri 10.30am–7.30pm, Sat 9.30am–1.30pm. Most, except for the malls, are closed on Sunday.

On Avda Apoquindo 9085, **Alba Pueblito de los Dominicos** is a collection of old-style buildings, comprising 200 shops where more than 300 craftsmen and women work. Handicrafts, antiques and plants are for sale.

Colombia A – Z

Getting Acquainted

Area 1,140,000 sq. km (439,600 sq. miles), bordering Panama with coasts on the Caribbean Sea and the Pacific Ocean.
Capital Bogotá
Population 40 million, of European, African and Amerindian descent. Nearly half a million belong to one of 60 tribes.
Language Spanish
Currency Colombian peso = 100 centavos
Weights & measures Metric
Electricity 120 volts
Time zone GMT –5hrs, EST
Dialing code 57 (Bogotá +1)

Government & Economy

Colombia's "limited democracy" is based on the constitution of 1991. The president and members of the senate and house of representatives are directly elected. Indigenous peoples have the right to two senate seats. Right-wing Alvaro Uribe has been in power since 2002.

Colombia has one of South America's strongest economies and is self-sufficient in energy. Agriculture is the most important source of revenue, and Colombia is the world's second-largest coffee producer. Manufacturing comes a close second. Colombia produces 60 percent of the world's emeralds and 80 percent of the world's cocaine.

Money

There are some legal *casas de cambios* (exchange bureaux) but generally you are advised to exchange cash and travelers'

checks (in US dollars) at a bank. Since a photocopy of your passport is often required, you can speed up transactions by taking a supply of spare photocopies with you from home. Do not change money on the street and avoid carrying large amounts of cash.

Credit cards are widely used, but American Express is accepted only in high-priced establishments in Bogotá. Amex is represented in Colombia by the Tierra Mar Aire travel agency.

Visas

Visitors to Colombia need a passport but, according to current regulations, do not require a visa. Check, however, since regulations may change. Visitors are given a 60-or 90-day stay on arrival. Stiff fines are imposed if passports are not stamped on arrival and if stays exceeding 60 days are not authorized by the Colombian Immigration Agency.

Extensions of 15 days for a maximum six-month period may be applied for. Exit stamps are necessary on departure.

Getting Around

From the Airport

Bogotá's international airport is at **El Dorado**, about 12 km (7 miles) from the city center. Registered yellow taxi services run to the city center at a fixed rate of US$8. Elsewhere they are on a meter. Local buses run to and from the airport during the day but luggage space is very limited. You can call a taxi on tel: 222 2111 or 311 1111.

Foreigners pay US$25 departure tax when leaving Colombia by air. Make sure that your documentation is stamped with the date of your arrival, so that you don't have to pay double the exit tax on departure.

By Bus

Several countries' foreign ministries are advising visitors to avoid overland routes, to travel by air and only to major cities. Bus transportation along the main routes is generally good, often luxurious, but deteriorates when heading into the more remote areas. Normally, the rougher the road, the poorer the bus. The alternative on main routes is a *buseta* (minibus) or *colectivo* (a shared taxi that is more expensive but much quicker).

From Ecuador, buses go to and from the border at Tulcan/Ipiales. From Venezuela, you can choose between the coastal route from Maracaibo to Santa Marta, or the highland route from Caracas and Mérida to Cucuta via San Cristobál. From Brazil, the only way to enter is via Leticia in the Amazon basin and then fly to Bogotá.

By Taxi

In main cities, taxis are cheap and relatively reliable. Always try to take a taxi that uses a meter; if not, agree a price in advance (all taxis are legally obliged to display a list of additional charges). At night women should not travel alone in taxis. Be very wary of old-looking vehicles, and always keep an eye on your luggage.

Crime

Although most Colombians are honest and friendly, theft occurs in the larger cities and visitors should look after valuables at all times. The 24-hour **Tourist Police Service** in Bogotá is at Carrera 7, 27–42, tel: 283 4930 or 334 2501. If you have lost documents, contact the police at Calle 46 and Carreras 14; for loss of valuables, go to Calle 40, 8–09.

Medical Services

The main medical centers in Bogotá are **Cruz Roja Nacional**, Avda 68, 66–31, tel: 250 66/231 9027/231 9008; emergency tel: 132; or **Centro Medico La Salud**, Carrera 10, 21–36, tel: 243 1381/282 4021. Make sure you have health insurance before you travel.

Newspapers

National daily papers include the liberal *El Tiempo*, the evening *El Espacio*, the business paper *La República*, and the conservative *El Nuevo Siglo*. *El Espectador* is a weekly newspaper. The English-language *Colombian Post*, published twice a week, is not widely circulated. **Drugstore Internacional**, Carrera 10, 26–71, sells US and European papers.

Postal Services

There are two postal systems in Colombia. The more reliable service is run by Avianca, the national airline. They have offices in most large cities, often next door to the airline office. The other system is state-run and less reliable. The General Post Office in Bogotá is at the Avianca Building in the center of the city, opposite Parque Santander. In small towns and rural areas use the Correos de Colombia.

Business Hours

Generally Mon–Fri 8am–noon, and 2–6pm. Banks are open Mon–Thur 9am–3pm, till 3.30pm on Fri. Many businesses shut on Monday.

Telephone & Fax

Telephone systems are automated and phone cards can be used. Telecom offices in all big cities have international communication facilities.

Parks & Reserves

Permits are sometimes required to visit Colombia's parks and nature reserves. For permits and information contact the **Office of Ecotourism and Attention to Visitors**, Caja Agraria building, Carrera 10, 20–30, 4th floor, Bogotá; tel/fax: 243 3095, www.parquesnacionales.gov.co.

Useful Addresses

Tourist Offices

Bogotá: Fondo de Promoción Turística, Calle 90, Carrera 18–35, Oficina 203. They have offices in other cities as well. Limited information is also available at the Edificio Centro de Comercio Internacional, Calle 28, 13A–15 and at the bus station and El Dorado Airport.

Tourist Agencies

Bogotá: Panamerican Tours, Carrera 11A, Calle 93A–80, tel: 635 4000, or Eco Guías, Carrera 3, 18–56A, Oficina 202, at the top of Avda Jimenez.
Santa Marta: Reales Tours, Carrera 1A, 20–09, tel: 214 418, can arrange trips to Ciudad Perdida, Parque Tayrona, Cabo de la Vela and the Guajira Peninsula.
Cartagena: There are many tourist agencies in Bocagrande, the modern beach resort.

Embassies/Consulates

Canada: Carrera 7, 115–33 14th floor, A.A. 110069, Bogotá, tel: 657 9800 (general), tel: 657 9951 (visas), fax: 657 9914.
UK: Edificio Ing. Barings, Carrera 9, 76–49, 9th floor, Bogotá, tel: 317 6690/6310/6321/6423, fax: 317 6298/6389, www.britain. gov.co
US: Building entrance: Calle 22D-bis, 47–51. Mailing address: Carrera 45, 22D-45 Bogotá. Embassy tel: 315 0811. Consular Section tel: 346 9150.

Where to Stay

Bogotá
Bogotá Royal, Avda 100, 8A–01, tel: 163 4177, fax: 121 8326. **$$$**
Hosteria de la Candelaria, Calle 9,

Hotel Price Guide

Prices for a double room including continental breakfast.
$ = US$20 – inexpensive
$$ = US$20–50 – moderate
$$$ = US$50 plus – expensive

3–11. tel: 342 1727. In a converted colonial mansion and furnished with beautiful antiques. **$**
La Fontana, Avda 127, 21–10, tel: 615 4400, fax: 216 0449. Recommended; good food. **$$$**
Tequendama, Carrera 10, 26–21, tel: 382 0300, fax: 282 2860. Full facilities including sports. **$$$**
Budget hotels, often dismal, are located between Calles 13 and 17, and Avda Caracas and Carrera 17. This area can be unsafe after dark.

Cartagena

Cartagena-Hilton, Avda Almirante Brion, El Laguito, tel: 665 0666, fax: 665 0661, www.cartagenahilton.com. A luxury hotel with several restaurants. **$$$**
Hotel de Caribe, Carrera 1, 2–87, tel: 650 155, fax: 653 707, www.hotelcaribe.com. A palatial building, close to the sea and the historic town center. **$$–$$$**

What to Eat

A few Colombian specialties worth trying are:
ajico: a soup of chicken, potatoes and vegetables.
arepa: a maize pancake.
arroz con coco: rice cooked in coconut oil.
bandeja paisa: a dish of ground beef, sausages, beans, rice, plantain and avocado.
carne asada: grilled meat.
cazuela de mariscos: seafood stew.
chocolate santafereño: hot chocolate accompanied by cheese and bread.
comidas corrientes: literally, ordinary meals; usually a fried piece of meat with beans and rice, found in many lower-priced restaurants throughout the country.
puchero: broth of chicken, beef and pork.
tamales: chopped pork with rice and vegetables wrapped in maize pastry.

Where to Eat

Carbón de Pal, Avda 19, 1016–12, tel: 214 0450. The place to go for grilled meats. **$$**

Restaurant Guide

Prices for a three-course meal for two, including house wine.
$ = US$20 – inexpensive
$$ = US$20–50 – moderate
$$$ = US$50 plus – expensive

Casa Vieja, Avda Jiménez 3–73; Carrera 10, 26–50; and Carrera 116, 20–50, Bogotá. The three branches of this restaurant offer excellent regional food. **$–$$**
La Fonda Antioqueña, Carrera 2, 6–161, Cartagena, has traditional Colombian food. **$**
Paco's, opposite the church of Santo Domingo, Cartagena, is also recommended. **$**
Refugio Alpino, Calle 23, 7–49, serves European food. **$**

Nightlife

Bogotá

There are several good bars in the zona rosa, Calles 81 and 82, Carreras 11, 12, 13 and 14. Nothing gets moving until after midnight on weekends. For taped tangos from Argentina, head for **El Viejo Almacén** at Carrera 5, 14–23.

Cartagena

A Caribbean trio plays on weekends at **Paco's** opposite Santo Domingo church – a good place to drink into the small hours. The bar attached to **La Quemada** has live salsa on Friday and Saturday. For discos, head for the **Bocagrande** district.

Where to Shop

For Colombian handicrafts, the best place is **Artesanías de Colombia**, Carrera 3, 18–60, Bogotá, next to the Iglesia de las Aguas. Other shops are at Carrera 10, 26–50 and Carrera 7, 23–40. Emeralds can be bought in the joyerías in Bogotá's **La Casa de la Emeralda**, Calle 30, 16–18 or in **Joyas Verdes Ltda**, Carreras 15, 39–15. The best antique shop in Bogotá is on Plaza Bolívar, next to the cathedral. Pre-Columbian pottery is sold in the **Centro Internacional**.

Ecuador A – Z

Getting Acquainted

Area 270,700 sq. km (104,500 sq. miles), bordering Colombia in the north, Peru to the south and east and the Pacific Ocean in the west.
Capital Quito
Population 13 million, 40 percent of whom are native Quichua.
Language Spanish and Quichua
Currency US Dollar = 100 cents
Weights & measures Metric
Electricity 110 volts
Time zone GMT -5hrs (Galápagos 1hr behind)
Dialing code 593 (Quito +2)

Government & Economy

Democracy was established in Ecuador in 1979. Former coup leader Lucio Gutiérrez came to power in 2003, with support from indigenous peoples who liked his promises to end corruption. The economy is based on oil, fishing, bananas, coffee and cocoa.

Visas

Visas are not required for a stay of up to 90 days. Permits (known as T3s) for a 30-day stay are issued at the border or point of arrival and can easily be extended. For visa extensions, go to Avda Amazonas 2639, open 8am–noon and 3–6pm. The immigration office in Quito is at Calle Independencia and Amazonas 3149, tel: 2454 122. The main police office dealing with tourist matters is on Calle Mantúfar. To enter the country, you will need a passport valid for six months, a return ticket and proof of sufficient funds for your stay.

Money

Travelers' checks and credit cards are more widely accepted than debit cards and in rural areas it is best to travel with small denomination notes.

On Sundays and holidays, when banks and *casas de cambio* are shut, you can exchange money in the major hotels. It is worth bringing most of your money in travelers' checks for safety, as these can be changed almost as easily as cash.

Major credit cards (particularly Visa and MasterCard) are accepted in the larger hotels, restaurants, and tourist-oriented shops.

ATMS are common throughout the country, but they can be unreliable.

Newspapers

The main daily newspapers are *El Comercio*, *Hoy*, *Tiempo* and *Ultimas Noticias*. Foreign papers are on sale in Quito.

Postal Services

It is worth having your letters certified *(con certificado)* for about 10 cents – you get a receipt which won't do much practical good, but means that your letter's existence is recorded somewhere.

The main post office in Quito is at Calle Eloy Alfaro 354 and 9 de Octubre (new Quito). *Poste Restante (Lista de Correos)* letters should be sent to Calle Espejo 935 and Guayaquil (old town).

Telephone

Ecuador's telephone network is run by Andinatel, Pacifitel, Etapa and a couple of private companies, and one of the best places to make calls is at the telephone company's office in each town. Debit cards for public telephones are not interchangeable between networks.

Hotels add hefty surcharges, although rates may be discounted after 7pm.

Since 2001, all numbers in the country have been changed to 7 digits.

There are numerous internet cafés in Quito, Guayaquil and Cuenca, many of which also offer an internet phone service, which is normally cheap if not of the best sound quality.

Embassies/Consulates

Canada: Avda 6 de Diciembre 2816 and Paul Rivet, Quito, tel: 223 2114, www.dfait-maeci.gc.ca/ecuador.
UK: Edificio Citiplaza, Avda Naciones Unidas and República de El Salvador, Quito, tel: 297 0800/0801, fax: 2970809, www.britembquito.org.ec.
US: Avda 12 de Octubre and Patria, Quito, tel: 2562 890, www.usembassy.org.ec

Getting Around

By Air

SAN-SAETA and TAME connect the principal urban centers – Quito, Guayaquil and Cuenca. Flying time Guayaquil–Quito is about 30 minutes. TAME and and SAN-SAETA offer daily service to the Galápagos.

Ecuador has international airports at Quito and Guayaquil. From Quito's **Mariscal Sucre Airport** there are buses to the old and new city centers, and taxi fares are around US$5. Taxis from Guayaquil's **Simón Bolívar International Airport** to the city cost US$4–5, and there are also buses. Ensure your carrier has arranged to get you to Quito if you are landing at Guayaquil.

River Transport

In the Oriente (Eastern lowlands), motorized dugout canoes are the chief form of public transport on Ecuador's main rivers. They can carry up to 30 passengers, as well as an unbelievable amount of cargo and livestock. Seating is on wooden boards (making your own cushion out of folded clothes will help on long journeys), and bags are usually stashed up at the front

By Bus

Buses in Ecuador are cheap, plentiful and the most convenient way to travel, even though many roads are unpaved, and landslides are common in mountainous regions. Some air-conditioned, luxury buses *(autobús de lujo)* cover the most popular routes. Always carry your passport when traveling by bus.

Many travelers enter Ecuador from Peru at the Tumbes–Huaquillas border post, changing buses at the frontier. Buses are frequent both ways. To Colombia, almost everyone takes the Quito–Ibarra, Tulcán–Pasto road.

Tours

For a useful list of some of the many excellent companies offering trips in Ecuador, check out www.lata.org, the website of the Latin American Travel Association in the United Kingdom. They can also give impartial advice on how to plan a trip to Ecuador.

The Oriente

Metropolitan Touring, tel: 298 8200, www.metropolitan-touring.com, offer luxury all-inclusive, 3–4-day tours down the Aguarico River from Lago Agrio to the Cuyabeno National Park aboard the Flotel Orellana *(see River Transport below)*. This area is excellent for wildlife. Cheaper and longer excursions can be organized in Misahualli. However, wildlife is very limited, and trips can be disappointing. Dayuma Lodge is well established and reliable.

end of the boat under a tarpaulin.

A much more comfortable (and expensive) alternative is the *Flotel Orellana*, a cruise ship which sails up the Aguarico River, close to the Peruvian border and the Cuyabeno Wildlife Reserve. Fully-inclusive packages can be booked through: **Metropolitan Touring**, República de El Salvador 970, Quito, tel: 298 8200; fax: 246 4702.

Excursions

Among Ecuador's snow-capped peaks, Chimborazo, Cotopaxi, El Altar and Tungurahua are certainly the most challenging, and 20 km (12 miles) north of Quito is **Mitad del Mundo**, where a monument and museum mark the equator. The road passes two dozen or so colorful billboards painted by prominent Latin American artists. On a clear day, a train or bus ride along the Avenue of the Volcanoes from Quito to Riobamba is highly recommended.

Pasachoa is a refuge for native birds and plants and has been declared a protected forest. It is run by the Fundación Natura, which is based in Quito. Ideal for a day trip from Quito.

The Galápagos Islands

On arrival, all non-Ecuadorian travelers to the Islands must pay a US$100 entrance fee in dollars (no credit cards). Keep the receipt: you may have to show it again.

There are daily flights by local airlines. Flights are heavily booked so you should confirm and reconfirm your seat and check in early at the airport. Note that if you want to be on Puerto Ayora, it can be difficult to travel between the islands.

The Galápagos archipelago is almost entirely a national park, and no visitor is allowed to enter it without a qualified guide on an organized tour.

For many, a trip on one of the largest cruisers is the most comfortable and convenient way to visit the islands.
The **Galápagos Explorer II**, operated by Canodros, is the most luxurious boat touring the islands. Contact any travel agency that specializes in Latin America or see www.canodros. com.
The **Santa Cruz**, run by Metropolitan Touring, has all the comforts of a luxury liner, including excellent food in its dining rooms. By traveling overnight, these cruisers can easily reach outer islands that smaller yachts sometimes struggle to get to.

The going is smoother on a large ship too. Both boats are based in the Galápagos, taking around 100 passengers on three- or four-day cruises – one covering the northern islands, another the southern. You can combine both trips to make a seven-day cruise. Passengers visit the islands in groups of 10 on motorboats (pangas) accompanied by English-speaking naturalist guides. The cost works out to US$200–300 per person per night on a twin-share basis (all inclusive, except for bar and air fare), depending on cabin and length of cruise.

Bookings for the Santa Cruz can be made at Metropolitan Touring (see above) in Quito or Guayaquil, or their US agents Adventure Associates

There are dozens of yachts operating cruises around the islands, most of which work out of Puerto Ayora, with a growing number based in Puerto Baquerizo Moreno. They can take from 6–20 people.

Galápagos Sub Aqua, Avda Charles Darwin, Puerto Ayora, Isla Santa Cruz, tel/fax: 05 526 350, www.galapagos-sub-aqua.com, offers scuba diving tours and instruction.

In the UK, many operators feature Galápagos cruises, including **Galápagos Adventure Tours**, tel: 020 7407 1478, www.galapagos.co.uk

Where to Stay

Quito

Many budget hotels are in old Quito, the colonial heart of the city; however, crime is on the increase in this area and it is safer to stay in the new town, which is where most of the shops and restaurants are located.
Café Cultura, Calle Reina Victoria and Robles, tel/fax: 222 4271. Converted mansion. Great Danish breakfasts. **$$**
Chalet Suisse, Calle Reina Victoria 312 and Calama, tel: 256 2700, fax: 256 3966. Excellent food, as well as a nightclub and casino. **$$**
Magic Bean, Calle Foch 681 and Juan León Mera, tel: 256 6181.

Attractive house with shared or private rooms. Good restaurant downstairs. Centrally located. **$**
Real Audencia, Calle Bolívar 220 and Guayaquil, tel: 251 2711, fax: 258 0213. In historical center. Well-furnished, spacious rooms. **$$**
Tambo Real, Calle 12 de Octubre and Patria, tel: 256 3822, fax: 255 4964. Good food. Opposite the US Embassy. **$$**

Guayaquil

Hostal Ecuahogar, Calle Sauces I and Avda Isidro Ayora, tel: 224 8357, fax: 224 8341. Youth hostel near airport and bus terminal. Airport transfers. Safe and friendly. **$**
Palace, Calle Chile 214, tel: 232 1080, fax: 232 2887. **$$**
Plaza, Calle Chile 414, tel: 324 006, fax: 324 195. Comfortable rooms with air conditioning and TV; good restaurant. **$$**
Ramada, Malecón and Orellana, tel: 256 5555, fax: 256 3036. www.hotelramadaecuador.com. Lovely rooms with view of the river, good restaurant, indoor pool. **$$–$$$**

Hotel Price Guide

Prices for a double room Including continental breakfast.
$ = US$20 or less – inexpensive
$$ = US$20–50 – moderate
$$$ = US$50–100 – expensive

Where to Eat

Quito

The main meal of the day is lunch (almuerzo), usually a soup followed by a main dish. There are many cafés for breakfast and snacks. Old Quito has little to offer but the streets surrounding Avenida Amazonas in the new town have many good restaurants.
El Campo Base, Calle Baquedano 355 and Juan León Mera, tel: 222 4504. Authentic Ecuadorian food; a popular venue for climbers. **$$**
El Marqués, Calle Calama 443 and Amazonas. Popular place for vegetarian food. **$**
La Choza, Calle 12 Octubre 1821 and Cordero, tel: 223 0839. **$$**

Restaurant Guide

Prices for a three-course meal for two, including house wine.
$ = US$20 or less – inexpensive
$$ = US$20–50 – moderate
$$$ = US$50 plus – expensive

La Viña, Calle Isabel la Católica and Cordero (behind Hotel Oro Verde), tel: 286 6033. Excellent international cuisine. **$$$**
Su Ceviche, Calle Juan León Mera 1232 and Calama, tel: 252 1843. Good place to try the local *ceviche* (marinated fish). **$$**
Taberna Quiteña, Calle Amazonas 1259 and Cordero, tel: 223 0009. Good Ecuadorian food with live entertainment. **$$$**
Zócalo, Calle Calama 469 and Juan León Mera. Terrace restaurant/bar with international food. **$**

Guayaquil

In Guayaquil, the most pleasant place to eat is aboard one of the boats moored along the Malecón.
For cheaper and often more fiery seafood meals, the area just north of Parque del Centenario is good. Calle Escobedo has popular street cafés serving breakfast.
El Caracol Azul, Calle 9 de Octubre and Los Rios, tel: 228 0461. Said to be one of the best seafood restaurants in Guayaquil. **$$$**
Galeria El Taller, Calle Quisquis 1313, tel: 239 3904. Good local dishes. **$**
Lo Nuestro, Calle Victor Emilio Estrada 903 and Higueras, tel: 238 6398. The most famous steak house in Guayaquil. **$$**

Public Holidays

- **January** 1 New Year's Day
- **January** 6 Festival of the Three Kings
- **March/April** Carnival (date variable, precedes Lent)
- **April** Holy Week; festivities on Good Friday and Easter Sunday (date variable)
- **May** 1 Labor Day; street parades
- **July** 24 Simon Bolívar's birthday
- **August** 10 Independence Day
- **November** 1 All Saints' Day; 2 All Souls' Day
- **December** 25 Christmas Day

Nightlife

Nightlife in Ecuador often involves bars with astonishingly loud music. In **Quito**, the new town has its share of discos, as well as a reasonably authentic English pub, the **Reina Victoria**, on the street of the same name. The best *peña* (folk club) is the **Taberna Quiteña**, which has two venues – Avda Amazonas and Calle Manabí in the old city.
El Pobre Diablo, Calle Santamaria 338 and Juan León Mera, is an authentic Ecuadorian café-bar with a friendly atmosphere.
In **Guayaquil**, many all-night discos play the latest American and Latino tunes, and some good Colombian salsa. They are not places for the faint-hearted.
Otavalo has a couple of *peñas* which are lively at the weekend. In addition to excellent local music, they regularly feature groups from Colombia, Peru and Chile.

Where to Shop

There are a number of large malls in Quito, including Megamaxi, on Calle 6 de Diciembre between Julio E. Moreno and Germán Alemán.
Otavalo market (Wed and Sat; daily June–August) is well worth the 30-minute bus journey from Quito. It is famous for hand-knitted clothing, jewelry, wood-carvings, tapestries, leather goods and embroidered textiles, and offers the best buys in Ecuador, but there are also stores in Quito, Guayaquil, Cuenca and Baños where similar goods are sold and prices are reasonable.
Cuenca is perhaps the best place to buy quality gold and silver jewelry. Shops and stalls on Avenida Amazonas in Quito sell everything Ecuador has to offer.
Ecuador (*not* Panama) is also the place for Panama hats, which are made by hand in the town of Montecristi but sold all over the country *(see page 213).*

French Guiana A – Z

Getting Acquainted

Area 91,000 sq. km (35,135 sq. miles)
Capital Cayenne.
Population 188,000; 65 percent of people are of Creole (African/Afro-European) descent.
Language French (official language), French Guianese Creole and English
Currency Euro (€)
Weights & measures Metric
Electricity 220 volts
Time zone GMT -3hrs, EST +2hrs
International dialing code: 594

Climate

The best time to visit French Guiana is August to December; the rest of the year, the rains are heavy and even during the dry period it is still very humid.

Government & Economy

French Guiana is an overseas *département* of the French government. The country receives large subsidies from the French government and the EU. The economy is closely bound to that of France. Major sources of income include shrimping, mining, and forest products. The European Space Agency operates a satellite launching facility at Kourou.

Business Hours

As a general rule, shops open Mon–Fri 8–11.30am and 1–4pm; Sat 8–11.30am. Banks open Mon–Fri 7.45–11.30am and 3–5pm.

Visas & Customs

All visitors except EU nationals need a visa to enter the country. There are no restrictions on the amount of currency visitors can bring in to the country.

Money

French Guiana is expensive. It is easy to change US dollars or travelers' checks in Cayenne. Major credit cards are widely accepted, and visitors can get cash advances from ATMS at post offices.

Tourist Information

French Guiana Tourist Board, 12 rue Lalouette, BP 801, 97338 Cayenne; tel: 296 500; fax: 296 501, www.tourisme-guyane.gf.

Information on accommodation is also available from **Syndicat National des Agents de Voyage**, BP 513, 97300 Cayenne; tel: 382 781; fax: 325 700.

Tourist Offices Overseas

France has a tourist office devoted to distributing information about French Guiana. Contact the French Guiana Tourist Board, c/o Horwath Axe Consultants, 12 Rue de Madrid, 75008 Paris, France; tel: 01 53 42 41 39; fax: 01 43 87 32 85.

Elsewhere, you should refer to the French tourist office:
Australia: French Govt Tourist Office, Level 20, 25 Bligh Street, 2000 NSW, Sydney, tel: 9231 5244, fax: 9221 8682, www.aufranceguide.com
Canada: French Govt Tourist Office, 1981 Avenue McGill Collège, Tour Esso, Suite 490, Montreal PQ, H3A 2W9, tel: 514 288 4264, fax: 514 845 4868, www.ca-ukfranceguide.com.
UK: French Govt Tourist Office, 178 Piccadilly, London W1J 9AL, tel: 0906 824 4123 (calls cost 60p per minute), fax: 020 7493 6594, www.ukfranceguide.com
US: French Govt Tourist Office, 444 Madison Avenue, NY 10022, tel: 212 838 7800, fax: 212 838 7855, www.usfranceguide.com.

Media & Communications

Daily newspapers include *France-Guyane* and *La Presse de Guyane*. There are no English-language newspapers available.

The BBC World Service broadcasts on MHz 17.79, 15.19 and 5.970. The Voice of America can be heard on MHz 13.74, 9.775, 7.405 and 5.995.

The whole telephone system is completely interconnected with that of France. The Internet is available in a few places in the capital, but access can be difficult elsewhere.

Getting Around

From the Airport

Cayenne-Rochambeau airport is 16 km (10 miles) from Cayenne. There are no buses; taxis cost US$25 (more at night). Exit tax currently costs about €27.

By Air

Air Guyane has regular services to Maripasoula, Saül, Régina and St Georges from Cayenne.
Air Guyane: Rochambeau Airport, 97351 Matoury, tel: 293 630; fax: 293 631, www.airguyane.com.

To rent a plane or book a charter flight contact: **Guyane Aero Services**, Zone d'aviation générale, 97351 Matoury, tel: 356 162; fax: 358 450. It is also possible to hire a helicopter. Contact **Heli Inter Guyane**, Rochambeau Airport, 97351 Matoury, tel: 356 231; fax: 358 256.

By Boat

Visitors can reach the interior of Guiana by boat. *Pirogues* (dug-out canoes) are equipped with outboard motors. Wooden *pirogues* can carry up to 12 passengers. Tours can be arranged; the average journey time is about five to six hours. Contact local tour agents in Cayenne or Kourou for details.

By Bus

Cayenne and its suburbs are served by a regular bus network. Buses do not run on Sunday. Routes and timetables are available from SMTC, 3 place des Palmistes, tel: 314 566.

Private coaches run between Cayenne and all the coastal towns to Saint-Laurent du Maroni. One service departs Mon–Sat at 5.30am from Av. Jean Galmot in Cayenne. It is advisable to book a ticket before departure. Bookings, tel: 312 666 8am–noon, 3–6pm.
Minibuses *(taxis colectifs)* run along the same route and are more comfortable than the coaches. Departures set out from the bus station, opposite the Laussat Canal in Cayenne. Information and bookings, tel: 307 305/305 225.

Car Hire

Most car hire agencies open 8am–noon and 2.30–5.30pm, and 8am–noon on Sat.
Avis, 77 rue du Lt Goinet, Cayenne, tel: 302-522; fax: 310-791; airport tel: 353-414, www.avis.com.
Hertz, ZL de Collery, Cayenne, tel: 351-171; fax: 351-048; airport tel: 356-069, www.hertz.com
Europcar, ZL de Collery, Cayenne, tel: 351-827; fax: 351-557; airport tel: 356 269, www.europcar.com

By Car

It is possible to hire cars in French Guiana but it is not advisable unless you are used to driving in developing countries. Driving along dirt tracks is dangerous in the rainy season.

Tipping

At hotels and restaurants the service charge is usually included in the bill; if not, 10 percent is usually left as a tip. Taxi drivers do not receive a tip.

Where to Stay

Cayenne

Bar Hotel La Bodega, 42 av. Général de Gaulle, tel: 302 513, fax: 294 284, www.labodega.fr. Intimate hotel; forest excursions offered. **$$**

Hotel Price Guide

Prices for a double room including continental breakfast.
$ = US$20–50 – inexpensive
$$ = US$50–100 – moderate
$$$ = US$100 plus – expensive

Best Western Hotel Amazonia, 28 av. Général de Gaulle, tel: 288 300; fax: 319 441, www.amazonia-hotel.com. Some rooms have kitchenettes. Air-conditioning, restaurant and swimming pool. **$$$**
Central, at the crossroads of rues Molé and Mecker, tel: 256 565/311 296; fax: 311 296, www.créol.net/centralhotel. Swimming pool. **$$**
Hôtel Ajoupa, Route du Camp du Tigre, tel: 303 308; fax: 301 282, e-mail: hotel.ajoupa@wanadoo.fr. With pool and garden. **$$**
Hotel Ket Tai, 72 blvd Jubelin, tel: 301 100, fax: 309 976. Restaurant and meeting room. **$$**
Phigarita, 42 rue Colomb, tel: 306 600; fax: 307 749. With air-conditioning, swimming pool. **$$$**

Kourou
Les Relais De Guyane, tel: 320 066. **$$**
Mercure Ariatel, Lac Bois Diable, tel: 328 900; fax: 326 160. Luxury bungalows, with swimming pool. **$$$**

Remire Montjoly
Motel Beauregard, PK 9, 2 Route de Rémire, tel: 354 100, fax: 354 405. Restaurant; bungalows with kitchen, TV, refrigerator. Recreation club on site. With pool, horseback riding, mini golf and tennis. **$$$**
Motel du Lac, Chemin Poupon, tel: 380 800; fax: 380 800. **$$**

Matoury
La Chaumiere, Chemin de la Chaumiere, tel: 352 300, fax: 352 503. Bar, banquet room, in-room TV, minibar, pool. **$$$**
Le Grillardin, PK 6, Route de Matoury, tel: 356 390; fax: 358 605. **$$$**

St-Laurent du Maroni
Chez Julienne, Route des Malgaches, tel: 341 153. **$**
Hôtel Star, 109 Rue Thiers, tel: 341 084; fax: 342 519. **$$**
La Tentiare, 12 Av. Franklin Roosevelt, tel: 342 600; fax: 341 509. **$$**
Le Relais des Trois Lacs, 19–23 Domaine du Lac Bleu, tel: 340 505, fax: 340 276, e-mail: r3lacs@nplus.gf. Has 16 rooms and two bungalows. **$$**

Roura
Amazone River, Bourg de Roura, Esplanade de l'Eglise, tel: 280 200, fax: 301 317. One *carbet* (wooden lodge) with hammocks, and café. **$**
Auberge des Orpailleurs, 62 Route de l'Est, tel: 376 297. Meals available; hammock space. **$$$**
La Crique Gabrielle, Dacca village, tel: 280 104, fax: 280 104. Forest inn with two bed and breakfast rooms, shared shower room. **$**

Sinnamary
Hôtel du Fleuve, 11 rue Léon Mine, BP 114, tel: 345 400; fax: 345 303, www.hoteldufleuve.com. With 121 rooms, two seminar rooms, swimming pool. **$$**
Sinnarive Motel, Savane Manuel, tel: 345 555. **$**

Accommodation Agencies

Club des Hôteliers (Hoteliers Club), Immeuble CTG, BP 49, 12 rue Lallouette, Cayenne, French Guiana, tel: 299 632.
Syndicat des Hôteliers, Restaurateurs et Cafetiers de Guyane (Guiana Federation of Hotels, Restaurants and Cafés), PK 9, 2 Route de Rémire, 97354 Remire Montjoly, French Guiana, tel: 354 100; fax: 354 405.
Relais Départemental des Gîtes de France (Guest Houses of France, Departmental Office), Immeuble CTG, 12 rue Lallouette, 97338 Cayenne, French Guiana, tel: 296 501, fax: 296 516.

Tourist Lodges

The following places offer traditional wooden lodges *(carbets)* located in areas of natural beauty, often deep in tropical forest:
Amazonie Détente, Valentin Falls, Mana River, tel: 325 288. Hammocks.
Campement de Saut Sonnelle, 30 minutes by boat along the Inini River from Maripasoula, tel: 314 945. Hammocks.
Degrad Cascades (La Marine), Cascades River, one hour from Tonnégrande by *pirogue*, tel: 399 365. Hammocks and beds.
Eden des Eaux Claires, 7 km (4 miles) north of Saül in remote *massif central*, tel: 309 111. Camp in tropical forest; beds or hammocks.
Gîte Quimbe Kio, village of Cacao, 97352, Cacao, tel: 270 122. Hammocks/beds.
Les Maripas (Guyane Excursions), PK 17, on the road to Degrad Saramaka, 97310 Kourou, tel: 320 541. Hammocks.

What to Eat

As a *département* of France, French Guiana has a high standard of food, particularly in and around Cayenne, with added color and variety provided by its rich racial mix. There is a wide choice of restaurants, mostly serving French food, but Vietnamese, Indonesian, Creole and Chinese food can also be found. Prices are relatively high at good restaurants, but a decent, cheap meal can be had at one of the many Asian cafés or food stalls.

Where to Eat

Cayenne
By the Canal Laussant are many Javanese and Creole cafés and

Restaurant Guide

Prices for a three-course meal for two, including house wine.
$ = US$20–50 – inexpensive
$$ = US$50–70 – moderate
$$$ = US$70–120 – expensive

Carnival

Carnival usually starts in January. While it's not the extravaganza of Rio de Janeiro or the Caribbean, it is a vibrant affair with a cultural mix of Creole, Brazilian and Haitian influences. Every weekend from Epiphany festivities are held until they reach a five-day non-stop climax before Ash Wednesday. In the colorful parades in central Cayenne, dancers dress in elaborate costumes, each day based on a different traditional theme.

food stalls, although some are not particularly clean and it is not a safe area at night.

DeliFrance, corner of Rue Justin Cayatée/Av. du Général de Gaulle. Good snacks, pastries, coffee. **$**

Hostellerie Les Amandiers, Pointe des Amandiers. The best in the city, facing an attractive park. Expensive but worth it. **$$$**

La Victoire, 40 rue du 14 Juillet. Chinese and Creole cuisine served at outside tables; tasty and good-value meals, friendly atmosphere. **$**

Les Pyramides, corner of Rue C. Colomb and Rue Malouet. Inexpensive Middle Eastern dishes, such as couscous and grills. **$**

Kourou

Ballahou, 1 rue Armet Martial. Good fish and seafood. **$$**

Le Provence, 11 Passage G Monnerville. Best French food in town, but pricey. **$$$**

St-Laurent du Maroni

Chez Felicia, Av. du Général de Gaulle. Creole cuisine. **$$**

Restaurant La Saramaca, Av. Félix Eboué. Excellent food but rather expensive. **$$$**

Restaurant Vietnam, 19 av. Félix Eboué. Good-value Asian dishes. **$**

Guyana
A – Z

Getting Acquainted

Area 215,000 sq. km (83,000 sq. miles)
Capital Georgetown
Population 800,000
Language English (official language), Creole, Hindi, Urdu and several Amerindian languages.
Currency Guyana dollar
Weights & measures Officially metric although imperial measures are widely used.
Electricity 110V (Georgetown), 220V (most other places)
Time Zone GMT – 4hrs, EST + 1hr
International dialing code 592

Climate

The temperature remains warm with equatorial humidity all year round, but not excessively hot; average temperatures are between 24°C (75°F) and 31°C (88°F). The best time to visit is July–November, between the two wet seasons, which are from May through June and from December through January. Average annual rainfall is 230 cm (91 inches).

Government & Economy

Guyana gained independence in 1966 and became a republic in 1970. The government is democratically elected and the president, who is elected by the majority party in the National Assembly, is head of state.

The economy is based on four export products: bauxite, gold, sugar and rice. Gold production has increased in recent years. Guyana is one of the poorest countries in the Western Hemisphere.

Visas

Visas are not required by visitors from the US, Commonwealth and EU countries. Proof of onward travel is necessary.

Customs

No duty is charged on personal goods, but there are high charges on items brought in for commercial purposes.

Money Matters

The currency is the Guyanese dollar, available in denominations of 1, 5, 10 (coins), 20, 100, 500 and 1,000 (notes). The value of the Guyanese dollar (G$) is revised weekly.

Most banks and bureaux de change buy only US or Canadian dollars and UK sterling. It is possible to change travelers' checks at a few of the larger stores and travel agents in Georgetown.

Tourist Offices

Tourism Association of Guyana, 157 Waterloo Street, North Cummingsburg, Georgetown, tel: 250 807 (24-hr emergency hotline: 56899), fax 250 817, www.interknowledge.com./guyana

Public Holidays

- **January:** 1 New Year's Day
- **February:** 23 Republic Day and Mashramani Festival
- **March/April:** Phagwah (Hindu Religious Holiday), Good Friday, Easter Monday and Eid-ul-Azha (Muslim Holy Day)
- **May:** 1 Labor Day, 26 Independence Day
- **July:** 1 Caricom Day
- **August:** Freedom Day
- **December:** 25 Christmas Day and 26 Boxing Day

Specialist Tour Operators

Wilderness Explorers, 61 Hadfield and Cross streets, Georgetown, tel: 262 085, www.wilderness-explorers.com

Trips Worldwide, 9 Byron Place, Clifton, Bristol BSB 1JT, tel: 0117 987 2626; fax: 0117 987 2627, www.tripsworldwide.co.uk.

Emergency Numbers

Police: 911
Fire: 912
Ambulance service: 913

Media & Communications

International direct dialing is available in most main towns and cities, and faxes can be sent from the Guyana Telephone and Telegraph Company, the Bank of Guyana Building in Georgetown, and larger hotels. Postal services are very good and cheap. The main post office is on Main Street in Georgetown.

The Guyana Chronicle is a state-owned daily newspaper. Other papers include The Mirror, The Kaieteur News, the liberal independent Stabroek News; and the respected and popular weekly Catholic Standard.

The BBC World Service (MHz 17.79, 15.19, 11.75 and 9.915), and the Voice of America (MHz 13.74, 9.775, 7.405, 5.995) are broadcast on radio. There are 14 TV channels, showing mainly US programs, but with increasing local productions.

Embassies/Consulates

Canadian High Commission corner of High St and Young St, Georgetown, tel: 272 081.
UK (High Commission): 44 Main Steet, PO Box 10849, Georgetown, Guyana, tel: 265 881–4.
US: Young Street, Georgetown, tel: 254 900.

Getting Around

From the Airport

Chedi Jagan International Airport is 40 km (25 miles) from Georgetown at Timehri. Minibuses (No. 42) to the center cost US$1, and will take you to your hotel for a small fee; taxis cost US$20–25 (double at night, cheaper to book a seat on a minibus on arrival). Departure tax is G$1,500.

By Air

Internal flights are the best way to get around Guyana. Guyana Airways has scheduled flights from Georgetown to Lethem. Charter companies include Trans Guyana Airways and Kayman Sankar. An airstrip at **Ogle**, about 20 minutes from the center of Georgetown by road, is used for domestic flights.

By Bus & Taxi

Minibuses and collective taxis run along the coast and to many destinations inland. This form of transport is cheap but slow. Taxis have an H in their number plates.

By River

Guyana has over 965 km (600 miles) of navigable waterways. There are frequent services but they tend to be erratic. Ballahoos are six-seater boats, corials are four-seater boats.

By Car

Most of the main roads are found in the coastal area. There is a highway being built between Bonfim in Guyana and Boa Vista in Brazil; when it is finished it will allow

Security

Georgetown is a colorful and attractive city but you should take care in some areas (avoid Tiger Bay and Albouystown in particular) and do not walk around the streets at night. Violent crime on the streets and highways is common, and there are many beggars, although most are harmless.

Car Hire

Camex, 125 'D' Barrack Street, Kingston, Georgetown, Guyana, tel: 276 976.
Trident Auto Rentals, 215 Camp Street, Georgetown, Guyana, tel: 250 675; fax: 256 864.

Guyana to connect with the network of roads in Latin America.

Where to Stay

Most of the luxury and business hotels are in Georgetown; quality ranges from good to reasonable.

Georgetown

Cara Lodge, 293 Quamina Street, tel: 255 301; fax: 255 310, www.carahotels.com. Small and luxurious; converted 150-year-old mansion, with good restaurant, bar and service. **$$$**
Florentene's Hotel, 3 North Street, Lacytown, tel: 262 283. Clean and economical; highly recommended. **$**
Le Meridien Pegasus, Seawall Road, tel: 252 853–9; fax: 260 532, www.lemeridien-pegasus.com. Pool, restaurants, tennis, gym. **$$$**
Rima Guest House, 92 Middle Street, New Cummingsburg, tel: 257 401. Safe and central budget hotel, with good value restaurant. **$**
Tower Hotel , 74–75 Main Street, tel: 272 011–5, fax: 256 021/265 691. Swimming pool and very good restaurant. **$$$**

New Amsterdam

Astor Hotel, 7 Strand, tel: 03 3578. Comfortable mid-range hotel; breakfast served; recommended. **$$**
Parkway Hotel, 4 Main Street, near the mosque, tel: 03 3928. Reasonable mid-range place; clean, friendly and safe. **$$**

Lethem

Savannah Inn, General Store, tel: 592 69716. Good and clean, mid-range. Can also be booked through Wilderness Explorers (tel: 262 085); organizes jungle tours. **$$**

Hotel Price Guide

Prices for a double room including continental breakfast.
$ = US$30 or less – inexpensive
$$ = US$30–50 – moderate
$$$ = US$50 plus – expensive

Jungle Lodges

There are many lodges and camps in the tropical forest interior, catering for the eco-tourism market. These establishments, whose facilities range from basic to up-market, usually run their own treks and nature safaris. Recommended:
Timberhead Rainforest Reserve, two hours from Georgetown by air and boat up the Kamuni River. Reservations with **Le Meridien Pegasus** in Georgetown (see above). Three comfortable lodges with inclusive facilities, meals, and guided activities. Good bird-watching area.
Dadanawa Ranch, 97 km (60 miles) south of Lethem, is a huge establishment, which runs horseback riding and trekking expeditions. Can be booked through Wilderness Explorers, 61 Hadfield and Cross streets, Georgetown, tel: 262 085, email: wilderness-explorers@solutions 2000.net.
Rock View Ecotourism Resort, Annai, a village 112 km (70 miles) from Lethem, tel: 64210; fax: 57211 (or book through Wilderness Explorers, above). Small, with some cheaper rooms, bars, and a zoo.

What to Eat

Guyanese cuisine is good and varied, combining influences from the Caribbean, Africa, Europe, North America, Asia, as well as indigenous cooking. Seafood is particularly tasty. Interesting Creole dishes include the traditional Christmas dish, pepperpot (meat cooked with hot spices and cassava juice); cow-heel soup and saltfish. There is a wide range of tropical fruits (often served in some excellent juice bars) and vegetables. Locally produced rum is the favored tipple, and the beer, *Banks*, is quite palatable.

Where to Eat

Many restaurants close on public holidays; cheaper places are often open only for lunch. Formal dress may be demanded in some of the capital's upmarket restaurants, the best of which are found within the luxury hotels.

Restaurant Guide

Prices for a three-course meal for two, including house wine.
$ = US$25 or less – inexpensive
$$ = US$25–50 – moderate
$$$ = US$50 plus – expensive

Georgetown
Browne's Café, Le Meridien Pegasus, Seawall Road, tel: 252 853–9. International and Creole cuisine, good English breakfast. **$$**
Eldorado, Le Meridien Pegasus, Seawall Road. International and Creole cuisine. Upmarket. **$$$**
Palm Court, Main Street, tel: 225 7938. Chinese and Creole food. **$$**
Sidewalk Café and Jazz Club, 176 Middle Street, tel: 270 152. Local and international cuisine; has shows by top-name musicians. **$$**

New Amsterdam
Brown Derby, corner of Church and Main Streets. East Indian and Chinese food. **$**
Circle C, Lot 7, Main and Charlotte Street. Good and cheap Creole cuisine. **$**

Outdoor Activities

Guyana's most popular sport is cricket. The Georgetown Cricket Club at Bourda is one of the finest grounds in the Caribbean.
The coastline is not ideal for water sports, but there are some good opportunities in the interior for trekking and river-rafting, which can be arranged by local tour operators.

Paraguay
A – Z

Getting Acquainted

Area 406,800 sq. km (157,000 sq. miles)
Capital Asunción
Population 6 million. Eighty percent of Paraguayans are *mestizo* (mixed race Amerindian and European). There has also been heavy immigration from Korea, Japan and Taiwan.
Language Spanish and Guaraní
Currency: Guaraní = 100 centimos
Weights & measures Metric
Electricity 220 volts
Time zone GMT -3hrs in east, -4hrs in the west (EST +3hrs, EST +1hr)
International dialing code 595 (Asunción +21)

Government & Economy

General Alfredo Stroessner was overthrown in 1989 after 35 years in office, yet both the Colorado Party and the armed forces remain highly influential in national politics.
Political reforms since the demise of Stroessner include the adoption of a new constitution in 1992, and a process of decentralization of power to local departmental and municipal government. Despite an attempted coup in May 1996, democracy seems assured. The ruling Colorado Party won the presidency again in April 2003, for Nicanor Duarte Frutos, extending their run to over half a century.
Agricultural products such as meat, soya and cotton account for the main bulk of exports, although the economy still relies strongly on contraband and drug smuggling.

Customs

Alcohol, tobacco and electronic items for personal use are admitted to the country duty-free.

Visas

US citizens need a visa, but visitors from the UK, Australasia, Canada, and most of Western Europe do not. Check with your local travel agent to see if requirements have changed.

Money

It is not possible to exchange guaraní outside the country – so only change what you will need. *Casas de cambio* will accept travelers' checks. ATM dispensers are fairly widespread and major credit cards are widely accepted.

Emergencies

A satisfactory ambulance service is not available; it's best to transport the patient by private means or taxi. Have someone phone the hospital, stating the nature of the problem and asking that a doctor receive the patient in the emergency room. To contact the police in an emergency, dial **442 111**.

For emergencies, contact any of the Asunción emergency rooms:
Centro Paraguayo del Diagnóstico, Calle General Díaz 975 and Colón, Asuncíon, tel: 947 722.
Hospital Bautista, Avda Rep. Argentina and Campos Cervera, tel: 600 171 or 607 944.

Business Hours

During the hot season, a long midday siesta is observed and many shops and offices open Mon–Sat 6.30am–noon, and 3–7pm. Banks tend to be open Mon–Fri 7.30–11am, although some stay open for longer hours. Dinner is served somewhat earlier than in neighboring countries, that is, around 8.30–11pm.

Religious Services

The state religion is Roman Catholicism. There is a Sunday Mass in English at Padres Oblatos de María Chapel, on Calle Gómez de Castro and Quesada. Other churches include the Anglican Church on Avda España 1261, the Mormon Church on Avda España and the Brasília Synagogue on Calle General Díaz 657.

Media

Radio is the most effective means of communication. One of the most popular is *Radio Ñandutí*. Two privately owned television networks operate in Asunción; all TV drama programs are imported from the United States and the neighboring countries. Channel 8 shows CNN in English.

The widest-circulating daily newspapers are: *ABC*, *Noticias*, *La Nación*, and *Ultima Hora* (an afternoon daily).

Telecoms

It is wise to send important letters by registered mail. All mail must be deposited at a post office counter. Long-distance calls can be made from ANTELCO office on N.S. de Asunción and Presidente Franco. Telex and fax services are also available. International calls are called either *ordinario* or *urgente*, urgent calls costing twice as much.

Public Holidays

- January 1
- February 3
- March 1, late March/April
  Maundy Thursday, Good Friday
- May 1, 14, 15
- June 12
- August 15, 25
- September 29
- October 12
- November 1
- December 8, 25.

Tourist Information

The *Dirección General de Turismo Paraguayo* is at Avda Palma 468, Asuncíon, tel: 491 230/441 530/441 620/494 110, e-mail: senaturpy@hotmail.com, website: www.senatur.gov.py. Information is available at the Touring & Automobile Club of Paraguay at Calle 25 de Mayo and Brasil.

Embassies/Consulates

UK: Avda Boggiani 5848, Asunción, tel: 612 611, fax 605 007.
US: Avda Mariscal López 1776, Asunción, tel: 213 715, fax: 213 728.

Getting Around

From the Airport
Asunción's **Silvio Pettirosi Airport** is 16 km (10 miles) from the city center; taxis can be reserved at agencies' desks, and cost approximately US$15; buses to the center cost US30¢, but luggage space is limited.

There is an international entry tax of about US$12 and a departure tax of around US$15 (it is cheaper to pay in guaranís). Domestic departure tax is about US$2.50.

By Air
Líneas Aéreas de Transporte Nacional (LATN), Aero Lineas Paraguayas (ARPA), Aeronorte, Líneas Aéreas del Este (LADESA), Aerosur, and Transporte Aéros del Mercosur (TAM) have flights to northern Paraguay and parts of the Chaco region. Varig Airways (RG) flies to Iguazú Falls from Asunción.

By Rail
Prices for travel on Paraguay's ancient trains are extremely cheap, but journeys are exceedingly slow.

By Bus
Buses are the main means of transport within Paraguay; the main terminal is a 20-minute cab ride from

the center of Asunción at Avda Rep. Argentina and Fernando de la Mora, tel: 552 154. "Executive" buses vary according to company. There is a luxury international bus service that serves Asunción and Ciudad del Este, Pedro Juan Caballero and Encarnación by way of Argentina, Uruguay and Brazil.

By River
There are several boats that sail up the **Paraná River** to **Concepción** every 2 3 weeks, a journey of 27–30 hours. An irregular passenger boat service shuttles downstream between **Buenos Aires** and **Asunción**. The journey takes five days and can be suspended during the dry season. (*For further details contact tourist information, see box, page 388.*)

By Car
Petrol is cheap and car hire relatively inexpensive; contact Touring y Automóvil Club Paraguayo, Calle Brasíl, tel: 210 550.

Taxis are inexpensive, averaging US$2 per journey in Asunción. Minimum charge is about US$80¢; more by night. One main taxi stand is in front of the Hotel Guaraní on the Plaza de los Héroes; or call RadioTaxi: 550 116/311 080.

Where to Stay

Asunción
Cecilia Hotel, Calle Estados Unidos 341, tel: 210 033/034, fax: 497 111. Has a good restaurant. **$$**
Chaco Hotel, Calle Caballero and Mariscal Estigarribia, tel: 492 066/9, fax: 444 223. Has a rooftop pool. **$$**
Excelsior Hotel, Calle Chile 980, tel: 496 743, fax: 496 748. The best in town. Modern, with conference facilities. **$$$**

Hotel Price Guide

Prices for a double room including continental breakfast.
$ = US$50 – inexpensive
$$ = US$50–100 – moderate
$$$ = US$100 plus – expensive

Guaraní Hotel, Calle Independencia Nacional and Oliva, tel: 491 131, fax: 443 647. Central, tried and tested. **$$**
Hotel de Yacht y Golf Club Paraguay, PO Box 1795, tel: 906 117, fax: 906 20. Sporty with all the trimmings. **$$$**

What to Eat

Paraguayan specialties include *surubí*, a tasty fish dish; *sopa paraguaya*, a rich cornbread made of ground maize and cheese; *soyo*, a beef and vegetable soup; *empanadas* and fresh tropical juices. Paraguayan beef is excellent. Also make sure you try *tereré*, a local ice-cold drink.

There are also a number of excellent Brazilian restaurants with succulent barbecue grilled meats and large self-service buffets.

Restaurant Guide

Prices for a three course meal for two, including house wine.
$ = US$50 – inexpensive
$$ = US$50–100 – moderate
$$$ = US$100 plus – expensive

Where to Eat

Asunción
Bar San Roque, Calle Eligio Ayala corner of Tacuary, near Plaza Uruguaya. Old-style café-restarant with an excellent selection of different cuisines. Closed Sunday. **$**
Bar Asunción, Calle Estrella and 14 de Agosto. Fast food and Paraguayan specialties. **$**
Amstel, Avda Rep. Argentina 1384. Expensive; serves good traditional food. **$$$**
La Preferida, Calle 25 de Mayo and Estados Unidos, tel: 491 126. Excellent international cuisine. **$$**
Sukiyaki, Avda Constitución near Brasíl. Japanese. **$$**
Tallyrand, Calle Mariscal Estigarribia 932, tel: 441 163/445 246. Highly respected local chain

Drinking Tips

Paraguayan beer is made according to German methods and is excellent. The national wine is not recommended. The local sugar cane liquor, *caña*, is popular and many liquors are imported at low prices.

serving French cuisine. Reservations essential. **$$$**
Bolsi, Calle Estrella 399, tel: 491 841/494 720. Asunción institution that has been serving local and Mediterranean food for over 40 years. **$$**
Il Capo, Avda Perú 291 and Calle José Berges, tel: 213 022, fax: 204 401. Classy Italian and international cuisine. **$$**

Theater Restaurants

A typical evening's entertainment is a restaurant floor show, with Paraguayan harp and guitar music, and sometimes the (indescribable and unmissable) bottle dance. Prices vary according to the quality of the show, but are generally about $10 per person. Recommended spots include:
Hermitage, Calle 15 de Agosto 1870, Asunción.
Ita Enramada Hotel & Casino, Calle Cacique Lambares and Ribero del Río Paraguay, tel: 332 044/333 041. Open 9pm–4am.

Tours

Check with recommended tourist agencies such as: **Inter Express**, Calle Luis A. de Herrera and Yegros, Asunción, tel: 490 111, fax: 449 156, e-mail: iexpress@interexpress.com.py or **Time Tours**, Calle 15 de Agosto and General Díaz, tel: 493 527.

Where to Shop

The street market in Calle Palma is pedestrianized on Saturday mornings and has a variety of goods; leather and lace goods are great value.

Peru
A – Z

Getting Acquainted

Area 1,285,000 sq. km (496,100 sq. miles)
Capital Lima
Population 27 million, of whom 45 percent are indigenous, 32 percent Amerindian and European *(mestizo)*, 12 percent white *(criollo)* and 2 percent black and Asian. The cohesive black population live mainly in the southern coastal cities.
Language The official languages are Spanish and Quechua. Near Puno and Lake Titicaca, Aymara is spoken.
Currency Nuevo Sol
Weights & measures Metric
Electricity 220 volts
Time zone GMT -5hrs, EST
Dialing code 51 (Lima +1)

Government & Economy

Since 1979 Peru has been run by a democratic government under a constitution. The country is divided into 24 departments and the province of Callao, which is where the country's main port is located.

Fishing, mining, and tourism play important roles in the economy. Petroleum is extracted from the Amazon jungle area, providing half the domestic demand.

In June 2001, Alejandro Toledo, the first Peruvian president of Andean indigenous extraction, was elected. His election ended more than a decade of rule by Alberto Fujimori (1989–2000), who fled to Japan in disgrace when allegations of widespread corruption and abuses during his period in office came to light. One lasting achievement of the Fujimori regime was its success in combating

extremist groups. The leader of the Shining Path guerrilla movement was captured in 1992, which led to the collapse of the group. Then in 1996–97, the leaders of the Tupac Amaru rebel group were wiped out. After these two successes, political violence in Peru virtually ceased, although human rights groups criticized many of the government's tactics, including the imprisonment of thousands of people merely on suspicion of links with terrorist groups, the suspension of civil liberties, and the armed forces' involvement in massacres, especially in remote rural areas.

Emergencies

24-hour travelers' hotline tel: 574-8000
Tourist police, Lima, tel: 225-8698.
General police emergency number, tel: 105.
The **Tourist Protection Service** can assist in contacting police to report a crime: tel: 224-7888 in Lima, or 0800/4-2579 toll-free from a private phone (the toll-free number cannot be dialed from a public pay phone).

Riots in southern Peru in June 2002 led Toledo to suspend his privatization plans. In 2003 a truth commission found that over 69,000 people had been killed in conflicts between rebel groups and the government – twice the figure originally thought. In June 2004, Toledo's presidency looked shakey following the resignation of his vice-president, two cabinet members and personal lawyer in the space of six weeks. Toledo attempted to stabilize matters by announcing a $2.5 billion social spending program and an anti-corruption plan.

Visas

Visas are not required by citizens of Australia, Canada, Ireland, New Zealand, South Africa, the UK, or the United States. With a valid passport, citizens of these

countries receive a tourism card which is usually good for 90 days.

A 30-day extension is available upon payment of US$20 and presentation of a return travel ticket. Contact the *Dirección General de Migraciones* in the Ministerio del Oficina de Migración, Avda España cda 7, Breña, tel: 330 4111.

A US$25 exit tax on international flights, and $12 for domestic flights, must be paid.

Customs

It is illegal to take archeological artifacts out of the country. Permits are no longer required for bringing camera equipment into Peru.

Money

On Plaza San Martín, in downtown Lima, hundreds of outdoor bankers run alongside the traffic exchanging US dollars – the rate is usually a little better than in the banks. It is legal to change with these *cambistas*, who generally wear a green jacket and carry a calculator, and usually quite safe. Banks will change your currency at a slightly inflated rate and good hotels have exchange services or will send a hotel courier to one of the *casas de cambio* for a better rate (remember to give him a tip). Travel agents accept payment in some foreign currencies and exchange small amounts. It is convenient to carry some US cash as well as travelers' checks, credit cards or cash advance card. It is not always possible to change checks, and cash dollars get a better rate. American Express will replace lost travelers' checks only in Lima.

Most international credit cards are accepted. Credit card loss can be reported in Lima. Visa: 372 5808, or toll free 0800 1 3333. Diners Club: 221 2050. MasterCard: 222 4242.

Medical Services

Most major hotels have a doctor on call. Three clinics in Lima and its suburbs have 24-hour emergency service and usually an English-speaking member of staff on duty: **Clínica Anglo-Americana**, Calle Alfredo Salazar s/n, San Isidro, tel: 221 3656; **Clínica Internacional**, Jr Washington 1475, tel: 433 4306 and **Clínica San Borja**, Avda Guardia Civil 333, San Borja, tel: 475 3141. The **Emergency Hospital Casimiro Ulloa** is on Avda República de Panamá 6355, San Antonio, Miraflores, tel: 241 2789. A recommended English-speaking dentist is **Victor Manuel Aste**, tel: 441 7502.

Business Hours

Most stores open Mon–Fri 10am–8pm and 1– 4pm.

Banks open 9am–12.30 or 1pm during summer (Jan–Mar). For the rest of the year they open 3–6pm, although the hours often change. *Casas de cambio* open 9am–6pm, while money changers are on the streets nearly 24 hours a day.

Communications

Both national and international calls can be made from public pay phones. It is advisable to buy a phone card (available from newsstands and supermarkets) but it must correspond to the telephone company of the phone you are using. Mobile phones can be rented from a number of shops in Lima.

Most of the country is serviced by Internet booths and cafés.

Useful Websites

www.peru.org.pe
A useful, if basic, site in English.
www.peruviantimes.com
Very informative online guide.

Embassies/Consulates

The following diplomatic representatives are all based in Lima:

Australia, Victor A. Belaunde 147, Via Principal 155, Building 3, Office 1301, San Isidro, tel: 222 8281.
Canada: Calle Libertad 130, Miraflores, tel: 444 4015.
South Africa: Via Principal 155 Office 801, San Isidro, tel: 440 9996.
UK: Calle Natalio Sánchez 125, 12th floor, Cercado, Lima, tel: 433 8023/4738, www.britemb. org.pe.
US: La Encalada, Block 17, Surco, Monterrico, tel: 434 3000, http://usembassy. state.gov/lima.

Getting Around

From the Airport

Bus services include **Transhotel**, Logroño 132, Miraflores, tel: 448 2179, airport, tel: 518 011; **CM Tours**, tel: 275 0612; and **VIP International Service SA**, tel: 446 4821, which run to and from **Jorge Chávez Airport**, Lima. Make reservations beforehand.

A bit more expensive but reliable are **Lima Taxis**, tel: 476 2121. A normal taxi will charge about US$10–15 to or from the airport (US$15–20 to Miraflores), and it's safer than trying to flag one down in Avda Faucett, outside the terminal.

You can also **rent cars** at the airport, where Avis, Budget, Dollar, Hertz and National have offices open 24 hours a day. An international driver's license is needed and is valid for 30 days. For additional days, you must obtain authorization from the **Touring and Automobile Club of Peru**, Calle César Vallejo 699, Lince, tel: 440 3270, fax: 422 5947.

By Air

Domestic airlines Aero Continente and Lan Perú and TACA serve most cities in Peru. For domestic flights there is an airport tax of US$3.50 at all airports. **Aerocontinente** is at Jr Bolognesi 125,16th floor, Miraflores, tel: 242 4260, e-mail: aerocont@aerocontinente.com.pe **Lan Perú** is at José Pardo 805, Miraflores, tel: 213 8200; fax 446 3157. **TACA Peru** is at Comandante Espinar 331, Miraflores, tel: 213 7000; fax: 445 3277. For trips over the Nazca lines or special short flights, **Aerocondor** has an office at Jr Juan de Arona 781, San Isidro, tel: 222 4130.

By Bus

Numerous buses operate morning and evening departures to most cities. Reliable companies include: **Ormeño**, Avda Javier Prado Este 1059, Lima 13 (domestic and international routes), tel: 472 1710, fax: 470 6474. Calle Carlos Zavala 177, Lima (domestic), tel: 427 5679.
Tepsa, Avda Javier Prado Este 1091, Lima, tel: 470 4664.
Civa, Avda 28 de Julio, corner of Paseo de la República, tel: 332 5236/332 5264.

From Bolivia, efficient minibus services will take you from La Paz to Puno.
Crillón Tours, PO Box 4785, Avda Camacho 1223, La Paz, Bolivia, tel: (591) 2 233 7533, fax: (591) 2 211 6482, www.titicaca.com/ctintro, runs several hydrofoil services across Lake Titicaca. The journey from Ecuador is also straightforward: take a bus to the Huaquillas border and walk through to Tumbes. Other buses operate from there.

By Rail

PeruRail runs a daytime passenger service on the Arequipa–Juliaca–Puno route. To reach the ruins at Machu Picchu, there are several options: the modern *Autovagón* departs from Cusco early for Machu Picchu (get off at Aguas Calientes) and returns in the afternoon. Travel agents in Cusco

Useful Addresses

Tourist Information Centers

Lima: Jorge Chávez International Airport (24 hours), tel/fax: 01-574 8000. Jorge Basadre 610, San Isidro, tel: 421 1627. Larcomar Entertainment Center, Module 14, Malecón de la Reserva 610, tel/fax: 445 9400.
Cusco: Velasco Astete Airport, tel/fax: 084-23 7364. Avda Sol 103, Oficina 102, Galérias Turísticas.
Also worth visiting for up-to-date information is the **South American Explorers' Club**, Calle Piura 135, Miraflores, Lima, tel: 445-3306, www.samexplo.org, or write to: Casilla 3714, Lima 100.

Hotel Price Guide

Prices for a double room including continental breakfast.
$ = US$50 – inexpensive
$$ = US$50–100 – moderate
$$$ = US$100 plus – expensive

sell all-inclusive day tickets for the trip. The Pullman also leaves Cusco in the morning, and there are much cheaper, slower and crowded trains for budget travelers. (*See Trekking, page 393*, for information on walking to Machu Picchu.)

The Lima–Huancayo passenger service, the world's highest train journey, is no longer operating.

Where to Stay

Arequipa
El Portal, Portal de Flores 116, tel: 812 782, reservations in Lima: tel: 9904 5055, www. portaldelmarques.com. Excellent views and rooftop pool. **$$**
Hotel La Casa de mi Abuela, Calle Jerusalem 606, tel: 241 206; fax: 242 761, www. lacasademiabuela.com. Constantly receives rave reviews. Large complex of bungalow-style rooms in a garden setting. **$**
Hotel Libertador, Plaza Bolívar on Selva Alegre, tel: 215 110, fax: 241 933. Reservations in Lima: tel: 442 0166/1995, e-mail: arequipa@ libertador.com.pe. The most traditional hotel in Arequipa. **$$$**

Cajamarca
Hotel Laguna Seca, Avda Manco Capac, Baños Termales, tel: 894 600, fax: 894 646, www. lagunaseca.com.pe. At the thermal baths, the waters of which enter the bathrooms of this hotel. **$$$**
Hotel Sierra Galana, Jiron Comercio 773, tel/fax: 82 2470. Reservations in Lima, tel: 446 3652, fax: 445 1139. Comfortable and central. **$$**

Cusco
Hostal Corihuasi, Calle Suecia 561, tel: 232 233, e-mail: corihuasi@amauta. rcp.net.pe.

Colonial-style house with warm and quiet rooms. Hot water. **$**
Best Western Los Andes de América, Calle Garcilaso 234–36, tel: 22 2253, fax: 232 203, www.bestwestern.com. Rooms arranged around an interior courtyard. Helpful staff; excellent buffet breakfast included. **$$**
Monasterio de Cusco, Calle Palacio 136, Plaza Nazarenas, tel: 246 419; reservations: tel: 23 7111; reservations in Lima: tel: 221 0826; fax: 421 8283, www.monasterio. orient-express.com. Elegant converted monastery. **$$$**

Iquitos
Explorama Lodge/Camp. In virgin rainforest. To make reservations in Iquitos, check at the administrative offices on Avda de la Marina 340, tel: 252 530, fax: 252 533. Reservations in Lima: tel: 244 764; fax: 234 968, www.explorama.com. **$$$**
Hostal La Pascana, Calle Pevas 133, tel: 231 418. Basic but comfortable budget hotel, with garden. **$**

Lima
Gran Hotel Bolívar, Jr de la Unión 958, Plaza San Martín, tel: 428 7672, fax: 428 7675, www.hotelbolivar.com. The doyen of Peruvian hotels. **$$$**
Hotel Crillon, Calle Nicolas de Pierola 589, tel: 428 3290, fax: 432 5920. The hotel's Sky Room stages the best folkloric show in Lima. **$$$**
Hotel Residencial Europa, Jr Ancash 376, Plaza San Francisco, tel: 427 3351. Very cheap and lively hotel in the heart of downtown Lima. **$**
Hotel España, Jr Azángaro 105, tel/fax: 428 5546, e-mail: fertur@terra.com.pe. Clean; shared bathrooms. Central budget hotel. **$**
Hostal El Patio, Calle Diez Canseco 341A, tel: 444 4884, fax: 444 1663, www.hostalelpatio.com. Colonial-style hotel in the heart of Miraflores. **$$**
Miraflores Park Hotel, Avda Malecón de la Reserva 1035, Miraflores, tel: 242 3000, fax: 242

3393, www.mira-park.com. Luxury business hotel; part of the Orient Express Group. **$$$**

Nazca
Hostal de la Borda, Km 447 off the Panamericana Sur, tel/fax: 52 2576. Reservations must be made in Lima, tel/fax: 440 8430. Near the airfield, *hacienda* with garden, swimming pools, hot showers and friendly service. **$$**
Nazca Hotel, Jr Bolognesi s/n, tel: 52 2293, fax: 52 2112, www.invertur.com.pe. Reservations in Lima: Invertur tel: 221 7020, fax: 442 4180. Comfortable and clean, with a swimming pool. **$$**

Puno (Lake Titicaca)
Hotel Libertador Puno, Isla Esteves, tel: 36 7780, fax: 36 7879. Reservations in Lima: tel: 442 1066, fax: 442 2988. www.libertador.com.pe. Large modern building with excellent view of Lake Titicaca. **$$$**

Trujillo
Libertador Trujillo, Calle Independencia 485, Plaza de Armas, tel: 24 4999/23 2741, fax: 23 5641. Reservations in Lima: tel: 442 1996, fax: 442 2988, www.libertador.com.pe. Beautiful building; good value. **$$$**
Los Conquistadores, Calle Diego de Almagro 586, tel: 203 350, fax: 235 917. Comfortable. **$$**
Hostal Trujillo, Calle Grau 581, tel: 243 921. Budget hotel, clean rooms with private bathrooms. **$**

Restaurant Guide

Prices for a three-course meal for two, including house wine.
$ = US$50 – inexpensive
$$ = US$50–100 – moderate
$$$ = US$100 plus – expensive

What to Eat

Peru's cuisine ranges from scrumptious seafood to potatoes – the staple in a variety of highland dishes – to tropical fruits from the Amazon jungle. Recommended

Drinking Tips

Peru has several **beers**, including Cristal, Pilsen, Arequipeña and Cusqueña, all of which are light lagers. Its best **wines** are Tacama, Ocucaje, Tabernero, and Vista Alegre. The national **cocktail** is *pisco sour* – made from *pisco*, a kind of brandy, lemon juice and egg white with a dash of cinnamon (the Hotel Grand Bolívar in Lima serves the *Catedral pisco sour*, claimed to be the best in Peru).

Travelers should drink only **bottled water** (and specify *sin hielo* – no ice – in other cold drinks) and refrain from eating food sold by street vendors.

The soft drink *chicha morada*, made with purple maize, is popular. It's different from the *chicha de jora*, the traditional home-made alcoholic brew known throughout the Andes. The lime green *Inka Kola* is more popular than its northern namesake.

Jugos (juices), are a delightful alternative to sodas and there are many choices available. Instant Nescafé is often served up even in good restaurants, although real coffee can be found. Tea drinkers would be advised to order their beverage without milk, to avoid receiving some odd concoctions.

dishes include *ceviche*, raw fish and/or shellfish marinated in lemon juice and onions. A typical chicken entrée is *ají de gallina* served in a lightly spiced creamed sauce. Also with a spicy sauce, but this one cheese-based, is *papa a la Huancaina*. For the adventurous, *cuy* or guinea pig is available stewed or fried. Hot peppers *(ají or rocoto)* are used liberally in many typical dishes.

The Peruvians have a variety of wonderful fruits including *chirimoya*, a large green fruit with creamy flesh; *lúcuma*, a small, tangy, nut-like fruit; and *tuna*, the sweet crisp fruit of the cactus. *Mazamorra morada*, a fruity pudding dating from colonial days, is a favorite.

Where to Eat

Arequipa
Sambambaias, Calle Luna Pizarro 304, tel: 241 209. High-quality international and local cuisine. **$$$**

Lima
La Gloria, Calle Atahulapa 201, Miraflores, tel: 445 5705. Delicious Mediterranean-style food. **$$$**
La Costa Verde, Barranquito Beach, tel: 477 2172/477 2424. One of the best, for great seafood and atmosphere. **$$$**.
La Rosa Nautica, Calle Espigon 4, Costa Verda, Miraflores, tel: 447 0057. Lima's best seafood restaurant, set on an ocean boardwalk. **$$**
Restaurante Royal, Avda Prescott 231, San Isidro, tel: 421 0814. High-class Chinese cuisine with service to match. **$$**

Cusco
El Truco, Plaza Regocijo 247. Nightly dinner and show; very good value. **$$**
Inka's Grill, Portal de Panes 115, Plaza de Armas, tel: 262 992. On the main square, great atmosphere and good food, with folklore show most nights. **$$$**
Kusikuy, Calle Plateros 348, tel: 26 2870. Typical local food. **$**
Pacha-Papa, Plaza San Blas 120, tel: 241 318/233 190. Highly recommended, serving traditional Peruvian food. **$**
Pizzeria Chez Maggy, Calle Plateros 339, tel 23 4861/23 2478. Excellent place for good pizza; there's another branch on Procuradores. **$**

Museums

Peruvian officials claim that Lima alone has more than 75 museums. See the Places section of this guide for details of the best. Most museums are closed on Monday (as throughout South America). The numerous colonial buildings, many of them well renovated, make central Lima something of an open-air museum.

Trekking

The Peruvian dry season, May through September, offers the best views and finest weather. For safety reasons and for greater enjoyment, parties of three or more should hike together. Groups are easily formed in Cusco, and the Tourist Office on the Plaza de Armas provides a noticeboard for this purpose. In Huaráz, contact the Casa de Guías, Parque Ginebra 28 G, Huaraz-Ancash, tel: 721 333.

Supplies should include a backpack, hiking boots, warm clothes, sleeping bags, insulated pad, tent and stove. This equipment can be hired at a number of adventure travel agencies, especially in cities like Huaraz and Cusco. The cost is minimal, but quality often suffers. Inspect hired equipment carefully before departure. It can get extremely cold at night, and by day the Andean sun burns quickly. Have a hat handy.

In the Cordillera Blanca, *arrieros*, or mule-drivers, are quite inexpensive and readily available.

It is not possible to hike the Inca Trail independently; you must pre-book with a tour operator. This is easily arranged either in your home country or in Cusco. Most organized treks provide all the necessary food and camping equipment for the 3–4 day trip, as well as porters to carry it, but make sure you understand what you will need to bring yourself.

Where to Shop

Each region has its own distinctive crafts, but if your time is limited, you will find that many cultures are well represented in Lima. Try: **Artesanías del Perú**, Calle Jorge Basadre 610, San Isidro, tel: 440 1925; **Mercado Indio** on Avda La Marina, from blocks 6 to 10 on your way to the airport; or at Petit Thours 5242, Miraflores.
Kunturwasi, Calle Ocharán 182, Miraflores, tel:444 0557, has a very good selection of Peruvian crafts.

If you feel the cold more than the average person, bring along extra warm layers or blankets.

All food should be brought from a major town; very little is available in the smaller villages. A variety of dried fruit, cheese, package soups, and tinned fish can easily be acquired. Drinking water should be treated with iodine. Add instant drink mixes like Tang to offset the unpleasant taste.

The unpleasant symptoms of altitude sickness *(soroche)* – nausea, exhaustion, headaches – can be significantly diminished by avoiding alcohol and physical exertion and not overeating for the first day or two, or longer if you need it. Drinking ample liquids helps the system adjust quickly. The sugar in hard candy stimulates the metabolism, and aspirin eases headaches. *Mate de coca*, tea brewed from coca leaves, is said to be the best treatment for any sickness.

Nightlife

Lima is full of colorful *peñas* where there is non-stop folk music and dancing into the early hours. Aim to arrive about 9pm to get a good seat. Barranco is the neighborhood where there is most going on.
Brisas del Titicaca, Calle Walkuski 168, Lima. An authentic *peña* with Peruvian dance shows. Popular with the locals and cheap.
Manos Morenas, Calle Pedro de Osma 409, Barranco. Good Peruvian food. Afro–Peruvian Dance group Wed and Thur; general Peruvian music Fri and Sat. Shows start 10.30pm.
La Noche, Avda Bolognesi 307, Barranco. A good, lively bar for a beer.

Suriname
A – Z

Getting Acquainted

Area 163,265 sq. km (63,037 sq. miles)
Capital Paramaribo
Population 440,000
Language Dutch (official language) Sranan Tongo, Hindi, Javanese, English, Chinese, French and Spanish are also spoken
Currency Suriname Gilder (SG
Weights & measures Metric
Electricity 110/220v AC, 60Hz
Time zone GMT –3hrs; EST +1hr
International dialing code 597

Government & Economy

Suriname has a democratically elected government, with one legislative house, the National Assembly. The president is head of state and head of government. Runaldo Ronald Venetiaan of the New Front is head of state and government. Major industries in Suriname include the export of bauxite and aluminum, shrimp, fish, bananas, and rice. The US is a major trading partner.

Visas

Visas are required by almost all visitors. Two good passport photographs, an application form in duplicate and a fee are necessary for the visa, which can be obtained upon arrival.
Visitors from the USA can contact the Surinamese Embassy at 4301 Connecticut Avenue NW, Suite 460, Washington DC 20008, tel: 202 244 7488/7590–2, fax: 202 244 5878.

Customs

All money should be declared on entry. The import and export of local currency is limited to SG100; there are no restrictions on foreign currency. Visitors to Suriname are required to exchange US$177 or SG300 on arrival. Children between the ages of 2–12 are expected to change half this amount.

Money

Most transactions should be made in cash; checks are not accepted. It is difficult to buy Suriname gilders abroad, so most travelers take US dollars into the country. The best place to change money is at banks but there is also a thriving (although illegal) black market.

American Express is accepted in most large hotels and tourist restaurants and shops, but Visa is not widely used.

Public Holidays

January 1 New Year's Day
March/April Good Friday, Easter Monday
May 1 Labor Day
July 1National Unity Day
November 25 Independence Day
December 25 and 26 Christmas Hindu and Muslim holidays are also taken, dates varying, according to the lunar calendar: **Holi Phagwah** (March or April, Hindu New Year); **Id ul Fitr** (end of Ramadan); **Id Ul Azah**; **Youm un Nabi**; and **Deepavali** (usually November).

Consulates/Embassies

Canadian Consulate, P.O.Box 1849/1850, Waterkant 92–94, Paramaribo, tel: 471 222, fax: 475 718.
UK: (Honorary Consulate), c/o VSH United Buildings, PO Box 1300, Van't Hogerhuysstraat 9–11, Paramaribo, tel: 472 870, fax: 475 515.
US: PO Box 1821, Dr Sophie Redmondstraat 129, Paramaribo, tel: 472 900, fax: 410 025.

Getting Around

From the Airport

All international flights land at **Johan Adolf Pengel Airport** which is about 50 km (32 miles) south of Paramaribo. There are several minibus companies, which charge about US$5 to the city center, or taxis which cost around US$25.

The airport at **Zorg en Hoop** in Paramaribo is used for domestic flights.

By Boat

There are various daytime ferry services, such as a daily four-hour journey up the Commewijne River. A ferry travels between Paramaribo and Meerzorg on opposite sides of the Suriname River, and smaller boats travel between Leonsberg (5 km/3 miles north of Paramaribo) and Nieuw Amsterdam. Or you can explore the rivers in *korjaals* navigated by highly skilled Maroons.

By Road

In Paramaribo, public transport consists of taxis or buses. It is possible to rent a car, but there is a general shortage of car parts in the country and most cars are not in very good shape; driving is on the left-hand side of the road.

There are no major roads in the interior except for the east–west highway which runs from Albina in the east to Nieuw Nickerie in the west. Buses operate on the coastal highway but they are a very uncomfortable way to travel. It is also possible to use taxis around the coastal regions.

There are road links from Guyana and French Guiana.

Rainforest and Coastal Tours

Much of Suriname's countryside is tropical forest, and many visitors take guided tours into its rainforest and coastal reserves. As the road system is minimal, the most practical form of transport is by small plane, or by boat up one of the many rivers.

Among the highlights for scenic and cultural interest are: the **Galibi**

Nature Reserve on Marowijne River near the village of Albina (turtle-nesting site in July and August); **Marienburg**, the last remaining sugar estate in the country, in the Commewijne district; **Jodensavanne**, south of Paramaribo on the opposite bank of the Suriname River, where an old synagogue has been restored; and the **Natuurpark Brownsberg** in montane rainforest, two hours from Paramaribo.

Suriname has an impressive national park system. Contact Stinasu (the Nature Preservation Foundation of Suriname) for more information and details of their inexpensive guided tours, Cornelis Jongbawstraat 14, P.O. Box 12252, Paramaribo, Suriname, www.stinasu.com

Business Hours

Banking hours are Mon–Fri 9am–2pm. Shops and businesses are open Mon–Fri 9am–4.30pm, Sat 9am–1pm.

Communications & Media

International direct dialing is available. There are no area telephone codes.

Offices of Telesur, the national phone company, in Paramaribo and throughout the country can be used to send telegrams.

De West and *De Ware Tijd* are Dutch-language daily newspapers. The BBC World Service (MHz 17.79, 15.19, 9.915 and 5.970) and Voice of America (MHz 17.71, 13.74, 9.455 and 5.995) are easy to receive.

Useful Websites

www.surinametourism.com
An on-line tourist guide in English.
www.parbo.com
Site dedicated to Paramaribo.

Tourist Organisations

There are two two useful organizations: **Suriname Tourism**

Foundation, PO Box 656, Dr JF Nassylaan 2, Paramaribo, tel: 410 357, fax: 477 786; and the **Suriname Tourism Department**, Communication and Tourism, Prins Hendrikstraat 26–8, Paramaribo, tel: 420 422, fax: 420 425.

Specialist Agencies

METS Travel and Tours, Dr J.F.Nassylaan 2, Paramaribo, tel: 477 088, fax: 422 332, www.metsresorts.com.
Trips Worldwide, 14 Frederick Place, Clifton, Bristol BS8 1AS, tel: 0117 311 4400, fax: 0117 311 4401, www.tripsworldwide.co.uk

Where to Stay

Paramaribo

Ambassador Hotel, Dr Sophie Redmonstraat 66, P.O. Box: 2632, tel: 477 555, fax: 477 903. A very good budget hotel, with a restaurant. **$**
Guesthouse Flair, Kleine Waterstraat 7, tel: 422 455/ 474 794. Clean, reasonable and recommended. **$$**
Torarica Hotel and Casino, Mr Rietbergplein 1, P.O. Box 1514, tel: 471 500, fax: 411 618, www.torarica.com. The best hotel in the city, with pool, restaurants and all facilities. **$$$**

Nieuw Nickerie

Hotel Ameerali, Maynardstraat 32, P.O. Box 6049, tel: 231 212, fax: 231 066. Clean, if small, rooms; comfortable. **$**
Hotel Luxor, St Jozefstraat 22, tel: 231 365. Old-fashioned and friendly place; clean rooms with private baths. **$$**

Hotel Price Guide

Prices for a double room including continental breakfast.
$ = US$50 – inexpensive
$$ = US$50–100 – moderate
$$$ = US$100 plus – expensive

What to Eat & Drink

The standard of food in Suriname is high but so are the prices as most produce is imported. The local cuisine matches the rich ethnic mix of the Surinamese people, and can be very good. Indonesian dishes, such as *bami* (fried noodles) and *nasi goreng* (fried rice) are spicy and served in cheap and cheerful food stalls. Manioc (cassava), sweet potato, plantains, chicken, prawns, and fish feature prominently in Creole cuisine; while among Hindustani specialties are *roti* (mixed curried vegetables and chicken wrapped up in a fried pancake) and *phulawri* (fried chick peas). Chinese cuisine is also plentiful and good value. **Parbo** is the locally produced beer, and is quite drinkable and cheaper than imported brands. The most popular spirit is rum.

Where to Eat

Paramaribo
Chalet Swiss, Lim-a-Po Straat. Good, cheap sandwiches (more Dutch than Swiss-style). **$**
Iwan's, Grote Hofstraat 6, off Watermolenstraat. Expensive, but one of the best Chinese restaurants. **$$$**
Natasha, opposite Torarica Hotel. Tasty and cheap Indian food. **$**
Sarinah, Verlengde Gemenelandsveg 187, tel: 430 661/492 045. Far from downtown but excellent Indonesian cuisine. **$**

Nieuw Nickerie
Incognito, Gouverneurstraat 44. Good Indonesian food. **$$**
Moksie Patoe, Gouverneurstraat 115. Good and varied menu in friendly bar and restaurant. **$$**

Restaurant Guide

Prices for a three-course meal for two, including house wine.
$ = US$50 – inexpensive
$$ = US$50–100 – moderate
$$$ = US$100 plus – expensive

Uruguay
A – Z

Getting Acquainted

Area 176,200 sq. km (68,000 sq. miles)
Capital Montevideo
Population 3.4 million
Language Spanish
Currency 1 Uruguayan peso = 100 centesimos
Weights & measures Metric
Electricity 220 volts
Time zone GMT −3hrs, EST +2hrs
International dialing code 598 (Montevideo +2)

Government & Economy

With the exception of the 1973–85 military dictatorship, Uruguay has enjoyed a liberal democratic system for the past century. Presidents are elected for five years, and cannot run for consecutive terms. The constitution has traditionally provided for a wide array of social services. Jorge Batlle of the center-right Colorado Party was elected head of state and government in March 2000. There are both presidential and National Assembly elections in November 2004.

Chief exports are beef, rice, leather products, automobiles, dairy products, wool, and electricity. An outbreak of foot-and-mouth disease, the recession in Argentina and the devaluation of the Brazilian currency, have all had a negative effect on Uruguay's economy. Current aims are to improve the country's infrastructure and to take advantage of a well-educated population to produce skilled labor and high-valued exports.

Public Holidays

Uruguay has a strong secular tradition whereby Christmas is known as Family Day; Holy Week is Tourism Week, celebrated with horse shows, etc. During Tourism Week, hotels must be booked in advance. Carnival is celebrated with lively parades of minstrels known as *murgas*, and businesses close on Monday and Tuesday of that week.
Other holidays are:
● **January** 1 and 6
● **April** 19
● **May** 1 and 18
● **June** 19
● **July** 18
● **August** 25
● **October** 12
● **November** 2
● **December** 8

Visas

Visas are not required for stays of up to 30 days by citizens of the UK, Canada, Ireland, New Zealand, South Africa, and the USA. A valid passport is required for most visitors.

Travelers must fill out a card at the customs counter, and this must be surrendered on departure. The stamp on passports is usually good for three months and can be extended for a small fee at the Oficina de Migraciones, Calle Misiones 1513, Montevideo, tel: 960 471.

Customs

There are no special restrictions on liquor, tobacco, or electronic goods brought in for personal use.

Getting Around

From the Airport
Montevideo's airport is at **Carrasco**, 30 km (19 miles) away. It's 30 minutes by taxi, and costs about US$30, but arrange the price beforehand; you can pay in dollars as well as pesos. Various bus services to the city center charge between US$1 and US$4. The trip takes up

to 55 minutes, and the bus terminates at either the Río Branco or Tres Cruces bus terminal.

International departure tax is US$12 (except for flights to Buenos Aires, for which US$6 is charged).

By Boat

The most enjoyable way to travel from Buenos Aires to Montevideo is by **night ferry**, which leaves at 9pm, arriving at 8am the following morning. The cost is around a third of the air fare, and includes a sleeping berth. A **catamaran** (buquebus) from Buenos Aires takes 2½ hours and sails three times a day each way.

Also from Buenos Aires, there are daily **ferries** and **hydrofoils** to Colonia (about 160 km/100 miles to the west of Montevideo). The journey can be rough on windy days. There is a connecting bus service to Montevideo, which takes about 3 hours.

By Air

Internal flights within Uruguay, though very cheap, can be scarce; the main airlines are **Pluna** (Calle Colonia and Julio Herrera, tel: 903 0273) and **Avlasur. Tamu**, the military airline, has suspended its national flights.

By Road

The nation's bus system is good, with a number of competing companies whose rates can vary. All long-distance buses depart from the Tres Cruces terminal in Montevideo.

In Montevideo, taxis are cheap though not always plentiful. The city bus system is a mixture of old British Leyland buses and ancient electric trolleys, but the service is fairly efficient. Bus No. 104 (catch it on Calle 18 de Julio) makes a slow but scenic tour of the beaches as far as Carrasco.

There is a daily bus service from Buenos Aires to Montevideo. The trip takes 10 hours. Buses also run on the Pan-American Highway from Rio de Janeiro to Montevideo and on to Colonia.

For information on driving in Uruguay, contact the Automovil Club de Uruguay, Calle Colonia 1251, tel: 902 5792, or the Centro Automovilista del Uruguay, E.V. Haedo 2378, tel: 408 2091.

By Rail

In January 1988, all passenger rail services were withdrawn. To check service details once you are in the country (a reintroduction of the line to the Brazilian border has been rumored), contact Uruguayan State Railways (AFE), Calle La Paz 1095, Casilla de Correo 419, Montevideo, tel: 940 805, fax: 940 847.

Business Hours

Most shops open Mon–Fri 9am–noon and 2–7pm, Sat 9.30am–12.30pm. In Montevideo, banks are open Mon–Fri 1–5pm.

Money

Most banks and exchange offices (casas de cambio) make a small charge for cashing US travelers' checks into dollars (rather than pesos). Credit cards and travelers' checks are widely accepted in Montevideo, but not elsewhere.

ATMS on the Cirrus network are widely available in Montevideo and Punta del Este. If you travel outside these cities, you will need pesos. There is no black market.

Media

There are five television stations in Montevideo; one is state-run. A large percentage of programs come from Argentina. Uruguayans are avid newspaper readers; dailies include El Observador and El País as well as the left-leaning República (good for film, theater and other social happenings). There are also a number of interesting weeklies – Busqueda is considered foremost.

Postal Services

Letters for overseas (extranjeros) should be sent by airmail (por avión). There are post offices (correos) throughout the country.

Telephones & Telexes

Antel, the national telephone company, operates telecentros in most towns; these are the most efficient places to make international calls. Internet and fax services are also available. Payphones require tokens (fichas) which can be bought at Antel or at newsstands. International calls are expensive, but rates are discounted Mon–Fri 10pm–7am, Sat 1pm–midnight, and all day Sunday.

Check with your home cellular service provider to establish compatibility if you want to use your cell phone in Uruguay.

Tourist Information

The main tourist office is on Plaza Fabini (Entrevero). It offers free maps, hotel information, etc. The tourist office at the Tres Cruces bus terminal is open 7am–11pm.

The **Ministerio de Turismo** is at Avda Libertador 1409, 2nd floor, tel: 900 4148, fax: 902 1624, www.turismo.gub.uy (Spanish only). There is an American Express office at Calle Mercedes 942, which is open Mon–Fri 1–5pm.

An online hotel information and reservation system, in English, is www.visit-uruguay.com.

Embassies/Consulates

Australia: Cerro Largo 1000, Montevideo, tel: 901 0743.
Canada: Plaza Independencia 749, Montevideo, tel: 901 3510.
UK: Calle Marco Bruto 1073, tel: 622 3630, fax: 622 7815, www.britishembassy.gov.uk
US: Calle Lauro Muller 1776, Montevideo 11200, tel: 418 7777, fax: 418 8611, http://uruguay.usembassy.gov.

Where to Stay

Montevideo

Belmont House Hotel, Avda Rivera 6512, tel: 600 0430, fax: 600 8609, www.belmonthouse.com.uy. Near Carrasco Airport. Surrounded by gardens and close to the beach. **$$$**

Columbia Palace House, Calle Reconquista 470, tel: 916 0001, fax: 916 0192. **$–$$**

Ermitage Hotel, Calle Juan B. Blanco 783, tel: 710 4021, fax: 710 4312. Good value hotel opposite Pocitos beach. **$**

Hotel Lafayette, Calle Soriano 1170, tel: 902 4646, fax: 927 367. First choice for top business people. **$$**

Hotel La Rochelle, Calle Fernández Crespo 1714, tel: 409 7176, fax: 401 3090. Centrally located hotel, close to Tres Cruces **$$**

Oxford House Hotel, Calle Paraguay 1286, tel: 902 0046, fax: 902 3792, www.oxford.com.uy. Classic English atmosphere. **$$**

Parque

Hotel Mediterraneo, Calle Paraguay 1486, tel: 900 5090. Small, attractive hotel *in a* converted mansion. **$**

Near Atlantida

Fortin De Santa Rosa, Ruta Interbalnearia, tel: 901 9120. Charming converted fortress, with a quiet beach a few meters away and an excellent restaurant. **$$**

Punta del Este

Hotels are invariably expensive, especially in season. Those recommended include:

Conrad Resort and Casino, Calle Biarritz and Avda Artigas, Parada 4, La Mansa, tel: 491 111, fax: 489 999, www.conradhotels.com. Enormous, centrally located, with spa and several restaurants. **$$$**

L'Auberge, Barrio Parque del Golf, tel: 482 601, fax: 483 408, www.lauberge.com.uy. Sophisticated boutique hotel in 18th-century tower. **$$$**

Hotel Price Guide

Prices for a double room including continental breakfast.
$ = US$50 – inexpensive
$$ = US$50–100 – moderate
$$$ = US$100 plus – expensive

Clarion, Avda Pedragosa Sierra and Avda Las Delicias, tel: 491 515, fax: 491 530, www.clarionpunta.com. **$$$**

Hotel Palace, Avda Gorlero and Calle 11, tel (toll free): 1-877 987 8482, fax: 424 4695. Traditional, with colonial garden. **$$**

Colonia

Recommended hotels include:
Rincón del Río, Calle Barbot 258, tel: 522 3002. **$$**

El Mirador, Calle Roosevelt s/n, tel: 522 2004.**$$**

Posada del Gobernador, Calle 18 de Julio 205, tel: 522 3018. **$$**

What to Eat

Breakfast consists of coffee and croissants; lunch is the main meal and is served from 1–3pm. Dinner tends to be quite late. On weekends, restaurants are jammed at midnight. Portions, particularly meat, are often enormous; it's quite all right to order one dish for two people.

Uruguayan food consists of two staples: beef and pasta. Uruguayans also like seafood. Try *calamares a la plancha* (griddled squid), *cazuela de mariscos* (seafood stew), and *lenguado* (sole) *a la provenzal*. Ice cream and pizza are excellent snacks, as is *chivito*, a steak and salad sandwich. For dessert, try a kind of custard called *isla flotante*.

Where to Eat

Montevideo

Arcadia, Plaza Independencia 759, tel: 902 0111. One of the best in town. Classic surroundings and food. **$$$**

Mercado del Puerto, Calle Piedras. Closed Sunday. Expensive grills, good atmosphere. **$$$**

El Fogón, Calle San José 1080, tel: 900 0900. Grilled beef a specialty; the seafood is excellent. **$$**

El Aguila, Calle Buenos Aires 694, next to Teatro Solis. Elegant service with a continental menu. **$$**

Restaurant Guide

Prices for a three-course meal for two, including house wine.
$ = US$50 – inexpensive
$$ = US$50–100 – moderate
$$$ = US$100 plus – expensive

Doña Flor, Calle Artigas and Avda España. Classy French cuisine. **$$$**

Grotto, Calle Luís de la Torre and Montero, Pocitos. Cool post-modern restaurant. **$$**

Punta del Este

La Bourgogne, Avda Pedragosa Sierra, tel: 482 007. Memorable French restaurant. Elegant surroundings and one of the best chefs in South America. **$$$**

Lo de Tere, Rambla del Puerto and Calle 21, tel: 440 492. Harbourside views and excellent fresh fish are the draws here. **$$**

Los Caracoles, Avda Gorlero 20, tel: 440 912. Well-established steak and salad house with lively atmosphere. **$**

Drinking Notes

For coffee or snacks, try the **Café La Pasiva** in Plaza Matriz Sarandi 600 or **El Lusitano** at Calle 18 de Julio across from the Plaza Cagancha. **Cakes** on the pedestrianized Rambla has superb cakes, coffee and beer. **Sokos** on Calle 18 de Julio, has good sandwiches and more substantial meals. Uruguayan wine is drinkable but nothing special. Beer is made with spring water and is very good, especially *Norteña*.

Bars & Nightclubs

You can hear jazz at **Alianza Francés** and Brazilian music at **Clave de Fu**, Pocitos. For tango dance and music, try **Tangueria del 40**, Hotel Columbia, in the Ciudad Vieja. The most popular discos are **Makao** and **Luna Gaucha** in Punta Gorda and **San Telmo** on Calle Maldonado 1194. You can gamble at the **Casino Parque Hotel**, the **Rodo Casino Carrasc**o and the **Radisson**.

Venezuela A – Z

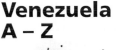

Getting Acquainted

Area 916,442 sq. km (352,143 sq. miles), with a 2,700-km (1,700-mile) Caribbean coast, and 72 islands.
Capital Caracas
Population 24 million. There is a mix of African and European descendants. The native population is fewer than 200,000. More than 80 percent live in urban areas, the largest of which are concentrated on or near the northern coast.
Language Spanish
Currency Bolivar (Bs)
Weights & measures Metric
Electricity 110 volts
Time zone GMT -4hrs, EST +1hr
International dialing code 58 (Caracas +212

Public Holidays

- **January 1** New Year's Day
- **February**, on the Monday and Tuesday before Ash Wednesday Carnival
- **late March/April** Thursday to Saturday Holy Week
- **April 19** Anniversary of the National Declaration of Independence
- **May 1** Labor Day
- **June 24** The feast day of San Juan Bautista
- **July 5** Anniversary of the Signing of Venezuelan National Independence Act
- **July 24** Anniversary of the birth of the Liberator, Simón Bolívar
- **October 12** Columbus Day (Anniversary of the Discovery of America)
- **December 25** Christmas Day

Government & Economy

Venezuela is a democratic republic. The election of former coup leader Hugo Chávez Frías in 1998 as president brought with it major changes in the country's political structure, and raised concerns over the growing concentration of power in central government.

Venezuela is the world's fifth biggest oil exporter, and the economy relies heavily on the petroleum industry. Since the devaluation of the bolívar in 2002, the Venezuelan government has found itself close to bankruptcy, and in 2002–3, a nine-week general strike devastated the economy, particularly oil production. Attempts by his opponents to oust Chávez are ongoing, and political demonstrations occur frequently. In early 2004, the economy grew by 30 percent, a sign that a recovery is on the way.

Emergencies

The nationwide emergency telephone number, **171**, is for police, fire and ambulance.

Visas

Entry is by passport and visa or passport and tourist card. If arriving by air, tourist cards (valid for 60 days) can be issued to citizens of the UK, the USA, Canada and Australia. If arriving by land, a visa must be obtained from a consulate before arrival – requiring a letter of reference, for which there is a charge. However, regulations sometimes change overnight, so double check in advance with your nearest Venezuelan consulate.

It is a good idea to carry your passport with you at all times (be sure to have photocopies of all documents in a separate location in case of loss) as the police mount spot checks and anyone without ID may be detained.

Tourist Information

Corpoturismo, 35th–37th floors, Torre Oueste, Parque Central, Caracas, tel: 571 3089/309 0247; www.venezuela.com/ corpoturismo) has overall responsibility for matters relating to tourism. There are no tourist information kiosks in Caracas; there is a booth at Maiquetía airport but the opening hours are irregular.

Money

Because of the constantly changing rate of exchange, it is advisable not to change more currency into bolívars than you anticipate using.

Currency can be exchanged at **casas de cambio** (most banks only exchange currency for their clients). Only accept US dollars if changing money in hotels.

The majority of banks do not change travelers' checks and except for the main hotels, restaurants, and expensive shops in the largest cities, few places accept travelers' checks, foreign currency, or credit cards. **ATMs** are widely available and give good rates of exchange, but are sometimes targeted by gangs of thieves.

Emergency Money
Western Union is represented by Grupo Zoom which has more than 40 offices in Caracas alone. For information, see www.western union.com. Intercambio offer a service called Moneygram and also have a national network. Details on www.italcambio.com.

Getting Around

From the Airport
The **Simón Bolívar International Airport** is in Maiquetía, 28 km (17 miles) from Caracas. The international and domestic terminals are very close to each other and there are shuttle buses every 10 minutes between the two. Shuttle buses also run to Caracas with stops by the Gato Negro Metro station (use

The Subway

The Metro has three lines providing stops all along the main corridors for business, shopping, and cultural attractions. A complementary system of Metrobuses combines Metro travel with buses which cover extensive routes from each stop. Tickets can be purchased singly for the Metro alone or *combinado*, good for a Metro ride and service on a Metrobus. Much more economical are the *multi-abono* tickets, valid for 10 rides for a flat fee. Tickets are available at many newsstands (those identified with a large M).

The Metro runs from 5am–11pm and is very clean, with excellent security.

this stop only during daylight hours) and at their terminal two blocks west of the Bellas Artes Metro station and Caracas Hilton (Calle Sur 17). It costs less than US$2 and usually takes just under an hour.

The black Anfitriónes de Venezuela taxis charge fixed prices (around US$25 to the center of town); tickets can be bought in the domestic or international terminals. Otherwise, the **taxis** which park near the departure area have a monopoly and charge nearly double the going rate. To avoid paying over the odds, call Tele-taxi on 753 4155/9122 (pre-paid phone cards are sold in dispensers next to the banks of phones in the terminal). Do not get into unlicensed taxis, as foreign visitors are sometimes mugged by these drivers.

Every state has at least one airport for commercial flights, except for Delta Amacuro. Travelers wishing to reach this state by air will have to fly in to Monagas' Maturín airport, then use public transportation or rent a car to reach the delta.

Avensa/Servivensa, Aserca, and Aeropostal dominate the domestic market. However, a number of regional or specialized airlines offer alternatives, in addition to scores of charter services.

Airport departure tax for international flights is US$20 and liable to change; for national flights it is roughly US$2.

By Bus

Cheap public transportation is found virtually everywhere. Long-distance east-bound bus lines operate from the Terminal del Oriente, Avda General Antonio José de Sucre, on the eastern outskirts of the capital. West-bound buses leave from La Bandera, at the junction of Avda Nueva Granada and the El Valle *autopista*, near Los Próceres, with the La Bandera Metro stop nearby.

Arrangements for interurban bus travel must be made at the *Terminal de Pasajeros* (passenger terminal), found in all towns and cities

By Ferry

Conferry in Caracas, tel: 782 8544, www.conferry.com, offers a service between Puerto La Cruz (tel: 281 267 7847) and Cumaná (tel: 293 433 1903), and Margarita Island (tel: 295 261 6397).

A catamaran service operated by Conferry plies between La Guaira, near Caracas, and Margarita,

Gran Cacique Express (Puerto La Cruz, tel: 281 63 0935; Margarita, tel: 295 98 339, fax: 800 22 726) has a passenger service from Cumaná to Margarita. **Naviarca** (tel: 293 31 5577/433 0909) also has services from Cumaná to Araya and Cumaná to Margarita. Neither of these routes has set schedules: the ferries simply depart when full.

There is a very inexpensive passenger-only service between Chacopata (on the Araya Peninsula, Sucre state) and Coche Island, continuing to Margarita (landing in Porlamar, by the shopping area).

By Car

Driving in Caracas is an exercise in self-preservation, so proceed with extreme caution. However, driving in the interior is pleasant, and the roads are of good quality, apart from the potholes. In many areas, driving is the *only* way to appreciate

landscapes, explore villages and mingle with local people.

Driving at night is not advisable since lighting, lane markings, and warnings of obstacles are poor to non-existent, and there are frequently animals in the road.

Health Matters

No inoculations are needed, but a yellow fever certificate is recommended if you intend traveling in the jungle. In 2002 the World Health Organization highlighted Venezuela as an endemic area for yellow fever, although this applies mainly to the upper Orinoco near La Esmeralda and Parima in Amazonas.

The incidence of cases of dengue fever is on the increase, primarily in poor urban areas. Malaria can also be a problem in some areas. It is essential to obtain proper advice and suitable medication before you leave your home country and also to take protective clothing with you. In the UK, contact the Medical Advisory Service for Travellers Abroad (MASTA), tel: 0906 8224100, www.masta.org.

For minor medical problems, the better hotels have physicians on call. Every town has a system to ensure a pharmacy is open 24 hours; these are marked with a *turno* sign.

In an emergency, contact the national emergency number **171**: **Ambulances** can also be called on tel: 545 4545/577 9209. **Centro Móvil de Medicina Permanente** is an emergency service with doctors who can make 24-hour house calls, tel: 483 7021/6092.

Two useful addresses are: **Hospital Universitario** (UCV), south from the Plaza Venezuela freeway exit, tel: 606 7111; and **Clínica de Emergencia Infantil** (Children's Emergency Clinic), Edificio Topacio, 4th floor, Avda Avila, between Avdas Caracas and Gamboa, tel: 577 6136/7381.

Business Hours

Generally Mon–Fri 8am–noon and 2–6pm. Most shops open Mon–Sat 9am–1pm and 3–7pm; but in high season, Mon–Sat 9am–7pm, Sun 9am–1pm.

Newspapers

The *Daily Journal* is the country's only English-language paper. Its "Week in Review" supplement printed on Monday provides a useful summary. *El Nacional* and *El Universal* are the two most important national papers.

Postal Services

The Venezuelan postal system (IPOSTEL) is extremely inefficient, but much better for international than domestic mail. For Europe or the US, mail takes 10 days to three weeks. For a small extra charge, you can have your letter certified *(certificado)* or ask for a return receipt *(con aviso de recibo)*.

Communications

Telephone

All numbers are seven digits. To make national calls, add a zero before the area code. CANTV is the national telephone company. Dial 122 for the long-distance operator.

Internet

In major cities, some travel agencies, hotels and cafés offer Internet services, but connections may be slow and prices high.

Useful Websites

www.think-venezuela.net offers comprehensive information in English, Spanish and German.

Embassies/Consulates

Australia: Quinta Yolanda, Avda Luis Roche, between 6th and 7th transversals, Altamira, tel: 261 4632, fax: 261 3448.
Canada: Edificio Omni, Avda 6 between 3rd and 5th transversals, Altamira, tel: 264 0833.
UK: Torre Las Mercedes, Avda La Estancia, 3rd floor, Urb. Chuao, tel: 993 4111/5280, fax: 993 9989, www.britishembassy.gov.uk
US: Calle F and Calle Suapure,

Colinas de Valle Arriba, tel: 975 6411, fax: 975 8971, http://embajadausa.org.ve

Where to Stay

El Litoral is the area of the Caribbean coast nearest Caracas and Simón Bolívar National and International Airport in Maiquetía which serves Caracas, but due to the natural disaster which devastated this area in December 1999, there are still few lodging options because of continuing problems with the infrastructure. Virtually all beaches were destroyed by mudslides, and vast areas are still in a state of ruin. The best option is Best Western Puerto Viejo, tel: 212 352 4044, www.bestwestern.com.

Hotels

Caracas

Avila, Avda George Washington, San Bernardino, tel: 555 3000, fax: 552 8367. Traditional flavor in quiet residential neighborhood. **$$**
El Cid, Avda San Felipe, between 1st and 2nd transversals, La Castellana. tel: 263 2611, fax: 263 5578. Modest, fully equipped suites with kitchens, in quiet side street in heart of La Castellana–Altamira district. **$$**
El Condor, Avda de Las Delicias 3, Sabana Grande, tel: 762 9911–15/762 7821, fax: 762 8821. An old favorite, near the main shopping centers. **$$**
Hotel Hilton Caracas, Avda Sur 25 and Avda Mexico, tel: 503 5000, fax: 503 5003, www.hilton.com. Well located near cultural attractions. **$$$**
Tamanaco Inter-Continental, Avda Principal las Mercedes, tel: 909 7111, fax: 909 7116, www.interconti.com. The best hotel in Caracas.**$$$**

Ciudad Guyana

Hotel Inter-Continental Guayana, Avda Guayana, Parque Punta Vista, tel: 286 713 1000, fax: 923 1914, www.interconti.com. Great location overlooking the river and Cachamay Falls, connected by jogging path to

Cachamay Park. Private dock and boats for river tours. **$$$**

Mérida

Posada de Luz Caraballo, Avda 2, 13–80, tel: 252 5441, fax: 252 0177, www.andes.net/luzcaraballo. Reliable, comfortable, economical and in the town center. **$$**
Posada Los Bucares de Mérida, Avda 4, 15–5, at Calle 15, tel/fax: 252 2841/0566. Typical vintage house with central patio, spotless comfortable rooms. Very friendly owners. **$$**
Posada Papá Miguel, Calle Piñango 1, La Mesa de Los Indios (5km/3 miles north of Ejido), tel/fax: 252 2529. Delightful house; restaurant has delicious home cooking. **$$**

Puerto la Cruz

Hotel Caribe Mar, Calle Ricaurte 12, tel: 281 67 3291/4973, fax: 281 67 2096. Good option for tight budgets. Near ferry terminal and Paseo Colón. **$$**
Gaeta Hotels, Beach hotel – tel: 281 65 1822/65 0411, fax: 281 65 0065; City hotel – tel: 281 65 0536. These two hotels have plain but comfortable rooms, and good locations. Continental breakfast included. **$$–$$$**

What to Eat

Pabellón, the national dish, combines rice, black beans, shredded beef and *tajadas* (fried ripe plantains). The Andes is known for *pisca* (a rich broth with eggs and bread), trout, and smoked cheese. Coro is famous for *tarkari de chivo* (curried or roasted goat) and goat's milk cheese. Zulia State has delicious coconut-based specialties like *conejo en coco* (rabbit cooked in coconut milk). The coastal region is known for *consomé de guacucos*

Hotel Price Guide

Prices for a double room including continental breakfast.
$ = US$50 – inexpensive
$$ = US$50–100 – moderate
$$$ = US$100 plus – expensive

(clams) and *empanadas de cazón* (shark meat pies), lobster, and fish such as grouper.

At Christmas, *hallaca* (a stew of chicken, pork, beef, spices, olives, raisins and capers wrapped in banana leaves and steamed) is the most traditional dish.

A typical and very popular Venezuelan dish is *mondongo* (tripe stew with chickpeas). *Arepa* is traditional flat round bread made from corn meal or wheat flour.

The beef is excellent throughout the country.

Where to Eat

The greatest concentration of restaurants in Caracas is in: **Barquisimeto**, along Avda Lara between Paseo Los Leones and the Barquisimeto Country Club; **Maracaibo**, along Calle 5 de Julio and Avda 4 Bella Vista; in **Maracay**, along Avda Las Delicias; in the city of **Mérida**, on Avda Chorro de Milla or Calle 24 facing Plaza Los Heroínas; **Puerto La Cruz**, along Paseo Colón and in **Valencia**, along Avda Bolívar Norte.

Most of the economical spots offer a daily *menú ejecutivo*, usually with soup, a main dish, dessert and a beverage for a low, fixed price.

Food in bars may cost 50 percent more and there is no need to feel reticent about asking for prices before you order as a beer can cost three times as much. You save the 10 percent service charge if you eat at the bar, not at a table.

Caracas
Las Mercedes and the **Altamira–Los Palos Grandes** zone offer a huge variety of restaurants and trendy, more upscale dining spots; **Avda Francisco Solano**, between Chacaíto and Avda Las Acacias, has a large

Restaurant Guide

Prices for a three-course meal for two, including house wine.
$ = US$50 – inexpensive
$$ = US$50–100 – moderate
$$$ = US$100 plus – expensive

concentration of Italian restaurants; **Candelaria** (recommended only for daytime visits) is popular for Spanish food and *tascas*.

An excellent source of information is *Miro Popic's Guía Gastronómica de Caracas*, updated annually, in English/Spanish, available in bookstores and hotels.

Ara, Centro Lido, 8th floor, Avda Francisco de Miranda, El Rosal, tel: 953 3270. Bistro-style menu in roof-top setting. Chic clientele. Live music and comedy. Closed Sun. **$$$**
Arábica Coffee Bar, Avda Andrés Bello at Los Palos Grandes, tel: 285 6748. Estate-grown, single-variety coffees roasted daily. Also a great choice of pastries. **$**
Aventio, Avda San Felipe and Calle José Angel Lamas, La Castellana, tel: 267 5422. Traditional, high-class French restaurant. **$$$**
Bar Basque, Alcabala a Peligro, La Candelaria, tel: 576 5955. Considered one of the best restaurants in Caracas. Tiny, with Basque home cooking. Closed Sun and Aug. Booking recommended. Zone best visited only by day. **$$**
El Buffet Vegetariano, Avda Los Jardines 4, La Florida, tel: 730 7490/7512. Healthy, generously served vegetarian fare. Fixed-price menu. No smoking or alcohol. Open 11.30am–2.30pm weekdays. **$**
El Portón, Avda Pinchincha and Calle Guaicaipuro, El Rosal, tel: 952 0027/0302. Traditional Venezuelan-style specialties, particularly beef; usually with live *música criolla*. **$$**
Le Petit Bistrot de Jacques, Avda San Felipe, La Castellana, tel: 263 8595. Authentic, intimate French bistro with classic offerings – *cassoulet, choucroute, steak frites*. Closed Sat lunch and Sun. **$$$**
Maute Grill, Avda Rio de Janeiro, Las Mercedes, tel: 991 0892. At the rear of the bar, the restaurant surrounds a traditional tree-filled patio. Excellent beef. **$$**

Mérida
Date con Rolando, Avda Urdanea and Calle 49. Snack bar on wheels serving high-quality fast food. **$**

Where to Shop

In the Caracas area, **Hannsi** in El Hatillo has the largest and widest selection of Venezuelan arts and crafts of any place in the country, with items for every budget. The most exquisite objects are found in **Casa Caruba**, Avda Andrés Bello between 1st and 2nd transversals, Los Palos Grandes.

The **Sabana Grande Boulevard** is an excellent commercial artery with hundreds of boutiques, jewelry stores, bazaars and assorted stores.

La Gruta, Prolongación Avda 2, tel: 634 828. "The Cave" has a great regional menu. **$$**
Restaurante Bimbo, Calle 23 (between Avdas 4 and 5), tel: 528 950. Traditional Italian with international dishes. **$$**

Puerto la Cruz
Brasero Grill/La Boite del Brasero, Paseo Colón (east end), tel: 67 4850/266 0923. Beef and seafood. Upscale crowd. **$$$**
El Parador del Puerto, Paseo Colón, tel: 265 0391/3950. Seafood specialties, elegant-looking dark interior. **$$–$$$**
Fuentemar, Paseo Colón, tel: 68 7623. Long-established place on the beach, with inside and outside seating. At the latter, a distinct soda-fountain-style menu; the formal interior has seafood. **$$**

Nightlife

Caracas is a swinging city by night and there are many and varied discos and nightclubs. *Caraqueños* usually eat at home at 8pm and between 9pm and 11pm when they go out to restaurants; the partying goes on until well into the early hours of the morning. There are many small clubs, restaurants, and bars on **Plaza Altamira Sur** and along the **Sabana Grande Boulevard**.

Language

Making Contact

Whether you need to know what time the next bus leaves or whether your hotel room is quiet, with a shower and a view of the beach, making yourself understood in the local language will be the key to the success of your stay in South America. The good news is that you can get by in the whole continent with just two languages: Spanish and Portuguese (with the obvious exceptions of the Guianas).

While people in many tourist establishments will speak English, once you are off the beaten track, hardly anyone will, and just making the effort to speak a few words will gain you a lot of appreciation. There are idiomatic differences from one country to the next, but you will soon pick these up as you go.

It would be impossible for us to give a complete language guide here, but the following are some useful words, phrases and tips that will hopefully ease understanding.

Portuguese

Although Portuguese, and not Spanish, is the language of Brazil, if you have a knowledge of Spanish, it will come in handy. You will recognize many similar words, and most Brazilians will understand you if you speak in Spanish. If you like to wander around on your own, you might want to get a Portuguese–English pocket dictionary. If you are unable to find one at home, they are on sale at airport and hotel shops and book stores in Brazil.

First names are used a great deal in Brazil. In many situations in which English-speakers would use a title and surname, Brazilians often use a first name with the title of respect: *Senhor* for men (written *Sr* and usually shortened to *Seu* in spoken Portuguese) and *Senhora* (written *Sra*) or *Dona* (used only with first name) for women. If *João Oliveira* or *Maria da Silva* calls you Sr John, rather than Mr Jones, then you should correspondingly address them as *Sr João* and *Dona Maria*.

There are three second-person pronoun forms in Portuguese. Stick to *você*, equivalent to "you," and you will be all right. *O senhor* (for men) or *a senhora* (for women) is used to show respect for someone of a different age group or social class or to be polite to a stranger. As a foreigner, you won't offend anyone if you use the wrong form of address. But if you want to learn when to use the more formal or informal style, observe and go by how others address you. In some parts of Brazil, mainly the northeast and the south, *tu* is used a great deal. Originally, in Portugal, *tu* was used among intimate friends and close relatives, but in Brazil, it's equivalent to *você*.

If you are staying longer and are serious about learning the language, there are Portuguese courses for non-native speakers. Meanwhile, here are some of the most essential words and phrases:

Greetings

Tudo Bem, meaning "all's well," is one of the most common forms of greeting: one person asks, "*Tudo bem?*" and the other replies, "*Tudo bem.*" This is also used to mean "OK," "all right," "will do," or as a response when someone apologizes, meaning, "that's all right, no worries." Other forms of greetings are:

Good morning (good afternoon) *Bom dia (boa tarde)*
Good evening (good night) *Boa noite*
How are you? *Como vai?*
Well, thank you *Bem, obrigado*
Hello (to answer the telephone) *Alô*
Hello (common forms of greeting) *Bom dia, boa tarde* etc.
Hi, hey! (informal greeting also used to get someone's attention) *Oi*

Goodbye (very informal and most used) *Tchau*
Goodbye (literally "until soon") *Até logo*
Goodbye (similar to "farewell") *Adeus*
My name is (I am) *Meu nome é (Eu sou)*
What is your name? *Como é seu nome?*
It's a pleasure *É um prazer*
Pleased to meet you *Prazer*
Good! Great! *Que bom!*
Cheers! *Saúde*
Do you speak English? *Você fala inglês?*
I don't understand (I didn't understand) *Não entendo (Não entendi)*
Do you understand? *Você entende?*
Please repeat more slowly *Por favor repete, mais devagar*
What do you call this (that)? *Como se chama isto (aquilo)?*
How do you say …? *Como se diz …?*
Please *Por favor*
Thank you (very much) *(Muito) Obrigado (or Obrigada, for a woman speaking)*
You're welcome (literally "It's nothing") *De nada*
Excuse me (to apologize) *Desculpe*
Excuse me (taking leave or to get past someone) *Com licença*

Pronouns

Who? *Quem?*
I (We) *Eu (Nós)*
You (singular) *Você*
You (plural) *Vocês*
He (she) *Ele (ela)*
They *Eles (Elas)*
My (mine) *Meu (minha)* depending on gender of object
Our (ours) *Nosso (nossa)*
Your (yours) *Seu (sua)*
His (her or hers) *Dele (dela or deles)*
Their, theirs *(Delas)*

Getting Around

Where is the…? *Onde é…?*
beach *a praia*
bathroom *o banheiro*
bus station *a rodoviária*
airport *o aeroporto*
train station *a estação de trem*
post office *o correio*

police station *a delegacia de polícia*
ticket office *a bilheteria*
marketplace *o mercado*
street market *a feira*
embassy (consulate) *a embaixada (o consulado)*
currency exchange *uma casa de câmbio*
bank *um banco*
pharmacy *uma farmácia*
(good) hotel *um (bom) hotel*
(good) restaurant *um (bom) restaurante*
bar *um bar*
snack bar *uma lanchonete*
bus stop *um ponto de ônibus*
taxi stand *um ponto de taxi*
subway station *uma estação de metrô*
service station *um posto de gasolina*
newsstand *um jornaleiro*
public telephone *um telefone público*
supermarket *um supermercado*
shopping center *um shopping center*
department store *uma loja de departamentos*
boutique *uma boutique*
jeweler *um joalheiro*
hairdresser (barber) *um cabeleireiro (um barbeiro)*
laundry *uma lavanderia*
hospital *um hospital*
Taxi *Taxi*
Bus *Onibus*
Car *Carro*
Plane *Avião*
Train *Trem*
Boat *Barco*
A ticket to... *Uma passagem para...*
I want to go to... *Quero ir para...*
How can I get to...? *Como posso ir para...?*
Please take me to... *Por favor, me leve para...*
Please call a taxi for me *Por favor, chame um taxi para mim*
I want to rent a car *Quero alugar um carro*
What is this place called? *Como se chama este lugar?*
Where are we? *Onde estamos?*
How long will it take to get there? *Leva quanto tempo para chegar lá?*
Please stop here (Stop!) *Por favor, pare aqui. (Pare!)*
Please wait *Por favor, espere*

What time does the bus (plane, boat) leave? *A que horas sai o ônibus (avião, barco)?*
Where does this bus go? *Este ônibus vai para onde?*
Does it go by way of...? *Passa em...?*
Airport (Bus station) tax *Taxa de embarque*
I want to check my luggage (on a bus, etc.) *Quero despachar minha bagagem*
I want to store my luggage (at a station) *Quero guardar minha bagagem*

Shopping
Do you have...? *Tem...?*
I want... please *Eu quero... por favor*
I don't want... *Eu não quero...*
I want to buy... *Eu quero comprar...*
Where can I buy... *Onde posso comprar...?*
cigarettes *cigarros*
film *filme*
a ticket for... *uma entrada para...*
a reserved seat *um lugar marcado*
another the same *um outro igual*
another different *um outro differente*
this (that) *isto (aquilo)*
something less expensive *a lgo mais barato*
postcard *cartão postal*
paper *papel*
envelopes *envelopes*
a pen *uma caneta*
a pencil *um lápis*
shampoo *xampu or shampoo*
soap *sabonete*
toothpaste *pasta de dente*
sunscreen *filtro solar*
aspirin *aspirina*
I need... *Eu preciso de...*
a doctor *um médico*
a mechanic *um mecânico*
transportation *transporte*
help *ajuda*
How much? *Quanto?*
How many? *Quantos?*
How much does it cost? *Quanto custa? Quanto é?*
That's very expensive *É muito caro*
A lot, very (many) *Muito (muitos)*
A little (few) *Um pouco, um pouquinho (poucos)*

At the Hotel
I have a reservation *Tenho uma reserva*
I want to make a reservation *Quero fazer uma reserva*
A single room (A double room) *Um quarto de solteiro (Um quarto de casal)*
with air conditioning *com ar condicionado*
I want to see the room *Quero ver o quarto*
Suitcase *Mala*
Bag or purse *Bolsa*
Room service *Serviço de quarto*
Key *Chave*
The manager *O gerente*

At the Restaurant
Waiter *Garçon*
Maitre d' *Maitre*
I didn't order this *Eu não pedi isto*
The menu *O cardápio*
The wine list *A carta de vinhos*
Breakfast *Café da manhã*
Lunch *Almoço*
Supper *Jantar*
The house specialty *A especialidade da casa*

água mineral com gás **Carbonated mineral water**
água mineral sem gás **Still mineral water**
Café **Coffee**
Chá **Tea**
Cerveja **Beer**
Vinho branco/tinto **White wine/red wine**
Um refrigerante (Suco) **A soft drink (juice)**
Um drink **An alcoholic drink**
Um cocktail **A cocktail**
Gelo **Ice**
Sal **Salt**
Pimenta **Pepper**
Açucar **Sugar**
Um prato **A plate**
Um copo **A glass**
Uma xícara **A cup**
Um guardanapo **A napkin**
Um tira-gosto **An appetizer**
Um lanche **A snack**
Carne **Beef**
Porco **Pork**
Frango **Chicken**
Peixe **Fish**
Camarão **Shrimp**
Bem passado **Well done**

Ao ponto **Medium rare**
Mal passado **Rare**
Verduras **Vegetables**
Salada **Salad**
Fruta **Fruit**
Pão **Bread**
Manteiga **Butter**
Torradas **Toast**
Ovos **Eggs**
Arroz **Rice**
Batatas (fritas) **(fried) potatoes**
Feijão **Beans**
Sopa **Soup**
Sanduiche **Sandwich**
Pizza **Pizza**
Sobremesa **Dessert**
(Doces) **(Sweets)**

The bill, please A conta, por favor
Is service included? Está incluido
o serviço?
I want my change, please Eu
quero meu troco, por favor
I want a receipt Eu quero um recibo

Money

Cash Dinheiro
Do you accept credit cards?
Aceita cartão de crédito?
Can you cash a travelers' check?
Pode trocar um travelers' check?
(cheque de viagem)
I want to exchange money Quero
trocar dinheiro
What is the exchange rate? Qual é
o câmbio?

Time

When? Quando?
What time is it? Que horas são?
Just a moment please Um
momento, por favor
**What is the schedule? (bus, tour,
show, etc.)** Qual é o horário?
How long does it take? Leva
quanto tempo?
Hour A Hora
Day O Dia
Week A Semana
Month O mês
At what time? A que horas?
At one-o-clock A uma hora
(two-, three-...) (duas,três...)
An hour from now Daqui a uma
hora
Which day? Que dia?
Yesterday Ontem
Today Hoje
Tomorrow Amanhã

This week Esta semana
Last week A semana passada
Next week A semana que vem
The weekend O fim de semana
Monday Segunda-feira
Tuesday Terça-feira
Wednesday Quarta-feira
Thursday Quinta-feira
Friday Sexta-feira
(Monday to Friday are often written
as 2a, 3a, 4a, 5a)
Saturday Sábado
Sunday Domingo

Numbers

1	um
2	dois
3	três
4	quatro
5	cinco
6	seis
half a dozen	meia
7	sete
8	oito
9	nove
10	dez
11	onze
12	doze
13	treze
14	quatorze
15	quinze
16	dezesseis
17	dezessete
18	dezoito
19	dezenove
20	vinte
21	vinte e um
30	trinta
40	quarenta
50	cinqüenta
60	sessenta
70	setenta
80	oitenta
90	noventa
100	cem
101	cento e um
200	duzentos
300	trezentos
400	quatrocentos
500	quinhentos
600	seiscentos
700	setecentos
800	oitocentos
900	novecentos
1,000	mil
2,000	dois mil
10,000	dez mil
100,000	cem mil
1,000,000	um milhão

Commas and periods in numbers
take an inverted form in
Portuguese: 1,000 is written 1.000
and 1.5 is written 1,5.

To help you understand the
addresses in this appendix, here's
what the Portuguese words mean.

Al or Alameda = lane
Andar =f loor, story
Ave or Avenida = avenue
Casa = house
Centro=the central downtown
business district, also frequently
referred to as a cidade or "the city."
Cj or Conjunto – a suite of rooms or
sometimes a group of buildings.
Estr or Estrada = road or highway.
Fazenda = ranch, also a lodge.
Largo (often written as Lgo) =
square or plaza.
Lote = Lot
Pça or Praça = square or plaza
Praia = beach
Rio = river
Rod or Rodovia – highway
R or Rua = street
Sala = room

Ordinal numbers are written with °
after the numeral, so 3° andar
means 3rd floor. BR followed by a
number refers to a federal
interstate highways, for example
BR-101, which follows the Atlantic
coast. Telex and telephone numbers
are given with the area code for
long-distance dialing in
parentheses. Ramal = telephone
extension.

Spanish

There is a colorful variety of local
idioms throughout Spanish South
America. An expression you will
hear everywhere in Ecuador, for
instance, and which is difficult to
translate, is no mas. Siga no mas
for example, means "Hurry up (and
get on the bus/move down the line
etc.)." Come no mas means "Just
eat it (It'll get cold/it's nicer than it
looks, etc.)." In Argentina, the
Spanish "ll", as in "llanos", comes
out like something between a **j** and
zh; while the familiar "tu" is
replaced by the archaic sounding

"*vos*." In Chile and to a lesser extent Peru, they are notorious for dropping the ends off their words, particularly those that end in "–ado", which become "ao" instead. It may come as a relief to know, that Colombians pride themselves on speaking the clearest and purest Spanish in South America.

In the Andes, *indígenas* all speak Spanish but you will hear Quichua words that have crept into the language: *wambras* translates as "guys," and *cheveré* means "cool."

VOWELS
a as in cat
e as in bed
i as in police
o as in hot
u as in rude
CONSONANTS are approximately like those in English, the main exceptions being:
c is hard before **a**, **o**, or **u** (as in English), and is soft before **e** or **i**, when it sounds like **s** (as opposed to the Castilian pronunciation of **th** as in think). Thus, *censo* (census) sounds like senso.
g is hard before **a**, **o**, or **u** (as in English), but where English **g** sounds like **j** – before **e** or **i** – Spanish **g** sounds like a guttural **h**. **G** before **ua** is often soft or silent, so that *agua* sounds more like *awa*, and Guadalajara like Wadalajara.
h is silent.
j sounds like a guttural h.
ll sounds like y.
ñ sounds like ny, as in the familiar Spanish word *señor*.
q sounds like **k**. *¿Qué quiere Usted?* is pronounced: Keh kee-ehr-eh oostehd?
r is often rolled.
x between vowels sounds like a guttural **h**, eg in México or Oaxaca.
y alone, as the word meaning "and", is pronounced **ee**.
Note that **ch** and **ll** are a separate letter of the Spanish alphabet; if looking in a phone book or dictionary for a word beginning with **ch**, you will find it after the final **c** entry. A name or word beginning with **ll** will be listed after the **l** entry.

Here are some basic words to help you get around:
My name is Mary *Me llamo María*
Hello, how are you? *¿Hola, que tal?*
I'm very well, and you? *Yo, muy bien. ¿Y usted ?*
Very well, thank you *Muy bien, gracias*
Good morning *Buenos días*
Good afternoon *Buenas tardes*
Goodnight *Buenas noches*
Welcome *Bienvenido*
Hello *¡Hola!*
Bye *Adios*
See you later *Hasta luego*
How are you? *¿Qué tal?*
Very well *Muy bien*
Thank you *Gracias*
Don't mention it *De nada*
Please *Por favor*
Excuse me *Perdón*
Yes *Sí*
No *No*
What is this? *¿Qué es esto?*
How much is this? *¿Cuánto es?*
Good morning, where is the tourist office? *Buenos días, ¿dónde esta el oficina de turismo?*
Straight *derecho*
To the left *a la izquierda*
To the right *a la derecha*
Town Hall *Ayuntamiento*
Bank *Banco*
Library *Librería*
Art Gallery *Sala de Exposiciones*
Pharmacy *Farmacia*
Bus stop *Parada de Autobús*
Train station *Estación de tren*
Post office *Correos*
Hospital *Hospital*
Church *Iglesia*
Hotel *Hotel*
Youth hostel *Albergue*
Camping *Camping*
Parking *Aparcamiento*
Sports ground *Polideportivo*
Square *Plaza*
Discotheque *Discoteca*
Beach *Playa*

Numbers

1	*uno*
2	*dos*
3	*tres*
4	*cuatro*
5	*cinco*
6	*seis*
7	*siete*
8	*ocho*
9	*nueve*
10	*diez*
11	*once*
12	*doce*
13	*trece*
14	*catorce*
15	*quince*
16	*dieciséis*
17	*diecisiete*
18	*dieciocho*
19	*diecinueve*
20	*veinte*
21	*veintiuno*
25	*veinticinco*
30	*treinta*
40	*cuarenta*
50	*cincuenta*
60	*sesenta*
70	*setenta*
80	*ochenta*
90	*noventa*
100	*cien*
101	*ciento uno*
200	*doscientos*
300	*trescientos*
400	*cuatrocientos*
500	*quinientos*
600	*seiscientos*
700	*setecientos*
800	*ochocientos*
900	*novecientos*
1,000	*mil*
2,000	*dos mil*
10,000	*diez mil*
100,000	*cien mil*
1,000,000	*un millón*

Days of the week
Monday *lunes*
Tuesday *martes*
Wednesday *miércoles*
Thursday *jueves*
Friday *viernes*
Saturday *sábado*
Sunday *domingo*

Months of the year
January *enero*
February *febrero*
March *marzo*
April *abril*
May *mayo*
June *junio*
July *julio*
August *agosto*
September *septiembre*
October *octubre*
November *noviembre*
December *diciembre*

Further Reading

Argentina

In Patagonia, by Bruce Chatwin, (Penguin USA, 2003). Chatwin's classic journey.

Natural Patagonia: Argentina & Chile by Marcelo D. Beccaceci, Victoria Lichtschein (Pangaea, 1998). Mostly photographic Spanish-English edition.

The Old Patagonian Express: By Train Through the Americas by Paul Theroux (Mariner Books, 1989). Theroux's self-indulgent travels by train from Boston to Patagonia.

Motorcycle Diaries: A Journey Around South America, Ernesto "Che" Guevara (Verso Books, 2003). The entertaining story of 23-year-old Che Guevara's road trip.

A Lexicon of Terror: Argentina and the Logacios of Torture by Marguerite Feitlowitz Oxford University Press (September 1999). Explores perversion of language during the Dirty War which claimed 30,000 victims.

The History of Argentina by Daniel K. Lewis (Palgrave Macmillan, 2003). Covers entire history from pre-Columbian times to 2001.

Bolivia

Marching Powder by Rusty Young (Sidgwick & Jackson, 2003). Bizarre world of Bolivian prison portrayed by English drug smuggler.

Bolivian Diary by Ernesto "Che" Guevara (Pimlico, 2000). Weighty narrative of last, doomed, 11 months of the revolutionary.

Bolivia in Focus: A Guide to the People, Politics, and Culture by Paul Van Lindert (Interlink, 2004).

The Incredible Voyage: A Personal Odyssey by Tristan Jones (Adlard Coles, 1996). Author sailed small craft from Dead Sea to Lake Titicaca.

We Eat the Mines and the Mines Eat Us: Dependency and Exploitation in Bolivian Tin Mines by June Nash (Columbia University Press, 1993). On life and death in the Bolivian tin mines.

Brazil

Futebol: The Brazilian Way of Life by Alex Bellos (Bloomsbury, 2002). Wonderful combination of history and anecdote.

Dona Flor and Her Two Husbands by Jorge Amado (Serpent's Tail, 1999). Colorful novel by Brazil's favourite author.

Tropical Truth by Caetano Velosa (Bloomsbury). The John Lennon of Brazil tells how Tropicalismo revolutionised the country's culture and politics.

Eat Smart in Brazil by Joan and David Peterson (Ginkgo Press, 1995). Recipes and vocabulary from *abacaxi* (pineapple) to *patinho de carangueijo ao vinagrete* (marinated crab claws).

Brazil-Amazon and Pantanal by David Pearson (Academic Press, 2001). Written by professional biologists, but accessible.

Chile

My Invented Country: A Memoir by Isabel Allende (Flamingo, 2003). Autobiographical account from Chile's acclaimed novelist.

Between Extremes: A Journey Beyond Imagination by Brian Keenan and John McCarthy (Black Swan, 2000). Travels along South America's backbone by the former Beirut captives.

Travels in a Thin Country: Journey Through Chile by Sara Wheeler (Abacus, 1995). Lone woman's travels along longest mountain range on earth.

Colombia

The Making of Modern Columbia: A Nation in Spite of Itself by David Bushnell (University of California Press, 1993). Remarkable examination of a country that is so much more diverse than its stereotype.

My Cocaine Museum by Michael T. Taussig (University of Chicago Press, 2004). Imaginative look at south Colombia's poor communities.

Colombia: Fragmented Land, Divided Society by Frank Safford, Marco Palacios (Oxford University Press, 2001). Most comprehensive single-source on Colombia's history

More Terrible than Death: Massacres, Drugs, and America's War in Colombia by Robin Kirk (Public Affairs, 2003). Compelling narrative by human rights investigator into affect of US role in drug war on Colombian lives.

One Hundred Years of Solitude by Gabriel Garcia Márquez (Perennial, 2004). Classic work of magical realism by Nobel Prize-winning author.

News of a Kidnapping by Gabriel Garcia Márquez (Penguin USA, 1998). Chilling, journalistic account of kidnapping of prominent journalists.

Ecuador

Galápagos: A Natural History Market by Michael Jackson, 1987 (Univ of Calgary Press, 1994).

The Voyage of the *Beagle* by Charles Darwin, 1835–1836 (Penguin USA, 1989). Darwin's epic voyage around the coasts of South America which led, 20 years later, to his theory of evolution by natural selection.

Eight Feet in the Andes: Travels with a Donkey from Ecuador to Cusco by Dervla Murphy (John Murray, 1983). An Andean adventure.

Ecuador: A Climbing Guide by Yossi Brain (Mountaineers Books, 2000).

Peru

Lost City of the Incas by Hiram Bingham (Triune Books, 2000). Bingham's enthusiastic account of discovery of Machu Picchu – a treasure.

The Conquest of the Incas by John Hemming (Harvest Books, 2003). Authoritative look at 16th-century Spaniards and Indians in Peru.

The Bridge of San Luís Rey by Thornton Wilder (Perennial, 2003). An acclaimed, sombre tale, by Pulitzer Prize-winner, about a bridge that collapses in 18th-century Peru.

Go and Come Back by Joan Abelove (Puffin, 2000). Tale of Peruvian jungle village for young people of 12 years of age and older.

Aunt Julia and the Scriptwriter by Mario Vargas Llosa (Penguin 1995). Entertaining novel set in Lima about a young writer's love affair with his aunt, and an enigmatic radio scriptwriter.

Venezuela

Venezuela in Pictures by Lincoln A. Boehm (Lerner Publishing Group,1998). Photographic guide.

Hungry Lightning: Notes of a Woman Anthropologist in Venezuela by Pei-Lin Yu (University of New Mexico Press, 1997). Well written, illustrated journal of the Pum way of life.

The Lost Fleet: The Discovery of a Sunken Armada from the Golden Age of Piracy by Barry Clifford (William Morrow, 2002). Dramatic story of shipwrecks and the dawn of the golden age of piracy.

Culture Shock!: Venezuela by Kitt Baguley (Graphic Arts Cente, 1999). Informative guide.

In the Rainforest by Catherine Caufield(Pan Books, 1986). Comprehensive study of the world's rainforests.

South America

The Argentina Reader: History, Culture, Politics by Gabriela Nouzeilles and Graciela R. Montaldo (Duke University Press, 2003) (also Peru, 1995, and Brazil, 1999). Comprehensive introduction to history, culture, and society.

Wines of South America by Jason Lowe and Monty Waldin (Mitchell Beazley, 2003). Comprehensive look at emerging wine-producing region.

Around South America: By Ship by Charles R Dillon (Writers' Club Press, 2001). The reader is taken through Panama Canal to every major city on coasts of South America.

Where to Watch Birds in South America by Nigel Wheatley (Princeton Univ. Press, 2000). Excellent reference guide to most important locations and specialties for birders.

The South American Table: The Flavor and Soul of Authentic Home Cooking from Patagonia to Rio De

Janeiro by Maria Baez (Kijac Harvard Common Press, 2003). Comprehensive cookbook that also touches on culture and geography.

The Explorers of South America by Edward J. Goodman (Univ of Oklahoma Press, 1992). Colorful look at nearly 500 years of exploration, with personal accounts.

Other Insight Guides

The *Insight Guide* series has 180 titles, spanning every continent. Apa Publications has also created two companion series of guidebooks. *Insight Pocket Guides* provide short-stay visitors with a range of carefully selected itineraries and include full-size pull-out maps. *Insight Compact Guides* are handy mini-encyclopedias, ideal for on-the-spot use.

In the *Insight Guide* series, South America and Latin America are covered by books on *Argentina, Buenos Aires, Brazil, Rio de Janeiro, Amazon Wildlife, Chile, Costa Rica, Ecuador, Mexico, Mexico City, Peru* and *Venezuela*. These companion guides give detailed, practical information backed up by entertaining essays and stunning photography.

Feedback

We do our best to ensure the information in our books is as accurate and up-to-date as possible. The books are updated on a regular basis, using local contacts, who painstakingly add, amend and correct as required. However, some mistakes and omissions are inevitable and we are ultimately reliant on our readers to put us in the picture.

We would welcome your feedback on any details related to your experiences using the book "on the road". Maybe we recommended a hotel that you liked (or another that you didn't), as well as interesting new attractions, or facts and figures you have found out about the country itself. The more details you can give us (particularly with regard to addresses, e-mails and telephone numbers), the better.

We will acknowledge all contributions, and we'll offer an Insight Guide to the best letters received.

Please write to us at:
Insight Guides
PO Box 7910
London SE1 1WE
United Kingdom
Or send e-mail to:
insight@apaguide.co.uk

ART & PHOTO CREDITS

Picture Spreads

INSIGHT GUIDE
SOUTH AMERICA

Cartographic Editor
Zoë Goodwin
Art Director **Klaus Geisler**
Picture Research **Hilary Genin**

Map Production: Berndtson & Berndtson Productions
© 2005 Apa Publications GmbH & Co. Verlag KG (Singapore branch)

Index